"Charlottesville, Virginia, my hometown, is now an emblem and a microcosm of the tensions and divisions roiling our nation. Mayor Michael Signer found himself in the center of a growing brushfire that culminated in the murderous Unite the Right demonstration in August 2017. Here he tells a difficult, unsparing but often engrossing story that illuminates just how hard it can be to face our past while also finding a healing and hopeful path forward."

Anne-Marie Slaughter, CEO, New America

"*Cry Havoc* chronicles how Charlottesville, VA, was torn apart by violence and murder in the summer of 2017, and how the small town has come together to heal since then. By telling the deep story of the rally that shocked the world, Mike Signer, the mayor of Charlottesville and an influential political theorist, not only takes us deep inside the life of one small American town, he points to lessons that could inspire the whole country to move towards a better future."

Yascha Mounk, author, *The People Vs. Democracy*

"Mike Signer does something remarkable in *Cry Havoc*. He takes responsibility. With candor and integrity, he describes his actions, his omissions, his ambitions, and his limits as a mayor in the midst of a consuming public crisis. This book will make every reader ask, '*What would I do? What choices would I make?*' And it will make every reader a more wise and skillful citizen."

Eric Liu, CEO of Citizen University and
author, *You're More Powerful Than You Think:
A Citizen's Guide to Making Change Happen*

"Michael Signer's *Cry Havoc* goes behind the scenes as neo-Nazis descended on Charlottesville, Virginia, in August 2017, transforming a small college town into an international flashpoint of extremist hatred and racial confrontation. The former mayor recounts, from his firsthand vantage point, the events of that tragic and dramatic weekend. This well-written, disturbing volume serves as a warning about what may be coming in America's increasingly divided society. We would be wise to

PRAISE FOR
CRY HAVOC

"Mike Signer had a unique vantage point on one of the inflection points of our time: the white-supremacist rallies and violence in Charlottesville in 2017. In this important new book, he explores where we've been, where we are, and—most important—where we should be headed if we can summon our better angels."

Jon Meacham, author, *The Soul of America*

"A report from the frontlines of Trump's America. Polarization, race, politicized memory, violence, and good-willed efforts of citizens and politicians to navigate it all. Mike Signer gives us his on-the-ground view of 'Charlottesville under siege,' revealing the deep vulnerabilities and promise of American democracy."

Daniel Ziblatt, Harvard University,
co-author, *How Democracies Die*

"Former Charlottesville Mayor Mike Signer, in providing an account of the tribulations in the lead-up to and aftermath of the Unite the Right rally, demonstrates the pain and struggle of a community defending itself from hate and constructing a collective path together toward a vision of belonging. He also offers an intimate glimpse into what it takes to carry the immense weight of responsibility and accountability to the public amid such turbulence. In doing so, Signer gives his readers firsthand insight into the necessary conflict that is at the heart of true bridging. But that through compassion, faith, and commitment to one another, extremism can be overcome toward a broad expansion of the circle of human concern."

john a. powell, Robert D. Haas Chancellor's
Chair in Equity and Inclusion,
University of California, Berkeley Law School

heed the lessons of Charlottesville, before one small city's dreadful conflict becomes the blueprint for violence from coast to coast."

Larry Sabato, Director, UVA Center for Politics

"*Cry Havoc* vividly recounts the disturbing events in Charlottesville and reminds us that the battle to preserve our democratic institutions is an enduring part of our national experience. Essential reading in a time of national peril."

Robert Dallek, author, *An Unfinished Life: JFK, 1917–1963*

"Incredibly compelling. *Cry Havoc* connects a richly detailed personal story of local politics with national trends that should scare us all."

P.W. Singer, author, *LikeWar: The Weaponization of Social Media*

"A complex, disturbing, valuable tale of racial disharmony, government failure, and one man's frantic attempts to save the day."

Kirkus Reviews

"Since the Unite the Right rally, I have tried to understand the events around the murder of my daughter. *Cry Havoc* is an important narrative of Charlottesville, providing unique insights to help make sense of the senseless, and moving us to a place of hope and courage."

Susan Bro, co-founder and president, Heather Heyer Foundation

"Mike Signer held the front and center seat during Charlottesville's darkest moments when our nation's democracy, values, and rule of law faced the worst of challenges. His brilliant, inspiring, accurate, and timely account is a must-read for every American concerned about the future of democracy, the civility of our discourse, and the harm of extremism."

Khizr Khan

CRY
HAVOC

ALSO BY MICHAEL SIGNER

Demagogue: The Fight to Save
Democracy from Its Worst Enemies

Becoming Madison: The Extraordinary Origins
of the Least Likely Founding Father

CRY
HAVOC

Charlottesville and American Democracy Under Siege

MICHAEL SIGNER

PUBLICAFFAIRS

NEW YORK

PublicAffairs
Hachette Book Group
1290 Avenue of the Americas, New York, NY 10104
www.publicaffairsbooks.com
@Public_Affairs

Printed in the United States of America
First Edition: March 2020

Published by PublicAffairs, an imprint of Perseus Books, LLC, a subsidiary of Hachette Book Group, Inc. The PublicAffairs name and logo is a trademark of the Hachette Book Group.

The Hachette Speakers Bureau provides a wide range of authors for speaking events. To find out more, go to www.hachettespeakersbureau.com or call (866) 376-6591.

The publisher is not responsible for websites (or their content) that are not owned by the publisher.

Print interior design by Linda Mark.

Library of Congress Cataloging-in-Publication Data has been applied for.

ISBNs: 978-1-54173-615-3 (hardcover), 978-1-54173-613-9 (ebook)

LSC-C

10   9   8   7   6   5   4   3   2   1

In memory of Paul Nace and Matt Seidman,
true believers in debate and democracy

Cry "Havoc," and let slip the dogs of war.
—Mark Antony
Julius Caesar, Act 3, Scene 1
WILLIAM SHAKESPEARE

CONTENTS

PART III | THE SUMMER OF HATE

PART IV | FIRESTORM

PART V | AFTERBURN

MAJOR CHARACTERS

Wes Bellamy	Vice-Mayor, 2016–2018
Bob Fenwick	City Councilor
Kathy Galvin	City Councilor
Maurice Jones	City Manager
Jason Kessler	Founder, "Unite the Right"
Terry McAuliffe	Governor of Virginia
Mike Signer	Mayor, 2016–2018
Kristin Szakos	City Councilor
Al Thomas	Chief of Police
Nikuyah Walker*	Activist and Mayor, 2018–2020

---

* Walker was selected to serve a two-year term as mayor in 2018. At the time this manuscript was completed in 2019, it was unknown whether she would serve an additional term after 2020.

PART I | CIVILITY

INTRODUCTION

WINTER IN SUMMER

WHAT HAPPENED ON THE WEEKEND OF AUGUST 11–12, 2017, IN Charlottesville, Virginia, was so horrific, was such a tear in the fabric of a small city's ordinary experience, that it strains one's power to describe. Hordes of white nationalists invaded the University of Virginia and then the Downtown Mall of the city, ostensibly to support the preservation of a statue of Confederate general Robert E. Lee. They clashed violently with counterprotesters along the way before a neo-Nazi terrorist drove his car into a crowd of counterprotesters, killing one young woman and injuring nineteen others.

The events were cinematic, to be sure, quickly branded into the nation's consciousness by a Vice News documentary that went viral. The video showed muscular, violent men chanting "Jews will not replace us" as they carried torches on the fabled "Grounds" of the university. It showed a melee near the quaint Downtown Mall, where right-wing activists, bearing handmade shields and helmets, cracked flagpoles onto left-wing counterprotesters and sent fists flying into faces. One counterprotester used a spray can as a torch; a white protester fired a handgun toward a black counterprotester (luckily, not hitting him). Others hurled newspaper boxes. Waves of neo-Nazis, wearing swastika apparel, rolled on foot into anti-racist activists wearing Black Lives Matter shirts. People fell onto concrete and blacktop, thrashing against each other. As the violence spread like wildfire, police from both the state and the city stood by impassively.

These scenes are available to anyone who types "Charlottesville" into Google.

But what stays in my memory were not these broad canvases of violence and suffering. It is instead individual vignettes, which I can slow down and replay in my mind, of men and women brought to anxiety and violence by extremism.

After taking an early-morning swim at the gym on Monticello Avenue, my friend Richard, an African American man in his late fifties who grew up in segregated Charlottesville, watching a militia of neo-Nazis unload from a rented tour bus. As they adjusted their shields and helmets, holding assault rifles, Richard said, they were smiling and cheerful, "like they were going to a party." Fearing for his safety, he retreated quickly back into the building from which he had come.

As neo-Nazis marched with tiki torches through Thomas Jefferson's famed "Lawn" at the University of Virginia, around Jefferson's Rotunda, and up to a statue of Jefferson, a group of UVA students linking arms and surrounding the statue, despite the melee unleashed on them, with pepper spray, punches, and blood.

At the rally, a man hurling a punch at a young female counterprotester as he walked by, knocking her back several feet. The untrammeled testosterone, the shocking violence, the mayhem in that blatant, unashamed act of battery.

After the rally disbanded, the two opposing groups walking next to each other along Market Street toward the municipal garage where they had all inexplicably parked, shouting and jostling and punching each other in the hot August sun, with cops walking alongside, doing nothing.

A group of white men throwing a young black man to the ground in the parking garage, beating and kicking him with their boots, with a police station just feet away.

At UVA's Zehmer Hall, where I'd been sent to the joint emergency operations center, receiving the text of a post: "It's time to torch these jewish monsters lets go 3 pm [sic]." Watching my wife sitting next to me, crying and shaking, as I contacted the secretary of public safety and called the rabbi of Charlottesville's only temple, and learned that the building had already been empty for hours (the Holocaust-era scrolls had been removed as well).

A little while later, hearing a scream from the control room. Rushing in to hear these words: "There's been a car crash." People in front of their screens with their hands clapped to their cheeks, watching the video of a car crashing into a crowd of people. And watching it myself, thinking it could not have been intentional, then scrutinizing it over and over, realizing, with horror, that it must have been.

On Fourth Street, normally a humble, approachable area, lined with an old-fashioned vinyl record store, a spa, a bank, and other businesses in red and white brick buildings, a young woman named Heather Heyer walking with friends after protesting neo-Nazis, her long braid swinging. The muscle car accelerating, then plowing into the crowd. One man literally thrown into the air. Heyer, spun through the air before hitting the pavement. She was declared dead at the hospital, where nineteen others were admitted with horrible injuries.

A bearded African American man at the intersection afterward, screaming, "There are people, bodies lying on the ground right now. We told City Council we did not want them here. They let them come. We told the police we did not want them here. They let them come. I had to jump out the way. I almost got hit by the car my motherfucking self."

The sound of a woman screaming: "Oh my god! We got hit by a car!"

At the city council meeting a week later, one I chaired as mayor of Charlottesville, the rage and grief on the face of a young African American man I knew as he shouted at us from the podium, "We told y'all numerous times this shit was going to happen. And y'all did nothing."

Me responding plaintively from the dais, saying, "We tried really hard to get the rally out and a federal judge forced us to have the rally downtown. I'm just gonna say. We did try."

An audience member shouting back, "Why did you have the rally in the first place?" Responding, "Because we were legally required to." My acquaintance shouting back from the podium, "This is what we want: we want Mike Signer, [Councilor] Kathy Galvin, [Chief of Police] Al Thomas gone. We want leaders in this community who will actually protect us."

During that same meeting, dozens of people standing and chanting, "Signer must go." I had to watch the video to remember the events. I'd blocked them out. They were that painful. They were that extreme.

What lingers with me the most, as I sift through these scenes and hundreds of others, is a feeling, as I walked the Downtown Mall, of cold. It was August in central Virginia, a warm day. But I felt a chill in the humid air. I felt it everywhere as the satellite trucks moved in, as the first white nationalists roamed the city, with their tattoos and their aggression, and as the anti-fascists edgily wove through the streets.

I felt it when I stopped to look at three young men crumpled on the sidewalk along Fourth Street, three hours after Heather Heyer was killed. They wore ragged camouflage and rebel flag garb. The guy in the middle had a gash on his forehead, and blood was trickling down his cheek. They looked stunned—as if even they didn't understand what they had unleashed. I almost shivered. A friend told me later he could "feel the evil in the air" on the Downtown Mall that day. I nodded my head. I'd felt it too. It had felt like winter in summer.

THAT WAS AN ALREADY-FAMOUS CITY CONVULSING AS THE WORLD watched, changing before their very eyes. Up until that point, Charlottesville had been a famous small college town known for Thomas Jefferson's home, Monticello (which appears on the "tails" side of the nickel), for the University of Virginia (a UNESCO World Heritage site), and for aesthetics that were college-town cool before college towns were cool. It was at once one of the nation's premier wedding destinations, and an AAA-bond-rated municipality that boasted Virginia's lowest unemployment.

The city, about ten square miles in area, has a population of just under fifty thousand. Despite its small size, it once named itself a "World-Class City" during a branding campaign, and the sweetly vainglorious title stuck. In 2016, the year I became mayor, the city received several honors, including being named the #1 place to visit in the United States by Expedia, the #4 city in the country for entrepreneurs by *Entrepreneur*, #3 of the nation's fifteen Best Places to Live by the *New York Post*, the #1 small city for foodies by Travelocity, and one of the healthiest small towns in the country by HealthLine.

Charlottesville was renowned for its local food movement, its wineries and horse farms in surrounding Albemarle County, and a culture that was friendly and laid-back and yet intellectual, curious, and creative. For a small city, we hosted a remarkable number of festivals: the Virginia Festival of the Book, the Virginia Film Festival, the Miss Virginia pageant, and the Tom-Tom Founders Festival (a smaller version of Austin's SXSW).

Not all was bright. For starters, there was a tragic undercurrent of poverty. Local civic leaders had worked with the Chamber of Commerce on the "Orange Dot" Project to analyze the stubborn problem of the city's underclass, finding in 2015 that 1,800 families in Charlottesville—representing about 25 percent of the population—were not self-sufficient.[1]

The issue was intertwined with a history of racist practices. Just within the past four generations, Charlottesville's poor and black residents had experienced the brunt of Jim Crow laws; segregated schools; a "Massive Resistance" campaign to shut down public schools, rather than comply with the Supreme Court's requirement, in *Brown v. Board of Education* (1954), that they be desegregated; and a 1960s urban renewal project that razed Vinegar Hill, the city's black commercial district, and relocated the residents to a public housing project with cinderblock walls. The original site was left empty for years afterward, pouring salt into an unhealed wound.

The city council had created a community-wide "Dialogue on Race" in 2009 intended to generate restorative new public policies, and it had formally apologized for Vinegar Hill in 2011. And yet there was still a raw, fractious quality to local politics, particularly when they touched on race and class. Charlottesville was a progressive one-party town that had voted for Bernie Sanders over Hillary Clinton in the 2016 Democratic primary, but there were often factions within the Democratic Party, with one breakaway bloc forming to demand more aggressive policies, often employing disruptive tactics and ad hominem attacks in the process.

Through all of this, Charlottesville was experiencing the same prosperity as other cities around the country during the "back-to-the-city" movement of the 2000s. Millennials and senior citizens alike were flocking to Charlottesville to live within walking distance of cafes and bookstores. The population was steadily rising along with spending power and tax revenues. But with a limited supply of housing and parking, Charlottesville began to get more expensive. It began to gentrify, with lower-income folks being pushed out of the most popular areas.

But still and all, the city had earned a reputation as quirky, intimate, engaging, and beloved by most of its residents. For many years, for instance, there were two alternative weeklies. One was called the *C-ville Weekly*; the other was called *The Hook*, in a playful reference to a local saying: Charlottesville was so charming, so intoxicating, even, that once you came, you were "hooked," and you'd come back.

This balance between the bucolic and the stimulating, which would be the envy of many cities around the world, would be fundamentally shaken in one brutal weekend. After the Unite the Right rally, and especially after President Donald Trump's extraordinary statement that there were "good people on both sides" of the mayhem, Charlottesville would become synonymous with white supremacy and with terrorism. The city's "brand" now commingled the pleasing contours of UVA and Monticello with swastikas, shields, swords, helmets, and that haunting chant: "Jews will not replace us."

WE USE METAPHORS DRAWN FROM THE NATURAL WORLD TO CAPture things that both delight and disturb us. Falling in love is like being in a heat wave. A political controversy is a tornado. A business crisis is a hurricane.

What happened in Charlottesville is no exception. But it's difficult to determine exactly which metaphor best captures the events this book describes. On the one hand, Charlottesville was like an earthquake. Earthquakes happen along fault lines, which take place when ancient plates underneath the earth's surface collide to release tremendous, violent energy. In this metaphor, the task we had in the city's leadership was to remain standing while the earth shook. The task ahead would be to anticipate tremors and stabilize society.

But Charlottesville also felt like a hurricane, a perfect storm—a weather system created by pent-up climatic forces gathering before descending in torrents of destructive wind and rain. Such a metaphor would imply that we needed to sail the ship of state through the squalls.

And the work ahead would not be to control hurricanes (you can't), but instead to prepare the city to survive them, perhaps through levees, weatherproofing, and better climatology.

But hurricanes aren't, in and of themselves, manmade (though climate change has made them worse), as the crisis in Charlottesville was. So perhaps a better metaphor would be fires, which often are caused by people. As I sought to understand these events through language, something our fire chief said to me in a security briefing before the rally came back to me. He said that the only model they could come up with for what they might have to deal with following the rally, as hundreds of violent people would likely disperse through the town, was that of the scattered brushfires that emerge even after a forest fire is put out.

So I decided it's fire, not wind and rain, that seems to be the best way to understand what happened in Charlottesville. I have used the word "firestorm" as much as anyone else, but I still had to look it up to learn exactly what it means. According to *Merriam-Webster*, it's a "very intense and destructive fire usually accompanied by high winds," particularly "one that is started by attack with nuclear or incendiary weapons and that creates a powerful updraft which causes very strong inrushing winds to develop in the surrounding area." Significantly, the word was first used in 1945—the same year that World War II ended with firestorms in Dresden and Hamburg, created by hundreds of massive, incendiary, oxygen-sucking bombs.[2]

This book is about a metaphorical firestorm. After one, the earth is scorched and barren. What happens next? The metaphor is generous. On the one hand, new growth can occur even after horrific fires, as we see in "slash-and-burn" agriculture—a method where forests are burned so the ashes can fertilize the ground for crops. In other words, even a firestorm can generate growth.

But there are other ways that fire can create. Consider a crucible, a container in which chemicals are melted together to create a new substance. *Merriam-Webster* refers to a place or situation where "concentrated forces interact to cause or influence change or development."[3] That's also how we might see Charlottesville: a fire that produced ingots of wisdom.

I will suggest in this book that there were actually five underlying brushfires that converged to create this firestorm. In each area, the conflict between ideas, ideals, and constraints created friction, heat, and combustion. First, the conflict between the freedom of speech and public safety in our First Amendment law. Second, our collective failure to come up with constructive ways to address a history of racism through our memorials and public spaces. Third, the clash between order and the passions of today's politics, and the fight to define "civility" itself. Fourth, the challenge of providing accountability in a crisis, to a public clamoring for real answers. Finally, how the newfound drive for equity can upend generations of policy and governance.

In each area, we were bedeviled not just by the difficulty of finding an answer, but by people demanding that one should be easy to find, and that we were flawed, even evil, if we couldn't. Supposedly simple answers dangled like sweets. On the First Amendment and repeated visits by white nationalists: "Deny the permit" and "Stop them from coming here." On the Lee statue: "Tear it down." On accountability: "Just tell the truth." On the civility debate: "Just let people be heard." On equity: "Just do the right thing."

So charged with energy, these demands could also be distracting and even dangerous, sparking blazes that could spread contagiously. In an age addicted to slogans that fit social media, and a press that struggles to cover complexity and substance, there was little appetite for leaders doing what leaders *needed* to do: grapple in the crucial gray area that lies between the seductive poles of black and white. This gray, mind you, was not mild or equivocal. It was the gray of smoke and of ashes.

THIS IS ULTIMATELY A STORY ABOUT GOVERNANCE UNDER FIRE IN a disruptive new era. This story is admittedly, and necessarily, mine—told in my voice, seen from my eyes, from the seat I had as the city's mayor during these events. In other words, while I have tried to tell the story as factually as I can, this is also a subjective account, and certain characters and events are certainly given shorter shrift than they would be given in other accounts. But because this account is told from my perspective, it also allows me to spend more time on certain aspects of the story that I saw as especially important, given my background in political theory, law, and American history.

I have tried to be as honest as I can, to describe not only mistakes and second-guessing, but my experiences in a very hot seat. In my role as the mayor in a city with a "weak mayor" form of government (there will be much more about this later), I fought hard to reconcile the irreconcilable as best as I could. When I became mayor, many of my friends and colleagues advised me that it would be safer to "take the title," focus on my ceremonial duties, and treat the office as the part-time job it's designed to be. But I wanted to use my term instead to reanimate the office, kick-start stalled projects, bring respect back to the council chambers, and lead where others had followed. In the process, I pushed boundaries, ruffled feathers, and, no question about it, made enemies.

These were the costs of the approach I took. We like to think of leadership in Hollywood terms: the successful IPO, scoring a touchdown, passing a bill, winning great cheers. But more often than not, it's a gritty slog up a field, battered from all sides, with a concussion or two along the way. The more I've gotten to know other mayors, businesspeople, and nonprofit leaders, the more I've heard those hidden stories of "wrestling in the gray." That's what real leadership is, and we need to understand it better. Where you find mistakes in this story, I would urge you to put yourself in the shoes of the person who made them—to think hard about what you would have done instead.

These were difficult experiences. But they were also rewarding. There is nothing like fighting for something you believe in where there's no easy answer, because, in the end, if you want to lead, that's just what you'll have to deal with. You might as well throw yourself headlong into the challenges. You need, in other words, to plunge into the real world.

Thinking about "the world" in this way is a crucial idea from the work of Hannah Arendt, the German Jewish philosopher who immigrated to America before writing the magisterial book *The Origins of Totalitarianism*, and who chronicled, as a journalist, the Nuremberg trials of Nazi war criminals, authoring *The Banality of Evil*, about the conviction of Hitler's henchman Adolf Eichmann.

I first heard Arendt's name from my grandmother, Esther Signer, who worked for a time as a secretary at the New School in New York, where

Arendt taught. I remember her telling me about the "great woman" in her office. After the Holocaust and World War II, Arendt was troubled by the widespread temptation to turn away from government and politics entirely. Even in 1968, over twenty years after the end of World War II, she observed that "more and more people in the countries of the Western world, which since the decline of the ancient world has regarded freedom from politics as one of the basic freedoms, make use of this freedom and have retreated from the world and their obligations within it."[4] She argued for the opposite: for turning back to the world, with all of its contradictions, meanness, faults, and even evil—for embracing the whole of it and plunging into it. That was the duty of the human being as a social, and therefore a political, animal. She called this *amor mundi*—love of the world. She approvingly wrote about "always taking sides for the world's sake, understanding and judging everything in terms of its position in the world at any given time."[5] She was urging us to get involved, to get our hands dirty with *realpolitik*, not despite of, but *because of*, the cost.

That idea suggests one light in which we can view the 2017 events of Charlottesville: as a case study for a surprising truth about how growth in a healthy democracy occurs—that it's *agonistic*. *Agon* is an idea from ancient Greece positing that conflict is essential to political life. The Greek playwright Euripides built productive conflict into his plots like an engine. His tragedies often featured harsh conflicts between protagonists and antagonists, but they drove the drama, and the lessons, forward.[6] In the words of one scholar, agonists believe so fervently in the centrality of struggle to democracy that they call for a revitalization of modern democratic culture "not in terms of the articulation of public goods which exceed partisan interests, but through a celebration of the continuous conflict of those interests."[7]

The struggle we see in the real world—the world as it is, not as we want it to be—can be uncomfortable and even ugly. But the cost of the struggle, on human beings, institutions, and society as a whole, is not only incidental to progress, but necessary to it. You can see this idea in much of America's history. Whether in Jim Crow laws or McCarthyism or the horrific bigotry and violence that took over the streets of Charlottesville, American democracy has responded to agony by pushing to perfect its first principles—for equality to *really mean* equality, for freedom to *really mean* freedom. In other words, progress not only won't happen without pain, but *depends* on pain. A crucible, in other words, needs a fire.

Even James Madison centered his greatest contributions on this very idea. We have a deceptive picture of Madison in our heads today. The Father of the Constitution, who was five feet four inches tall and weighed only a hundred pounds, is caricatured as intellectual and somewhat effete. We praise the elegance of the checks and balances in the constitutional system he designed much as we might celebrate the artistry of an architect's blueprints. But the inevitability of conflict, even violence, was woven into his theory of how society's factions needed to be balanced against each other, lest one of them consume the country.

In a democracy, Madison went to great pains to teach us, people are free to disagree, and power is up for the taking. Even in a time of peace, this can be ugly. The system endures, however, because it embraces rather than rejects this conflict. I will argue in this book that the agonizing events of Charlottesville will still help the nation move forward from them, that we will become more democratic, more free, and more pluralistic as a result.

But this progress won't be without agony. It will be because of it.

1

THE HOOK

CHARLOTTESVILLE'S CITY HALL IS AN UNREMARKABLE 1970s-style building whose only notable feature is a frieze at its rounded corner featuring three US presidents—Thomas Jefferson, James Madison, and James Monroe—in bronze. Just out front, in the center of the Downtown Mall, stands the Freedom of Speech Wall, a slate wall that runs for over fifty feet, where members of the public are encouraged to express their views on any subject in multicolored chalk that is conveniently provided. The chalk is wiped off three times per week—unless the rain does the job first—and it always fills up again quickly, usually within a few hours. Carved into one segment of the wall is the text of the First Amendment of the US Constitution. On the opposite side is a quote by the late US Supreme Court justice Thurgood Marshall:

> Above all else, the First Amendment means that government has no power to restrict expression because of its message, its ideas, its subject matter, or its content. To permit the continued building of our politics and culture, and to assure self-fulfillment for each individual, our people are guaranteed the right to express any thought, free from government censorship.[1]

The monument also includes a podium that serves as a contemporary soapbox. Inscribed on it is a quote from John Milton's *Areopagitica*:

"Give me the liberty to know, to utter, and to argue freely according to conscience, above all liberties."[2]

This is the center of one of America's most celebrated small towns, drawing thousands of locals and visitors every year for its shopping and restaurants, for weddings, brewery tours, and romantic getaways. But in 2017 it became a stage for terror and for a political furor that still burns on today. The murderous disaster on this promenade transfixed the world. My time in City Hall as mayor, from 2016 to 2018, gave me a front-row seat, in the historic backyard of three American presidents, to one of the greatest tests that contemporary American democracy has seen.

Democracy's power as a beacon of hope for all people and its confounding changeability were illuminated for me by my paternal grandfather, Herbert Signer, a lifelong proofreader for the *New York Times* who as a young man served as an army jeep mechanic in World War II, servicing the vehicles that helped liberate the prisoners of the Nazi concentration camps of Europe. He and my grandmother were active members of the American Communist Party in the postwar years, but they resigned from the party in 1956, when Soviet premier Nikita Khrushchev disclosed Joseph Stalin's war crimes and purges. After that, they were completely apolitical. I only learned about their early political activities years later, when I was in college.

"If there's one thing I've learned," Grandpa had told me, "it's that everything becomes its opposite." What did he mean? I asked. He talked about how communism—so idealistic, so aspirational—had become fascism instead. He cited examples of ambitious social justice schemes as well. Public housing towers in America, for instance, had seemed like such a good idea at the time. They would help needy folks by putting them in new, safe housing—together. But the projects ended up concentrating poverty and crime instead and gave already marginalized people a sense there was no way out. An idealistic ambition had become its opposite. This, to him, was a key problem in our country. It was, in contemporary parlance, a feature, not a bug, of liberal democracy.

He told me this with a sense of mystification, almost wonder. He could finish the Sunday *New York Times* crossword puzzle in minutes. He had answers for many things. But not this. This was an exception and a paradox. It was something I'd have to reckon with on my own. No wonder that I would later become so fascinated by the problem of how democracies can collapse at the hands of their own citizens. I'd go on to write a PhD dissertation on the subject. Later, when promoting democracy became the announced goal of US foreign policy in the George W. Bush administration, the dissertation became a book about the challenges that demagogues abroad, such as Venezuela's Hugo Chavez and Iran's Mahmoud Ahmadinejad, posed for democratization.

Little did I know that in 2016, with the election of Donald Trump, America would see a demagogue ascend to the presidency, unleashing for me and millions of others profound worries about our own democracy's ability to self-destruct—to turn into its opposite—and what we should do in response.

IN 2012, AT THIRTY-NINE, I FOUND MYSELF AT ONE OF THOSE CRITical turning points in life that determines everything afterward. Since college, I'd been driven to achieve. I had earned a PhD from the University of California at Berkeley and a JD from the University of Virginia; practiced law at the prestigious law firm WilmerHale in Washington, DC; and directed national security policy on a presidential campaign. I had run for lieutenant governor of Virginia, authored the book on demagogues and democracy and started another on James Madison, became a visiting professor at Virginia Tech, and founded a successful law practice.

Amid all of this, it had been difficult to carve out space for a family, but that changed that same year, when I married Emily Blout. Emily and I had first met in 2008 during the Obama campaign, when she was working on Iran policy at a DC-area nonprofit. With huge, expressive eyes and long, tousled brown hair, she was effervescent, passionate, and principled. She represented the opposite of so much I had seen and come to dislike in politics, but what I loved about democracy. We were living at the time in a one-bedroom condo in Arlington, Virginia, just over the Potomac River from the capital. Emily was writing her PhD dissertation, and I was practicing law, teaching, writing a book on James Madison, and serving on boards, including the Virginia Board of Medicine and the Center for National Policy.

In 2013, I would turn forty. As I reckoned with a life half-over, I realized that whether I was counseling clients, authoring white papers, teaching courses, attending lunches and panels, or advising campaigns, most of my life related to influencing powerful institutions.

I found myself wanting a smaller, more local life, a life defined by community, not influence. I came back again and again to something I'd first experienced in elementary school, when I had attended week-long summer enrichment programs at the University of Virginia, and then again when visiting my two younger sisters, who attended UVA as undergraduates, and again as a law student at UVA—the sense of being part of a small, close-knit community. My interest in returning to Charlottesville had been brewing for years. The year after I'd graduated from law school, I'd worked in Richmond as counsel to then governor Mark Warner, but I'd chosen to live in Charlottesville, over an hour away. I'd bought a small red house in a historically African American neighborhood called Fifeville near the Downtown Mall, where I could walk to the coffee shops and music venues I'd loved during law school.

My passion for Charlottesville had become a family joke, as a plot in the making. I'd proposed to Emily at the Foxfield Inn in Charlottesville in a gazebo filled with flowers, and we'd gotten married in Charlottesville at the historic Clifton Inn.

And so, entering midlife, I convinced Emily to give Charlottesville a try. In 2013, the year after we got married, we moved back to the Hook.

IN FACT, WE MOVED INTO THE SAME SMALL RED HOUSE IN FIFE-ville. Fifeville had been populated by railroad workers and African American employees of the University of Virginia for generations, and it featured densely packed, low-slung bungalows with distinctive angles in the eaves. It was quiet, friendly, intimate, and diverse.

Life became busy quickly. I opened up a local law office, working with local tech and finance companies. I became a lecturer at UVA. I chaired the local Democratic Party's campaign for city council. I also chaired the Emergency Food Network, a small nonprofit that provided three days of food to thousands of people a year, where I saw firsthand the problems faced by the working poor.

In the Fifeville Neighborhood Association, I joined a committee charged with advising the city council on a controversial plan to redevelop the West Main Street corridor linking the University of Virginia and the Downtown Mall. Shortly thereafter, when I became president of the association, we faced an issue that had come up before: a local liquor store was generating crime and litter. It was owned and operated by the state Alcoholic Beverage Control (ABC) Authority, and its five-year lease was ending. A generation earlier, the store had been located in the African American neighborhood over the objections of many of the residents with whom I had spoken. We'd watched dozens of instances of open-air drug deals and public urination. People passed out on the nearby streets from drinking, and thousands of discarded "airplane" liquor bottles littered the area.

A campaign to relocate the store somewhere else had garnered the endorsement of the pastors of two African American churches. I gathered several hundred signatures on petitions, and the majority of the signers were African American. Every member of the city council supported a resolution asking the state to relocate the store.

A local African American activist, however, suddenly turned the effort into a referendum not on public health and safety, but gentrification. Blaming the critique of the store on "the influx of white people moving into the neighborhood," he launched a new petition drive to keep the store where it was. He appeared before Charlottesville City Council, where he attacked me and tried to convince the councilors to change their position. Unexpectedly, a liquor store had become a point of pride. I was surprised and caught off-guard. Clearly, I had missed something. I said I was "listening and learning"—and I meant it, especially regarding the topic of race and class in this small southern town.

Regarding the store, the activism still led to progress. The state overhauled the store's appearance, put in security cameras, and instructed employees to actually enforce the liquor laws. Littering—and the crime rate—dropped. The Charlottesville Planning Commission gave the association a "neighborhood of the year" award. Although the results were not what I had hoped, I still thought we'd made a difference on a local issue.

That fall, the mayor of Charlottesville, a Sikh American who had previously been the city's planning director, announced that he would not be running for reelection. I was encouraged to run for city council, and I said yes. In doing so, I moved from a career previously dedicated to high-level federal and state issues to the more granular and gritty issues of a city. There was a lot to learn. Meanwhile, in late September 2014, Emily gave birth to tiny, yelling, blessedly healthy twin boys. The campaign started in earnest just three months later.

I campaigned on a "One Charlottesville" platform of bridging divisions in the city. As much as I wanted to focus on policy, I was counseled by activists and former mayors alike that my campaign would also need to be intensely local and one-to-one. Whether I won or lost would depend not on speeches, on how much money I raised, or on how many mailers I sent out, but on the number of voters I met personally and how they responded to me. My plan was to personally contact every one of Charlottesville's regular Democratic primary voters multiple times. That goal would be achieved in part by holding a large number of house parties where I could have conversations with small groups. There, I hoped to delve into the issues they cared about.

Ultimately I would knock on around 2,000 doors and hold about a dozen house parties. I had a motorcycle at the time—a cherry-red Honda Shadow 750 American Classic Edition, and I would put my literature into its saddlebags, pick a neighborhood, and ride out to knock on doors. These were friendly but demanding folks, and they ran a wide gamut—there were political refugees from West Africa, elderly folks and people with disabilities, and students who had just started voting. Almost everyone I met was highly informed, and many of them asked tough questions. They told me how much they appreciated the fact that, rain or shine, I physically came to their door to introduce myself and ask about their concerns.

I kept on knocking. Our system ranked each person I met from 1 to 5 according to their enthusiasm for my campaign and had specific targets for 1's and 2's to ensure my election, and we were on track. But then I had a setback: just a few weeks before Election Day, I made the mistake of taking yet another long walk to canvass a neighborhood, this time in cheap dress shoes. The tops of my feet began hurting, badly: plantar fasciitis. Just when I needed to be out there the most, I was sidelined. My field director put me on the phones instead. After I spoke with someone, we would send a follow-up note, and my field of support continued to grow.

By the time of the election, we had identified about 1,300 voters who we believed ranked 1 or 2 in their enthusiasm. It was what we needed to win. Confident on election night, due to the literal expenditure of shoe leather, I ended up receiving 1,855 votes, a pleasant surprise. Although I had broken the record for fundraising on a council race, I think I would have won with much less, just based on voter contact alone. What mattered was that people had met me, or knew I'd stopped by their house. It was the essence of democratic politics—getting to know people's stories, and hearing them, with attention, focus, and care.

But getting elected was one thing. I would now have to deliver.

And not just as a city councilor, but as the mayor.

2

"SIMPLY BECAUSE THERE'S PASSION"

AT MY FIRST CITY COUNCIL MEETING, THE CHARLOTTESVILLE city manager asked for nominations for mayor. Mine was the only name submitted and seconded. The vote was then called, and the vote for me was unanimous. I was mayor, just like that. And yet earning the votes to be mayor had required extensive discussion beforehand with my soon-to-be colleagues. Wes Bellamy, a twenty-nine-year-old African American teacher in the Albemarle County Public Schools, had suggested that he be vice-mayor and I be mayor, and our colleagues had agreed. We'd been meeting along with the other Democratic nominee, Kathy Galvin, once a week for the past several months to discuss our plans.

One thing I realized, as I moved to the mayor's center seat, was that I'd never wielded a gavel before. Another was that the room looked decidedly different from behind the dais than it did from the podium in front, where I was accustomed to speaking as an activist. Some council chambers are completely horizontal, with the speakers and elected officials sitting at the same level. But in Charlottesville, the council hears speakers from behind a raised dais. As a citizen, it always somehow felt daunting. Now I was on the other side.

The meeting had begun unevenly. Prior to the meeting, a local activist who had run unsuccessfully for council in the past staged a small protest near the Freedom of Speech Wall. With about a dozen other people, he protested the amount of money that I and the other candidates had raised. The group then marched into the chambers carrying signs alleging corruption, which gave an edgy, rambunctious feel to the meeting that followed.

My first priority as mayor would be to bring order and efficiency to the proceedings. No longer would meetings go past midnight with no clear direction. No longer would decisions be kicked to ineffective citizen committees like the West Main Street committee I'd sat on for two years. No longer would a circus-like atmosphere predominate, with personal attacks, back-and-forth conversations with audience members, and long discussions with no item up for actual decision. We had already begun to work on a new set of governing procedures that would create more efficiency and transparency, which we thought would make the council more effective.

In this first meeting, I read a statement that referenced the cynicism about politics and government in society, which we saw in Charlottesville as well as in nasty comments online and in the toxic politics of Donald Trump. I said we had an opportunity to rebut that cynicism with governance itself. Schoolchildren should be able to watch us on TV and think they might want to be on a city council someday too. The city council should become an exemplar for our citizens of collegiality, of deliberation, of transparency, and of good government. We could disagree without being disagreeable.

I said that as mayor, I wanted to avoid "symbolic victories." I brought this up for a reason. Symbols seemed to be replacing real issues in our politics. I'd already seen in Charlottesville how much symbols could wreak havoc with reality. One week, the liquor store meant one thing to many folks; the next week, racing across Facebook, it had come to mean something else entirely. The meaning of many such symbols could so easily be changed because the symbols themselves were free-floating signifiers, batted about like balloons, up for grabs. The fight over holding and defining the symbols *became* the issue.

Call it the "politics of symbolism." I wanted the new Charlottesville City Council to get rid of it and to get back to substance.

I had a second goal in that first meeting. I told my constituents that I didn't want the council to "play to the public's passions." The Founding Fathers had built entire political institutions to check collective rushes to judgment, like the US Senate, the federal judiciary, and the Electoral College. In Federalist Paper No. 49, for instance, James Madison described the "danger of disturbing the public tranquility by interesting too strongly the public passions," worrying that the "PASSIONS, therefore, not the REASON, of the public would sit in judgment." His solution was that "reason, alone, of the public, . . . ought to control and regulate the government."

But I also knew what I'd seen in prior years on the dais: acrimony, personal attacks, and squabbling between councilors and the audience. Not to mention audience members openly shouting at councilors from the crowd.

Sure, I could have started smaller than the politics of symbolism and governing the passions. But I was eager to tackle practical problems through the lens of truly thoughtful ideas, informed by history and the values of our democratic system. Alarmed by the surge of Trumpism on the national scene, I hoped we could address the waves of surging, usually symbolic politics sweeping across our ten square miles of city.

Little did I know how hard that would be.

DURING MY FIRST MEETING AS MAYOR, A LAWYER NAMED JEFF Fogel came to the podium. Originally from New Jersey, he had a long history of suing the city (sometimes successfully) on social and racial justice issues. Fogel said, "Now what I don't understand here is why it is that people with passions are somehow in your mind to be dismissed simply because there's passion." He continued: "And I think it's about time that we got the respect, those of us who have worked our butts off in this area, even if you don't like the way we express ourselves. And why are you afraid—afraid—of controversy?"

As I watched him remonstrate with me, I saw not only a gadfly taking on the new mayor, but a local instance of a debate that has been occurring for thousands of years. This is an essential dilemma to democracy. We require our leaders to be responsive. If their constituents are angry, then who is government to say they ought to be more polite? Who were the ancient Greeks, anyway, to lecture us about the passions? Who was the new *mayor* to say anything about it? On the other hand, those very principles about deliberation prevent a meeting from becoming a shouting match, allowing people with strong opposing opinions to participate in the same government, to work together under the same rules, and to accept the results, even if they don't win.

Thus appeared the first licks of flame of a brushfire I would come to know well as mayor: the challenge of keeping order in a tumultuous time. The fraught status of the most ancient underpinnings of democratic self-government: civility, efficiency, and deliberation.

AFTER THE MEETING, I HAD TO START ACTUALLY BEING MAYOR.

The only formal, written duties of the mayor in our "council-manager" form of government (more on this below) was to set the meeting agendas and to run the meetings. But from the outset, I wanted to take a new approach from that of the prior two-term mayor. While he had taken a largely passive role in the public eye, I wanted to take a more vigorous, proactive stance.

I began with the literal office. The mayorship came with one specific perk: an actual large office right across from the city manager's office. It was used for occasional meetings, but not actual work, and so had become by default the storehouse for dozens of random artifacts: gifts from the Sister City program, including plaques from Ghana and books from France, for example, and assorted items from Charlottesville's history—municipal awards and the like. A large "Office of the Mayor" sign was coated with dust and leaning in the closet.

Emily and I began by decorating. We were hyper-sensitive to the potential issue of a new mayor buying up things to create fancy digs, so we purchased some cheap furniture at a President's Day sale from places like World Market with my city-issued credit card (checking with the city manager first for approval). For under $600, we got two small couches, a coffee table, a rug, and a few other odds and ends. I brought my desk and laptop from home. We put my diplomas and books in the room and a few plants. I bought an inexpensive Mr. Coffee espresso maker and put it in the staff kitchen.

I hung around. I met frequently with Paige Rice, our clerk of council (the only staff member who exclusively reported to the city council). I met with staff. I poked my head into meetings. I showed up unannounced to events. It made some of them uncomfortable to have the mayor around so much. None of them reported to me. In fact, the convention in place at the time, common in council-manager forms of government, was that councilors (including the mayor) were not supposed to communicate with staff directly without the city manager—their boss—being in on the email, or even in the room.[1]

From my new office in City Hall, I had identified a suite of initiatives I wanted to lead from the Office of the Mayor. Among others, I wanted to pass the long-delayed $35 million West Main Street plan, which would better connect the university and the Downtown Mall; redevelop the Downtown Mall's crumbling and unfinished Landmark Hotel into a thriving mixed-use project; mandate a long-overdue efficiency study and plan for the city; create a "311" system for tracking complaints by citizens; develop a new regionalism approach for the city's often conflicted relationship with Albemarle County, which surrounds Charlottesville like a doughnut; increase support and incentives for technology businesses and stimulate our creative economy; implement an "Open Data" policy for the city; expand our support for affordable housing; and strengthen voting rights in the city.[2]

In putting my plans together, I began holding open office hours on the first Wednesday of every month. I convened a Mayor's Advisory Council on Innovation and Technology with several dozen members that generated ideas like a pilot project on automated vehicles and expansion of our incentives for technology businesses. To create a system for support and research beyond what our lone clerk could provide, I started a "Mayor's Fellows" program with the Batten School of Public Policy and Leadership at UVA, where I was teaching. I had a monthly breakfast with a vice-provost at UVA charged with city relations, and another monthly meeting with the chair of Albemarle County's Board of Supervisors. I joined the United States Conference of Mayors, which put me into a new network of peers. On the Landmark Hotel, I reached out to the owner myself, while pushing the council to support a new approach and staff to negotiate a deal with the owner. I even started calling citizens on their birthdays to wish them happy birthday from their mayor.

There was a problem, however. I was doing all these things within a form of government that gave the mayor much less formal power than my approach implied. The little-known fact is that almost 50 percent of American cities have this very same "council-manager" form of government. And my vigorous approach to the "weak mayor" office would have consequences down the road, when people would be confounded by just how little power I really had over things like policing, public events, and city communications, compared to the whirlwind of activity I was generating.

The model had been devised in Staunton, Virginia, a small, picturesque town just an hour west of Charlottesville. In 1905, with a population that had recently exceeded ten thousand, Staunton had a mayor with veto power; a city council that ran a number of committees charged with the major functions of government, such as highways and sewers; and a duplicative board of aldermen. But having part-time councilors direct important things like highways and sewers was creating a disaster. The city found itself over half a million dollars in debt as a result of what was called "honest graft": contractors would place bids for city contracts well above their ordinary prices, and thirty different committees, some with as many as fifteen elected officials, often had corrupting relationships with the contractors.[3] As a consequence, the city's street department was paving only about one block a year, while many other streets went unpaved and were just reverting to mud.

Local leaders came up with a new idea: scrapping the current system and instead concentrating the executive and administrative powers of government in a single appointed official who would manage all the different departments. They envisioned him as a sort of body politic unto himself: "In him would combine the duties in other cities imposed upon paid heads of departments; he would be the manager or superintendent of the city's work."[4] Like the board of directors of a corporation and the corporation's CEO, the city manager would occasionally report to city council, which would shift from operational functions to policy development. The council would have certain specific duties, such as making land-use decisions in zoning appeals, running the public meetings, where the councilors would hear directly from citizens, and voting on the budget prepared for them by the city manager. But otherwise, the city manager would implement the policies the council approved.

That basic framework spread quickly through many American cities. Today, 48 percent of all US municipalities have a city or town manager or executive, and over 105 million people live in these cities. Sixty-two percent of cities with populations greater than 100,000 have this form of government.[5] It is usually firmly embedded in both state and city law. As a contemporary example of how a council-manager government works—an example directly relevant to this book—Charlottesville's city manager is vested by state law as the city's "emergency manager." When an emergency is declared, he or she—rather than elected officials—may alone legally direct what the government does, whether on law enforcement, events, communications, or cooperation with entities like the Virginia State Police and the Virginia Department of Emergency Management.

But as with other systems whose very success ensures that we take them for granted (think Medicare or the sewers), many of the people who live in these cities don't even know they have a council-manager government, let alone how it works. This is doubly the case in a time of crisis. During natural disasters like hurricanes or fires, for instance, the "weak mayors" in a council-manager government often speak on behalf of the government. There's nothing wrong with serving as a spokesperson, of course. But they are not the ones calling the shots. It's the city manager or county executive, often standing just stage left or stage right, who's in charge.

My new approach created a new picture of the mayorship for both City Hall and the citizens at large. Over the course of my two years as mayor, the clerk of council who had been with the city for eight years and worked with two prior mayors, would estimate in a March 2019 email that I increased the work of the office by a factor of ten. But given my ambitions for the mayorship, I found the limitations of the council-manager form frustrating. And when there was a crisis, it would be just as frustrating for the public to have a mayor who was not in fact as strong as they thought he was.[6]

The real picture of my power was complicated not only by the new approach I'd taken, but by the mystical envelope that I stepped into when I received the title of mayor.

"MAYOR." "THERE'S THE MAYOR." "HI, MAYOR." "WELCOME, MAYOR."

That title was like pixie dust surrounding me wherever I went in the city. Even in my part-time role, with a city manager running the actual day-to-day operations of government, I found myself suddenly clothed with the honorific persona while I went about my everyday life.[7] One time, at a local running shop, there was a small sensation that the mayor was there buying shoes in person, rather than online. The owner took a selfie with me and the store tweeted it out. Whether I was at the library or on a bus, people would whisper to their kids, "There's the mayor!" At the gym, as I huffed on the treadmill or sweated through a set on the bench, I often felt eyes on me. I did ribbon-cuttings and made speeches launching festivals.

This was the ceremonial power of the office, the fact that we ritualistically enjoy elevating one human among us, through such titles, to a place of veneration.[8] With the example of strong executive-type figures looming large in American history (Richard Daley in Chicago, Fiorello La Guardia and Rudy Giuliani in New York), mayors are often the subject of public fascination, even obsession. Albemarle County, which is two and a half times the size of Charlottesville, has a chair of its board of supervisors. There was no legal or functional difference between my role as mayor and that of Albemarle's chair. Yet the local media, constituents, and stakeholder groups treated me differently. I came to believe the difference lay in the title, and in the broader ceremonial associations that came along with it.

After I finished my term as mayor and became a plain city councilor, I saw how accurate my assessment of the magic cloak was when the requests and the recognition stopped almost instantly. This despite the fact that in our system, a councilor has virtually the same actual powers as the mayor. The title made all the difference.

BUT THERE'S A FLIP SIDE TO THE FASCINATION: MAYORS GET AN extra helping of criticism along with their adoration. Two weeks after becoming mayor, I traveled with the United States Conference of Mayors for an event at the White House. The event began when President Barack Obama sat down before a group of about two hundred mayors and, with a broad smile, joked, "Y'all feeling underappreciated recently?" Every mayor got the joke instantly, and the room burst into laughter. One mayor asked how Obama got through all the attacks. Obama explained that our twenty-four-hour news cycle was out of sync with our policy. He gave two examples: his administration's response to the Ebola epidemic, and its successful resolution of the Gulf oil spill. Both had created a sense of crisis on the news and social media that was out of whack with what government actually was doing.

The image of an enmeshed system of gears came to mind—the small wheels of social media frantically spinning, the progressively larger wheels of actual government action through policy, and of justice and truth, moving slowly and methodically, but powerfully. The president's responses offered us a glimpse into his own challenges, but it was also an astute commentary on our political times—the confluence of the politics of symbolism with a raging passion for, well, passion. He was encouraging us as mayors to think about the long game: to fireproof our work from the passions raging around us, and to focus on the *solutions* rather than on the *symbols about* the solutions.

He had done it in Washington, I thought. Couldn't we at least try to do it in Charlottesville?

3

"IS MIKE YOUR DADDY?"

| FEBRUARY 2016 |

During my second month as mayor, on Saturday, February 20, Donald Trump won the South Carolina primary. Wherever I went, a dark, sick feeling followed me like a shadow. It was with me at Kroger, when I shopped for groceries late on Sunday night, bagging them myself. It was haunting: a demagogue could actually become president of the United States. My book *Demagogue: The Fight to Save Democracy from Its Worst Enemies*, published seven years earlier, had argued that this was virtually impossible because of the strength and resilience of American constitutionalism—I believed that our "constitutional conscience" protected us from electing someone who would play on our prejudices and passions.[1] But it was that very foundation bolstering the republic that seemed to be turning into quicksand before my eyes.

In some unconscious way, the goal of bringing order to our unruly meetings took on greater urgency for me. During our weekly breakfasts that year, Wes Bellamy, Kathy Galvin, and I had frequently talked about the common impression that city council's meetings were a circus. We had decided to establish, for the first time, governing rules for our meetings. Working with our clerk, we researched rules in other bodies in Virginia and around the country.

We learned that even though the council was supposed to be under Robert's Rules of Order, it had been operating for years under a "small group exception" to the rules. That's why things seemed so screwy in meetings. These rules of parliamentary procedure prohibit members from interrupting each other. Nobody can speak without recognition first from the chair of the meeting. You also aren't supposed to allude to the motives of anyone else (this is why you always hear "my friend" and "the honorable"). Deliberation was the goal—not just debate. The city council was supposed to move from one point to another through this formal process. That's what we were there for. Robert's Rules allow debate only when a motion is properly moved, seconded, and on the floor.[2]

That's also why many city councils around the country speed through their agendas. They do have debates, but they occur only after formal motions are made on the basis of an agenda item. Even then, the debate is supposed to be constructive. It is supposed to allow an official to explain his or her position to the public and to allow officials to work together on the measure. Well-crafted governing rules were all devised to achieve that end. In some councils, we learned, they had even added time limits for speaking. Other councils would not allow the member making the first motion to speak again, to prevent one member from dominating and speechifying. In Charlottesville, the opposite was happening: debate *before* a motion. That's why so little was moving forward, why the debates so frequently devolved into plain argument.

I worked with the others to craft a new set of governing procedures that were modeled on several others in place around Virginia, including Williamsburg, Arlington, Richmond, and Staunton. We discussed the rules and had our first vote in favor of them at a work session one Saturday afternoon in February. Going forward, we would now be under the traditional requirements of Robert's Rules of Order, with the mayor having all the powers those rules normally provided the chair of a meeting.

In an open letter to the public, I explained why I wanted to enforce Robert's Rules, whose purpose, I noted (citing *Robert's Rules for Dummies*), was to "ensure public confidence." Following parliamentary procedure, I said, would ensure that minority opinions were heard. It would also "focus debate on actions and issues rather than personalities." These standard procedures would require members of the council to recognize me as chair of the meeting before they could have the floor, and they would allow discussion of a matter only after a motion had been introduced. For support, I again cited *Robert's Rules for Dummies*, which says that this set of rules "helps keep things on track by requiring that no discussion be undertaken until somebody proposes an idea for action. Everything your group ever accomplishes gets its start through *motions*."[3]

It seemed like such a no-brainer.

ALMOST AS QUICKLY AS WE PASSED THE NEW RULES, THEY, AND I, came under fire. On February 11, a citizen named Nikuyah Walker emailed the council, saying: "The fact that you all expended energy on these potential changes is scary." Walker, an African American woman who had grown up in Charlottesville, earned a bachelor's degree at Virginia Commonwealth University in Richmond and worked for non-profits in the city before taking a job in the city's parks and recreation department. She sent the council frequent emails, signing them with "Blue Skies" and poetry excerpts, and she frequently appeared before the council to talk about issues affecting the city's low-wealth African American community.

Of the new rule giving the mayor the authority to recognize members of the council before they could speak (one of Robert's Rules), Walker asked, in her email, "Is Mike your daddy?" She said the new rules showed the "emergence of tyranny." It had begun, she thought, with "general feelings of insecurity and inadequacy" among council members, followed by a "pattern in which some individuals assume the role of 'father' to the others" and the other councilors taking the role of "dependent 'children' of such persons." On the role of "father," she meant me.

Walker went on to assert that this "pattern of co-dependency" was "pathological" and that it could "produce a vicious spiral that, if not interrupted, can lead to total breakdown of the group and the worst of the available outcomes." She continued: "In psychiatry, this syndrome is often discussed as an 'authoritarian personality disorder.' In common parlance, as being a 'control freak.'" She ended her email with a section on the "methodology of tyranny." "Tyranny does not have to be deliberate," she said. "Tyrants can fool themselves as thoroughly as they fool everyone else."

I remember bemusedly reading the email, thinking, "Wow. That's the first time I've been called an authoritarian and a tyrant in the *same* email." Little did I suspect that the woman who wrote the email would end up becoming our next mayor, that I would support her ascent to that position, and that, in a surreal capsule of the paradox of how to govern our way through the storm of passions converging on us, she would end up exercising some of the same powers, as mayor, for which she was now criticizing me so harshly as an activist.

But I'm getting ahead of the story.

IT HADN'T HELPED MATTERS THAT I'D ADMINISTERED THE THREE-minute limit for each comment in matters by the public with a very firm hand. Starting in my first meeting, I began stopping each speaker precisely at the three-minute mark. I was worried about how a slippage in each of the twelve comments could become half an hour overall, and I wanted to signal a new direction toward more efficient, cleanly run meetings. But it hardly endeared me to the speakers, or to a crowd accustomed to a long history of easygoing, long-running meetings.

For those twelve speakers' slots, we'd also decided to put in place a lottery rather than a "first-come-first-served" approach, in part to address the phenomenon of the same handful of speakers monopolizing the lion's share of those slots, and in part to open slots to those who couldn't come to wait in line if they weren't going to get a slot. That change also became controversial. The local nonprofit news organization *Charlottesville Tomorrow* quickly put up an online poll on the issue, and 69 percent of the respondents were against the new policy. *C-ville Weekly* published a cover story titled "Winning the Lottery"; it began by noting that the new policy "has some doubting the new rule's integrity." It quoted one activist who said the lottery was a "deliberate attempt to limit public comment" and that the council, "under the new leadership of Mayor Mike Signer, already seems 'sort of perturbed by things they've heard during public comment.'" Louis Schultz—a regular who spoke during every meeting, often shouting at the councilors—said the change was about "controlling what you can say as a citizen."

It got even worse. Because the rules gave the mayor the power to evict people from meetings, and even bar them from coming back, in the case of disorderly conduct—a power that was just restating prior rules—Jeff Fogel, the lawyer who had often sued the city, said I was "reminiscent of an authoritarian figure."

I was surely the only authoritarian in history distracted by day-care bills. I bemusedly responded to the reporter writing the piece: "I want to be crystal clear the point of this is to open this up to more people, make the process more accessible and to connect us with the broader section of Charlottesville's populace."[4]

Despite my determinedly cool public posture, I began waking up early in the morning, usually around 4:00 a.m., my mind spinning with the critiques I was hearing. Were they right? Should we have let the chaos of the meetings continue, if that's what people wanted?

But there was the other side. I knew from being approached while buying groceries at Reid's, filling up my tank on Preston Avenue, and standing in line to buy bagels at Bodo's that many folks supported bringing the meetings under control—and, by extension, concentrating on the actual governance of the city, on solutions, not just theatrics. I began referring in my mind to these people as the "silent majority." The question was whether we could serve them if the voices of the minority of citizens who hated the new rules, and by extension the whole project of bringing deliberation back to the council, were louder, and if these vocal residents were more extreme in their claims.

4

RACE, POLICY, AND THE PAST

| MARCH 2016 |

Trump's seizure of the Republican nomination continued to unfold on the national stage, featuring relentless blasts against virtually every institution I'd spent my career trying to respect, whether it was the press, Congress, the federal court system, or our foreign allies.

But in Charlottesville, I was determined to prove government could work. During my sixth meeting as mayor, we voted 4–1 to move the West Main streetscape project ahead. This was the same project whose steering committee I'd sat on for the Fifeville Neighborhood Association, and it had been delayed for decades, revealing the council's inability to make a decision. Through significant amendments I'd helped usher in, the project would now also embrace the history of the minority neighborhoods surrounding the street and turn an asphalt desert at the street's far end into a small park. It was a complicated project that showed we were working. We were providing grounds for faith in government.

But I was disheartened by how difficult it was for this news to break through in the narrative about what the new council was doing. Instead, the media, and many constituents, stayed focused on the controversy over our new rules, and especially the lottery system. Coming under intense fire for an issue I felt was symbolic at best—whether we chose twelve people to talk to us at random or because they were first in line at 6:00 p.m.—I began coming to grips with what Obama had teased the group of mayors about—"Y'all feeling underappreciated recently?"—with that big grin.

It was around this time—just about two months into my mayorship—that the second brushfire approached.

ONE FRIDAY IN MARCH 2016 I WAS SITTING WITH WES BELLAMY on the outside patio of a burger place on the Downtown Mall. I had a beer, and Bellamy, who doesn't drink, had a pint of ice water. By this point, we had become close. Soon after I started campaigning, I had invited him to have breakfast at our house—making hash browns and eggs, served with hot sauce—and had learned that we had similar intellects and an almost identical sense of humor. After we both won two of the three Democratic slots in the June Democratic primary, we were on the same ticket. Over the course of the campaign that followed, we had developed the rapport of an older and younger brother. He had a huge smile and an outgoing personality, and he always hugged everyone. He even hugged people who didn't like him, calling them "Bro." He was an intuitive and empathetic politician.

But there was another side to Bellamy. He could be impatient, demanding almost instantaneous action on items big and small. He could be divisive, casting issues—particularly on race—as absolute and us against them. He also could say different things to different people. When I first had him over to my house for breakfast, the fracas about the liquor store run by the Alcoholic Beverage Control Authority was kicking up. When I had explained my perspective to him on why the store should be moved, he had looked at me, nodded, and said, "You're right. It's the right position." Two days later, I was shocked to see him on Facebook cheering my opponents on.

So I usually had a mix of emotions when we talked about politically controversial topics, particularly about what we might do on the council. It felt like getting on a roller-coaster ride blindfolded. It was all complicated by the fact that, no matter how many people told me to watch out, and even to watch my back, I *liked* Bellamy. I found his enthusiasm infectious, and we could crack similar jokes—which goes a long way on a long night behind the dais.

Bellamy asked me if I had heard about the petition just launched by a Charlottesville High School student named Zyahna Bryant to remove the Robert E. Lee statue from Charlottesville's Lee Park. I had. Another councilor, Kristin Szakos, was in the middle of her second four-year term and well known for championing racial and social justice issues. She had called me just the day before about the issue. I'd told her I was open to discussing the idea of removal, but that I'd want to be very careful—very deliberate. I'd then done some research online and learned the statue was historically protected. I'd learned that the donor, Paul Goodloe McIntire—a Charlottesville benefactor so storied that our largest park was named McIntire Park, and that the chamber of commerce still bestowed an annual McIntire Award—had dedicated the statue to his parents.

Bellamy told me he was thinking about publicly calling for the statue's removal, and soon. I told him I might be sympathetic, but not if the issue wasn't approached with tact and precision. The Virginia legislature had passed a law in 1987 prohibiting the disturbance or removal of war memorials, and it had been used by plaintiffs to stop similar efforts. Bellamy said he thought a judge's recent decision to limit the law's reach to statues installed after 1987, which had allowed the City of Danville to remove a Confederate flag from a courthouse on city-owned property in 2016, had created a legal opening for how Charlottesville could remove the Lee statue. He argued that the fact that we had a Democratic governor in place, Terry McAuliffe, created a window of opportunity to prohibit the Republican-majority General Assembly from passing a law that would expressly prevent Charlottesville from acting.

This was the same argument Szakos had made on the phone: that the Danville judge's decision opened a narrow window for action during McAuliffe's last year in office (Virginia's governors are limited to a single four-year term). I told Bellamy I thought it could be a disaster if done rashly. It could lead to both fury and inaction. He seemed to recognize as much. In a reflective moment, he said that Levar Stoney, who was running for mayor of Richmond, had told him, "If you do this, that's all you'll be known for." But he also seemed to relish that outcome. I found the derring-do unsettling. "Give me a month," I told him. He said he would think about it. But I could tell he wouldn't.

The next day, Saturday, March 19, the famed founder of the Equal Justice Initiative, Bryan Stevenson, was in town for an event at our Paramount Theater. Stevenson, among other accomplishments, had won a MacArthur "genius" grant in 1995 for his work to bring fairness and equity to the criminal justice system. I talked with him at a cocktail reception beforehand. He was warm, friendly, and interested in the nitty-gritty of local government. During his powerful talk, he urged the audience to do two things: "get proximate" to injustice—to really get near it, to feel it—and "change the narrative." The second idea struck home with me, and I would come back to it as a touchstone in the months and years ahead.

After Stevenson finished speaking, it was time for Q&A. The Paramount is a very large venue, and there were at least a couple of hundred people there, spread through the rows. Bellamy was sitting in the middle, a few rows away from me. He rose and loudly challenged Stevenson on the topic of the Lee statues. Bellamy seemed impatient, even pushy. I could see that the audience was uncomfortable, and that he wanted that discomfort. Even Stevenson, who had been talking about very material issues of criminal justice reform and the fact that thousands of people have been wrongly imprisoned in America, seemed taken aback by the question, focused so overtly on a symbolic issue rather than the practical issues of injustice that he was asking us to confront.

The next morning, I was sitting in the pews of the First Baptist Church, a warm, inviting historic building on West Main Street, with burnished wooden rafters that gently arched upward. The pastor had invited me to hold an informal town hall after the service. Bellamy was there, too, and rose during the service to address the congregation. He announced that he would be holding a press conference that week to call for the Lee statue's removal. He said, "If you want it gone, then let the mayor know." (Notably, Bellamy and Szakos only focused on the statue of Robert E. Lee, even though there was another equally large statue, of Confederate General Thomas "Stonewall" Jackson, three blocks away, surrounded by trees in a park adjacent to the Albemarle County Courthouse. The Lee statue was situated on top of a gently rising hill in the more open Lee Park and more visible from the Downtown Mall. But this inconsistency between the different levels of outrage apportioned to the two statues would become increasingly important as the controversy intensified.)

Sitting there, my first reaction was anger. Most municipal bodies have traditions that enhance collegiality and the ability to work together. Chief among them is not campaigning against each other. At that moment, I could sense the dynamic that would come to poison many of the coming months: that if I didn't agree with his approach, I would be attacked, maybe even called a racist.

Bellamy left. In my town hall that followed, I had a conversation with the crowd about the statue. I asked folks, all African American, to raise their hand if they wanted it moved. Only two did. Importantly, this was just one meeting at one church and therefore not representative of anything other than itself and the fact that there were dramatically different opinions among local black folks on both statues, not to mention among the citizens of Charlottesville at large. In general, many younger African American residents wanted the Lee statue removed, though they could care less about the one of Stonewall Jackson, while many older ones saw both statues in a more complicated light, arguing that even though they might be offensive to many, they should be kept as "teachable moments" about history. It was not a clear-cut issue either way.

We had a city council meeting the following night, Monday the 21st, and the room was crowded with proponents and opponents of statue removal. A ragged, tense mood invaded the cramped council chambers. Bellamy and Szakos announced that they would hold a press conference the following day—Tuesday—at the base of the Lee statue.

That press conference drew hundreds of people with strong feelings both for and against the statue's removal, including dozens of "Virginia flaggers"—rebel-flag-wearing defenders of "southern heritage." The pictures were vivid—Bellamy holding a bullhorn, shadowed by Virginia "flaggers" holding large rebel flags aloft. In our next meeting, he told me he wanted to "rip the Band-Aid off" the racism he felt lingered underneath everyday life in Charlottesville.

But what if that Band-Aid—the social norms that prevented shouting matches and name-calling, that allowed us to deliberate together—

was actually healing us? And even if it wasn't, was removing the statue the right path to come to terms with our racist past?

WHAT I WANTED TO DO WAS TO SLOW DOWN, EXPLORE THE ISSUE, and treat matters as holistically as possible. I wanted to build consensus and focus on solutions—not symbols. My philosophy and temperament were different from Bellamy's. In a parallel universe that unfolded from that same moment sitting on the Downtown Mall, I imagine us trying to achieve consensus. In that universe, we would have worked with area stakeholders to plot a path forward. We would have brought in different perspectives and opposing views as part of a process. Perhaps through a series of conversations with leaders on both sides, and a strategy involving steady, careful pressure, we could even have succeeded in changing the state law. We could then have more readily implemented some of the inventive ideas that were being proposed—like removing the Lee statue from its pedestal. I'm not saying these things would have been easy. But I could at least envision how, instead of creating a symbolic sensation, we could actually have changed things on the ground.

Instead, with the rallying cry already launched, and with the community already up in arms, we blundered headlong down a path that ended up frustrating almost everyone: defenders of the statues, those who wanted them gone, and supporters (including me) of a "third path" where we would add more context, such as plaques and signs explaining the statues' history, and new monuments representing freedom and civil rights.

I felt particularly passionate about the need to move with care because I was teaching, at that very moment, a class at UVA titled "Race, Policy and the Past." I felt the readings and discussions that had been on my mind from the class illuminated the path ahead and the wisdom of charting a pragmatic way out of the brambles of our pitiless history.

I'D BEEN INVITED BY UVA'S BATTEN SCHOOL OF LEADERSHIP AND Public Policy to design the class the previous year, after there had been conversations on campus about the challenge of addressing past racial injustice through present policy. I was initially concerned about being a white man teaching a class about race and gladly agreed to the school's request that I meet with a group of students before moving forward with the course. In the school's basement, I met with about a dozen graduate students of mixed races. What I heard surprised me. They weren't concerned about trigger warnings. They weren't particularly concerned about my race. What they wanted, they said, was substance. They said they were frustrated by all the shouting and posturing that had occurred at the school in the past year on the topic of race. It sounded a lot like what we were also hearing about the city council.

I went to work designing a syllabus that focused on dilemmas in policymaking and the narrow path forward on actual solutions to racial injustice. The students were diverse in their ethnic backgrounds and life experiences but uniformly eager to get started. We began by examining the debates over the Confederate flag in South Carolina through both popular and academic articles. We read a philosophical essay titled "Deontology, Utilitarianism, and Rights," where I introduced the basic polarity that would guide the class—the difference between purely moral reasoning, based on the pursuit of a moral duty (which philosophers call "deontology"), and reasoning focused instead on outcomes, on what the effect of the policy and principles will be (called "utilitarianism").[1]

It was the same distinction we were facing on the dais. Bellamy was saying the Lee statue *should* be moved as a moral matter, irrespective of whether or not it *would* be moved, or what the practical effect of moving it would be in terms of racial and social justice in Charlottesville.

With that framework firmly established, we delved into various topics of racial injustice in American history, including inequities in criminal justice, educational disparities, and the horror of the lynchings that had occurred throughout the American South, as well as the economic enslavement of African Americans even after Jim Crow ended. We then shifted to the reparations debate. Throughout the course, the goal was to give the students a deeply informed way of thinking about the challenges and scope of *actually* remedying past injustice through present policy. As illustrations, we worked on case studies demonstrating the powerful element of pragmatism embedded in many social justice victories, including Abraham Lincoln's tortured path to the compromises of the Emancipation Proclamation and Lyndon Johnson's embrace of the Civil Rights Act despite a past of embracing racism and racists.

Closer to home in Virginia, the class included a close examination of a practical effort at both reconciliation and reparation: the Virginia legislature's 2005 attempt to provide a remedy for the thousands of African American victims of Massive Resistance through the creation of a scholarship program. Initially funded with $1 million from a philanthropist, the program granted scholarships for Virginia public colleges, universities, and community colleges to any Virginia resident who had not been able to attend public school because of the school closures that some areas had enforced after *Brown* to avoid integrating. It was narrowly tailored to provide a specific benefit to specific victims, and the funds could only be used for education.

The program illuminated the challenges in shifting from rhetoric to action on redressing grievous racist actions. It was more narrow than the reparations that had been implemented elsewhere—for instance, for Japanese American internment victims, or for Jewish Holocaust survivors. At the same time, it was a rare example of a successful reparation for African American victims of systemic racism (despite the fact that the program's materials go out of their way to characterize it not as a reparation but as an attempt to "restore" an education to the victims of Massive Resistance).[2]

The program bore the firm imprint of *realpolitik*. My students learned that legislators had to engage in the nitty-gritty of transactional politics to pass the legislation through the conservative Virginia General Assembly. When a progressive legislator who had helped get the program approved spoke to my class, we learned that to get the initiative passed, it had been crucial not to frame it as "reparations." The legislator had succeeded in getting the vote of one of her Republican colleagues only by agreeing to vote for a judge she wanted confirmed.[3]

The program was at once intriguing and disappointing to some of my students, who had just studied the soaring language of civil rights idealism and the thundering vision of nationwide reparations. The program's own final report soberly considered the question, "What are the measures of program success?" It gave these answers: "The existence of the program is a success in itself as an acknowledgement of local and state government culpability in denying education through school closures." "Each participant," it said, "should be considered a success."

Through such examples, I wanted my students to grapple with what it takes to move from rhetoric to reality. That policymaking was substance, not symbols. That rectifying injustice would require programs to be put in place, and that the programs needed to have measurable outcomes. Given the fact that I was mayor, it was ironic, to say the least, that the city council had ended up with the very problem I was trying to teach about: the allure of a purely symbolic victory, in this case grounded on the notion that a statue's removal could be a victory against racism itself.

The simplicity of this particular symbolic victory was understandably alluring, however. Tackling Charlottesville's racism both systematically and substantively, rather than through the single issue of removing a statue, would be very complicated indeed.

PARTICULARLY IN THE SOUTH, AMERICA'S PAST OF RACIAL DIScrimination can seem like buried embers, ready at any moment to burst into flame. This is particularly the case with the memorials to the Confederate cause, which were erected, in many cases, in the first decades of the twentieth century. Nine black churchgoers at a Bible study in Charleston, South Carolina, had been slain by Dylann Roof, a white supremacist, in 2015. Photographs later emerged of Roof carrying a Confederate flag; Roof later said his intent had been to incite a "race war." For many, the flag all of a sudden acquired a new meaning. By removing it, they felt they could repudiate Roof's twisted, demonic project. Republican lawmakers, led by Governor Nikki Haley, joined with their Democratic colleagues to swiftly remove the flag.

The Southern Poverty Law Center (SPLC), a nonprofit civil rights organization based in Montgomery, Alabama, then cataloged Confederate place names and other symbols in public places in the South and across the nation. It recorded 1,740 Confederate symbols, including statues, schools, and roads, and noted that 113 had been removed since the Charleston attack. The report observed that many of the monuments (as in Virginia) were ostensibly protected by state laws. It went on to report that others were shielded by civic leaders fearful of a "strong backlash among many white Southerners who are still enthralled by the myth of the 'Lost Cause' and the revisionist history that these monuments represent."[4]

In Virginia, the SPLC's list included thirty-one streets or highways named after Confederate generals in Alexandria; in Fredericksburg, there were two monuments (The Heights at Smith Run and the Thomas R.R. Cobb Monument and Marker), as well as the Lee Hill Community Center and the Lee Hill Elementary School; and in Petersburg, there were three monuments (Hagood's Brigade, Old Men and Boys Monument, and To the Memory of A. P. Hill), a street named Confederate Avenue, Robert E. Lee Elementary School, J. E. B. Stuart Elementary School, and General Mahone Boulevard and Highway. In other words, the problem was multifaceted.

Meanwhile, other elements of southern history remained entirely unmemorialized, whether it was the black middle class decimated by redlining, urban renewal, and segregation; those buried in deteriorating black cemeteries; the courageous black politicians and business leaders who emerged during Reconstruction; or the victims of economic enslavement and Jim Crow. How were *those* parts of our past seen, felt, and reckoned with through our built environment?

For me, those questions led into the brambles of physical memory itself as a mechanism for justice, truth, and democracy. My undergraduate alma mater, Princeton University, had just found itself in a sticky controversy when a group of students had begun a campaign to remove Woodrow Wilson's name and images from the campus, because he was an avowed racist and eugenicist. Wilson is deeply linked with Princeton. Prior to becoming governor of New Jersey and then president, Wilson had been a professor at Princeton and later the university's president. Princeton's prestigious Woodrow Wilson School of Public and International Affairs is, obviously, named after him.

With angry people on both sides, I thought the university had responded admirably. Between the first option of doing nothing and the second of deleting Wilson altogether, they found a third path: to recontextualize Wilson by telling the full story of his offenses while retaining him, and to use the controversy as a prod for new efforts focused on redressing the historical wrongs begun under the ideas Wilson espoused. The school decided to keep the name of Woodrow Wilson for the School of Public and International Affairs, but to rename West College for the African American novelist and Princeton professor Toni Morrison; it would also rename Dodd Auditorium for the African American professor and Nobel Prize winner W. Arthur Lewis and expand programming focused on diversity and multiculturalism.

A professor at UVA pointed out to me that the new National Museum of African American History and Culture in Washington, DC, holds a unique statue of Thomas Jefferson. He is surrounded in shadowy light by stacks of bricks painted with the names of his slaves—and the bricks are taller and wider than the statue. The museum, under the direction of the famed African American historian Lonnie Bunch (who now heads up the entire Smithsonian Institution), had chosen to include, not remove, Jefferson—but to dramatically recontextualize him.

Likewise, Montpelier, the home of James Madison, had recently launched a dramatic effort to tell the full story of race in James Madison's life and legacy. With the benefit of a $10 million gift from the philanthropist David Rubinstein, the museum converted the entire basement of the mansion into a rich, provocative journey through slavery and its legacy—including a documentary that connected enslavement to practices like mass incarceration today.

In Rome, I had walked through colonnades and forums built through the labor of slaves and traipsed around colosseums where slaves had fought for the entertainment of elites. They had not been torn down. They remained as fraught testaments to an age whose casual brutality we had gradually transcended. In East Berlin, I had seen a massive Soviet communist statue in a central square—remaining, but deteriorating. That deterioration itself, and the dynamism of capitalist Germany unfolding around the statue, were themselves a kind of recontextualization.

However, these shades of nuance in the gray area between black and white were easily overcast by the broad shadow of a bracing May 19, 2017, speech by Mitch Landrieu, the mayor of New Orleans, in which he explained his decision to take down that city's four Confederate monuments:

These statues are not just stone and metal. They are not just innocent remembrances of a benign history. These monuments purposefully celebrate a fictional, sanitized Confederacy; ignoring the death, ignoring the enslavement; and the terror that it actually stood for. After the Civil War, these statues were a part of that terrorism as much as a burning cross on someone's lawn; they were erected purposefully to send a strong message to all who walked in their shadows about who was still in charge in this city.[5]

The thundering power of Landrieu's purely moral—going back to the class I'd taught, his *deontological*—approach came to my own doorstep in the coming months, when people asked me how I would feel, as a Jew, if I had to walk by a statue of Adolf Hitler, or of Josef Mengele, in Charlottesville. Wouldn't I want them torn down?

And I was forced to answer my truth. The fact was, I found the idea of tearing down *all* memorials that offend *anyone* to be Orwellian. I felt this absolutist approach would destroy too much history, and too much art, while purging the public realm of offenses as surely as some college campuses have been cleared of objectionable but provocative ideas. As a general matter, I believed that objectionable—even offensive—ideas can serve a useful purpose; they can challenge and provoke us to learn, to understand the good more deeply by the very contrast with the bad.

And so instead of taking the absolute, black-or-white view so common to the deontological approach I'd taught about, I found myself instead gravitating toward the murky gray of pragmatism, the model that had featured so prominently in our case studies of leaders like Lincoln and LBJ. I would approach the problem of Confederate statues on a case-by-case basis. My position on any particular statue *would depend*. It would depend on why the statue had been constructed. It would depend on whether it had any redeeming artistic merit (art historians considered the statues of Lee and Jackson to be high-quality equestrian statues, and both were in the Historical Register). It would depend on whether people of good faith cared about it remaining as a historical testimonial—as a "teachable moment." It would also depend on the process by which we decided to remove it, and the values embodied in that process.

In fact, as I considered my own position, the story of one New Orleans monument in particular stuck out to me: the memorial of the Battle of Liberty Place, a thirty-five-foot stone obelisk that had been erected in the middle of Canal Street in 1891. It celebrated the 1874 victory of several thousand paramilitary fighters from the Crescent City White League, many of them former Confederate soldiers, against a contingent of mostly black police and state militiamen who supported the federal Reconstruction government.[6] It had been relocated, but was still in the city.

As I was forced to wrestle in the coming months with nuances within the statues debate, and their freighted symbolic meanings, I came back in my mind to the Liberty Place memorial. Because it had been designed specifically to memorialize the crushing of a black-led revolt by Confederate soldiers, the monument seemed distinctly unredeemable. It had been designed *expressly for* white supremacy, rather than *influenced by* or in *general service* of it. Further, it lacked any redeeming artistic merit that could somehow be weighed against its shameful history (after all, much important art has been created by artists who embraced cruel ideologies—for anti-Semitic artists alone, I think of Richard Wagner's operas, Leni Riefenstahl's films, and Ezra Pound's poems). For those reasons, to me, it did not seem like this particular monument could be worth recontextualizing.

It seemed more often than not that we weren't really talking about anything that would happen with the Lee statue—in part because of the certainty of protracted litigation even if we did move ahead to try and move it. We were shadowboxing instead with what the statue (and one's position on the statue) meant—what it *stood for*. We were, in other words, squarely in the middle of the very politics of symbolism I'd pledged to avoid as mayor, where the battle to deconstruct the monuments became a battle to redefine them as well.

In the months to come, we would hear that the statues were important as symbols because their removal would repudiate systems and legacies of oppression and white supremacy. It wasn't whether this repudiation would happen in practice. It would happen at the level of the statues themselves—at the all-important level of signs. A few months later, the Reverend Tracy Howe Wispelwey, an active voice in the clergy movement that would advocate for the statues' removal, would write to the council in favor of taking the statues down, calling them "symbols that uphold a belief": "When we talk about beliefs and ideologies, these things cannot be re-contextualized," she said. "We can confront it, name it and all of the pain and violence it has caused. . . . Institutionally the practice is public repudiation."

In taking down symbols, the logic went, we could change society. That was the idea, and it was potent. And it would take on growing force in the months ahead.

In combination with the lessons from my UVA class, the Bryan Stevenson lecture, and conversations around town, I came up with the idea of creating a Blue Ribbon Commission of thoughtful citizens and charging them with a broad mission: to change the narrative by telling the full story of race in Charlottesville through our public spaces.

I had to come up with the idea quickly, as things had already started breaking so fast. At the council meeting before Bellamy's press conference—three days after he raised the issue with me on the Downtown Mall—I made a statement that cited Landrieu's position on the statues in New Orleans. We needed, I said, to heal the wounds created by slavery and racism in our community, and for me, the decision was not about one or two men or statues. It was how we reckon today with the city's shameful decisions, during the Jim Crow era, to celebrate the Confederacy in our public places.

To make an informed and deliberative decision, I said, the commission would fully engage with the community, evaluate a full range of options, examine costs and fundraising possibilities, and determine the appropriate location to which the statues might be moved. I also said we should receive a full legal review of any obstacles from our City Attorney's Office.

My colleagues agreed in the meeting that the idea should be on a future agenda. Knowing that we could take action on a good process felt like a victory—not a huge one, but a real one—but I still felt unsettled. Rick Turner, the head of the local NAACP, emailed me saying that "many people" were "baffled" that I hadn't been at the press conference about the statues. I explained that I didn't think it was appropriate for the mayor to be advocating against the government he's a part of. A growing mass of grudging and critical comments online began stalking me like a shadow.

These were warning flares of how much some of my constituents were looking for me to take an absolute moral stance on the statues, and how much I might disappoint them if I didn't deliver. There were dark insinuations that I was countenancing racism—even that I was a racist in not calling immediately for the Lee statue's removal. I found this particularly upsetting. I took the cause of diversity personally and I had always been an ardent supporter of racial equality. I had attended majority-minority public schools. I had an African American cousin and an African American sister-in-law. Whenever I'd heard a racist comment or studied the evils of racism—intentional or implicit—in American history, I had been chilled to my bone, but also resolute about the need for action.

While in law school at UVA, when an African American student was physically attacked by someone using the "n-word," I'd led the campus response, swiftly founding an organization called the UVA Coalition for Progress on Race, which later established the law school's Center for the Study of Race and Law. While serving as counsel to then governor Mark Warner, I'd worked on issues like improving Virginia's record with entering into contracts with minority businesses. I'd run several "election protection" programs in Virginia as a voting rights attorney, helping to ensure that African American citizens could vote, and have their votes counted. As a candidate for lieutenant governor, I'd made the restoration of rights for ex-offenders—who then suffered under a blatantly racist policy of disenfranchisement with clear roots in Virginia's Jim Crow past—one of my top issues, which I mentioned in every single speech I made. As mayor, I'd led a drive to make Charlottesville the first city in Virginia to require city agencies to register voters.

I was sure about my anti-racist compass. But there was something new here I wasn't sure how to handle. There was an unsettling "you're with us or against us" tenor that was at war with my deep impulse to resist symbolic victories. If you didn't *signal* that you were on the right side, the argument seemed to go, then you were *already* supporting racism and white supremacy. And that felt awful. The idea that I could be cast in the same lot as racists, people I had been taught my entire life to loathe, made me sick to my stomach. I wondered for the first time—and not for the last—whether I just might not be smart enough to figure out an approach on the statues that could at once be principled and pragmatic, that could mirror what I was hearing among my constituents, and navigate between the hazardous shoals toward actual progress.

I wondered how so many older African Americans in the community who I'd already heard arguing that the statues were "teachable moments" (more on this later) could be so easily dismissed by Bellamy and his followers as just the "elders," implying (or stating outright) that they had been co-opted by white supremacy—that they were too frightened, or too afraid, to assert that the statues should go. Particularly on such a fraught issue as race and history, where I believed the oldest generation probably possessed the most wisdom, I found myself unable to cast their views aside as "false consciousness" (the academic term for people unaware that their own views have been warped by forces beyond their knowledge and control). Indeed, I found myself wondering whether I, as an indisputably privileged white man, could be a leader on these fraught issues of race at all. Should I just shut up and sit down, say nothing, and let others take the lead?

But at the same time, as a fierce supporter of so many policies I knew were critical to progress on racial justice, and especially given the proactive stance I'd decided upon as a new mayor, I felt like I not only had a role as an ally, but a duty to lead as an ally. It was a call to do the best I could.

5

"BROADEN THE APERTURE"

| APRIL 2016 |

OUR JUNIOR US SENATOR, TIM KAINE, HAD BEEN MAYOR OF Richmond at a time when that city had faced similar issues. I'd known Kaine since 1999, when he was Virginia's lieutenant governor, and now I reached out to him for advice. We talked for about an hour. I took scrupulous notes. Kaine suggested we create a small commission that would focus on positive steps. Instead of talking about taking down statues, he thought we could instead try and "broaden the aperture" of the problem. He noted the challenge of trying to "cleanse history" while also avoiding "whitewashing" it. He submitted that the overarching question could be, "What's the best way to tell the whole story of Charlottesville history?"

He told me how Richmond, when he was on the council, had gone about deciding to add the Richmond native and African American tennis legend Arthur Ashe to Monument Avenue, rather than to take down the avenue's statues of Confederate generals. They had named a new courthouse for the civil rights hero and attorney Oliver Hill. They had taken two bridges named after Confederate generals—J. E. B. Stuart and Stonewall Jackson—and renamed them for civil rights leaders, despite "getting a lot of grief" for it. They had, he said, treated the questions as broader issues of how to describe who Richmonders had become.

This was the possibility he was suggesting for the Blue Ribbon Commission's "broad aperture"—not just to advise on the statues, looking through a narrow aperture, but to take on the broader charge of engaging with, and thereby expanding, our history itself.

He told me a story about a controversial mural that was to be put along the floodwall in downtown Richmond. The thirteen planned paintings included one of Robert E. Lee. The Richmond City Council had appointed a diverse commission of seven people who ended up devising a plan to put smaller photo versions of all thirteen murals in a public space with a comment book, to gather public opinion in a gradual manner. During the process, the commission ended up including some new subjects in the mural—but Lee stayed. The controversy had begun "very focused" on Lee, but had then "broadened to all the murals." It was, he said, "an interesting use of a public process."

Kaine was suggesting that a good process could provide opportunities to tell new stories, to change the narrative in a way that would build up rather than tear down.

THE CONVERSATION HAD A SIGNIFICANT IMPACT ON ME. I BECAME even more laser-focused on the possibilities of recontextualization. A few months earlier, a stir had been created in New York when a sculptor put up a bronze sculpture of a young girl, hands on hips, sassing Wall Street's famous *Charging Bull*. She was called *Fearless Girl*, and it was astonishing how the new context changed the old.

Other models came to mind. In Richmond, I had worked in the historic Capitol building designed by Thomas Jefferson, a wedding-cake design that was the oldest continually operating government building in the Western Hemisphere. Segregationist Harry Flood Byrd's tall statue stood feet away as a shameful memorial to the leader of Massive Resistance, but it was emotionally dwarfed by a more powerful memorial that had recently been erected on the Capitol grounds to Virginia's civil rights hero Barbara Johns and the other brave students who desegregated the schools that had been closed in Prince Edward County.

Germany had also recently made a decision to allow the republishing of Adolf Hitler's hateful book *Mein Kampf*, but in such a heavily annotated form that the lies and outrages of the original version could now only be read through the lens of contemporary values and lessons. It became a best seller. The *New York Times* reported that the edition's success was "proof that the attempt by a team of historians to annotate, criticize and contextualize the original much-reviled work was worth it."[1]

6

CHANGING THE NARRATIVE

| MAY 2016 |

ONE DAY DURING MY NEW MONTHLY OFFICE HOURS, A RAIL-thin, goateed, curiously intense man appeared in my doorway. He introduced himself as Joe Draego, vigorously shaking my hand. He began by telling me he was a tolerant and open person. He then brandished a sheaf of pages printed out from a website talking about the threat posed to the world by single Muslim men of a certain age, who Draego said would rape women wherever they were. He demanded that we ban single Muslim men from living in our city.

Such a thing would obviously be unconstitutional, but I also told him I didn't think we should ever make public policy based on stereotypes. I was thinking of the internment of Japanese Americans during World War II, for which Congress paid reparations in the 1990s. He glared at me, shook my hand, and ominously left my office. I was left to wonder what would happen next. It would only take until the next month to find out.

IN OUR NEXT MEETING, THE COUNCIL AGREED TO CREATE A BLUE Ribbon Commission on Race, Memorials, and Public Spaces with the broad mission of changing the narrative by telling the full story of race through our public spaces. The resolution I'd prepared, working with my colleagues and our staff, gave them about a dozen specific instances to examine where race was featured in public places. This was the broad aperture Kaine had suggested. For a moment, at least, we seemed to be on the same page.

Dozens of people applied to be on the commission, but my hope to get a balanced set of members who were open-minded on the issue turned out to be naïve. In the actual closed session to appoint the members, Wes Bellamy, Kristin Szakos, and Bob Fenwick came in clearly prepared to support a bloc of four candidates in lock-step. These candidates had all expressed a desire to remove the statues, and it was a plain attempt to rig the outcome. They were unmoving and successful. It seemed that the position of a majority of the commission on the most critical issue of the statues had been predetermined.

Just as the Blue Ribbon Commission prepared to sail into the fray, we were presented with an opportunity also to take an immediate step forward. Lehman Bates, the pastor of Ebenezer Baptist Church, requested a meeting in my office. He cleared his throat and told me about a request he had from several women in his congregation for specific renovations of the neglected and nearly forgotten African American Daughters of Zion Cemetery located just a couple of blocks from the Downtown Mall. The cemetery had been there since 1873. The cost of renovation would be $80,000, and they had a proposal ready.

I loved the idea. It was exactly what I'd been looking for: a way to change the city's narrative by telling the full story of race through our public spaces. Harkening back to the framework of my UVA class, it was utilitarian, focused on what we would practically accomplish rather than the moral mission we would express. The council's strategic reserve for onetime, off-budget allocations like this was limited by policy to $25,000, but I told him I thought I could put together the support—given how this need fit into the debate we were having—for an exception.

My colleagues were instantly supportive. We were able to make a case to staff for exceeding our usual threshold, and we did so within a couple of weeks—making progress, not waves.

But the $80,000 for the Daughters of Zion restoration barely registered in social media traffic and news stories, which were still consumed by the statue controversy. The social media squalls were frustrating, at best. A student group named "UVA Students United" was routinely attacking me on Facebook for my "racist" position on the statues. I could not believe how ad hominem and divorced from the facts the dialogue online had become. And the really aggravating thing was how little I could do about it. I realized that fighting back against trolling was a losing cause, because it would only give more oxygen to toxic, baseless assertions. I could imagine the headline: "Mayor Confronts Charge He's a Racist," with a parade of articles to follow.

No way. So I bit my tongue, pulled my punches, and held my fire, which felt like an act of unholy will. I was bottling up my natural impulses, which I knew could not be psychologically healthy. I knew I needed to keep my faith that the good would balance out the bad in the long run, but it felt very much like an open question.

We were twelve months away from the first invasion of Lee Park by white nationalists.

7

"HEIL SIGNER"

| JUNE 2016 |

IN JUNE 2016, EMILY AND I TOOK A LONG-PLANNED TRIP TO Mexico. When we were at the airport for our return flight, I got an alert on my phone, clicked through, and saw a headline on the website of right-wing radio host Rob Schilling that said, "Heil Signer." The story was about Joe Draego. According to Schilling, because I'd had Draego removed from the meeting, I was leading a "totalitarian police state." Schilling complained about our public comment procedures not allowing "defamatory attacks on individuals or groups."[1]

The sandy beaches I'd just been on were *terra firma* compared with the shifting, treacherous terrain I was about to step on—the First Amendment.

Just before we left for our vacation, Draego had appeared before the city council. He began ranting about the Koran and the prophet Mohammed before attacking Muslims as "monstrous maniacs." I stopped him from speaking further, looking down at my packet to cite a rule we had included in our new governing procedures prohibiting "defamatory attacks on individuals or groups." Draego then lay down behind the podium in protest. Our officers carried him out by his arms and legs.

John Heyden, an older man with heavy, horn-rimmed glasses, blue overalls, and a long white beard, who often showed up at council meetings to make speeches in support of white pride, then also lay down, with obvious effort, in solidarity with Draego. He seemed comfortable enough, so we let him stay there. Speakers walked around him to address us. At one point, Szakos leaned over to me and asked, "Is he asleep?"

My decision to eject Draego, though, would soon land us in court. It was my first experience as a defendant on a First Amendment case, with words I'd uttered, and decisions I'd made, all in the heat of the moment, scrutinized to see whether I had acted against free speech.

IN THE CHARLOTTESVILLE CITY COUNCIL, ONE GOAL OF THE PROvision prohibiting "defamatory attacks on individuals or groups" in our new rules was to prevent speakers from attacking individual staff members, who had no way to defend themselves during a council meeting. Our attorney at the time said the rules passed legal muster. The courts had created a "limited public forum" doctrine to afford public bodies greater discretion in limiting speech in order to be able to conduct business. For instance, a planning commission could require that only public comments about zoning be heard during an open meeting. A public library could announce that only suitable children's books could be read during a reading hour, rather than any book anyone chose.

These allowances were all conditioned on the priority of order. As a general matter, public bodies were allowed to maintain order through such rules, applied without discrimination, for the sake of doing the public's business as they defined it.

Then we got the news that Jeff Fogel—the same local attorney who had attacked my focus on the passions in my first meeting as mayor—was suing us on behalf of Joe Draego.

THE DRAEGO LAWSUIT WOULD ALLEGE THAT THE RULE AGAINST defamatory attacks violated the First Amendment. We had outside counsel from the Virginia Municipal League representing us. That November, Federal District Judge Norman Moon would issue a preliminary ruling in favor of Draego and against our new rule. Our outside attorney said the decision was shocking. He felt it represented a radical departure from general case law, which defers to local governments in maintaining order and preventing disorder.

The decision wended its way through some complex areas of public forum law before coming to the key point: that the issues of the "forum's decorum and order," as presented in our legal briefs as the rationale for the rule preventing group defamation, were "not compelling." From that one key finding, the court ruled that "with no compelling interest urged to support the rule, it is facially unconstitutional."[2] The court went on to find that I had engaged in an "inconsistent application of the group defamation rule."[3] The court observed that John Heyden, the overalls-wearing antagonist who had lain down on the floor after Draego was removed, had made comments in support of whites and against blacks, spoken against "radical Islamic terrorists" as "killers" at a prior meeting, and described "radical Islamic zealots who only want to kill us" and "vicious animals intent on killing."

The decision concluded that although those statements were "not materially different from Plaintiff's view that Muslims are 'monstrous maniacs' who commit 'horrible crimes,'" I hadn't stopped Heyden. The judge found that this constituted proof that the city council "did not adhere to the bounds it set for itself during the public comment period, and the nature of that non-adherence indicates it removed Plaintiff because of hostility to his views."[4] The judge went on to write that the video he had reviewed "reveals that Plaintiff's statements during both public comment periods did not elicit any disruption." He said that the audience "remained respectful," that the public comment period "proceeded apace," that other citizens had been given the opportunity to speak, and that the council's "intervening agenda items were addressed without incident."[5]

But there was a problem. I had *not* ordered Draego removed because of my "hostility to his views," noxious though I found them. The video available on the council website—that the judge reviewed—did not show what I had been watching there in the chambers, live. It only captured the speaker at the dais, with audience members visible over his shoulder. It did not capture the actual body language among the audience members around the entire chambers.

Heyden was a known character and an irritating curmudgeon, but not someone who I thought was going to incite a disturbance inside the council chambers. Not so with Draego. As the chair of the meeting, charged under our rules with maintaining order in the room, I vividly remember watching as the crowd around the chambers emotionally and physically responded to his descriptions of Muslims. In the background, as always, was Trumpism. Donald Trump had been attacking Muslims for months by this point. Our progressive, diverse town was correspondingly on edge—physically so. As Draego spoke, I saw people moving angrily in their seats, gasping and stirring, beginning to rise in outrage.

In the moment, I strongly felt his speech could lead to an eruption of disorder, maybe even violence against him, and among the crowd. In other words, it was the need to maintain order—decided on the spur of the moment, based on what was happening in the room out of the camera's scope—that led me to cite the group defamation rule, which the new rules specifically described as a means for maintaining order. If the case had gone to trial, I was eager to testify about these very perceptions. Alas, our attorney advised that the judge's preliminary opinion had been so harsh that the city should settle to avoid a punitive judgment at trial. So that's what we did.

This was my first personal experience with the delicate balance between free speech and public safety in First Amendment law—how much can turn on a perception, an idea, or, in this case, inaccurate facts provided by a self-interested litigant.

Meanwhile, the Blue Ribbon Commission began holding public meetings on the Confederate statues. John Edwin Mason, the commission's vice-chair, was a youthful but white-bearded African American professor of history who also happened to be a neighbor of mine. Before his appointment, Mason had expressed a clear desire to take down the statues. At one of the commission's first meetings, he said, "It would be a dereliction of duty simply to make this a public opinion poll. . . . Of course we're going to listen. . . . but that's not all we're going to do." He said, rightly, "We're going to be talking about a history of blood and rape and the exploitation of human beings." And, he said, "if you think that slavery had anything to do with *Gone with the Wind*, then you're going to ask why is anyone upset by these statues?"

It seemed his mind was already made up on the statues. Perhaps the whole Blue Ribbon Commission, the idea of broadening the aperture, would end up being a waste of time.

Then again, maybe it wouldn't.

8

"HAVE YOU EVEN READ THE US CONSTITUTION?"

| JULY 2016 |

ONE OF THE MOST MEMORABLE MOMENTS AT THE 2016 Democratic National Convention was the speech of Pakistani American Khizr Khan, with his wife Ghazala Khan standing resolutely by his side. They were Gold Star parents: their son, Humayun, who was in the US Army, had died in the Iraq War in 2004. In his speech, Khan confronted Donald Trump in the second person. Holding up a pocket copy of the US Constitution, he said, plainly, with a slight tremor in his voice: "Donald Trump, you are asking Americans to trust you with our future. Let me ask you: Have you even read the US Constitution? I will gladly lend you my copy. In this document, look for the words 'liberty' and 'equal protection of law.'"

The convention roared. I noted with surprise that the couple was from Charlottesville. I resolved to meet the Khans and recognize them in their hometown.

MEANWHILE, THE RACE AND MEMORIALS BRUSHFIRE IN CHAR-
lottesville kept taking unpredictable turns. The Blue Ribbon Commission held a "Civil War discussion"—an attempt to understand more about
the conflict in which Robert E. Lee and Stonewall Jackson had served
as Confederate generals. This decision led to a surprising discussion
among locals about what the statues meant and what to do about them.

Joan Burton, an older African American woman from Charlottesville, told the commission that she was a descendant of enslaved people
who had been brought to Virginia as the property of Peter Jefferson and
John Wells, who had in turn left them to Thomas and Martha Jefferson
in their wills. "History has to be an open book for all of us," she said.
"Although I'm disturbed by the [Lee] statue, I don't want it taken down."
Even after the Unite the Right rally in 2017, Burton stuck to her views,
telling a TV reporter, "When I was a child, this was a white park. It was
for whites-only, as was most of Charlottesville." She added, "It symbolizes what we were, and it also symbolizes how far we've come." Burton
said she would rather the statue be "put in the context, as has been proposed in Richmond, rather than removed."[1]

These sorts of comments would continue during the commission's later meetings. On August 12, Pat Edwards, an African American woman who had been born and raised in Charlottesville, and had
left for many years before returning to retire in the historically African American Starr Hill neighborhood, rose to tell the commission the
story of recently visiting Monticello, Thomas Jefferson's home. She said
she had visited often in her youth, and at that time the tour guides
and displays had called the enslaved people of former times "servants."
They had ignored the issue of Sally Hemings, the mixed-race enslaved
woman with whom Jefferson had had a long-term relationship—"Sally
who?" But under new leadership, she noted, Monticello had recently
begun embracing the full story of Jefferson's enslaved family.

"Truth has come to Monticello," Edwards said. She expanded: "And
so what I'm here to urge you tonight is to tell the whole truth. Don't hide
the truth. They did not remove Monticello, they did not take it and put it
somewhere else. Tell the whole truth. Expand it." She told the commission, "Make it true. And then we'll see where the chips fall." Jefferson

was a "complex man in a complex time in a complex nation," she said. "But we cannot escape the truth. And to do anything that removes it, and hides it, is just wrong."

It was striking that she employed the same strident language of moral duty, of the clear rights and wrongs central to deontology—in such stark contrast to the murky gray of pragmatism—as those who wanted the statues taken down.

9

"TO UN-ERASE THIS HISTORY"

| AUGUST 2016 |

I N THE MUGGY MONTH OF AUGUST, CHARLOTTESVILLE, WITH UVA students out of town, becomes quiet and slow-moving, and by tradition the city council cancels the first biweekly meeting. But in 2016, a crisis hit when the air-conditioning in the hallways of a public housing tower suddenly failed.

The air-conditioning issues at Crescent Halls intensified the climate of suspicion and frustration around the city's approach to race and class. The tower was funded and controlled by the independent Charlottesville Redevelopment and Housing Authority (CRHA), which in turn was partially funded by the US Department of Housing and Urban Development. As a body, we had a single member—Wes Bellamy—representing the city council on the CRHA board; we otherwise had no direct role in the CRHA, including the maintenance of its properties. But angry residents, many of them African American, flooded city council chambers nonetheless, looking for responsiveness and accountability. Bellamy made remarks to try to pacify the residents, telling them that help was on the way, but he was interrupted by a wave of boos. Many residents shouted and disrupted the meeting. Others walked out while he was talking.

Again, I was unable to quiet people with my voice alone. I needed to suspend the meeting. I wanted to engage, to be reasonable and accessible, and waded into the hallway to try and talk to some folks. A well-known local woman who had been appearing at the podium for many years got close to my face. Wagging her finger at me, she yelled that I was a "piece of shit." She then charged that I'd said there was prostitution going on behind the liquor store in Fifeville, by implication impugning a historic African American neighborhood. But I had not said this; she was confusing me with another city councilor, Bob Fenwick, who had in fact made that assertion in the local press.[1] She then shoved my shoulder with her hand. I noted to our city manager the next day that it was, technically, an assault. I would never have pressed charges, but the touch lingered like a burn.

Meanwhile, Trump was stampeding across the country openly stoking flames of fear, flagrantly displaying his own prejudices with a swagger America hadn't seen in public for a long time. On July 19, at a speech in a predominantly white suburb of Lansing, Michigan, he addressed African Americans: "You're living in poverty, your schools are no good, you have no jobs, 58% of your youth is unemployed. What the hell do you have to lose?"[2] For him to describe the nation's thirty-seven million African Americans, including thousands of my neighbors and friends in Charlottesville, through such blanket stereotypes was disgusting to me and to countless others in the city, and it added an ominous shadow to our community-wide discussion of race.

In the Blue Ribbon Commission's August 24 meeting, John Edwin Mason, the African American UVA history professor and vice-chair of the commission who came onto the body supporting statue removal, made a powerful and surprising statement. He said his subcommittee might, in the end, not recommend tearing down the statues. But they were "certainly going to come back and say we're going to have to have the courage to face the history that those statues were designed to erase," he said. He expanded: "Charlottesville has not had the courage to face that history. Because it's painful. It's really, really painful. We have to understand what the suffering of slavery was all about. We have to understand the lash. We have to understand the blood. We have to understand the torn flesh. We have to understand that the rape and sexual exploitation of women was a routine part of slavery and the slave trade." With that charge from the commission, Mason said, the city could create something new that had "emotional and visual weight to bring this history to the fore, to un-erase this history."[3]

It seemed there might be momentum to create new memorials that would tell the full story of Charlottesville, past, present, and future, after all.

PART II | *IN EXTREMIS*

10

TRANSACTIONAL OR TRANSFORMATIONAL?

Septem ber brought Labor Day and the traditional inten-sification of the national political campaigns. It seemed impossible that Trump would win, particularly after the tremendous Democratic National Convention. (And October saw the release of the 2005 Access Hollywood tape showing Trump boorishly boasting about sexually assaulting women.)

The Khans had by now become international celebrities—and they were from our hometown, and everyone wanted to meet them. I helped to organize a local Democratic event with the Khans where we focused on pluralism and Charlottesville. I introduced Khizr Khan by saying that, in a time of demographic, cultural, and technological change, we had a choice about whether to embrace change as the key to a brighter future, or to reject it by accepting old stereotypes and stale thinking. This, I said, was the heart of the generous, innovative, diverse constitutional-ism that Khan had articulated for the country.

I was genuinely moved as he spoke about Thomas Jefferson and his love of our country. When he brought up the death of his son, it hit me just how real and raw that must be, and I teared up again. Dahlia

Lithwick, a columnist for *Slate*, was there, and we spoke afterward about how refreshing and moving it was to hear such unabashed, warm feelings being expressed in a political setting.

Khan later dropped off a book at my office in City Hall about the foundations of the Abrahamic faiths. When we recognized the Khans with a proclamation at a city council meeting, I gave him a copy of my book on James Madison, inscribed with a joke—that I hoped in reading it, he would shift his allegiance, even slightly, from Charlottesville's beloved Thomas Jefferson, whom Khan frequently cited, to Madison, whose ideas I felt were even more necessary for our tumultuous time.

SEPTEMBER BROUGHT NOT JUST A RETURN TO COUNCIL MEETINGS, but a new semester at UVA and a new iteration of a class I had taught there for two years—"Leadership, Statesmanship, and Democracy." It was an odd experience. By day, I was teaching James MacGregor Burns's classic *Leadership*, which employs mini-biographies of historic leaders to illustrate his famous distinction between "transformational" and "transactional" leadership. As examples of different concepts, he brings up Mao Tse-tung, Mahatma Gandhi, Franklin Roosevelt, and Martin Luther King Jr. We began working through his provocative contention (similar to the lesson from my "Race, Policy, and the Past" class) that, despite a poor reputation, transactional leadership—designing pragmatic, even utilitarian, advances while compromising with other stakeholders—can actually be a powerful tool for moral advancement.

The class surfaced in academic language the very practical dilemmas I faced when confronted by folks on either side of the statue issue in the very nonacademic arenas of my office, the street, the grocery and hardware stores, or the council chambers. Despite the voices calling for restraint in the Blue Ribbon Commission's public hearings, the folks who wanted the statues and the procedures gone were louder and more intense than those who didn't—more adamant that theirs was the morally right path. Should I echo them? Or should I try to include the quieter folks in my leadership—in the approach I would take to the issue? If I didn't throw my lot in with those demanding removal, would that be principled policymaking—or patronizing stupidity? It was a whisper of what was to come when haters and bigots and neofascists would invade the town, and many expected me to mirror—indeed magnify—Charlottesville's public fury at them, all while performing my required, sworn duties as a councilor and as mayor.

I was not the first politician to allow the intensity of criticism, particularly on social media, to generate inner uncertainty about my own approach—to worry that by *not* pursuing a more overtly symbolic politics, that I was actually *denying* the people (or some segment of the people, anyway) what they wanted and maybe needed, and in the process self-destructing.

Despite all the classes I'd confidently taught on leadership and race, I was faced with the task of reconciling outrage with prudence, one diametrically opposed constituency with the other. I wasn't sure reconciliation was even possible. And that made determining the path forward that much more challenging. I felt like I was cutting my own path through the bracken, entirely unsure whether I was headed toward a clearing or a cliff.

Meanwhile, I was struggling with the increasing amount of work the statue issue was superimposing on what had already become a full-time job, despite its part-time pay of $16,000. I was making a living through my strung-out law practice and teaching. But the mayorship—the constant flow of emails and requests from constituents, over-the-transom developments from staff, and requests from the media for comment on breaking developments like Crescent Halls—had worked its way into every nook and cranny of my life. At this time, the council had only our clerk as our single staff member. I was mindful of the thousands of emails in her inbox and the two dozen boards and commissions she had to serve, not to mention all the paperwork and reimbursements and proclamations and resolutions. And so I found myself shuffling through hundreds of emails late every night, trying to figure out which ones to even respond to—while alternating between trying to ignore social media, where I knew all the action was happening, and being drawn down rabbit holes for hours, where I saw with a sinking heart the polarization, ad hominem attacks, and gross oversimplification that are the unfortunate coin of that realm.

Meanwhile, the Blue Ribbon Commission continued to hold its public hearings, drawing large numbers of folks on opposite sides of the statue issue. We were hurtling toward their December deadline, and nobody knew what they were going to do.

11

"WE WILL BUILD THIS WORLD FROM LOVE"

DURING ROSH HASHANAH, THE BEGINNING OF THE JEWISH New Year, Rabbi Tom Gutherz from Charlottesville's Congregation Beth Israel spoke about how the new year works for Jews: that you revisit what has happened in the past year and get a fresh start. Time works in cycles, he said, and Rosh Hashanah is a chance to make adjustments in life. It represents rebirth. I loved the strange rhythm of celebrating the new year first on Rosh Hashanah, then atonement a week later on Yom Kippur. The cycle happens every year, so you listen to the echoes of your own life as you reflect on what you're becoming.

At the morning Yom Kippur service, Rabbi Gutherz sang a song I'd never heard before called "Olam Chesed Yibaneh." Suddenly close to weeping, I had a surge of deep feeling, of *need*, that felt almost liquid. While fasting that afternoon, I found myself looking up the Talmudic roots of a repeating motif of the song: "Build this world from love." This love of the world is at the core of Judaism, central to *tikkun olam*, the call to repair the breach in the world.

Under the hot and often harsh glare of the public eye, that emotional call to action was now taking on a new poignancy for me.

MEANWHILE, THE BLUE RIBBON COMMISSION—WHICH HAD BEEN handpicked by a majority of the city council to ensure a vote to remove the Lee statue—continued to confound expectations. More testimony from local African Americans continued to disrupt the notion that the statues symbolized one thing and one thing only. At the commission's hearing on October 19, 2016, Eugene Williams, an anti-segregation leader who was perhaps Charlottesville's greatest living African American civil rights hero, said, "I come before you tonight to ask that you not recommend the removal of the Lee and Jackson statues from their current site. In my opinion, they recall the history of a certain era. Removing them does not change history." He continued to explain his view that the politics of symbolism could detract from real action: "The funds that would be used to remove these statues . . . could be spent to tell the story of African Americans from the time of slavery to the present."

At that same meeting, the commission's vice-chair, John Edwin Mason, announced a stunning conclusion: "To me, the statues do many different things—they embody the myths of the Lost Cause (and represent Jim Crow). . . . These statues for me are this history, this unstated history, this history that is very painful." He continued: "But if we don't understand this history, we don't understand the world in which we're living. And so, for me, that's why these statues have to remain in Charlottesville, absolutely they have to remain in Charlottesville."

At its next meeting, the commission voted 7–2 to keep the Lee statue and "transform it in place." Mason put up a series of ten tweets explaining what had happened. Condensed into a single paragraph, they read:

Last night Charlottesville's Blue Ribbon Commission voted on recommendations about the fate of the Confederate statues. We did not recommend that the statues of Lee and Jackson should simply remain in their respective parks. We recommended that they should remain "on the condition that" their meanings are transformed & histories retold. Over the last few meetings commission conversations have made it clear that we understand how the statues embody the Myth of the Lost Cause and that they make many Charlottesvillians uncomfortable in the parks. For us, transformation and reinterpretation are the key elements in our recommendation. The commission's conversations also made it clear that we don't see this as an easy option. Transformation [of] parks and reinterpretation of statues will take creativity & commitment from City Council & from citizens. The recommendations about the statues must also be seen in the context of our recommendations to create a more accurate & inclusive story of the city, paying particular attention to histories that have been slighted. Among other things, we recommended that the new, more accurate story include proper memorialization of enslaved people.

A year later, Mason's thinking would continue to evolve in thoughtful directions, even after the horrific Unite the Right event. In late 2017, after the violence, in an essay he contributed to a University of Virginia Press anthology, he wrote that although the monuments clearly reflected the "centrality of white supremacy throughout American history," that was "not all they [could] be": "Transformed, they can also reveal history that has been denied and overlooked." He said that, "at the time [of the commission's final report]," while he understood the "power and cogency of the arguments of those who wanted to remove the Lee statue from its park," he had told himself that "both options . . . were good," but that "one was better." And the city council's decision to remove the statue "disappointed" him.

But the violence of the Unite the Right rally, tethered to the Lee statue as a symbol for ascendant white nationalism, would change everything for Mason—as it would for so many others. "Heyer's death changed my mind," he wrote in his essay. "The man who killed her and injured many others added another layer of meaning to the statue. It is now covered in blood."

He would conclude that "it cannot be allowed to remain in the heart of Charlottesville."[1]

But then I'm getting ahead of the story.

12

DIZZYING AND DESPONDENT

| NOVEMBER 2016 |

THE ELECTION OF DONALD TRUMP HIT OUR PROGRESSIVE OASIS like a tsunami. The morning after, I almost expected to see trees uprooted, telephone poles snapped. But there was an eerie calm. I had breakfast with a genial, thoughtful friend: breakfast burritos at Café Cubano under autumnal willow oaks. It was a pleasant morning, and my friend, a scholar of Russian literature, gave a glass-half-full take on the election, suggesting that Trump's radical campaign gambits were just "opening bids." I reacted with frustration. I felt the real danger wasn't his policy positions; it was that by normalizing lies and bullying his opponents, Trump would convert a politics grounded on deliberation into one founded simply on performances and the will to power, with potentially devastating consequences for the republic.

After all, if we went all the way and merged entertainment with politics completely—giving up the Madisonian ghost—then demagoguery would become the norm. And what then? Facts would become elitist. Constitutionalism would fade away. And then the cultural integrity at the core of our democracy, the internal, enduring strength that Alexis de

Tocqueville had chronicled back in the 1830s, would crumble. America would be hollowed out.

That week, I launched a personal mission: I would do whatever I could, from my small platform as the mayor of Charlottesville and the author of a book on James Madison, to stop Trump from ascending to the presidency. In a long-scheduled talk at the Political Theory Colloquium at UVA about my book on Madison, I argued that Federalist Paper No. 68, authored by Alexander Hamilton, showed that the Founding Fathers wanted to stop demagogues from becoming president. The essay specifically said the electors should stop men with "talents for low intrigue, and the little arts of popularity," from being elected to the office, calling on the electors to prevent "foreign powers" from gaining an "improper ascendant in our councils."

Soon enough, I was making this argument on National Public Radio and in an article for *Time*, which brought hundreds of emails and calls my way. As one of the only elected officials in the country demanding that the Electoral College take on the role of providing a check against a demagogue's election, I quickly became a touchstone for groups seeking changes to the practices of electors. The Hamilton Electors, for example, a small group of potentially breakaway electors, were promising to challenge "faithless elector" laws in many states that prevent electors from voting for anyone other than the winner of that state's popular vote. I was asked to join daily conference calls with the remnants of Hillary Clinton's senior leadership team, who debated among themselves the admittedly daunting prospects of trying to challenge Trump in the ancient institution.[1]

But at the end of the day, Clinton had no appetite for a full-bore assault in the Electoral College, especially given the daunting combination of state laws and party pressures that would be necessary to make a difference. (The Republican electors who would need to break away from Trump to ensure a victory for another candidate, after all, were usually Republican Party operatives.) A substantial breakaway group of electors was highly unlikely. When the 538 electors met separately in the 50 states on December 19, 2016, the movement died with a whimper. Just two Texas Republican electors broke from Trump, and five Clinton electors defected.

The aggressive steps I and others would eventually take in Charlottesville in response to Trumpism must be considered in light of this central fear: that democracy in America might, at long last, be turning on itself. The riot that seemed in the offing during Joe Draego's incendiary comments had just been one lick of flame. Thousands of Charlottesville residents, millions of progressive Americans, were about to start behaving differently as they considered how to resist the brushfire barreling toward us. Over one hundred thousand people, for instance, most of them women, were about to wear woven pink "pussy hats" in a march on Washington, DC, on January 21, 2017, the day after Trump's inauguration.

And this would happen just as a minor local right-wing blogger, who wanted to be a celebrity in the new political landscape, was preparing to throw a Molotov cocktail into the mix. Jason Kessler was about to break news about some tweets Wes Bellamy had written.

THE CITY COUNCIL RECEIVED AN EMAIL THROUGH OUR COLLECtive email address under the pseudonym "David Golbergshekelstein" on November 25, 2016. The demonic email address he used was "6million-neverforget@gmail.com," the subject was "vice-mayor," and the salutation was "To all the goyim concerned." It began, "My great-grandparents, grandparents, parents, nieces and nephews were all victims of the holocaust." It continued, "As a Jew, I found the remarks made by our vice Mayor . . . to be tremendous." It continued, "I hope this Wes gentlemen gets elected again to combat the scourge of white skin that has afflicted this city for too long. Black lives matter!" It was signed, "Professor, Doctor, Holocaust survivor, David Goldbergshekelstein." I responded, "I reject your hateful, racist, anonymous (because this anti-Semitic name is obviously made up), and cowardly message in its entirety." But I suspected my admonition would fall on deaf ears.

The email linked to the website of a Charlottesville local named Jason Kessler that featured a trove of tweets authored by Wes Bellamy— which would soon become national news. We had seen Kessler previously that year at council meetings. A short, squat man who appeared to be in his early thirties, he would show up to trumpet Trumpist talking points, usually with a mocking smirk on his unshaven face. It was the first time, but not the last, that I would see Kessler in light of the actor Heath Ledger's haunting portrayal of the Joker in the 2008 film *The Dark Knight*—a figure who delighted in toying with others, creating pain and destruction for pleasure, intelligent but horribly twisted. It was the first sign of a malignancy that would later infect the town.

But Kessler had found a dagger to twist in the council's side. On November 24, he'd written a blog post on the website cited in the email to council exposing tweets that Bellamy had written between 2009 and 2014. The tweets were a horror show of misogyny, reverse racism, homophobia, bravado, and belligerence. Among others:

Does it make males uncomfortable wen [sic] girls are so up-front about sex?? . . . It only makes faggots uncomfortable. . . .

I'm all for equal opportunity . . . but a Female Principal with a school full of female teachers is fkn a sure fire way to fk up our lil boys smh.

I DONT LIK WHIT PEOPLE SO I HATE WHITE SNOW!!!!!

Eat it while she asleep if she moan it aint rape.[2]

To someone who had been working hard to develop a good relationship with the twenty-nine-year-old Bellamy—in conversations with others he often said I was like his "big brother"—I felt immediately betrayed. I was as bothered by the attitude toward women and LGBTQ folks as by the persona lurking under the surface.

Bellamy didn't help matters by responding to the email, and to the council, "I don't think those tweets were made by me as my twitter handle has only been @ViceMayorWesB since January." (While the Twitter handle might have changed, however, elementary Twitter sleuthing by Kessler and several reporters revealed that it was the same account that had been used to create the older tweets.) He said, "Unless I'm a profit [sic] of some sort, it would be essentially impossible for me to have that name during that time." He said, of his early twenties, "I'll be the first to admit I had a lot of growing up to do, but please be respectful."

But when Kessler proceeded to publicize more tweets, Bellamy had no choice but to admit they were his. He owned up to the tweets and publicly apologize for them, but that hardly settled the matter.

By late October, the Blue Ribbon Commission on Race, Memorials, and Public Spaces had held seventeen public hearings. On November 1, it now conducted a straw vote on whether the Lee statue should be moved outside the city. Sitting in the meeting, City Manager Maurice Jones sent the council a note informing us that the commission had just voted 6–3 to "recommend keeping the statues in their current locations but adding significant context." The commission recommended that both the Lee and Jackson statues "remain in place on the condition that their histories are re-told and meaning transformed based on wide ranging historical analysis."

It was a stunning development. It meant that commissioners like John Edwin Mason, who had come onto the commission wanting the Lee statue moved—and who had been chosen by a bloc of councilors in part for that purpose—had changed their minds. It meant we could now focus on transforming the Lee statue in place while adding new memorials around the city. The pragmatic (utilitarian) view had prevailed over the moral (deontological) view. Or so I thought.

As it turned out, the pro-removal forces were not so easily daunted. During the commission's pivotal meeting, the chair, Don Gathers, condemned the commission's vote. Gathers, a deacon at First Baptist Church and an avowed firebrand opponent of the statues, said the vote meant the commission had "bowed down to a segment of society in our area that has no real relevance here anymore." He continued, "Unfortunately, the commission didn't vote to capture the lightning in a bottle when we had the chance to do so."[3]

Statue opponents began a hectic push to reverse the commission's initial vote. Three days after the meeting, the members of a Facebook group called "Take Down the Robert E. Lee statue" urged their followers to "visibly show both the Commission and the City Council (who will ultimately decide whether or not to remove the statues) that we want these monuments to a racist heritage removed from our city center, so we can start to change the narrative in our central public spaces."

And they did. On November 10, dozens of activists came wearing white shirts with large, hand-lettered words saying, "We are the 52%," a reference to the percentage of Charlottesville's population who had been enslaved during the Civil War. They attacked the members opposing removal—white or black—as upholders of white supremacy.

The next step was crucial, and so much turned on it.

During the next meeting, on November 28, Maurice Jones emailed the councilors advising that the commission had responded to the activists by voting unanimously to send us two recommendations, rather than one. He explained, "They then proceeded to prioritize their recommendations through a vote on each recommendation." The commission voted 7–2 to move the Lee statue to McIntire Park "for further interpretation of the statue and the issues surrounding the Civil War and segregation in our City." It then voted 5–4 to keep the statue in place "and transform the historical context of the park." Notably, the commission also voted to keep the nearby Jackson statue in place.

Reading the email, I immediately started to worry. In the old parable about King Solomon adjudicating between battling mothers, there's a reason splitting the baby is the worst option of all. Where we'd wanted clarity, we'd now be effectively plunged back into the same dilemma that had led us to create the commission in the first place. However, there was a striking commonality between these two recommendations, as different as they were otherwise: they would both still keep the Lee statue inside city limits. The commission had not voted to remove the statue from the city.

But this was a meaning fixed in time: December 2016, still months before white supremacists and neo-Nazis began invading the city intent on glorifying these very same statues. Their meaning would change, fundamentally and forever, nine months later, when a terrorist would kill for them.

13

"IT'S AN ISSUE OF RIGHT AND WRONG, SIR"

| DECEMBER 2016 |

IN DECEMBER, CHARLOTTESVILLE BECOMES QUIETLY FESTIVE, A college town emptying of its students, and a southern town reckoning with the always surprising chill of winter. But Jason Kessler heaped more fodder onto the fire, launching an unsuccessful effort to recall Bellamy from office. Bellamy had been on a meteoric political rise up to this point. Earlier that year, Governor Terry McAuliffe had appointed him to the Virginia State Board of Education, a prestigious post. But the governor now quickly asked him to resign. He would also soon leave his position with the Albemarle County Public Schools.

A reporter at the *Washington Post* hounded me about whether I thought Bellamy should resign from the city council. Sitting in my car before a town hall meeting, I provided a response that threaded the needle, stating that he had apologized, and the matter was now between him and the voters of Charlottesville. The reporter, eager to get a story, tried to force me to admit that by making that statement I was effectively calling on him to resign. I terminated the call as quickly as I could. The statement she used, which straddled the matter, was the best I could manage.

But my equivocal position did not put me in good stead with Bellamy—or with his base.

There were critics on all sides. The next week, a student in my leadership class at UVA—a conservative who had served in the military—confronted me in front of the entire class about why I hadn't called for Bellamy's resignation. "It's a moral issue, sir," he said. I explained to him that it was more complicated than that—that he'd apologized, that we'd worked on many things together, that he couldn't be forced from the council under our rules, and that I still wanted to get things done together, a desire that would be imperiled by a public condemnation of him.

But my student wasn't interested in any of that. He said, with disgust, "It's an issue of right and wrong, sir." It was the competing political frameworks—deontology versus utilitarianism—right there in the classroom, and there I was again siding with the pragmatic side of the argument.

MEANWHILE, WE RECEIVED, IN OUR FINAL DECEMBER MEETING, the official report from the Blue Ribbon Commission, an impressive document that walked, in double-columned pages, through the dozen-plus areas on which we'd asked for advice. The commission had responded with thoughtful recommendations about how to augment our physical history to address our past. But on the critical issue, the commissioners only concluded, in the negative, that the two statues "belong in no public space unless their history as symbols of white supremacy is revealed and their respective parks transformed in ways that promote freedom and equity in our community." That "unless" was the shooting match. It meant that if that history could be revealed and the parks transformed, they were recommending we keep the statues.

On the "transform-in-place" option of recontextualization, the commission specifically noted that "numerous Charlottesville African American residents who have lived through decades of suppression of their history oppose removal on the grounds that it would be yet another example of hiding their experience. For them, transforming the statues in place forces remembrance of the dominance of slavery and Jim Crow white supremacy." They called for new memorials "to be done clearly, unambiguously, and on at least the same scale as the statue exists now, such as by lowering, covering, de-centering, or otherwise indicating the rejection of the Jim Crow–era narratives that dominated when the statue was erected." A new design that reduced the centrality of the sculpture and countered the "Lost Cause" narratives, they concluded, could achieve a "real transformation of both the space and the narrative."[1]

This response perfectly echoed what I'd been hearing in the community and what I had concluded on my own that year. The question now was whether the city council would listen.

MEANWHILE, JASON KESSLER BEGAN PACING THE BRICKS AT nearby Mudhouse Coffee on the west end of the Downtown Mall, aggressively approaching passersby and asking if they were Charlottesville residents. If so, did they want to expel Bellamy from office? He would then push paperwork toward them to sign, part of a one-man petition drive to recall Bellamy from office under Virginia law (an effort a judge would later reject for falling far short of the number of signatures required). I watched him do this several times at close range, mystified by the burning rage and sense of self-importance of this lonely man driven down such a lonely path.

(The several times I passed him, he wouldn't even make eye contact with me.) I thought he seemed drawn to make himself into some kind of a figure and wanted a *mano-a-mano* fight with the object of his obsession.

There were chilling episodes to follow. A video went up on You-Tube featuring one of Kessler's city council performances, when he had brought a boombox to the podium of Tom Petty singing "Don't Back Down" before he began a rant. The video had been edited to feature not only Pepe the Frog icons (a favorite icon of the alt-right) but also video-game-style targets on councilors, with noises of gunfire in the background. It was so concerning I immediately contacted the chief of police and city manager, who stationed additional officers at a pre-holiday budget work session.

Meanwhile, Kessler used a holiday-card photo I had put up on Twitter with my family. Pepe the Frog icons had been edited over the faces of our twin two-year-old boys.

The intent to create a threatening environment was clear. But the Tom Petty lyric captured my feeling as well. This was no time to back down.

14

"YOU GOTTA GET ME OUT OF THIS"

JANUARY 2017 BROUGHT MY FORTY-FOURTH BIRTHDAY, WHICH Emily and I celebrated like true parents of twin two-year-olds: with Chinese take-out, a bottle of sparkling wine, and bedtime soon after the ball dropped in New York City. The Lee statue's grim silhouette loomed over my thoughts about the city council. When I ran into a local architect named Pete O'Shea, a sociable fellow who had designed Charlottesville's cherished Freedom of Speech Wall, I told him I was looking for creative ways to resolve the statue dilemma in order to accomplish the transform-in-place mission the Blue Ribbon Commission had endorsed. I told him I was looking for something that would help to unify the community.

O'Shea sent me an intriguing, stirring idea, visualized in a slide deck that depicted several large glass "lenses" installed around Lee Park. These ten-foot-high windows of glass would be etched with meaningful sayings and historical facts. The goal would be to prevent any visitor from seeing Lee except through new truths and create a new narrative.

The design was not only beautiful and transformative but met my other criteria as well. Raising money for artistic projects is notoriously difficult. A sculpture meant to memorialize the victims of the Vinegar Hill urban renewal, with a price tag of $300,000, had languished for several years, with only a few thousand dollars raised. But I thought the public would support allocating perhaps $500,000 to the transformation of Lee Park, and O'Shea's project could be done within that kind of budget. It could also be done quickly. The design was versatile and well-suited to community engagement, as ideas from many different groups could be incorporated in the lenses. Finally, I believed it would meet the circuit court judge's strict interpretation of the Virginia law in question, as it would plainly neither "disturb" nor "interfere" with the Lee statue.

But in my vision, the lenses would only be one part of a new scheme. In addition, I envisioned a series of visible markers at each of the dozen or so sites the Blue Ribbon Commission had been asked to study, including the slave auction block, the Drewary Brown Bridge (which featured small, aging plaques to prominent local "bridge-builders" who had worked for reconciliation), and the Daughters of Zion Cemetery. I imagined a glowing blue light and a kiosk at each site and an app that would take visitors on a journey—Charlottesville's attempt to change the narrative by telling the full story of race through our public spaces. That tour would culminate at the transformed Lee statue.

I talked these ideas over with the city manager, Maurice Jones, who was open to them but said the matter would depend "on the will of council." I conferred with Councilor Kathy Galvin, who strongly supported them. Councilor Bob Fenwick had sent signals in the prior months indicating that he would oppose removing the statue. But he was being especially coy with the public and with me about his current stance. I knew he had told others that he was the "swing vote." I suspected he would oppose the scheme of linked memorials and could very well flip to support removing the Lee statue. I knew Councilor Kristin Szakos would oppose the idea. The paramount question, then, was what Wes Bellamy would do.

I had two meetings with Bellamy about the concept. The first was with O'Shea at a local coffee shop. They got along very well, and Bellamy seemed excited about the idea. It seemed to give him a way out and forward on an issue that had consumed most of his waking moments of late. We'd often discussd how, in a roundabout way, the whole issue had made him the subject of Kessler's monomania.

We had a second meeting with Jones and our city attorney, Craig Brown. Bellamy still seemed very interested in the idea. He asked some tough questions about the cost and the flexibility of the idea, but they seemed intended to move it ahead. I began to feel cautiously optimistic.

Meanwhile, I got ready for the council meeting. We'd be voting on the Lee statue on the same night that I'd give the mayor's annual State of the City address. By tradition, this was a speech where the mayor listed the city's major accomplishments and suggested policy proposals for the upcoming year. I had worked intensively on my speech.

In the afternoon, I agreed to meet for coffee with two UVA professors, Jalane Schmidt and Lisa Woolfork. Both were African American, and they had helped found Charlottesville's Black Lives Matter chapter. I had stopped by both of their houses while canvassing neighborhoods during my city council run. Schmidt, upon learning that I was the same person who had spearheaded the push to relocate the liquor store from Fifeville, had shaken her head, said, "Uh-uh," and closed the door in my face. Woolfork had engaged in a spirited and wide-ranging conversation with me about her teaching at UVA (she taught a class on *Game of Thrones*). She had criticized my campaign theme, "One Charlottesville," for potentially being exclusionary of anyone who did not rally to the cause of unity. I found her argument thought-provoking and had enjoyed the conversation.

During our meeting about the statue proposal, both professors expressed anguish at my position on the statues. They said that as relics of the Confederacy, they had the effect of diminishing African Americans' sense of belonging in Charlottesville. I asked Woolfork when she had come to this conclusion. She did not answer, but it was clear it was recent. I asked them about the experience in Richmond with adding the Arthur Ashe statue to Monument Boulevard, and Schmidt laughed derisively. When I asked them about the opinion I'd heard from so many other local African Americans about retaining the statues as teachable moments, they said they didn't believe the voices were representative.

I appreciated their intellects, their passion, and their request to meet and talk, and I thought it was a constructive meeting. It was clear that there was little common ground between us, but I would still be surprised by the intensity with which both would later frame me as an opponent.

I met with Bellamy about an hour before the meeting. He said he hadn't eaten, so I volunteered to buy him pizza. Over dinner, he mourned the "statue thing." When I brought up the idea of incorporating the lenses again, he smiled supportively and said, "You gotta get me out of this." We continued eating our pizza, talking, as we often did, about the cost of holding local office on our family lives. We both had young children and working wives. He had just been through almost a year of savage attacks and threats on social media.

I really thought he was going to support the compromise and that we would be able to move ahead. How wrong I was.

I WAS SPINNING MULTIPLE PLATES AS I WENT INTO THE MEETING. I needed to try to pull off a compromise on the statue issue, but I also had to deliver my State of the City speech. Hundreds of spectators were crammed into the chambers, and despite the fact that it was January, the room felt overheated. The crowd was definitely not there for my speech. They were there for one thing: the vote on the Lee statue. Dozens of signs saying "REMOVE THE STATUE" rose above the crowd. Among the speakers in the public comment period beginning the meeting (still featuring the "lottery") was Woolfork. Reading steadily and almost rhythmically, she described the Lee statue as "coercive." She said, "Its size and proportions are designed to force those who stand at its base to look up. This bodily position, looking up, is a posture of reverence and awe, even if you don't feel it." She went on to quietly scorch anyone who disagreed: "It is coercive in that a vote against moving it is a vote in favor of a racist relic, a vestige of a falsely mythologized past that has managed to maintain its power in the present, the power to control our conversation, to contort people of good will into bad choices."

Squarely addressing the argument I'd been making for months, and that I'd just made to her hours earlier, she said, "You can resist the seductive power of inaction disguised as recontextualization. You can resist the allure of the Confederacy and the alt-right." Her comments eerily prefigured the central role that the ideal of "resistance" was already taking—and was about to take—in Charlottesville's stance against the new tilt of the country.

THE AUDIENCE WAS RESTIVE, BUT I AT LEAST HAD THEIR ATTEN-tion for my speech, which was scheduled in the agenda before the discussion of the Lee statue. I began by recalling my campaign goal of "One Charlottesville," which I said had been meant to focus on what united us rather than what divided us. I went through our accolades—our AAA bond rating, the fact that we had the most jobs that had ever been recorded for the city, the $6 million surplus from the prior year, our #3 ranking among Virginia cities for LGBTQ policies by Human Rights First, our #4 ranking by *Entrepreneur* for cities nationwide for entrepreneurs, Expedia ranking as the #1 place to visit in the United States, HealthLine naming us one of the healthiest small cities in the country.

I continued where I'd begun a year earlier: with the need for respect. When I had watched the city council previously, I had too often seen acrimony and a body that got stuck, whether in arguments with staff or arguments with citizens. We needed political will to solve our problems, even the most difficult ones. We needed deliberation to work our way through the issues. And we needed collaboration and compromise to get things done. We needed, in other words, substance rather than symbols. I explained my four priorities as mayor—innovation, infrastructure, governance, and reconciliation—noting that the past, as William Faulkner said, is never past. I observed that surveys showed that our deepest value in the Charlottesville area was history. We had injuries in the past on race and class that continued to haunt us, and we needed to strive to recognize, address, and overcome them.

I went on to reel off a top-ten series of victories across the four categories, most of which I had spearheaded, usually behind the scenes and through the power of coalitions and coordinating with staff: increasing the funding of public schools by over $2 million; renewing and expanding the technology tax credit (which was expiring) from five to seven years; lowering building heights on West Main Street for neighborhood protection and historic preservation; moving the $35 million West Main streetscape ahead; making major progress on parking, including preventing privatization of the Water Street Parking Garage and purchasing a $3 million lot for more parking downtown; making progress on reconciliation, including stopping the rezoning of the African American Booker Hill neighborhood and rehabilitating the Daughters of Zion Cemetery; becoming the first Virginia city to require city agencies to register voters; creating a new Open Data Policy; passing a new regionalism policy with Albemarle County on the environment, education, housing, and transportation; and instituting the new governing procedures, which brought more transparency, effectiveness, and efficiency to our meetings.

It had been a good year, I said, but not for everyone. I talked about attending the memorial service of Holly Edwards, a vice-mayor known for her work on racial and social justice, the week before, where I had been painfully reminded that the city was leaving some citizens behind—that we were, for some, a beautiful but ugly city. Because Charlottesville was in demand, our assets were also in demand, and when there isn't enough supply—whether of housing or parking—costs go up. Given those dynamics, we needed to work hard on providing equity.

Hard experience in campaigns had taught me the danger of unfurling a Christmas-light string of ideas when what people really wanted was the star on top of the tree. So I'd decided to propose just one big idea in my first State of the City speech. We'd ended the prior year with a substantial budget surplus, and all our economic indicators remained strong. Given the contrast between Charlottesville's abundance and our endemic underclass, I announced that we should invest some of the largesse by doubling our spending on affordable housing over the next five years. The proposal would amount to adding $1.6 million to this area each year, equating to $8 million in new dollars over five years.[1] The idea would be unanimously supported by the council when we passed our new budget several weeks later.

The screen behind me then showed a photo of Khizr and Ghazala Khan. As bad as our national politics had been in the past year, my experience thus far as mayor had given me faith that there was no problem we couldn't solve if we worked together. I was painfully aware that we would be inaugurating not only a new president the coming week, but a style of politics that trafficked in stereotypes and in coarse language that demeaned the nation that Thomas Jefferson, James Madison, and George Washington had envisioned.

I said we needed to pursue a vision of pluralism, inclusivity, and authenticity, where everyone felt comfortable being themselves. As an example, I described how I myself often felt like an outsider—but that I'd always felt welcome in Charlottesville, a community that embraced authenticity and uniqueness. I explained how I'd been born in India to a single mother, and how my biological father had died there in a car crash while she was pregnant. I told how my birth name is Atri, the name of a revered ancient Indian prophet, and that it had been given to me by the guru of the village where I was born. I recounted how my mom and I had come back to the United States when I was close to two, and how she later married my dad, Robert Signer, who adopted me. I told how I'd been close growing up to his wonderful, boisterous family of New Yorkers and New Jerseyites. I spoke of my pride in my Jewish heritage, and how I'd heard my first hurtful ethnic slur when I was in elementary school. And I talked about how I'd attended majority-minority public high schools, where my closest friends had been black, Pakistani, Ukrainian, Vietnamese, and Peruvian, and noted that my first cousin and sister-in-law were African American. Finally, I expressed my appreciation for my sister and her wonderful wife, who are social workers with two daughters.

The applause that followed felt gracious and welcoming. After a trying year, with this personal celebration of diversity, pluralism, and authenticity I felt closer to Charlottesville than ever before. But my speech would be quickly forgotten because of what happened next.

NOT JUST THE LEE STATUE, BUT THE BLUE RIBBON COMMISSION'S full slate of recommendations was on the agenda. It ran a wide gamut, from increasing our support for the local Jefferson School African American Heritage Center to adding new memorials throughout town celebrating unheralded civil rights heroes. But the only item anyone cared about was the Lee statue.

On the council, Bob Fenwick was the first to speak. A crusty and quixotic army veteran in his early seventies, he drove a white van around town for his handyman business hand-lettered on the sides with the slogan "HOMEWORK WITH BOB FENWICK." He began: "Enough symbolism. Enough symbolism. Enough of the declarations, proclamations, good intentions, written promises. We have been down that road more than once. It's time to show me the money. . . . It's time to invest in our citizens." He talked about the urgent need to invest in programs that would change people's lives and establish equity. It was confusing what he was saying, exactly. He said he was against symbolism . . . but was he against moving the statue, or not? It was about to get much worse.

Bellamy was next. He quoted Martin Luther King Jr.'s famous passage from "Letter from a Birmingham Jail" describing how he had reached the "regrettable conclusion that the Negro's great stumbling block is the white moderate who is more devoted to order than to justice, who prefers a negative peace, which is the absence of tension, to a positive peace, which is the presence of justice." Virtually gesturing at Fenwick, sitting to his right, he said that King was "essentially talking about what we may have just heard." He talked about receiving death threats, being called the n-word, and being stalked by Kessler.

In combination with his personal story, his defiance, and his invocation of the horrific racism in our midst, Bellamy's citation of MLK was a blunderbuss, meant squarely for the older white man to his right and, I felt, the mayor in the middle of the dais. It was also red meat for the crowd. But while he was whacking Fenwick, he also seemed to indicate support for the compromise that he and I had worked out. "The Band-Aid has been ripped off," he said. "I'm willing to extend an olive branch of sorts. I believe we can honor our past and correct its wrongs and still move forward as a group."[2]

It was my turn to explain the underpinnings of my position. I recounted that the Blue Ribbon Commission's recommendations were to keep the statue in Charlottesville. We should move ahead, I said; we should do something rather than kick the can down the road. I recalled how an African American man had told me at an NAACP meeting that the statues should be teachable moments that should prod us to teach and learn. Instead of treating the southern states as territories to be further vanquished, Abraham Lincoln had sought to bring them into the fold of the union, and that, I believed, suggested the power of the "add rather than subtract" approach.

In the wake of Bellamy's reference, a compromise approach was available to us: first, renaming the parks to better reflect our values today; second, transforming Lee Park with a new monument that would exceed the Lee Statue in visual and emotional power and create a new conversation worthy of our present values; third, transform Jackson Park by creating a monument to the slave auction block, which was just a small plaque in the sidewalk; and fourth, creating a new web-based utility that would allow locals and visitors to understand the complete history of race in the city.

This multifaceted approach, I said, would create a dynamic path ahead that would change the narrative by telling the full story of race through our public spaces. While the Lee statue was tall and dominant, the world was full of inventive artists eager to create an even bolder new memorial that would recontextualize Lee while testifying to our current values. We had before us an exciting opportunity, one that could embrace the living, changing nature of history, that would make clear not only where we'd been, but where we were going.

I felt these remarks contained ideas that could actually move us forward, complementing the agreement I thought I had with Bellamy.

As expected, Szakos then put a motion on the table to move the Lee statue. We would direct staff to give us options within sixty days for how to do it. Notably, this motion ignored the Blue Ribbon Commission's recommendation to move the statue to McIntire Park. (Szakos also moved to disband the Blue Ribbon Commission.)

Bellamy swiftly seconded the motion. This stunned me. I thought he supported the compromise motion I was ready to make.

There was a pregnant pause. Fenwick then spoke. "And my vote will be to abstain," he said. There was another long moment where everyone took this in. After six months, the chamber was ready for an answer one way or another. Galvin and I had already spoken out in favor of recontextualization. Fenwick's seven words meant we'd be plunged into no-man's-land.

Pandemonium broke out. "Shame on you, Bob!" someone in the crowd shouted. From the back of the room, the activist Nikuyah Walker began demanding that Fenwick provide an explanation. I threatened repeatedly to eject her from the meeting for the interruptions, leading to catcalls.

Meanwhile, Bellamy began openly grilling Fenwick on the dais about what he was thinking. Fenwick admitted that he wanted the motion to come up again in a future meeting and suggested he would actually support it if he got "certain things" in return.

Bellamy retorted that Fenwick was "holding the motion hostage."

Szakos restated her motion to remove the Lee statue, and we proceeded with the voting again. Fenwick again abstained, leaving us again in deadlock. Galvin then introduced a motion to recontextualize the Lee statue, with the language I had provided about a new installation linked with the set of other monuments. Bellamy voted against that motion, along with Fenwick and Szakos. I was astounded all over again. Nothing—not removing the statue, not recontextualizing it, was getting a majority. We were, Galvin said in exasperation, "in limbo."

Szakos then made her same motion to remove the statue a third time. Laughter and gasps of surprise emanated from the crowd. Fenwick stated that he wanted "to see something concrete" before he supported removing the statue. He seemed to want to exact some specific programs that he alone could take credit for in exchange for his vote. He kept on mentioning a planned field house at Tonsler Park, located in majority-minority Fifeville.

I said, "I feel like this is putting the public through agonies." I called the question. He abstained for a third time.

Fenwick's bizarre actions led to screams from the activists, to more cries of "Shame on you, Bob," and to calls to "Shut it down!"

I was literally nauseated by the spectacle of so much work going up in smoke. I'd already had to suspend the meeting once for violations of the rules. I was coming down with a twelve-hour stomach bug during the meeting. After I called a second suspension to restore order, I went into the bathroom tucked away behind the dais and threw up.

And that was the easy part.

The next day brought another email from Nikuyah Walker. She wrote to Fenwick, Galvin, and me, "Just to be clear—You are the same kind of white people who closed schools after Brown vs. The Board of Education instead of forcing integration. . . . Thank you Kathy and Mike for being open about the fact that you are overseers. We appreciate when people show us who they are" (underlining hers). I was getting accustomed to the intensity of opinion on virtually any issue related to race. But I didn't think I could ever get used to damning anyone who disagreed with the removal of the statue as the equivalent of an "overseer" of slaves.

And this didn't address at all what the Blue Ribbon Commission had said about the statue, or what the hundreds of folks the commission had heard from, or I had talked to, had said, including so many local African Americans.

The order issue surfaced, too. Another email came to me alone, from a local white therapist: "I hope you feel shame. I hope you could not sleep last night. I hope you stayed awake wondering why you shut down citizens who were telling you to your face that you are failing them. I hope you are struggling to regain the humanity that you have lost." She directly linked my efforts to establish order in the room to structural racism—merging the two brushfires. "I lost my humanity in the name of decorum," she wrote. "I wanted to shout across the room to you—'ending racism will require ending business as usual.'"

But it wasn't that simple. It wasn't that black and white.

DURING THE SAME WEEK, MAYORS OF MAJOR AMERICAN CITIES around the country announced that they would become "sanctuary cities" and defy the federal forces that were attempting to intimidate and deport undocumented immigrants. The speeches were bold, defiant, in some cases spectacular. I received an email from Kathy Galvin a few days after Trump's inauguration noting that Boston's mayor, Marty Walsh, had taken a stand on Trump's first set of executive orders, including lifting the ban on the Central Intelligence Agency's "black site" prisons, pursuing extreme immigrant and refugee vetting, and instituting gag orders on climate change at the Environmental Protection Agency. "We should do the same [as Walsh]," she said. "I will stand with you. . . . I'm sure all of Council will, with all of our diverse staff, advisory groups . . . etc. Unity is the word, quick is the action. Let me know but we must do it now."

The next day, Friday, January 27, Trump issued the first version of his Muslim travel ban. Our worst fears were materializing before our very eyes. I called a friend I'd made at the local mosque, who invited me to an event that had been called for Saturday afternoon. I arrived at the mosque—a nondescript, office-style building constructed on an obscure pocket of land in the heart of the low-lying African American neighborhood of Orangedale. In a room with fluorescent lighting sat three dozen plainly terrified political refugees.

An Afghani translator for American troops told of being hunted by the Taliban. A bald, bearded, husky Syrian who had been a professional Olympic-style wrestler described refusing to serve in Bashar al-Assad's army and watching as his son was murdered in front of him by machine-gun fire. An Iranian told of starting an activist group and newsletter and of being hounded until he feared for his life.

I listened to the anxiety in their voices. Over and over, they expressed bewilderment that they had escaped the frying pan only to fall into the fire.

I came home that afternoon feeling as if my hair was on fire. What could we do? It needed to be strong, big, mirroring and magnifying our progressive community's values. We needed to send the strongest possible signal to our embattled community to assert our solidarity with them and affirm the strength of our alliance—while repudiating as loudly as we possibly could the outrage of the Muslim travel ban. Conferring with friends and family, I swiftly put together the idea of holding a press conference in front of City Hall to declare that we would stand with our immigrants and refugees. Through a feverish few hours, too many cups of coffee, and dozens of cross-cutting conversations—looking at what other cities were doing minute-to-minute—I landed on creating a major event on the Downtown Mall where I would stand with a broad range of other leaders. We would declare Charlottesville, which I knew all too well from my scholarship on James Madison was the ancestral home of America's deepest principles of religious toleration, "a Capital of the Resistance" to religious intolerance and bigotry.

In my part of the event, I desperately wanted not only to provide a bracing rhetorical call for these principles, but to announce specific policy measures that would support immigrants and refugees but not actually employ the divisive term "sanctuary city" (we had been advised by the refugee community that this term could actually backfire). But there was a problem.

Virginia is what's called a "Dillon's Rule" state. According to Dillon's Rule (named after the judge in two 1868 legal cases in Iowa), cities are not allowed to take any action unless they have been expressly allowed to do so by the state government sitting in the state capital. "Home rule" by cities and counties is not only not allowed—it's actively prevented. Under Dillon's Rule, judges will strike down any local decision that is not expressly allowed by the state legislature. (In legal scholarship, this is called "preemption.") Because of this rule, the city actually couldn't do much directly for these embattled people that wouldn't lead immediately to a successful lawsuit. We couldn't decide to give undocumented residents driver's licenses, for example—that was something that could only be done by the state government. Nor could we bar US Immigration and Customs Enforcement (ICE) agents from the city.

But we could provide new forms of help outside the confines of Dillon's Rule. I knew that our agencies, including the local jail and our police and prosecutor, were quietly supportive of the undocumented. We had a practice of issuing only fines the first two times an undocumented person was stopped for traffic violations, for instance, so that they would not go to jail or be put at risk of deportation for such minor offenses. We needed to get the word out that our government was compassionate. We needed more federal resources to back up our plan, though, so I contacted our senators, Mark Warner and Tim Kaine, to ensure that we could refer local residents to their offices for help. We also needed legal and social services help, so I convened an emergency meeting of lawyers who would be willing to help these residents on legal issues. These folks needed bulldog attorneys on their side in deportation cases, so I also connected with Legal Aid about the idea of the city council giving them a donation for legal services. All of these steps were successful.

Armed with this list of action items, I arrived at the event. A friend brought a bluegrass band and an amp system to the event where we would announce the plan.[3] About seven hundred people crowded onto the Downtown Mall in front of City Hall. Lined up in a row were Khizr Khan; Jeff Legro, UVA's vice-provost for international affairs; Pam Northam, the wife of Lieutenant Governor Ralph Northam (who was running for governor at the time); Hodari Hamilton, the pastor of Charlottesville's oldest African American church; Tom Gutherz, the rabbi of Congregation Beth Israel; Elaine Thomas, the pastor of the liberal St. Paul's Memorial Presbyterian Church; and Harriet Kuhr, the executive director of the International Rescue Commission.

There were also two refugees to tell their stories: Edgar Lara, the son of an undocumented single mother, who had served in the US Marines and currently worked with a nonprofit called Sin Barreras (Without Borders), and Ahmed al-Syra, a political refugee from Palestine who was scheduled to take his citizenship oath at the annual ceremony at Monticello in February.

Wes Bellamy and Kathy Galvin were also there, standing resolutely with the line of speakers.

It was a chilly but bright day. I was stunned by how many people showed up. As I looked out on the crowd, I experienced a powerful, even joyful sensation: the solidarity was real. A local band called Chamomile and Whiskey played a bluegrass version of Woody Guthrie's anthem "This Land Is Your Land."

Khan began with eloquent remarks about the enduring power of our Constitution but was soon loudly interrupted by someone in the crowd. I looked over to see Jason Kessler, wearing sunglasses and shouting through a bullhorn. He appeared to be filming himself for Facebook Live while Khan was talking. He kept shouting out sexually explicit lines from Bellamy's notorious Twitter feed. He also seemed to be attacking Khan for being a Muslim. I could see people crowding Kessler, shouting over him, and trying to shame him. This was all about a hundred feet from the Freedom of Speech Wall, and right in front of City Hall. Khan, unperturbed, kept going. The cops were hovering nearby, obviously uncomfortable, but going out of their way not to put their hands on anyone. It was a case study in the difficulty the police face in handling disruptive but constitutionally protected speech—even hate speech—at a public event in a public space.

And yet the event still felt like a tent revival for the resistance against Trump that was taking shape around the country. Hundreds of people were smiling, cheering, and waving. And in the weeks ahead, it spoke to the moment. *C-ville Weekly* would publish an article titled, "Unprecedented Activism Galvanizes Charlottesville," observing that since Trump's election as president, at least seven new groups had sprung up. "Mayor Mike Signer declared Charlottesville the 'capital of the resistance' at a January 31 rally," the article noted, "and it's hard to keep up with the ongoing protests."[4] I was proud of the city.

It's worth noting that the day after the event, right-wing radio host Rob Schilling pointed out that I did not have a permit for the event. When a reporter raised the question the next day, I confirmed with our city manager, Maurice Jones, that I hadn't needed one. He said, "It was a press conference, right?" I confirmed that yes, I thought it was.

In Charlottesville, we had at that time a formal requirement that any event that would have over fifty people in attendance and that would occur on a public right-of-way—like the Downtown Mall—needed a permit. Yet I hadn't heard of people getting permits for events related to quick-breaking news—such as the press conference Bellamy and Szakos had called at Lee Park to protest the statue. Similarly, I hadn't thought to get one, either. Jones explained that in Charlottesville, our practice was to extend considerable deference to events that were called in relation to the news—that were free-speech events, as opposed to, say, a large picnic. But it made for an awkward answer when a reporter shoved a mic in my face, and I answered that we just didn't enforce the rule.

That tension—between a liberal approach to speech and enforcing buttoned-up rules—would prove to be far more important later, when the stakes were much higher.

15

GRENADE GAME

| FEBRUARY 2017 |

I N MY OFFICE HOURS THE NEXT WEEK, A LATINX COUPLE CAME TO tell me about rumors spreading through the local population: people were being sent to ICE if they got a traffic ticket. The husband, a burly, garrulous auto mechanic, had come to the United States from Central America. His wife was a native of the Charlottesville area. They told me about the terror sweeping through their community. Their friends, they said, were afraid to drive. They were being told that Charlottesville police were rounding them up and deporting them.

It was plain terror, based on rumor and intimidation—right there in my office. I had to think this was exactly Trump's intent—to intimidate these populations out of the country. They knew hundreds of people. I worked with them to set up a community meeting where the hidden Latinx community could hear directly from local government officials. Not only would they learn about our actual policies and approaches, but we could learn from them and find out how we could do better. It took some work to find a location, but we ended up at a local Christian church whose politically conservative pastor was also a strong supporter of protecting this community. We soon realized that at the event itself, members of the Latinx community would not want us to use last names or other information that might put them at risk, so we were careful to instruct anyone involved with the event not to ask for attendees' names.

At least 150 community members crowded into the church, many wearing faded blue jeans, baseball caps, and sweatshirts. The showing from our government officials was just as impressive: our elected prosecutor—or commonwealth's attorney, in Virginia's parlance—was there, along with several police representatives, members of the Albemarle County Board of Supervisors, and an assistant city manager. I was the emcee of the event. Story upon story was told about terrorized and terrified people. The most emotional moment came when a nine-year-old girl stood, took the microphone, and described her fear of her parents being taken away from her. We then heard from a police officer, the prosecutor, the assistant city manager, and other government officials, who reassured these folks that local officials were not hunting them down, not seeking to expel them, and in fact had inclusive policies in place.

Afterward, I worked with the city manager and our Office of Human Rights to create a pamphlet that would explain just how our city agencies approached undocumented people and what their rights were if they were ever confronted with federal immigration officials. It would be another determined show of solidarity from a local Virginia government.

I also convened a meeting on March 2 of an ad hoc group meant to put more flesh on the bones of the resistance idea. I invited faith leaders, immigration lawyers, the leadership of the refugee community, and other activists. We discussed specific ways to recognize the contributions of immigrants and refugees to the local community through interfaith exchanges and programs in our public schools and other institutions. This exciting initiative would become Welcoming Greater Charlottesville—which developed a documentary highlighting the incredible stories of these courageous people too often in the shadows, a community ID program, and educational programs. It continues to promote religious and cultural tolerance and pluralism.

But the statue issue was still smoldering in the background.

WES BELLAMY AND I HAD A MEETING IN MY OFFICE AROUND THIS same time. I confronted him with my shock at his turn against the compromise. He threw up his hands. "It was all Bob, man!" he exclaimed. "He tricked both of us!" He explained that Fenwick had put him—Bellamy—in the position of needing to pursue removal. If Fenwick had voted against removal, the idea went, he would have constituted a majority of three votes, along with myself and Galvin. Bellamy could have been in the minority, voting for removal. But because removal would not have the votes, he could then support the compromise measure with a clear conscience. Fenwick's surprise abstention upended this whole scheme, depriving Bellamy of the political cover he needed as the most public advocate of removal to later support the compromise. At the same time, Fenwick's action breathed hope into Bellamy's sincere desire to remove the statue—as he surprised even Bellamy, who had not planned for the scenario that Fenwick would support removal.

We sped toward a second council meeting where we would revisit the statue vote, presumably now with Fenwick having gotten some of the concessions he wanted in exchange for a vote he was prepared to give, despite his own misgivings about symbolic victories.

EVEN FOR OUR MEETINGS, THE NEXT MEETING FELT LIKE A CIR-cus. There were now large "SAVE THE LEE STATUE" signs among the crowd with pictures of the statue on them, along with a whole new crop of blue "REMOVE THE STATUE" signs. Several officers stood prominently in the aisles in case of an outburst. During the "Matters by the Public" part of the meeting, several people spoke in favor of removing the Lee statue, including the president of the local NAACP. Others spoke against, including a white woman from a neighboring county who appeared in full Civil War dress—a white bonnet and a pink southern frock. A local African American man who said his great-grandfather had been a slave observed that not many African Americans were in the chambers and said it was because "we're more concerned about getting our kids an education." He said, "This disgusts me. And you are supposed to be our leaders?" He called out white liberals and their "white guilt." He said, "Our parents did not teach us to hate this statue."

We heard from a twelve-year-old girl who said she had five dogs named after Civil War generals. We heard from a histrionic white woman who said she had traveled from Florida; she started crying, saying, "I want my respect, because I have followed these men through battles." She said she had cleaned up cigarette butts at the statue that day.

There were frequent outbursts during these speeches, and it took all my energy to run the meeting calmly. I was prepared to have people escorted out again but wanted to do everything in my power not to. So I had come into the chambers with a carefully prepared statement about how we could disagree without being disagreeable. I introduced the police officers present to everyone and asked the audience to use hand gestures (thumbs-up or thumbs-down) to agree or disagree with speakers. Anyone who interrupted the order and decorum would be called out, and if it happened again, they would be escorted out of the room.

In the end, despite a very high level of energy in the room, only four people had to be taken out, and in my view, they just looked rude. I felt I earned a lot of buy-in from the crowd by talking through the rules at such length before anything got started.

However, what I regret, in retrospect, was that my focus on running the meeting well risked creating a disconnect with the very real emotions in the room, particularly among African Americans, who were exhausted and angered by a dehumanizing past and present, and their white allies, who employed their privilege and their voice to express fury at a system that has so often fallen far short of its ideals.

I had put a lot of thought into my statement for voting against moving the statues. I said I would be voting for a plan that would tie together Lee Park, Jackson Park, the slave auction block, and the former local field office of the Freedmen's Bureau in such a way that we could challenge and transform the Jim Crow legacy of these settings and forever change the narrative in Charlottesville. We could create a magnificent new memorial to civil rights victories in Lee Park and tell the truth about our history of systemic racism near the slave auction block in Jackson Park. And this dynamic conversation using our public spaces could all happen regardless of whether the Lee statue was moved.

I explained how numerous African American residents had told the Blue Ribbon Commission they supported maintaining the statues as "teachable moments." They believed that to move forward, we must push against the past. We must see these monuments for what they were and defy them in order to overcome what they represented. This was a more uncomfortable reality, to be sure. But this dialectical exhibit, coming into being through an underlying process of visible thesis, antithesis, and synthesis, would be part of the vibrancy and dynamism of the progressive project in Charlottesville. (This was the first and last time I would allude to Hegel in a public speech.)

The decision could also backfire by alienating groups from each other, I said, explaining that the project could unintentionally damage progressive goals. Attempts to cleanse the public realm of irritants to progressive aims, to barricade liberal values behind seeming victories such as removing a statue, could lead to more fury in the long run. Indeed, we had seen just that violent cycle playing out in the Trump campaign, where an intense attack against progressivism in general seemed to resonate with millions of people.

But my statement did not change any minds. In this second meeting on the issue, Fenwick, who seemed to have gotten what he wanted through his gambit of abstention (Bellamy and Szakos had readily agreed to support his call for expanded hours at the field houses at parks in majority-minority neighborhoods), voted for removing the statue, becoming the decisive vote in a 3–2 decision.[1] The crowd burst into loud whoops and hollers.

Technically, however, the motion was not to move the statue. It instead directed the city manager to come back to the council in sixty days with options for moving it out of the city. In terms of symbolic versus actual action, that fact would turn out to be momentous. The three members of the council in favor of the measure had not decided among themselves what should be done with it, and Kathy Galvin and I had not committed to anything at all. So not only was there no imminent action afoot (such as the city manager hauling the statues off that night), but nothing had actually been decided yet. This outcome afforded ample time for a legal challenge.

Later in that same meeting, we unanimously voted to rename Lee and Jackson Parks (with specific names to be decided in a later meeting). And we voted for a recontextualization project that would tie new monuments in Lee and Jackson Parks together, redo the slave auction block, and recognize the Freedmen's Bureau, which had been near Jackson Park. We included $500,000 for a new memorial near the Lee statue—which could fund the "lenses" concept, among others. Because I doubted anything would happen soon with the Lee statue, due to the likelihood of protracted litigation, I thought the decision on the new memorial was the most impactful action we'd taken. It could lead to change *actually happening*—rather than more merely symbolic victories.

A FEW DAYS LATER, I HAD LUNCH WITH A FORMER TWO-TERM mayor who told me that not once in his four years as mayor did anyone try to disrupt the meeting. How much had changed. For me, maintaining order during that second statues meeting had been particularly frustrating, including the overt measures I'd had to introduce to prevent people from jeering and standing up and shouting, like having them use thumbs-up and thumbs-down gestures. Though it was successful, it had felt ridiculous. We needed to be able to deliberate, to exchange ideas, and to explain our positions. But people had become so accustomed to the distilled, potent, extreme positions that performed well for Facebook, YouTube, and Twitter audiences that they had become simultaneously disinterested in the give-and-take of actual decision-making. Meanwhile, those who served in public office became something like memes on social media, simplistic symbols to be either deified by the online crowd or lustily taken down. (I would only later learn from Emily, who was then teaching in UVA's media studies department, about an emerging academic discipline that studies just how social media has enabled "character assassination," defined as "verbal and non-verbal assaults and accusations aimed at a person's morals, integrity, and public image."[2])

And, worse, many online commenters believed—now, with justification from Fenwick—that this energy could force elected officials into changing their positions. The metaphor that came to mind for modern-day politics was a grenade-field. It all resulted in intense forces of fury exploding on left and right and being hurled at individuals from silos all over the Internet. To survive while reaching your destination, you had to weave through the explosions. It was like a video game. But to extend the metaphor, people were watching it—watching you try to survive—the same way young people today watch other people play video games on YouTube as if it were a spectator sport.

It wasn't always like this. There were still extended times where things were quiet and we could be more deliberative. We would often deal with more substantive issues (budget work sessions, for instance) and no grenades would go off. But I felt the balance was grotesquely off between the theater of deliberation and the theater of the grenade game, and that in the latter, symbols, rather than actual change, often *were* the victories. Worse, the grenade game had become 24/7. The grenades were going off in my Twitter feed until midnight.

I saw a disturbing pattern of local reporters writing about my tweets as if they were actual news. Denver Riggleman, for instance, a distillery owner in nearby Nelson County who was running for governor (he was ultimately unsuccessful, but would be elected to the US House of Representatives in 2018), tweeted,

> If Charlottesville Mayor Mike Signer wants to keep poking the rest of Virginia in the eye with this sort of nonsense with our statues and making statements about Charlottesville being the "capital of resistance," he is going to wish that he would be allowed to make Charlottesville a sanctuary city, because I am coming.

I was walking into a clothing store at the time to return a pair of pants and paused to tap out a response on my phone: "Newby Gov candidate @denver4governor's inexperience is showing. Doesn't he know I voted AGAINST moving Lee statue?!" He shot back, "@MikeSigner I lead men. I was responsible for their success or failure. You failed . . . I won't. I'm not all talk no action #realexperience." I responded: "Love getting trolled by a Gov candidate! Come visit & learn about our 3.9% unemployment & AAA bond rating. Didn't happen thru rhetoric. Thx."

And then, all of a sudden, it became a headline in the *Daily Progress*: "Charlottesville Mayor and Gubernatorial Candidate Riggleman in Twitter Spat over Statue."[3] The piece went through the individual tweets *as if they were news*. It was all so ridiculous, but it was significant, too. Somehow, these words we were writing on our phones were *becoming what politics was*. And maybe government, too. And I have to admit there was also excitement in it, just as in a video game: in surviving the blasts, dancing along, prevailing, being resilient, eluding your enemies, reaching the end, grabbing the jewel.

MEANWHILE, THE OLD BRUSHFIRE FROM MY FIRST MONTHS AS mayor—the battle over how to maintain order—burned on. At the one-year mark of passing the new governing procedures, we were due to ratify them. In late January, I had opened the *Daily Progress* to read a letter from a UVA professor named Walt Heinecke, who had been a sort of council gadfly in recent years, titled "Resist Council's Assault on Democracy." Cleverly invoking my longtime concern about demagogues, he wrote, "These changes, taken together, undermine free speech, the ability to dissent, and our democracy in Charlottesville. The way they were implemented smacks of demagoguery." He then flipped my support of resistance against me, asking ominously, "What happens when citizens resist and Councilors ignore the resistance?"[4]

What would happen, indeed?

16

"DISTURBANCE OR REMOVAL"

| MARCH 2017 |

THE PROCEDURES WE HAD PASSED AT THE START OF MY TERM AS mayor were only temporary. They came up again in March 2017 for a vote to make them permanent. We ratified them 4 to 1, Fenwick voting against. This small but important victory would have consequences in the months ahead, as I would have to use the new rules to try to reckon with the passions erupting in our chambers.

Meanwhile, the predicted lawsuit quickly materialized. On March 20, a series of plaintiffs filed suit under Virginia's statute preventing the "disturbance or removal" of war memorials. The statute had first been passed in 1904 and applied only to counties. It had been amended several times since, including in 1997 to apply to cities, and credible arguments had been made that it applied only prospectively to statues installed after the amendment had been made. In 2016, a judge in Danville, Virginia, had allowed the removal of a Confederate flag from the city's courthouse on that basis. Many also argued that the Lee statue was not even a "war memorial," as the statue's benefactor had dedicated it to the memory of his parents.

For those reasons, even though I disagreed with the removal decision, I felt the council could do it legally. But I also knew we would be sued and thought it likely that a local judge would order an injunction to forbid removing the statue while the lawsuit was in process. And I knew that lawsuits like this took a long time to resolve, that it might even go to the Virginia Supreme Court—and that we would be stuck that whole time with passions stirred up and nothing actually happening to address and resolve them. It would be a fire with plenty of tinder, and not a drop of water in sight.

It was not a good feeling to see this coming, but that's exactly what happened.

17

"OUR MAYOR IS A NEO-FASCIST"

I was in a meeting at a new day job I'd taken in January 2017 as general counsel of a quickly growing software firm that made mobile apps for companies around the world. My phone started lighting up with texts from both TV stations and the *Daily Progress* about an activist who was holding a protest at the Landmark Hotel, replete with a hand-lettered sign declaring "OUR MAYOR IS A NEO-FASCIST."

Did I have any comment?

A friend walking by the scene relayed a description to me. There were just a handful of people, and the handmade sign likened me to Mussolini. The organizer holding up the sign was the very same one who had led the small, disruptive protest on my first day as mayor. He told a reporter that, in crafting a complex set of incentives on parking, zoning, and economic development that would put redevelopment of the vacant hotel on track, I had "flip-flopped" and "lied" about "taking an aggressive stance" against the owner of the hotel during my campaign for council. He said, "The trains ran on time in fascist Italy. But it catered to big business. And I think Mike Signer is catering to big business."

I wrote a statement that took the high road, but the paper still put the story, along with a photo of the sign, on the front page the next morning. The "rally," the story noted, was attended by six people.[1]

It was stupid. It was silly. But combined with the other issues churning away, it set me back. I told my mom about the episode while I was at Toys R Us buying a new diaper pail, and she just started laughing, and then I did, too. I realized that what really bothered me was not being able to respond. If I had taken the bait—and decried the attack—I would have gotten caught in the troll's trap. There would have been another story: "Mayor Defends Against Charge He's a Neo-Fascist." But by not responding, I was also bottling that frustration inside. It was a double-bind.

But there was a third path: to keep it all in perspective. To see it as something about the activist, not about me. To laugh it off and move on. Pulling punches was not at all intuitive to me. But in this new age of social media, it was the only path forward.

IRONICALLY, IN THIS SAME MONTH I OPENED UP MY INBOX TO FIND an email from two political scientists asking mayors across America to give candid, anonymous answers to questions about "mayors' experiences with the public." Their interest, in the wake of the 2016 election, was "heightened levels of acrimony facilitated by an instant communication environment." They wanted to know whether mayors had experienced "negative interactions with the public either in office or on the campaign trail." Their survey asked about psychological problems experienced as a result of such negative interactions.

It reminded me that mayors often receive undue attention through the public fascination with their ancient ceremonial role, and because of the reputation of controversial, larger-than-life municipal titans like the Daleys of Chicago. I answered honestly. When I received the results of the survey the following November, I saw that of 283 mayors, 48 percent said they had received disrespectful comments or images on social media, and 31 percent reported being harassed. Thirty-nine percent reported increased levels of irritability, sleep disturbances, problems concentrating, or an exaggerated "startle response," and 18 percent reported intrusive memories and nightmares.

But only 16 percent said such negative experiences had caused them to think about leaving public office or suspending their campaigns. That's the club to which I already had the dubious distinction of belonging.

We were just two weeks away from the first invasion.

PART III | THE SUMMER OF HATE

18

"THAT DAY WE FINISH THEM ALL OFF"

| MAY 2017 |

SATURDAY, MAY 6, 2017, BROUGHT A SUNNY DAY AND A SPEAKING invitation at Charlottesville's annual Festival of Cultures, which took place at Lee Park. Dozens of ethnic and national groups had installed colorful booths around the Robert E. Lee statue featuring crafts and foods from their cultures. In my remarks, I celebrated diversity. A few dozen folks sat on folding chairs; others staffed the kiosks under bright tents. After I finished, I heard something unsettling: someone told me that Richard Spencer, a UVA graduate and notorious alt-right leader, had been stalking around the festival with followers in tow. He and his young, buzz-cut male followers had made "Heil" salutes at an event celebrating Trump's victory in Washington, DC, on November 19, 2016, and he had been at the center of controversy when he had been punched in the head by a black-hooded man following President Trump's inauguration.[1]

I was told that Spencer and his followers had made disturbing, aggressive remarks to several people present in the park. The mood was tense. One organizer told me he had recently received bystander training and felt equipped in case they came back. It was chilling. I placed a call to the city manager to let him know. I didn't hear anything more that afternoon.

It was a warm May evening, the temperature just right, and after putting the boys to bed, Emily and I were looking forward to a lazy night. I received a text and looked down at my phone to see a photo of Lee Park with what looked like a hundred torches. The park was only a few blocks from our house. Emily and I asked our neighbors, a political science PhD student and an elementary school teacher, who were having a glass of wine on their porch, if they could be on hand if the boys woke up. They said of course.

We arrived at the park a couple of minutes later. Whatever had happened had only just ended. A handful of cops were roaming around. There were a few charred tiki torch stumps on the ground. I asked what had happened. An officer told me, "We cleared them off." I quickly gathered that Spencer and about one hundred of his followers, clad in their eerie uniform of khakis and white dress shirts, had crowded into the park. I learned that Jason Kessler had called the gathering a "funeral procession for the dead." Under Spencer's lead, the group chanted, "We will not be replaced," "Blood and soil," and "Russia is our friend." Kessler said the Russia reference was because "Russian people are a white people." Spencer told his followers: "We will not be replaced from this park. We will not be replaced from this world. Whites have a future. We have a future of power, of beauty, of expression."[2]

I knew that pictures of this event would quickly race around the world. I headed back home and wrote a statement that was worded as strongly as I thought I could make it, but I also tried to recognize that at least some of the participants may not have been out-and-out neo-fascists: "The event involving torches at night in Lee Park was either profoundly ignorant or was designed to instill fear in our minority populations in a way that hearkens back to the days of the KKK. Either way, as Mayor of this City, I want everyone to know this: we reject this intimidation. We are a Welcoming City, but such intolerance is not welcome here."

Without quite realizing it, with that statement I was throwing a match into the alt-right's tinder. The following day, Sunday, I began receiving the first waves of anti-Semitic tweets. One said, "I smell Jew. If so, you are going back to Israel. But you will not stay in power here. Not for long."

That night, there was a candlelight vigil at Lee Park convened by far-left groups, including Solidarity Cville and Black Lives Matter. I was not invited. I went anyway, dutifully bringing a couple of candles from home, but with a sinking feeling in my stomach. It was unlike any other vigil I'd been to. A sheet was draped over the statue with dripping red letters reading "BLACK LIVES MATTER. FUCK WHITE SUPREMACY." In an eerie monotone, a male speaker spent several minutes attacking me and Kathy Galvin for voting against removing the "racist statues." The mood was inflammatory and divisive. I saw many people looking around at each other uncomfortably. I left after about fifteen minutes but tried to put the best possible face on the experience, tweeting out a photo of folks holding candles with a statement that "these are the kinds of torches I like to see." But my heart wasn't in it.

On Monday, a blizzard of requests arrived on my iPhone. The *New York Times*, the *Washington Post*, Associated Press, and *All Things Considered* wanted interviews. A Reddit post, put up by someone called "NuckFigures," included a photo of me and Khizr Khan from the "Capital of the Resistance" event along with a caption reading, "Photo of Kike Signer (Mayor of Charlottesville kvetching in the articles) posing with that paki shitskin 'gold star father' the judenpresse pumped up during the election last year."

In contrast with the "neo-fascist" attack, something about these new attacks made me feel calm, strong even. I think, without fully realizing it, I was living out a lesson I'd taken from visiting Israel and watching how the native *sabras* conducted themselves. *Sabra* is a colloquial term of endearment for native Israelis; it is derived from the native prickly pear, which has a tough, thick skin but a sweet interior. Israelis, too, can be thorny, blunt, and a little unfriendly on the outside, but tenderhearted on the inside. Spending time with them, I had come to understand at a bone-deep level the personal necessity of rejecting—even destroying—the stereotype of the weak and easily bullied Jew.

I began responding with a dry, self-confident voice (I was "droll to the trolls," I told Emily). When one called me a Bolshevik "on the side of evil," I responded, "Apparently this troll doesn't know about our unemployment rate (2.9%-lowest in Va) and AAA-bond rating. Oh well!" Someone said I was a "slimy spineless white coward," and I responded, "Another profile in courage here—anonymous trolls lecturing elected officials about cowardice. Yawn."

In an interview with the reporter Michael Edison Hayden, who was covering the alt-right for *Newsweek*, I described the challenge of how much oxygen we should give the alt-right. I said that the people doing this had a "juvenile mentality and are beneath our contempt."[3] I was trying to put things in context, to minimize them while condemning them at the same time—and while keeping the city's firm hold on the moral narrative. But it was a difficult balance, to say the least. When the Associated Press interviewed me for a story about my tweets to the anti-Semitic trolls, it appeared across the country titled, "Mayor Trolls the Trolls." David Duke ominously tweeted about me, "Mayor Mike Signer is doing exactly what his fellow tribesmen in #NOLA did—cry out in pain as they strike you." I saw Duke as a pathetic footnote in American history and responded, "When David Duke—David Duke!—takes time out of his busy schedule to compose a thoughtful message like this, I KNOW I'm doing something right."

Yes, I enjoyed writing that. But it also put me on the radar of an entire universe of anti-Semites. Suddenly, more people were following me, tweeting at me with a whole new level of stereotype—hook-nosed Protocols of the Elders of Zion stuff. Emily was worried. I was surprised by the strange sense of *sangfroid* that I found—or that found me.

At this point, the Anti-Defamation League (ADL) contacted me and asked to schedule a call, which Emily joined. The rep informed us that the ADL had compiled a file on me containing eight hundred attacks. It was a sobering conversation. Among other points of advice, he suggested that I look out for information online that could allow my family to be "doxed" (attacked online using information gathered online), and that we watch for indicators I was being physically followed (such as suspicious cars). Afterward, we unlisted our house from the online white pages, and I asked our clerk of council to remove information about my family and my children from my council bio. The ADL connected me with an FBI agent in Richmond. When we spoke, he informed me that nothing online—even references to gas chambers—rose to the level of a "credible threat." This was the legal term for a planned, imminent act of violence, which the Supreme Court said was required to intervene. He was operating within the same legal framework the city would be required to adopt in the coming months.

Emily was understandably troubled by the confluence of my outspoken confrontation with hate, and my seemingly nonchalant approach to the anti-Semitic bigots online. Talking quietly by ourselves, she worried about the possibility of a rogue actor targeting us. But I also saw how the position was resonating nationwide. *Time* magazine included my quote about how the protesters were "beneath contempt" emblazoned along the bottom of its opening pages. The *New York Times* editorialized about the Spencer event and cited the stance against hate with approval. When I received an email with a cartoon attached showing Robert E. Lee pushing the green button on a gas chamber, and a picture of me photoshopped into it—complete with a Star of David on my lapel—it was unnerving. But in a perverse way, the cartoon seemed to be a measure of the power of my stance against extremism.

While the nation was looking for resolve and unity against modern-day white supremacists, however, Charlottesville continued to splinter. The following Monday, there was a regular city council meeting. I felt it was a time for us to present a united front and was glad when each councilor made a statement condemning the rally. But I was discomfited when Wes Bellamy took a "you're with us or against us" approach. He said: "The choice is yours—to this city, to this area, and even to this Council, whether you can be on the side of justice and equity with us, or whether you can stand on the side of those from Saturday night." This comment essentially grouped everyone into two sides—those who were for removing the statue, and those who were now with Spencer.

WITH THAT GAUNTLET THROWN DOWN, I FACED AN OBVIOUS question about the position I'd originally taken on the statues. Now that a noxious actor like Richard Spencer and I seemed to be "on the same side" of the issue of the Lee statue, should I change my position?

That was the obvious question. But I knew that in reality I wasn't aligned with the alt-right in any way at all. I knew they would despise the Blue Ribbon Commission's compromise position of transform-in-place. They would fight tooth and nail any effort to illuminate the history of white supremacy around the statues, or to erect new statues that would transform the parks as surely as the *Fearless Girl* statue had transformed Wall Street's *Charging Bull*. They wouldn't even want us to rename the parks, or remove the plaque that described Lee as a "hero of the Confederacy."

Moreover, I didn't want to let Spencer and his ilk push me around. This opportunistic maneuvering by a renegade bunch should not destroy the idea I'd heard so often in the African American community, an idea that clearly had moved the Blue Ribbon Commission: to concentrate on teachable moments, especially given the new attention the city was getting.

The alt-right, and the often obnoxious pro-Confederate history "flaggers" who had been flooding our council meetings and swarming all over social media, obviously made the discussion around recontextualization harder. But I also kept thinking about the danger of symbolic politics overtaking real politics—just as I'd mentioned on my very first day as mayor. I saw the new politics about the statue as almost entirely politically manufactured by the far right, a fake symbolic hook for other unrelated outrages for Trumpists. As long and hard as I thought about it, I still felt that the picture of Charlottesville today overcoming Charlottesville of yesterday, in the same place, *was the truth*, which is exactly what I'd heard so many in the black community saying.

Around this time, I walked by an elderly African American neighbor as she was tending the roses in her front yard. Her family had been in Charlottesville for generations, and they owned a well-maintained brick house whose front porch was a place where people tended to convene. Black and white neighbors alike would stop and say hello. I asked her what she thought about the controversy. She said, "I want those statues to stay there so my grandchildren know what happened here." More than any other comment, that one would stick with me. So, despite Spencer, and despite the attacks on my stance at the candlelight vigil, I decided I would maintain my position.

But I still had a knot in my stomach that didn't seem to go away. I knew that the Spencer visit had changed things. I knew that people who had been certain of their position previously, including many African Americans, were now uncertain. They didn't know what to make of the new developments or even how to behave.

Was the tide turning against the recontextualization position? Would I find myself marooned on an island of my own making?

I WAS AT MY DAY JOB WHEN I SAW A VOICEMAIL COMING IN FROM a Florida number. I didn't answer it—I didn't answer calls from unknown numbers anymore—but when I listened to the voicemail a few minutes later, it was an audio clip of Hitler ranting about Jews. The next night, we received a strange envelope at home. In beautiful script that had been added to an old Christmas card, it read:

> *You should buy a one-way ticket to Tel Aviv, make Aliyah,*
> *LEAVE WHITE CHRISTIAN SOUTHERNERS and*
> *their heritage THE HELL ALONE, AND STOP BEING*
> *SUCH A GODDAMN BOLSHEVIK KIKE. Go and destroy*
> *monuments w/your Semitic cousins, ISIS, to your hearts [sic]*
> *content! Enjoy living your life knowing that no matter the*
> *level of Jewish nepotism, scheming, blood money, lies and*
> *propaganda, white southerners like Robert E. Lee were men*
> *of honor, truth, beauty and nobility that your hook-nosed*
> *cabal of Talmudic propagandists will ALWAYS envy and*
> *seek to destroy. NOT THIS TIME!*

And then I learned that a group of KKK members from North Carolina had filed a request for a permit for a rally in Charlottesville.

I WAS IN A MEETING WITH RABBI TOM GUTHERZ AT CONGREGA-tion Beth Israel a few days later. We were unpacking recent events in a rather scholarly way when the executive director of the synagogue came in, alarm in her eyes, and said she'd heard the news about the KKK.

My God, I wondered. What can happen next?

The city manager confirmed what she had told us. He said that, so far, the applicants seemed to have followed the proper procedures. They were applying for a "free speech event." I knew this request would be explosive, and that it would create a First Amendment paradox of the first order.

THE PREVAILING DOCTRINE IN OUR FEDERAL COURTS REGARDING freedom of speech is sometimes called "First Amendment absolutism." It holds that with extremely narrow exceptions, even the most offensive speech must be allowed and even enabled by government. Central to this tenet is a 1949 Supreme Court case called *Terminiello v. Chicago*. In *Terminiello*, a suspended Catholic priest, Arthur Terminiello, was invited to speak at a political rally for the Christian Veterans of America by one Gerald L.K. Smith, a notorious anti-Semite who had been an acolyte of the Louisiana demagogue Huey Long. Long had been assassinated in 1935, but Smith was still active on the political far right. When Terminiello arrived at the rally, there were about 800 people inside the auditorium and 1,000 angry protesters outside. The crowd outside then grew to 1,500, and the people inside the hall could hear them yelling, "Fascists, Hitlers!" and "Damn Fascists." Some protesters threw bricks through the windows of the building; one young woman's coat was torn off. The police arrested over a dozen people, all on the outside.[4]

Inside, Terminiello railed to his supporters, "We will all be drowned in this tidal wave of Communism which is going over the world." He threatened to collect the names of the protesters, charging that they had been "imported from Russia," and asked those in the crowd to send him their names "immediately." He went on to attack Jews and communists, telling those inside the hall how to deal with the "howling mob" outside it: "We don't want them here; we want them to go back where they came from."[5] The speech "stirred the audience not only to cheer and applaud but to expressions of immediate anger, unrest and alarm." One member shouted that "Jews, niggers and Catholics would have to be gotten rid of." Another yelled, "Yes, the Jews are all killers, murderers. If we don't kill them first, they will kill us." There were shouts of "Kill the Jews" and "Dirty kikes."[6]

Terminiello was arrested by the Chicago police, and then convicted by a jury, for "breaching the peace" under a city ordinance.

In a 5–4 decision, however, the Supreme Court struck down the jury's decision—and the ordinance—on the grounds of freedom of speech under the First Amendment. Justice William Douglas wrote a famous opinion finding that the "vitality of civil and political institutions in our society depends on free discussion." The Court applied an "imminent danger of unlawful action" test, ruling that Terminiello's speech could be stopped only if it was "likely to produce a clear and present danger of a serious substantive evil that rises far above public inconvenience, annoyance, or unrest." Emphasizing the value of disorder, Justice Douglas wrote that free speech's very function was to "invite dispute." He said, "It may indeed best serve its high purpose when it induces a condition of unrest, creates dissatisfaction with conditions as they are, or even stirs people to anger."[7]

Justice Robert H. Jackson vehemently dissented from the Court's holding reversing the lower court. He wrote that the choice was "not between order and liberty," but between "liberty with order and anarchy without either." He argued that if the Court did not "temper its doctrinaire logic with a little practical wisdom," it would "convert the constitutional Bill of Rights into a suicide pact."[8]

Who was this Supreme Court justice, little known today, who could equate the lack of "a little practical wisdom" with a "suicide pact"—without seeming hysterical? Jackson's path suggested that the right approach to the First Amendment might come through the pragmatic, utilitarian course that had featured so prominently in my seminars on leadership and race, instead of soaring deontological pronouncements. There was a plainspoken harmony in his words, a commitment to practical application, a worldliness without world-weariness, that I found magnetic upon my first reading of the case as a graduate student in political science at Berkeley in the late 1990s. There, I learned that Jackson had been the chief prosecutor for the United States in the Nuremburg trials. But he had never graduated from law school; instead, he had attended two years of law school and then chosen the path, still technically available in some states (including Virginia), of "reading into" the law. (Those taking this path study law under a mentor and then pass an examination.) After becoming a lawyer, Jackson had worked in corporate law and Democratic politics. He had taken a low-level position in the Internal Revenue Service before joining the Justice Department, rising from the Tax Division all the way to solicitor general and then attorney general. This was all during Franklin D. Roosevelt's term in the Oval Office, and Roosevelt appointed him as a Supreme Court justice in 1941.

At every turn, it was practice—not theory—that guided Jackson. He delivered his opening statement at Nuremberg in firm, steady tones before the Nazi defendants in the dock. He said that the four great nations in charge of the prosecutions would "stay the hand of vengeance and voluntarily submit their captive enemies to the judgment of the law," and that this was "one of the most significant tributes that power has ever paid to reason."[9]

It was—and is—significant that Jackson, representing the United States and the civilized world, expressly chose to put "reason" over "power." Often, pragmatists see reason as power's weaker sibling. If you're committed to the practical application of principles, rather than the principles themselves, the logic goes, then you also are going to be more skeptical about reason, which places such faith in abstract principles. But Jackson saw it the other way.

And this is how he approached the problem of dangerous speech as well in *Terminiello v. Chicago*. He assailed the majority for judging what happened at the rally in the abstract, as if Arthur Terminiello had "spoken to persons as dispassionate as empty benches, or like a modern Demosthenes practicing his Philippics on a lonely seashore." It was practical application, lived context, that concerned Jackson. "The local court that tried Terminiello was not indulging in theory," he observed. It was instead "dealing with a riot and with a speech that provoked a hostile mob and incited a friendly one, and threatened violence between the two." The trial judge's instruction to the jury on whether Terminiello had "stirred the public to anger, invited dispute, brought about unrest, created a disturbance or molested peace and quiet by arousing alarm" was not about "harmless or abstract conditions," Jackson said. It was about "concrete behavior and specific consequences disclosed by the evidence."[10]

If Jackson had had his way, the Supreme Court would have had no right to announce a "nation-wide rule that disables local and state au-

thorities from punishing conduct which produces conflicts of this kind."
In an eerie prefiguring of the forces that would come to Charlottesville
and other American cities seventy years later, he observed that clashes
between protesters and counterprotesters were increasing across America, where each "parade is met with counterparade." Locked in this dangerous dance, these events had the "potentiality, and more than a few
the purpose, of disorder and violence." They all shared this in common:
"appeals not to reason but to fears and mob spirit." They were a "show
of force designed to bully adversaries and to overawe the indifferent."[11]

Jackson linked Arthur Terminiello himself to the instability of democracy at the hands of demagogues. He cited Hitler on the "strategy
of the mass demonstration as used by both fascism and communism,"
noting that Hitler had said, "We should not work in secret conventicles
but in mighty mass demonstrations, and it is not by dagger and poison or
pistol that the road can be cleared for the movement but by the conquest
of the streets." Jackson argued that the "present obstacle to mastery of
the streets by either radical or reactionary mob movements" was the "authority of local governments," which he said "represent the free choice of
democratic and law-abiding elements, of all shades of opinion but who,
whatever their differences, submit them to free elections which register
the results of their free discussion."[12]

It was precisely such local elected officials, themselves dependent
on public opinion for their support, who Jackson said should be in
charge of determining peace and order. He predicted that the effect of
the majority decision in *Terminiello*, if not the goal, would be to "paralyze
and discredit the only democratic authority" that could "curb [totalitar-
ian groups] in their battle for the streets." Jackson's conclusion should
chill anyone who watched the videos of the militias marching through
the streets of Charlottesville with their swastikas and their shields, after
a federal judge ruled against our attempt to relocate the rally to safer
grounds. "Wholesome principles" of pragmatism and deference to on-
the-ground officials were being abandoned in favor of a "dogma of absolute freedom for irresponsible and provocative utterance," which "almost
completely sterilizes the power of local authorities to keep the peace."

The black-and-white approach contained a hidden vulnerability. Speakers could "incite mob action while pretending to deplore it."[13]

Jackson observed the cunning inversions through which one could employ the "invocation of constitutional liberties as part of the strategy for overthrowing them." This was, he observed, "a dilemma to a free people which may not be soluble by constitutional logic alone."[14]

Little did I know how relevant Jackson's reasoning would be to some hard choices we would have to make in Charlottesville, with the world watching on, as we faced off with adversaries intent on warping the First Amendment to advance authoritarian aims.

IN THE WAKE OF KESSLER'S RIGHT-WING CAMPAIGNS AND SPENcer's torch parade at the Lee statue, local activists from the "Antifa" movement had begun a campaign to out anyone connected to Kessler and Spencer. They had been putting flyers in UVA buildings that read, "Know your local Nazis." They featured pictures of people who were friends with Jason Kessler, and the pictures included one of a local man who worked in a small family business. He had recently come to see me during my office hours to talk about crime in Charlottesville, and had told me a moving story about a black friend of his who had recently been murdered, with the crime as yet unsolved.

I didn't approve of him being friendly with Kessler, but he wasn't a Nazi. It seemed this term had become another untethered signifier hurled around in our politics of symbolism, in this case by some locals associated with the loose organization calling itself Antifa. Antifa is the self-adopted nickname of organizers and protesters around the world who have fiercely resolved to oppose what they see as neo-fascist, or outright fascist, political actors. The movement has roots in the violent confrontations in Europe between socialists protesting authoritarian figures like Oswald Mosley, the British fascist who emerged in parallel to Adolf Hitler in the 1930s.

In 2019, Nicole Hemmer, an expert on the history of the American right and then a professor of presidential studies at UVA's Miller Center, described to me what she called "anti-fascist ideology": today's antifascists believe that the lesson from the rise of fascism in the 1920s and 1930s was that "if you do not cut it off at its root, it will grow, it will become empowered, it will become nearly impossible to stop. And so what you have to do is, by any means possible, stop fascism where you find it." Anti-fascists now face a particular challenge in the United States, where she said nonviolence is "lionized." "Anti-fascists also make room for violent resistance," she told me. "They say that the only way to combat a violent ideology like fascism is with violence." Antifa activists, she said, are trying to "gain acceptance for the idea that sometimes protest, sometimes resistance, is violent."[15]

With the incipient election of Trump and the racism and sexism of the forces around his campaign, the movement had gathered steam in the United States. In February 2017, Antifa protesters created violent disturbances around a speech planned in Berkeley, California, by alt-right provocateur Milo Yiannopoulos, a former Breitbart editor who frequently said outrageous things about immigrants. Masked Antifa activists had broken store windows and thrown rocks and Molotov cocktails at police during a rally against the speech.

According to *The Atlantic*, Antifa is "heavily composed of anarchists," and its activists therefore "place little faith in the state, which they consider complicit in fascism and racism." They instead choose "direct action," which requires confrontation, including physical force. They often surge in what they call a "black bloc," dressed in black and wearing concealing masks.[16] The nature of their activity, at once organized and violent, would lead the progressive mayor of Berkeley, Jesse Arreguín, to say they should be prosecuted as a gang.[17] At times, they became involved in shocking cycles of violence with the far right.

In April 2017, the Republican Party of Multnomah County in Portland, Oregon, was planning to participate in an annual parade when activists got involved. A group called the Direct Action Alliance declared, "Fascists plan to march through the streets," and warned, "Nazis will not march through Portland unopposed." The alliance said it believed "fascists" had infiltrated Republican ranks. A group called Oregon Students Empowered created a Facebook page called "Shut down fascism! No nazis in Portland!"

After Antifa successfully forced the cancelation of the parade, Trump supporters planned a "March for Free Speech," where an ex-con appeared draped in an American flag, making racial slurs and Nazi salutes.[18]

Antifa also often turned against elected officials. They interrupted so many city council meetings in Portland that the council decided to meet behind closed doors. They trailed Mayor Ted Wheeler to his house often enough that he began "taking refuge in a hotel." One Antifa email threatened, "The police cannot stop us from shutting down roads."[19]

These same tactics would become familiar soon enough in Charlottesville, but at the time it felt new, strange, and alarming. It was a complicated situation for me. On the books, I had been an "anti-fascist" since writing my doctoral dissertation on democracy's historic and urgent need to confront and defuse demagogues, and I sympathized with the activists' concerns. Setting aside my personal commitment to nonviolence and the rule of law, I had also been struck by the emotional and physical courage of those seeking to stop fascism in its tracks. But as I came to understand the contemporary movement going by that same name better, I was unnerved by how broad their brush was. In writing *Demagogue*, I'd taken pains to argue that the term "demagogue" could lose its meaning and power when used too loosely—that the charge should be specific, rather than broad and general. So, too, with fascism. Sometimes, I almost felt that these activists called nearly anyone they disagreed with a "fascist," which meant it was hard to distinguish incipient tyranny from boorish bigotry. I also saw a radicalism, and an anarchism, that made me uncomfortable, not only because it counseled an approach that would corrode many democratic norms and institutions, but because it didn't seem that government could provide solutions to the problems they were protesting.

In those respects, the movement reminded me of the protests against the World Trade Organization in Seattle in 1999, four years after I graduated from college. There, too, idealism had given way to fury, and specific policies were incinerated by rage against the machine. Radicalization swept up the young and well educated. Liberalism became anarchism, and the generic nature of the accusations tended to classify virtually anyone and anything remotely part of the "establishment"— whatever that even was. At the same time, I felt Antifa's blunderbuss approach undermined the prospect of identifying specific changes government actually could enact to address their complaints.

LIKE SO MANY, THOSE JOINING THE ANTIFA MOVEMENT WERE RE-
acting to Trumpism: it was a function of fear and frustration spinning
into fury. But they were stuck in a paradox that could become a quag-
mire. For every success against hatred, there was the risk of provoking
even greater outrages on the other side. Meanwhile, the slow breakthroughs that have always marked true progress against prejudice—the
resolve, organization, conscience, and institutional courage that, in the
end, halt demagogues—were diminishing.

In the contest between Kessler and Bellamy, the fight between
Spencer and Antifa, it seemed we might be tripping into something
resembling the "horseshoe theory." That idea, originated by the French
political theorist Jean-Pierre Faye, describing European politics, theo-
rized that the far left and far right are drawn to each other like the arms
of a horseshoe.[20] You can't simplistically apply this concept to American
politics and society. For one, in European politics, there are more parties and they are more internally homogeneous than in America, and
it's easier to observe similarities between radical socialist or communist
parties and nationalist or conservative authoritarian ones.

In our case, the theory seemed to echo how the extreme left and
extreme right were almost magnetically pulled closer to each other
than to the middle. There was insight to be gleaned through the theory. It wasn't that the far left and the far right were *similar*. It was
that the human beings within both movements were, in a time of
accelerating unreason, *drawn to each other*, and in that process, slip-
ping into a pattern of *mirroring each other's extreme actions*. The far
right made a move, and the far left reacted in kind. The far left made
another move, and the far right responded in kind. And both were
deeply cynical about government's ability to solve problems. It was an
explosive recipe.

IN APRIL, MEMBERS OF THE CHARLOTTESVILLE CHAPTER OF
Showing Up for Racial Justice (SURJ), a national organization that describes its goal as "undermining white support for white supremacy,"[21]
went from distributing flyers to physically targeting Kessler in public.

One night, Kessler went with friends to Miller's, a bar on the Downtown Mall, where they sat and had beers. A notice went up on SURJ's Facebook page, and soon, a couple dozen SURJ members surrounded Kessler. He sat smirking while they sang "Fuck white supremacy" to the tune of "Shoo Fly, Don't Bother Me" and chanted, "Nazis, go home!"

Sure enough, none other than the civil rights attorney Jeff Fogel, who had sued the city council for our rules prohibiting disorderly defamation, was soon arrested for assault after he allegedly bumped into Kessler in one of these confrontations. (Fogel was later acquitted of the charge.) A volatile scene then unfolded at the jail, with more SURJ members showing up to shout at the police for arresting Fogel.

Watching this on Facebook Live, I had a sick feeling. I was already disturbed by the phenomenon of "liberal intolerance," which had also been on display at many American universities. At many venues, speakers with controversial, usually conservative, views were being shouted down or outright barred. In a conversation about the violence at the bars on the Downtown Mall, Rabbi Gutherz asked me what I would think if the shoe were on the other foot—what if Jews were being harassed in public spaces by anti-Semites, as had happened in the lead-up to *Kristallnacht* (Night of Broken Glass) in Germany in 1938? It was not a hard thought experiment. For all the talk about fascism, it's also reminiscent of fascism to prevent someone you disagree with from speaking at all.

And then there was that feeling I just couldn't shake that this was the mayhem that the alt-right, like Heath Ledger's Batman, *wanted*. Before August 12, one Unite the Right organizer named C. J. Ross—a member of a militia organization called the Virginia Three Percenters—sent a Facebook message stating that the rally's purpose was "to crush and demoralize Antifa to the point where they don't return to the park." In a message to a "Mountaineers Against Antifa" Facebook group, Ross wrote, "I can assure you there will be beatings at the August event. . . . That day we finish them all off."[22]

Thus the stage was set for the alt-right to battle the far left in the streets of Charlottesville.

19

"DON'T TAKE THE BAIT"

| JUNE 2017 |

O N June 6, 2017, Judge Richard E. Moore of the Charlottesville Circuit Court issued a temporary injunction preventing
the city from moving or selling the Lee statue; meanwhile, the lawsuit by
the statue defenders proceeded on the merits. This became a perverse
situation, with passions on all sides riled up, yet everyone now stuck
in a state of suspended animation. There was no outlet for all those
emotions.

But my mind was only partly on the statue. The most press-
ing task at hand was to somehow figure out a way, as the part-time mayor
in a council-manager form of government, to deal with the upcoming
KKK rally. Exchanges between Antifa members and the alt-right were
intensifying, and I was deeply worried about the potential for violence
between the protesters and counterprotesters. I called City Manager
Maurice Jones and former mayor Alvin Edwards, who was now the pastor of Charlottesville's largest African American church, Mount Zion
First African Baptist. He was a local touchstone for leaders seeking

discreet, effective wisdom, and I thought he could help us come up with a strategy that emphasized public safety.

From Maurice Jones, I learned that the Charlottesville Police Department was actively working with the KKK to ensure that the rally would be peaceful, as required by constitutional case law. The KKK members had acceded to the department's suggestion to hold the rally near the Jackson statue instead of the Lee one, for ease of access. They were also going to keep the event brief, to an hour. They had agreed to go where they were directed to park and to speak.

Looking toward the next council meeting, where the statues would come up yet again, amid widespread unrest and anger about the KKK's imminent visit, I felt like I was swimming upstream against impossibly strong currents of politics and culture. I thought that perhaps people were looking for a voice to call us back to best civic practices, much as I'd managed the most disruptive voices during our recent council meetings. But I could just as easily second-guess that idea. What if the Constitution would be cold comfort? What if people wanted rage and defiance from me instead?

On the legal merits alone, I thought our strongest ground under the First Amendment would be to focus on preventing intimidation. The US Supreme Court, in *Virginia v. Black* (2003), had upheld Virginia's statute preventing cross-burning on private property, reasoning that the prevention of "intimidation" constituted a compelling government interest. No matter where you were on the ideological spectrum, you should be able to distinguish free speech from intimidation.

Right?

IN OUR NEXT COUNCIL MEETING, WHILE STAFF WORKED ON THE issue of exactly how to remove the Lee statue, I'd put another big item on the agenda: renaming both Lee and Jackson Parks. Again, chambers were crowded and restive. Again, I knew I'd have to use a strong hand to keep the meeting from getting out of control. I began by reading, very firmly, our rules preventing interruptions and giving the mayor the right to remove disorderly members of the public, and again, I introduced the police officers to the crowd.

Both a community survey and our Historic Resources Commission had preferred neutral names, like "Market Street Park" and "Library Park." But the day before the meeting, Councilor Kristin Szakos had suggested to me that we choose the seemingly bolder names of "Emancipation Park" and "Justice Park," respectively. Candidly, I was so frustrated by the turmoil around symbols that I just wanted to find a compromise that could get her and Bellamy on the same page with me and the others. Assuming that Szakos was on the same page as local justice advocates, I checked with Bellamy, who agreed. We went on to rename the parks with efficiency, even alacrity. (This would turn out to be a mistake, as the public would later revolt against all names related to the Civil War era or civil rights. A year later, we would yet again, embarrassingly, rename the parks, now to the more neutral-sounding "Market Street Park" and "Court Square Park.")

There were several far-right speakers at the June 2017 meeting. At least a couple dozen people from Showing Up for Racial Justice were in the audience, and they were doing their best to be disruptive and interrupt the speeches. The speakers plaintively complained about being harassed and shut down in public. When the SURJ members began hissing and singing and booing, I threatened to have them escorted out. After I called them to order, they refused to stop. With the step-by-step help of several officers, they were walked out of the meeting.

During this unpleasantness, I was forced to find a strange groove with the audience, where I basically entered a conversation with the whole crowd, securing their collective assent to the rules through head-nodding before proceeding. Granted, it again felt silly being forced to do this among a room full of adults. But it also felt more under control. When I allowed the conservatives to speak, people shouted back at me, "But he's a white supremacist!"—as if the *status* of someone being a white supremacist should prevent them from being able to speak. I responded by saying that this was freedom of speech, and we would just have to get through it. Of course, we were also now prohibited, thanks to Jeff Fogel and Joe Draego, from stopping defamatory attacks on groups that threatened disorder.

We voted 5–0 to rename Lee Park as Emancipation Park and Jackson Park as Justice Park. We ended up getting cheers and smiles. I felt spent.

But I also felt like we'd made some progress in the project of changing the narrative while providing at least a semblance of order against chaos.

We were careening toward the KKK event on July 8. I was not involved in our security plan, given my limited role in the council-manager form of government. Indeed, I didn't even know what the plan was; nor did I have the right to demand to know it. So I decided to do what I could within the gray area of mayoral authority and exhort everyone to keep our faith in the democratic process.

In the meeting, I tried to make the case for calm through a range of observations and arguments. I noted that Stephen Carter's 1998 book *Civility* had said the "general problem" of the day was that "everybody tries to find ways to put their own cherished positions beyond debate." I referred to Peggy Noonan's recent *Wall Street Journal* article, titled, "Rage Is All the Rage, and It's Dangerous," where she observed that "we look down on each other, fear each other, increasingly hate each other." She keenly observed that Trump's power lay in being able to trap us in increasing cycles of rage, whether for him or against him—but controlling us nonetheless.[1] I said those trends had come to Charlottesville in recent weeks and argued that the danger was that the alt-right, like some sort of body-snatcher, could take us over and turn us into our opposite.

Our democratic system had been set up for us to be able to debate, I explained. To deliberate. To push, to argue, and, ultimately, to make a decision. And then to act. The surge in intimidation was particularly pernicious because it changed the rules. Now, it wasn't persuasion, or facts, or debate, or even a vote, that won the day—but power and force. In this new world, we were deeming the victor based not on who wins under the rules, but on who bloodies their opponent the most. Ironically, it is our very rules for competition that make us great.

The reason Trump always seemed to pick fights, I asserted—the reason he did so many things that seemed irrational—was not only that he preferred conflict, but that he wanted conflict that got in his opponents' heads. We could not let rage take over. When we let someone get in our heads that way, when we start playing by their rules, when we take their bait, then we are letting them tell our story. I said our story in Charlottesville had too much promise for that to happen.

I concluded by trying to remind everyone to have sympathy with each other. As human beings, we all had dignity and all deserved the protection of the law. It was that very law that allowed us to defeat those who would prey on us; it was those rules that maintained our freedom and our dignity. That was the faith of the democratic project itself. Our constitutional principles make us stronger together than apart.

I closed by promising the crowd that we could, and would, confront and defeat these dark forces, and that we would do so on our own terms.

There was no applause. Just silence. It felt somber, serious, and dark. And it was about to get darker.

AT THE NEXT CITY COUNCIL MEETING, ON JUNE 19, KESSLER WAS back, burrowed into a row with a malicious smile playing across his face. He then rose and strode up to the podium. He was wearing a black hoodie. He made most of his angry address staring directly at Bellamy, but he also took a shot at me, saying it was "really rich when Mike Signer, professional victim, comes up here and talks about Trump being to blame for the lack of civility," when I was not speaking up against Bellamy's tweets. He then turned back to me: "Mike Signer is an embarrassment to this city. He thinks he's some kind of James Madison. He's not. I've already outshined you. You will never be half the warrior for our civil liberties that Richard Spencer is."

When his three minutes were up, I cut him off and said, "You're done." He shot back, "I'm not done. I'll be back on August 12." That was the date he'd requested in the permit application for the Unite the Right rally.

A young African American man later came up to the mic. He stated that the KKK was a terrorist group and said, "To tolerate it is allowing racism by proxy. Revoke this permit. Resist this siege of terrorism that is coming into our town, trickle by trickle by trickle until it pours, until it bleeds. . . . Are you gonna wait for another Portland?" Looking at me, he said, mockingly, "It's your choice, sir—Mr. Resistance. How are these group attacks on our city not the equivalent of yelling fire in a crowded theater?"

A young woman then came up on behalf of SURJ. She cited the Portland mayor's recent (failed) attempt to ask the city council there to take back a permit. She cited a provision in Charlottesville's event ordinance that allowed for cancelation for public safety. "Charlottesville claims to be a Capital of Resistance, but acquiescing to white suprem-acists seems pretty far from resistance to me," she said. "By giving the KKK this permit, the city has legitimized their white supremacist views." Criticizing the "ghost town approach," she criticized the "knowledge they will occupy this space and will do so with the city's blessing."

Another woman stood and called out the "extremely unconsciona-ble actions of the white members of this City Council." Looking at me as "the one who declared the city the Capital of the Resistance," she said, "But your actions speak louder than your words. . . . By allowing them to come, you are telling us with your actions that you do not care about the black community in Charlottesville, that you do not care about the Muslim people in Charlottesville. . . . They are not here for free speech. They want to cause havoc."

A red-haired woman in a denim jacket rose next and said, "The City of Charlottesville is planning to protect the KKK. . . . You can go on and on about their right to speak, but . . . [y]ou approved a permit." She demanded that we "rescind the permit" and asked everyone in support to stand. A majority of the room stood up.

I was sweating in my jacket. The air in the chambers felt at once hot and thin, as if the oxygen was being consumed by the brushfire of the First Amendment.

KESSLER HAD BEEN POSTING ALERTS ABOUT HIS ALLIANCE WITH the Proud Boys, a white nationalist group with a bizarre ritual of beating each other up after reciting breakfast cereal names. According to Kessler, they were planning to come to Charlottesville. On the dais at the same meeting, Kathy Galvin grilled City Manager Maurice Jones on whether the group could be prevented from coming to the city on the grounds that they were a gang. Jones said there wasn't enough evidence that they were coming to Charlottesville planning to do violence, conclud-ing, "I'm not sure how we can deny them the opportunity to come."

Our city attorney, Craig Brown, then said, "I don't think you can start rounding up people because of what they might do." I explained that the legal standard to stop free-speech activity under the First Amendment was an "incitement to an imminent unlawful act"—requiring specific evidence of a planned violation of the law. Governments weren't allowed to stop events from happening because of a fear about what they *might* cause. That's how the courts had balanced the First Amendment with our interest in the avoidance of violence.

I also knew, as a general matter, that elected officials were not supposed to be involved in the permitting decision in Charlottesville. In the council-manager form of government, permitting decisions were made by our administrative staff. To have politicians involved in this function when they weren't ordinarily involved would increase the likelihood of a court finding that our decision was not content-neutral—that it stemmed from the objectionable nature of the content.

During this time, I often had the feeling of being an unwilling actor in a jailhouse theater, being forced to read from a script lest I be whipped by my captor. This was the legacy of *Terminiello*—and it was also the bind handed down to cities like Charlottesville by the case of *National Socialist Party of America v. Village of Skokie*.

IN 1977, SKOKIE, ILLINOIS—A CITY OF ABOUT SEVENTY THOUSAND people—had an ordinance requiring anyone requesting a permit to use a park for a rally to post a bond of $350,000. The leader of the Nazi Party of America, Frank Collin, announced plans to protest the bond requirement by holding a march on Skokie's sidewalks. Over forty thousand of Skokie's residents were Jewish. Collin said his march would include thirty to fifty demonstrators marching in single file in front of Skokie Village Hall, wearing Nazi garb and armbands with swastikas on them.

The elected officials of Skokie decided to take legal action to stop the parade by filing for a preliminary injunction in circuit court. One resident testified that twelve thousand to fifteen thousand protesters were expected, along with physical clashes between protesters and counterprotesters. During the hearing, the mayor also testified that he expected violence.

The lower court responded by enjoining the Nazis from marching, walking, parading, or otherwise displaying the swastika on or off their person. The Nazi Party, aided by the American Civil Liberties Union (ACLU), sued the city on free speech grounds, launching a complicated legal journey that involved a trip to the Illinois Appellate Court, the Illinois Supreme Court, and the US Supreme Court, and then another tour back through the Appellate Court before the Illinois Supreme Court issued a sweeping ruling on free-speech grounds. It would establish profound precedents for how governments like Charlottesville would need to handle—and support—free speech, including hate speech.

The village of Skokie argued that the "fighting words" doctrine should apply in allowing them to prevent the Nazis from marching while wearing swastikas. (In the "fighting words" case, *Cohen v. the United States*, from 1971, a man wearing a "Fuck the Draft" jacket in a courthouse was arrested under a "fighting words" doctrine, and the Court went on to reject his arrest, ruling that free speech could only be curtailed for "those personally abusive epithets which, when addressed to the ordinary citizen, are, as a matter of common knowledge, inherently likely to provoke violent reaction.") The village's argument was that the Nazi symbol, on the village streets, before Holocaust survivors, would be just such a "fighting word." At the case's end, the Illinois Supreme Court and then the US Supreme Court rejected that argument, ruling instead in favor of the doctrine of First Amendment absolutism.[2]

The Illinois Supreme Court's opinion contained the decision's famous reasoning about the First Amendment. The Court cited the Supreme Court's ruling in *Cohen* that "it is often true that one man's vulgarity is another's lyric. Indeed, we think it is largely because governmental officials cannot make principled distinctions in this area that the Constitution leaves matters of taste and style so largely to the individual." The justices ruled that the swastika, "as offensive to the principles of a free nation as the memories it recalls may be, is symbolic political speech intended to convey to the public the beliefs of those who display it." They circumscribed the experiences of the public upon seeing the march: "We do not doubt that the sight of this symbol is abhorrent to the Jewish citizens of Skokie, and that the survivors of the

Nazi persecutions, tormented by their recollections, may have strong feelings regarding its display. Yet it is entirely clear that this factor does not justify enjoining defendants' speech."[3]

The Court then looped back to *Terminiello v. Chicago*: "Starting with *Terminiello* . . . it has become patent that a hostile audience is not a basis for restraining otherwise legal First Amendment activity." The rule was instead whether "actual behavior," not just the anticipation of violence, would be "sufficient to sustain a conviction under a statute."[4] The true chilling effect in terms of free speech could be found in that anticipation. To allow anticipated behavior to stop an event with Nazis and swastikas would equate to the prior restraint of speech and the governmental suppression of offensive ideas.

The ACLU's website today crows about the decision, praising its own "controversial stand for free speech." The ACLU admits that the "notoriety of the case caused some ACLU members to resign, but to many others the case has come to represent the ACLU's unwavering commitment to principle." The site explains that many of the laws the ACLU cited to defend the group's right to free speech and assembly in *National Socialist Party of America v. Village of Skokie* were the same laws it had invoked during the civil rights era, "when Southern cities tried to shut down civil rights marches with similar claims about the violence and disruption the protests would cause."[5]

There were just too many ironies to count. But as the Charlottesville mayor, I knew irony would be no help at all. I had studied this history in law school and to pass the Virginia Bar. To become a city councilor, I had sworn to uphold the Constitution, and the Supreme Court had clearly stated what the law was.

Those were the facts—and my duties—as I saw them. But it still felt awfully lonely up there.

THE LAW WAS CRYSTAL CLEAR. ABSENT ANY EVIDENCE OF A "CREDible threat"—the constitutional term for a planned act of imminent, specific violence, or an incitement to one—not only could the city not stop the KKK from coming, but it had a duty to facilitate the speech so that it could be safely expressed.

To make matters even more complicated, from online chatter and the fervent speeches in our chambers, it was clear that hundreds or even thousands of counterprotesters were planning to come to "defend C'ville," and that we could face violent conflicts with Antifa activists similar to the ones that had already occurred in Berkeley and Portland, melees we'd all watched with chagrin.

I worked with other leaders to devise a strategy to try and avert the clashes. I sat down separately with City Manager Maurice Jones, Police Chief Al Thomas, UVA President Terry Sullivan, and the Clergy Collective, a multi-faith organization that the former mayor and pastor Alvin Edwards had cofounded. They all agreed that this ragtag group traveling from North Carolina clearly wanted specific things from our famous little city: provocation, publicity, confrontation. So why give them everything they wanted, while also creating a potentially unsafe situation?

The alternative coalesced into a slogan: "Don't Take the Bait." I reached out to a coalition of community partners—a brewery, an art park, a philanthropist, the Human Rights Commission, the Jefferson School African American Heritage Center, the University of Virginia, and the Clergy Collective—to create a new ad hoc organization called "Unity Cville" that would offer the community a slate of alternative events focused on social justice, community, and systemic racism. It would provide an alternative to the KKK show. The hope was that the KKK would just fizzle, outshined by the community itself while we preempted the kind of violence that had broken out in Portland and Berkeley.

They all agreed to support this effort. I conveyed their support to the city manager and police chief and the other councilors. Everyone was on board.

On the day of the announcement, I walked over to City Space, a city-owned meeting space, where the four other councilors, along with City Manager Jones, Chief Thomas, and the other community leaders who had joined our fresh new group were all gathered to make a series of speeches endorsing "Unity Day." Jones and Thomas led off, all the councilors followed suit, and then the other leaders. Reports of the event were carried in all our media.

I had taken extra care to talk with Bellamy beforehand, as he was the only African American city councilor, had already experienced threats, and was close to some of the members of the community who might want confrontation. He told me he wasn't even planning on going to the event, but that he supported the "Don't Take the Bait" idea.

We continued to press this line in the days ahead. The *Daily Progress* published an article where I called the KKK a "ridiculous sideshow" and said, "This rump, out-of-state arm of a totally discredited organization will succeed in their aim of division and publicity only if folks take their putrid bait." Bellamy told the paper it was "absolutely imperative that we don't stoop to the levels of hate groups like the KKK." He continued, "I also know they want us to fall for their trick of getting angry, acting with pure emotion and getting locked up while they stand to the side and watch us while saying they're having a 'peaceful protest.'"[6]

His support of the "Don't Take the Bait" message was particularly important. It seemed to signal that unity, which so often seemed elusive, might in this case be within our reach.

I BOARDED A PLANE TO ATTEND THE UNITED STATES CONFER-ence of Mayors annual meeting in Miami on June 22. One warm after-noon, at a lavish party featuring seafood buffets and high-end cocktails, I saw New Orleans mayor Mitch Landrieu, dressed perfectly in short-sleeved white linen. I asked him about his May 19 statues speech and said it had created a pickle in Charlottesville, particularly because our state law offered litigious opponents a ready means to stall any quick resolution to the problem. I told him about the recommendation from the majority-minority Blue Ribbon Commission that the statue stay within the city.

"I never meant it to be a national thing!" he protested about his speech. I nodded my head, a little amused, as his powerful and magnif-icently detailed speech could not have been intended for anything but a national audience.

Bill Clinton had given the lunch address as the mayors, broken into small groups at circular tables, munched on a plated meal. During his remarks, he mentioned Landrieu's work on the statues in New Orleans and condemned the evil legacy of slavery. But he didn't say anything one way or the other about what should be done with those statues in New Orleans specifically—or Confederate statues around the country generally. Afterward, I made my way through the long line. I introduced myself and talked with Clinton for three or four minutes, telling him about our experience and dilemmas in Charlottesville, especially the current quandary after the Blue Ribbon Commission's recommendations, the council's vote, the lawsuit, and the injunction.

He listened carefully and then told me he thought the "*process*" would be the key. He described how when Northern Ireland and the British came to a peace agreement, the process had been central. I thought about that one word, "process," throughout the next day. In our case, there had been clear shortcomings in the last stages of the Blue Ribbon Commission's process for making a decision on the statues, as well as in the two agonizing meetings of the council around Fenwick's abstention. And then the court system had stopped the city from taking any action at all. So the public was both torn and stymied. All the while, by virtue of the fires that had been stoked and the fact that nothing had happened, the opposing forces were only primed for confrontation even more. In other words, virtually nothing about the process was leaving us in a better place than before. I wondered if the same fate would befall our "Don't Take the Bait" strategy.

I was right to worry.

The next morning, I had breakfast with two other mayors, Andy Berke of Chattanooga, Tennessee, and Pete Buttigieg of South Bend, Indiana—both friendly, can-do fellows. I'd met Berke when we were both on a panel about innovation in cities at Charlottesville's Tom-Tom Festival. I'd known Buttigieg for a decade through the Truman National Security Project, which we'd helped found as young DC-area professionals back in 2005, hoping to bring progressives back to the center on national security issues.

They were both "strong mayors"—the chief executives of their respective cities, rather than a city manager. They had both seen the national press coverage of the torch parade. Over eggs and coffee, they listened empathetically as I described the unusual path that had brought such a friendly, progressive city to the brink of seeming disaster. I described the brushfires that were consuming every meeting I had to run, and the way in which, at every turn, I had to improvise my authority through the council-manager system.

Berke suggested I read *A Prayer for the City* by the journalist Buzz Bissinger, about Ed Rendell's reign as mayor in Philadelphia, which I did soon after.[7] The riveting volume showed how common dilemmas are in the governance of complicated, fractious city politics, especially on issues like race and rights. It gave me some solace. There is fellowship, after all, in misery.

MEANWHILE, THE POLICE WERE ENGAGED IN A STRATEGY OF outreach to the counterprotesters. Unfortunately, in the supercharged environment on the left (which I had already concluded could be self-destructive), the approach would backfire. In the weeks before the KKK event, Charlottesville police officers began visiting the homes of activists with the stated goal of creating a bridge for communication and attempting to understand their goals for the counterprotest.

But these attempts were swiftly condemned by Antifa activists and the Rutherford Institute. The Rutherford Institute, based in Charlottesville, was a tiny legal outfit that became famous for supporting Paula Jones in her lawsuit against Bill Clinton, and it had become well known for its quirky and aggressive stances on arcane First Amendment issues. The institute's president, John Whitehead, had published a long, detailed complaint against the city's "defamatory attacks" policy in March 2016, just days after they were put in place, arguing that the rules "violate[d] the letter and spirit of these constitutional rights by imposing obstacles to transparency and citizen engagement."[8]

In a June 27, 2017, letter, he said the practice of home visits "smack[ed] of intimidation" and "serve[d] as a potent example of the kinds of totalitarian tactics that this nation, its founders and all those who truly value a robust First Amendment have historically opposed."[9] Speaking with a journalist, he also called the visits "overkill," likening them to the tactics of Nazi Germany and the KGB. "The police's job is to show up at the protest and keep the people safe," he said. "They should back off." A local attorney named Pam Starsia, who with her husband Joe—a lacrosse coach at UVA—helped lead the SURJ chapter, had held a press conference in front of police headquarters on June 23. In her remarks, she charged that the home visits were intimidating and chilling of the counterprotesters' First Amendment rights.[10]

Any prospect of productive communication between the police and Antifa activists effectively died.

20

"SAILING INTO THE WINDSTORM"

| JULY 2017 |

TWO DAYS BEFORE THE KKK CAME, A *WASHINGTON POST* RE-
porter called me to tell me something he'd heard from one of the
Klan members: that they would be heavily armed. He had gone so far
as to say it could be "like Greensboro"—the infamous 1979 massacre
where the Communist Workers Party had demonstrated in a "Death to
the Klan" march that led to a shootout. Four Communists and one other
individual were killed, and eleven other demonstrators and a Klan member were injured.

I had been operating in the same *sabra* mindset that had gotten me
through the trolling. But this news alarmed me. And, not for the first
time, or for the last, I grappled with the almost unbelievable reality that
Virginia law did not allow the city to stop people from bringing firearms
to the rally. I feared that it was a powder keg.

IT COMES AS A SHOCK TO VISITORS FROM STATES WITH MORE REG-
ulation of firearms that Virginia has an "open-carry" law. Unless someone

is already barred from owning firearms under state law (for instance, for being a felon), he or she is allowed to carry virtually any firearm in public, as long as it is openly displayed.[1]

The Virginia General Assembly had also passed, in 1987, the Code of Virginia's section 15.2-915, which stated, "No locality shall adopt or enforce any ordinance, resolution or motion . . . governing the purchase, possession, transfer, ownership, carrying, storage or transporting of firearms, ammunition, or components or combination thereof." Such a state law was possible because Virginia is an anti-home-rule Dillon's Rule state. As a progressive city, we knew that we would instantly be sued if we tried to prohibit firearms at the KKK event—and that we would lose in court, where any Virginia judge would rigorously enforce the state law.

Some creative legal scholars contended that, by virtue of permitting an event, a city could claim the authority to regulate firearms within the permitted area. But the statute had been written in a particularly airtight fashion, and our counsel said he thought it would certainly prevent us from prohibiting weapons. Any contrary action would likely give rise to immediate injunctions and a summary judgment against the city—giving another victory to white nationalists.

In these incendiary times, Dillon's Rule also perversely prevented the city council from prohibiting firearms in council meetings themselves. It was the reason we'd had to sit through so many "flaggers" openly carrying firearms in our charged, hostile, and overheated meetings on the statues—even though Charlottesville *courts* legally prohibited guns. How could that be? Because, in Virginia, courts are a separate branch of government from the legislature, administered and overseen by the Virginia Supreme Court. And the Virginia Supreme Court, free from oversight by the legislature, had allowed courts to prohibit guns from courtrooms. A city, however, under the thumb of the General Assembly and its 1987 law, could not prohibit them.

So despite the chilling call from the *Washington Post* reporter, I knew we'd be forced to watch the KKK come to town, hands tied. The call had worried me, so I dutifully called both the police chief, Al Thomas, and the city manager, Maurice Jones. Thomas was somewhat reassuring. He told me they had heard this sort of rhetoric for months, and they had a plan in place that would keep the two groups separated. It sounded new, however, to Jones, who told me that the assumption all the way through had been that the Klan, on the condition of the police basically escorting them to this event and facilitating their safety, was going to be in and out. He said he would talk with the police to see if they'd heard any information that would rise to the level of a "credible threat"—a promise of active violence—that could stop the rally. Conversely, however, as long as the Klan framed any potential violence as defensive, they were, as far as the Constitution goes, in the clear.

And that evidence never came.

THE MORNING THE KKK CAME TO CHARLOTTESVILLE, JULY 8, Emily and I woke up early with the boys. We had coffee, they had Cheerios, chattering and babbling, and we played for a while and read books. When our friend Trish came over to stay with them for the day, we went to the launch of the Unity Cville program at the Jefferson School African American Heritage Center. There were many African American leaders there, and the local chapter of the NAACP was supporting the "Don't Take the Bait" strategy. It had organized events all day at Jack Jouett Middle School in Albemarle County, far away from downtown Charlottesville.

The NAACP rally highlighted the theme "steadfast and immovable." Janet Boyd Martin, the chapter president, told a local TV station, "It seems that the country nowadays is just everybody protesting about one thing or another and it's in such a state of unrest, . . . and it hasn't always been like that, we just want people to realize that the NAACP, 108 years we're still here, and we will be about our business of our mission."[2]

At the Jefferson School, the energy was at once nervous and upbeat—caffeinated defiance. We chatted with a few folks and then headed to a security briefing that Chief Thomas was conducting. Both the Charlottesville police and visiting officers from around the state who had come to help were there. Hundreds of officers were milling around the Albemarle County auditorium. They sat down when Thomas came to the front of the room. He started his remarks by saying they would need courage that day. Although they might be in physical danger, he asked them to treat everyone they encountered with respect.

We then headed back to the morning session at the Jefferson School. It was spectacular—diverse and heartening and wide-ranging, with several hundred folks in attendance. I spoke briefly. I said that over a year ago we'd begun a journey to finally tell the truth about race in our city, and that this had made us a target for organizations opposing that very mission, but we wouldn't be intimidated away from the work. This was a message I felt could unify both those who wanted the statues gone and those who supported the transform-in-place message. After a sustained burst of warm applause, that seemed, at least for the moment, right.

Then we went over to the "People's Picnic" at the IX Art Park—a large asphalt area decorated with cheerful, somewhat haphazard folk art and surrounded by painted trees. This event was markedly less well attended—a couple hundred people—and markedly more white. People were starting to peel off to go to the protests to come. We were there for half an hour or so—I made the same speech—before heading off to the First United Methodist Church to attend an interfaith meeting convened by the Clergy Collective. To get there, we walked through Justice Park (the new name for Jackson Park, with the Stonewall Jackson statue, where the KKK had been relocated) and saw various pieces of the protest to come assembling—liberal clergy members and their congregants wearing clothing decorated with rainbows, Black Lives Matter members with black T-shirts, SURJ members prepared for direct action, some Antifa members wearing bandannas and armbands who clearly were not from Charlottesville.

At First United Methodist, the mood was markedly more volatile and conflicted. It turned out that the message that Jones and I had delivered to the Collective, asking them to help not take the bait, had been controversial. The interfaith group at the church had already split into three separate groups. Some of them favored the "Don't Take the Bait" strategy and wanted to go to the planned Unity Day Concert and sing and pray together. Others wanted to bear witness to evil and confront it, believing that this was a moral duty that flowed from their faith. A third group wanted to stay behind at the church and pray for everyone else. There were a couple hundred people there along with the clergy who belonged to the Collective. After sermons and prayers, the organizers gave people two options. The first was to go to the concert; the second was to go to Justice Park.

We headed to the concert. There were probably about four hundred people there. Clearly, many more were going to Justice Park. We were at the concert for most of the next three hours. It was a wonderful event, with the musicians expressing belief in the power of love, and a nice range of faith singers. Chamomile and Whiskey sang inspirational bluegrass, and a gospel choir of African American women belted out songs. Emily and a friend went over to the KKK rally, and Emily sent me back texts and some video, telling me how it all just made her sick to her stomach, both the presence of the Klansmen and the spectacle of the entire affair. As we headed toward the end of the afternoon, Jones sent several email updates to council members that made it seem like things were wrapping up fairly peacefully.

I put up a tweet about how it seemed that the day, all in all, had gone well. But then, just as the concert was wrapping up, just as it seemed that the KKK had come and gone without incident, Maurice Jones sent an update saying there had been some trouble with counterprotesters.

CONCERNED, I HEADED BACK WITH EMILY TO THE SITE OF THE rally. We walked by a row of police officers holding tear-gas guns in Justice Park. They were in full riot gear. A few ragtag protesters roamed around nearby, and they looked traumatized. A clump of people also stood farther away. It looked like a conflict zone after urban warfare, like a scene on a tattered film reel. As we walked toward the command center, I noticed an acrid scent in the air. It was tear gas, an odor I was fortunately not familiar with. Emily started complaining about her eyes and nose hurting.

I called the city manager on my cellphone and asked if I could come into the command center. I was admitted into a large conference room with long windows overlooking dozens of counterprotesters, who were raggedly milling around (Emily stayed outside). There were four live video feeds from cameras on TV screens at the end of the table.

There was a lot of agitation in the room about the tear gas being released, and a corresponding pressure to figure out what to say—and do—about it. The story going around the table was that a bloc of protesters had physically pursued and pressed into the police after the Klan had left. One person at the table, then another, reported that an officer on the ground had seen a counterprotester release "pepper gel." It was only in response to this, I was told, that the officers had let off three tear gas canisters.

I took all this in for a while and watched the surveillance videos playing on the screens on the wall. I listened to a description of how the counterprotesters had locked arms to prevent the police from going back up the street. I heard they had been chanting "Cops and the Klan go hand in hand." I learned that twenty-three people had been arrested, and three people had been taken to a hospital—albeit two for issues related to the heat, the other related to alcohol. I decided I would issue a statement supporting the police.

In retrospect, this was a mistake. I should have let the professional staff that had actually been in charge provide any responses from the city. The most fundamental problem was that I didn't know what had actually happened. There had been hundreds of local officers from the Charlottesville Police Department (CPD) there, and hundreds of Virginia State Police (VSP) officers, who were under an entirely different command structure, and I had no role in the command structure for either. Our chief of police wasn't there during these discussions, and I hadn't spoken with him. I hadn't been onsite to see what had actually happened. I hadn't been able to speak with the counterprotesters, either, to get their view. And in our council-manager government, I had no official role whatsoever in communicating about police decisions.

But I was still the city's mayor. Sitting there at the time, I felt intensely frustrated by the self-destructive approach of some of the counterprotesters. I felt their behavior bordered on anarchism. The KKK had been on their way out of the city after an hour, with minimal disturbance. Three years earlier, I had attended the Citizen Police Academy as a neighborhood association president and had relationships with many of the local officers. Embattled as they were in this time of increasingly hostile language, I felt they were, in general, caring and dedicated servants, in a low-paid profession, and they generally managed that balance admirably. I wanted to have their back.

I drafted a Facebook statement making the points I was hearing around the conference table. Overall, the day had been a victory. What could have been a day of rage and indiscriminate and violent confrontation had instead been a day of prayer, education, testimony, and protest. I then sympathized with and celebrated the police.[3] Thousands of people had followed the advice not to take the bait, to deny the KKK members the confrontation and celebrity they desired. But at the end of the day, our police had succeeded in executing their strategy of protecting both the First Amendment and public safety.

And then I supported the Charlottesville Police Department's assertion of an inciting act. I wrote that after the rally concluded, there had been a disturbance, during which counterprotesters apparently released pepper spray and officers released three canisters of tear gas.

Having written this statement on my own, I carried my laptop over to Al Thomas, then to Maurice Jones, and to our communications director, Miriam Dickler, who all okayed the statement. I then put it up and put it out of my mind.

That, it turns out, would be impossible.

I HEADED OUT TO FIND EMILY, WHO WAS AT A PIZZA PLACE WITH our boys. They were happily at Christian's eating cheese pizza cut into little squares. We were just a couple of blocks from the site of the mayhem. She looked over the statement, her big eyes widening with concern. She shook her head. She wasn't happy. She thought it was a mistake to get involved with the tear gas issue.

She was right.

We were exhausted. We gave the boys a bath, read a story, and went to bed. The next morning was Sunday, July 9, and we tried to sleep late, but that only goes so far with two-year-olds. It was already hot outside by 10:00 a.m. I inflated our wading pool, put it on our small gray porch, and filled it up. The boys splashed happily as Emily and I talked over the prior day. She framed the events from the counterprotesters' perspective; I countered with what it must have been like from the point of view of the police. I watched a video online that showed the counterprotesters pushing like a wall into the police. Their chant, "Cops and the Klan go hand in hand," shouted over and over again, had mesmerizing intensity. Then a new chant: "Whose streets? Our streets!"

I could see how the police had felt under threat.

On Facebook, I saw dozens of angry attacks on me from groups such as Black Lives Matter for siding with the police. The nastiness, cynicism, and anarchism of the attacks on the police were in direct parallel to what I had seen in council chambers so many times, where the idea of order had become somehow suspect and oppressive. I was literally being described as a fascist, and I found the vitriol dispiriting and infuriating.

For a few moments, the thought of resigning in protest floated into my head, as a sort of dark, seductive escape route. But it was followed just as quickly by a series of more sober counterarguments. If not me, who? If I gave up in the face of cynicism and anarchism, wouldn't I be giving up on the kind of leadership I'd been trying to teach about? Even if it was a no-win situation, wasn't that precisely when leaders were needed the most?

I was left torn and in the middle. Emily and I went back and forth all Sunday afternoon on a new Facebook statement. With the police narrative in mind, I'd initially believed the tear gas was probably necessary to maintain order. But in conversations with residents and reviews of social media posts online, I also saw how traumatizing it had been for people—particularly those fearful of the police to begin with—to experience a painful and frightening chemical used against them. At the very least, I concluded, the public needed a swift, transparent explanation of exactly why the tear gas had been used. I ended up putting up a new post that day, July 9, stating that the use of tear gas was "unsettling" to many, and asserting that the police "owed an explanation" to the people of Charlottesville about what had happened.

Maurice Jones let me know that night that Chief Thomas was very upset with the tone of the Facebook statement. He sent me the following text:

> Mr. Mayor, the statement you posted is causing significant heartburn in law enforcement circles. It appears to be casting doubt on their efforts to keep everyone safe on Saturday.

I responded:

Thanks for letting me know. There's a lot of heartburn all around. Our system is set up so they work for you, not for me. I'm the political barometer and most directly accountable to the people. People are very upset by what they saw. There was a clear understanding going into this that there would not be a riot presentation. Yet that's what happened. The pepper spray assertion is another matter. The state police may have been the problem. But as much as I want to defend the police at first blush, I think the public does not need a defensive response from all of government. Al and you have your jobs and I have mine. Together we will get through this.

He responded:

Yeah but if we lose the morale of the police department when they did nothing wrong then we all have a problem. Ours was not a defensive response, it was the truth.

I responded:

The problem is, I'm not sure they did nothing wrong. It is most likely a mixed story. A great victory during the day. But the second chapter after the rally—while it didn't result in any serious injuries—probably could use improvements. I am hearing this from extremely reasonable people who were just watching. I would like to know more about the VSP role and decisions. I am going to be walking this line myself in the coming days—supportive yet for improving. I would very much encourage Al to do the same.

He responded:

We are all about continuous improvement and said as much in Al's statement. Check out what happened in Berkeley and Portland to see what could have gone wrong here without careful planning and execution. The tone of your statement implies that one, we wouldn't have told the truth about what we found in the aftermath and two, that the pepper spray story is in doubt, which from our end it is not. There is video evidence of

> people reacting to the spray before the tear gas was released and an empty canister was found by the police. All we asked for was 24 hours to gather more information and to give the Chief some time to digest what he learned in the debrief.

I responded:

> I'd like to fix this if we can. I think I can amend the statement without too much harm. Please call if you can.

I put up a revised version of the statement on Facebook on July 10 that softened the tone considerably. The changes made clear that the first statement from July 8, referencing the counterprotesters' alleged use of pepper gel, had been written in consultation with the chief of police and the city manager, and it was based on information they had at the time. I added that Chief Thomas had said he would thoroughly review the whole event, not only to understand what went right, but also to determine where we could improve. I promised that he would present a report to the city council in the near future, where he would also answer our questions.[4]

(But I was wrong about that. The report never came, as discussed below.) Another brushfire, about accountability in a time of crisis, had just been lit. It felt horrible. The counterprotesters were already angry, and now the police force felt I had thrown the department under the bus. I didn't know how I could have struck a better balance, other than just being silent—which is what I should have done.

Underneath, the issue was worse than I suspected at the time. Six months later, the independent investigation we commissioned would show a high level of disarray. There was no evidence that the counterprotesters had released pepper gel; therefore, there was no evidence of the initial rationale that had been provided for the police decision to turn to the use of tear gas. The report would find that, after the declaration of an unlawful assembly, a Virginia State Police first sergeant had asked Chief Thomas for permission to use tear gas, which Thomas denied. The denial, however, was not communicated to either state or local supervisors at the scene. A VSP field sergeant then approached Major Gary Pleasants of the Charlottesville Police Department and asked for consent to deploy tear gas. Pleasants said, "Absolutely." Pleasants mistakenly believed the VSP sergeant was acting on the authority of a VSP supervisor. Through a bullhorn, Pleasants issued a dispersal order to the crowd and announced three times that chemical agents would be used. However, the report found that no warning went out over the radio to either VSP or CPD officers on the ground. Multiple counterprotesters reported receiving no warning about the tear gas.

In the aftermath, Chief Thomas, who never wanted tear gas used, confronted Major Pleasants, who responded, "You are damn right I gassed them, it needed to be done." Pleasants explained that the Charlottesville police had been "under attack." The VSP major in command told the investigators that only a VSP senior official was supposed to have been able to deploy tear gas—not a field sergeant. Thomas also told the investigators that he'd seen no evidence that pepper gel had been used to attack the police.[5]

There was no question that the counterprotesters had been extremely confrontational with the police. I had seen video of them shouting, "Cops and the Klan go hand in hand." They had pushed into a line of cops wearing riot gear and bearing shields, and had linked arms across the street the police were trying to open. But the police had also played a role. On top of the disorganization, on top of the crossed lines of authority, and on top of the apparently baseless assertion about the pepper gel, there was the question of whether both the VSP and the CPD could have just waited out the counterprotesters. No matter how aggressive the counterprotesters were, could the police have disengaged from conflict and engaged instead in de-escalation? We can't know the answer, because no sustained de-escalation ever happened. The escalation instead happened, tear gas was used, and the stage was set for a cycle of deeper mistrust between the police and counterprotesters.

It would take six months for the real story to come out. In the meantime, I needed to keep going, because the First Amendment brushfire was raging anew.

I received an email from Claire Guthrie Gastañaga, the ACLU's executive director in Virginia and an old friend of mine from

Virginia Democratic politics: "Heads up. We're solidly with John on this." "John" was John Whitehead, the president of the Rutherford Institute, and "this" was the institute's position on what had happened at the KKK event.

The Rutherford Institute, the ACLU, the Charlottesville Legal Aid Justice Center, and the left-leaning National Lawyers Guild all sent a letter to the city council on July 17 (and a similar letter to Governor McAuliffe on the same day). The first sentence set the tone: "We write to express concerns over the outsized and militaristic governmental response to those who chose to peacefully exercise their First Amendment rights to assemble in public and engage in peaceful, nonviolent protests."

The letter went on to complain that the police, "prior to any clear and present danger of violence, descended on the scene dressed in riot gear, driving armored vehicles, and carrying weapons typically used only in war zones." Instead of controlling the KKK, "law enforcement may have played a role in provoking the unrest that ensued, and certainly made those demonstrating against the Klan feel like enemies of the state." The letter said that the Constitution "obliges law enforcement to refrain from tactics that intimidate and chill non-violent counter-protest, even when the target of protest is law enforcement itself."

The group's first demand would knock the city on its heels in the critical weeks to follow: to "acknowledge that the deliberate choice to use warzone tactics on July 8th—instead of planning for de-escalation—is inconsistent with Charlottesville's values and good policing." The letter went on to cite the benefits of de-escalation training and passive policing, arguing that the "show of force" by the police "appeared to be premised on intimidation, rather than de-escalation." It requested an independent investigation into law enforcement's actions to determine whether any of them were unlawful, and asked for measures to "ensure accountability for any unlawful tactics used."

Crucially, it demanded that the independent investigation not be conducted by the local or state agencies participating in the law enforcement response on that day. In other words, the groups behind the letter were requesting a federal investigation of the Charlottesville Police Department.[6]

SOON AFTER THE KKK EVENT, I CONVENED A BRAINSTORMING session of democracy-related organizations in the Charlottesville area to discuss the creation of a "Civility Alliance." In attendance were leaders from Monticello, Montpelier, Morven, the Sorensen Institute for Political Leadership, the Institute of Politics at UVA, the UVA School of Law, and the Presidential Precinct, an organization that educated foreign students in the history and institutions of American democracy. David Toscano (a former Charlottesville mayor), the minority leader of the Democrats in Virginia's House of Delegates, was also there.

It was a rich discussion that touched on rules of competition, making friends with people who disagree with you, and learning to listen. Along the way, we discussed specific action ideas, such as bringing in a consultant to manage a local civility campaign of some sort. Toscano suggested the idea of a "Declaration of Interdependence." I talked about convening civility conversations at local businesses, nonprofit organizations, and civic groups.

In retrospect, it seems sweet, almost innocent, to have spent time on this initiative, this paper barricade, while a firestorm barreled toward our little town.

Meanwhile, there were lessons to be drawn from the "Don't Take the Bait" strategy. It was clear that the strategy had worked, but only in part. We had created a powerful set of events alongside the main event. But there had also been no way, functionally, to dissuade people from the main event. And it had backfired, in part, driving more people to confront the KKK, in order to signal their resistance to what they felt was a dismissive and paternalistic attitude from the established powers in a progressive city.

And I couldn't ignore the conflict between my feelings as an elected official and those of my erstwhile activist self—the progressive, the anti-racist, the anti-fascist (on my own terms). Even though I wanted to ignore this tiny, retrograde, criminal group from another state by refusing to take their bait, and by rendering them as pathetic as I felt they were, I still found it heartening that so many people had turned out to repudiate the KKK. It was a *good* thing that a thousand people were there, even if many of them had arrived in groups with anarchic intent. That some of them had directed their anger at me, as the city's figurehead, could not obscure their overall value, and valor.

Meanwhile, the Unite the Right rally loomed. Jason Kessler had applied for a permit, but it had not been granted. What would we do now?

THE MONDAY AFTER THE KKK RALLY, JULY 10, I WAS AT MY DAY job, trying to work on contracts and various corporate matters, but having a hard time concentrating. The next day, Tuesday, my attention started turning to August 12. I started thinking we needed a big new idea.

I called Professor A. E. Dick Howard at UVA's School of Law. He was an old friend of mine who had been the officiant at our wedding in 2012, and I wanted to ask for his legal advice on whether and how we could put Kessler's rally at a different location (as there wasn't evidence that met the legal standard to deny the permit). Kessler wanted the rally in the former Lee Park (now named Emancipation Park), where the Lee statue stood, just a block away from the pedestrian Downtown Mall. With the intense publicity the Unite the Right rally was already drawing, and after the melee that had followed the KKK event, I felt there was no way hundreds or even thousands of angry protesters and counterprotesters could safely coexist in the small park and the densely compressed surrounding urban streets. It seemed like a recipe for havoc.

Howard thought it would be very difficult to change the location because of the strictness of case law on content-based decisions. The objectionable content of the Unite the Right event would likely be seen as the core of our decision, and the proximity of the Lee statue to Lee Park would lead most courts to give Kessler the benefit of the doubt in viewing the rally as a free-speech event. He suggested I call Leslie Kendrick, another UVA professor and a leading First Amendment expert. Sitting in my car in our day-care parking lot, I called her that afternoon. We talked about "content-neutral" reasons that would allow us to make that decision, including, most significantly, the fact that the event would likely far outstrip the crowd estimate of four hundred included on the permit application.

Later that night, I called Mayor Pete Buttigieg of South Bend. He had been a naval reserve officer and had served a tour in Afghanistan, so I specifically wanted his advice on whether there might be insights for our situation from the military's work on counterinsurgency and civic unrest. I trusted his judgment on both substance and politics. It was at once a discomfiting and revelatory conversation. After hearing me out, he said, "That's tough." He agreed we should try and relocate the rally, but he also suggested there was likely no single solution. I realized I was looking for a silver bullet, when one wasn't available.

He suggested a metaphor from the navy—"sailing into the windstorm." Just getting through the storm with the boat intact, he said, would be a victory. I took a new perspective from that conversation: that we should start thinking about the project in terms of preventing worse things from happening, rather than in terms of achieving some sort of victory. My quest for another such silver bullet at the KKK event—"Don't Take the Bait"—had not worked perfectly because of the reality on the ground. That was a hard lesson, but when I realized the wisdom of Buttigieg's advice, it felt strangely reassuring.

The next day, I called Sylvester Turner, the vigorous, charismatic mayor of Houston, Texas, whom I'd also met at the Miami mayors meeting. He called me back from a trip in Turkey, and after hearing me out, gave me one simple, strong piece of advice: "You've got to separate the groups," he said. "You've got to get green space between them." He told me this had worked to defuse tensions in events about police brutality in Houston. Thinking about the city's landscape, I quickly landed on a new idea: McIntire Park. This was a large park with softball fields located a couple of miles away from the Downtown Mall, near Charlottesville High School—which had a large parking lot to boot.

This was five days after the KKK event.

That week also brought a small but momentous action on the statue front. Acting upon direction from the city council, but within his administrative authority as head of our government, City Manager Jones quietly had the old interpretive plaque that stood in front of the statue of Robert E. Lee removed—the fading, yellowing one that referred to Lee as a "hero of the Confederacy." It was a proximate result of the KKK madness the week before.

Meanwhile, though the Kessler permit still had not been granted, we began receiving hundreds of intense emails demanding that we revoke it. The social media traffic against me became really wild. I texted Governor Terry McAuliffe on July 11, asking for five minutes of his time for "advice on how to deal with the upcoming alt-right rally here on

August 12, which might draw thousands of people, in the wake of the good and bad from the KKK rally last week."

The governor called me the next day, and we talked for about twenty minutes. I discussed the quandary of the request for the August 12 event to occur near the Downtown Mall, and he said I needed to focus on protecting public safety. I floated the idea from Sylvester Turner of moving the rally to a green field, where the two sides could be separated. McAuliffe agreed and suggested "moving the rally to a field somewhere." He told me a story about how, as Democratic National Committee chair, he had also attempted to relocate a protest. For him, it had been at the 2004 Democratic National Convention. He had wanted to move a planned protest to a different site; the DNC had then been sued, but had prevailed in litigation. I also told him that the Virginia State Police needed to provide some evidence of their claims of being attacked during the KKK event, in connection with the tear gas, and that it was creating a big problem for us. He said he would look into it. However, I never heard back from him or his office about the tear-gas decision. Coupled with the city's refusal to account for the decision, this lack of explanation and accountability from the state added significantly to the brushfire of accountability that would soon sweep over the city.

On Thursday, July 13, I dropped the boys off at day care. I headed to City Hall, where I again met with Maurice Jones, and told him about the McIntire Park idea. He seemed intrigued but noncommittal. Separating the groups in the parking lot near McIntire Park might be extremely difficult, he said, but he would give it more thought. What I'd taken from the other conversations, however, was that the event simply could not happen safely in downtown Charlottesville. It was too crowded. The windstorm would be too dangerous for us to sail into, and I wasn't sure we would be able to come out safely on the other side. I talked with Bellamy about the idea of separating the groups, and he agreed we should pursue it.

Jones and I talked about the August 12 permit request a little more and discussed a few more content-neutral reasons that the public safety challenges of the downtown location were insurmountable. We talked through the chess game that was likely to follow over the next few weeks. He said he would need to offer the alternative of McIntire Park to Kessler. Kessler would likely turn it down, but at least then we'd be on record as having made a good-faith, content-neutral bid. If we insisted, we would then probably get sued. We might lose, but it would mean we could ask the governor, and maybe even the National Guard, for help. And then it would be less in our hands.

The emails continued to pour in asking us to revoke the permit. I felt we were debating yet another symbolic victory. The permitting process was an administrative decision out of the city council's control. Council opposition to it would fit on a bumper sticker or in a tweet, but in practice, given First Amendment rules, we would lose in court if we intervened. Trying to deny the permit could then backfire, handing an important victory to the alt-right while painting the city as feckless and defenseless.

There were also emails demanding that the city council "drop the charges" against the counterprotesters who had been arrested during the KKK protest. A meme saying "Mayor Signer, drop the charges" appeared on a Facebook page created by an Antifa group from Richmond. Of course, in our system of government, I did not control the charging of defendants; that was up to the prosecutor and the police. Maybe the people making this demand didn't know that, or maybe they didn't care.

July 17, the following Monday, brought the first council meeting since the KKK rally. The feeling was raw and turbulent. Watching the incendiary online traffic, the chatter among members of the alt-right on Twitter, often using the hashtag #unitetheright, as well as Reddit threads and posts on the virulent white supremacist website The Daily Stormer, I again had that eerie feeling of being an amateur firefighter trying to protect a small patch of forest from an approaching blaze. During one of our conversations, Bellamy sounded genuinely worried. He said the KKK members had been "clowns," but the Unite the Right rally might be worse: "These guys are *serious*," he said.

The city, too, was catching that fever. The citizens of Charlottesville were watching the same thing I was watching online, and they had the same sense of impending doom. At the council meeting, the chambers felt particularly hot and crowded. The audience was bristling with hand-lettered "REVOKE THE PERMIT" signs on white and fluorescent green posterboard, and the body language was edgy and angry, with frequent whoops and hollers.

I began with a few key points. We had begun a journey to tell the full story of race, I said. The Blue Ribbon Commission had been convened for that purpose, and we had enacted many of their recommendations already. We'd set up events to take the spotlight away from the KKK, and the community came through. I thanked all the community members who had organized the events, including the NAACP, the African American Heritage Center, the Downtown Pavilion, the Clergy Collective, and the Mount Zion First African Baptist choir. While many went to those events, thousands also went to the protest. That was absolutely their right, I said, and we should be proud of the headlines showing that the counterprotesters had outnumbered the pitiful KKK by a factor of two hundred. No matter what one had chosen to do on July 8, the important thing was we had spoken with one voice, sending a clear message that we rejected racism and intolerance in this community.

I acknowledged that there had been both praise and criticism of the policing. We'd received hundreds of emails from ACLU supporters and hundreds more asking us to revoke the August 12 permit. Many had asked the city council to drop the charges against the July 8 counterprotesters, including several people who had been arrested for wearing masks—ironically, in violation of a law originally set up to prevent the KKK from wearing masks in Virginia. We took all of this very seriously, I said, but we also had to be clear with the public about what we could and could not do. It was essential that anyone advocating for change and improved government understand the structure of local government in Charlottesville and Virginia. I explained that we had a city manager form of government, where the police report to the city manager; the city manager, in turn, had operational authority over the police—the council did not. The council had no authority whatsoever over the prosecutor—or commonwealth's attorney—who was separately elected. We could not, in other words, "drop the charges."

However, I said, I was asking that the content of all of the emails—close to a thousand of them—be conveyed to the city manager and to staff for evaluation of any actual actions we could take. In addition, I asked that the Commonwealth's Attorney's Office be apprised of the complaints.

I concluded by explaining, as best I could, the law underlying the permit quandary for the Unite the Right rally. It was crucial for people to understand that the permit had not actually been issued yet.

This piece of information was technically and constitutionally important. The city was trying to reserve all of its options, rather than putting the ball back in Kessler's court. At the same time, the councilors, as elected officials, were being kept out of all aspects of the permit decision, to keep it as removed from political and content-based considerations as possible. But I couldn't say that from the dais. It could make it seem like the city was gaming the permit, being calculating rather than bureaucratically dispassionate in determining whether ultimately to grant it.

Protecting freedom of speech should always be a sacrosanct obligation, I emphasized. As a scholar of the US Constitution and as an attorney, I was passionately devoted to the First Amendment, and as a city councilor, I had sworn an oath to uphold the Constitution.

Borrowing from the conversations I was having with First Amendment scholars, I said what I *was* able to say, and what might be helpful in the inevitable court case to come: that there were grave concerns about *logistical aspects* of the event, including the potential crowd size, methods of ingress and egress, parking, and the fact that so many public assets would be so proximate to the proposed site, and therefore vulnerable in the event of any unrest. Each of these concerns was a determinedly content-neutral factor, which would matter regardless of the ideas or viewpoints expressed at the event. We had to examine those issues in the permitting decision and explore whether there were other locations in the city where the First Amendment could be equally upheld without the logistical challenges of the downtown location.

This statement was meant—as early as possible—to express my strong opinion that moving the event to a location like McIntire Park would be both safer for the city and protective of freedom of speech.

In my conclusion, I declared, with pride, that we had come out of the difficult day of the KKK rally stronger than before—more committed to diversity, to racial and social justice, to telling the truth about our history, and to unity.

I only wish that had been the case.

IN "MATTERS BY THE PUBLIC," THE SECTION BEGINNING EACH council meeting, UVA professor and Charlottesville Black Lives Matter cofounder Jalane Schmidt came to the podium wearing a Black Lives Matter T-shirt. She was carrying something in her hand, and she began by shaking the object and saying, "Mic check." The audience shouted "Mic check" behind her.

She then brought the object up to Bob Fenwick and put it on the dais in front of him. It was a tear gas canister. "You dropped something, Councilors," she said to him. "I want you to pass that down the row, please. I want you each to touch it. I want some accountability. I want you to imagine that thing hitting your flesh at high velocity, as it did for many of us."

She went on to charge that the counterprotesters' backs had been turned when the tear gas had been discharged. She talked about how three people had been arrested for being masked in violation of the law, when they were covering their faces to avoid the tear gas. "To a hammer, everything's a nail," she closed.

She was followed by more people telling more angry stories of fear about the police. The director of the local Legal Aid office came up and made several direct challenges. Who had ordered riot gear to be deployed, and why? Who had ordered an unlawful assembly to be declared, and why? And who had ordered the use of tear gas—and why?

Heading into the Unite the Right rally, those questions would go unanswered by those in our government who could actually answer them. This failure to understand the events of the July rally and its aftermath help explain both the growing rage from the left and the defensiveness of the police during the August rally.

Another commenter was a blond woman I had not met before. She said, "Everyone knows me as the call-out queen. It is taking everything in me, right now, not to call you out, Mike Signer."

But first she gave her account of being brutalized by the police. She described encountering military-grade weapons as another counterprotester, a black woman, was being handcuffed, and others were yelling at the officers to let her go. She recounted how after some folks decided to try to prevent the officers from taking the counterprotester away, she was thrown down by one officer, and another officer pulled her away. Officers then "threatened to arrest my comrades," she said. An officer pulled out an "assault rifle" and pointed it at her comrade's head. The police threw her (the woman who was speaking) to the ground again, and she ended up on her knees. She began to have a panic attack, and medics took her blood pressure and pulse.

In telling her story, she went over her three-minute deadline. I said, "Listen, we will read your statement. We have to proceed with our rules, we have rules here, this is not civil. Everyone else kept to three minutes." The crowd then interrupted and jeered me, and cheered her on. I asked her how much longer it would take, whether she could finish in one minute. "Listen, I am a victim of domestic violence," she said. "I was in a relationship for two years," she said. She said she was experiencing posttraumatic stress disorder.

"Look at me, Mike Signer," she announced, staring at me. "You let this happen. Chief Thomas let this happen. You did this. You did this to our community. We are stronger than you. . . . It is a shame what you let happen on Saturday."

I will not attempt to explain what it felt like to be linked, however remotely, to the woman's experience of domestic violence. I just knew I had to sit and listen, as best as I could.

AN ANTIFA ACTIVIST NAMED EMILY GORCENSKI THEN STOOD UP AND cited section 3.4.5(b) of the city's regulations, which granted grounds to reject a permit if there was a clear and present danger to public safety. She read from a packet, copies of which she later gave to council. It contained a series of threats that she said she had gathered from online searches. The quotes included: "I can assure you, there will be beatings at the August event." One post called for "all able-bodied men and women ready to fight." On The Daily Stormer, she told us, the alt-right was "advertising this event gleefully." A notorious alt-right man who went by the name "Based Stickman" would be attending, she said, and "his group are pretty prone to starting violence." The Daily Stormer was saying that "military members [were needed] to crack the skulls of black people."

She concluded by observing that Kessler had even stood in front of the police department with a private security force, a biker gang that prides itself on violence.

It was startling. The staff listened and took copies of the packet, and I later asked our attorney about it. She said firmly that nothing we'd heard, even taking the city ordinance into account, met the Supreme Court's "credible threat" test of a *specific* statement advocating, or planning, a *specific and imminent* act of violence. It was the same thing I'd heard from the FBI when we'd talked about the online comments about me. Under existing constitutional case law, and under the approach adopted by federal, state, and local intelligence and police agencies, such general threats and descriptions of violence, as alarming as they were, could not be used to stop the event.

It seemed crazy. But it was, at least at that moment, the law.

A YOUNG BLACK MAN WHO DIDN'T GIVE HIS NAME THEN CAME TO the podium, wearing a T-shirt that said, "All lives can't matter if black lives don't matter." He said he'd been onsite as a counterprotester and had been tear-gassed. "When I wake up right now," he said, "I can hear tingling in my head, the effects of all the bombs in the street." He said there had been no pepper gel from the counterprotesters. He ended with a warning to Kessler: "We will be out there. If August 12 is coming, the permit is allowed, they'll be there, we [are] going to be there also. We ain't running, we ain't hiding. If they use force, we're going to use force also." This led to whoops, hollers, and loud clapping.

Another young black man then came up, wearing long dreadlocks. He provided an intricate and eloquent argument against the idea of order itself. He said that people of color were "continually told to sacrifice their emotions, their hurt, their very humanity in the service of white comfort." They were "continually asked to police [themselves] when no such expectation is placed on white folks." He said, "Instead of being empowered to draw on righteous anger and indignation at injustice, we're told to be smaller, quieter, or even just quiet." In a biting criticism of Charlottesville's image as a bastion of progressive tolerance, he said: "This is the price we pay for inclusion in progressive visions of our communities defined through the lens of whiteness, the loss of the very parts of ourselves that could be most valuable in the creation of freer and more human communities. Any truly progressive city would reject placing that burden on oppressed folks." This was not the first time we would hear the challenge to civility as a mask for white supremacy, but it was the most powerful articulation of it that I remember. The audience gave him an ovation as he left the podium.

A white musician with a long gray goatee then came up. Directly addressing me as a lawyer, he argued that "law and morality have nothing to do with one another." He said, "This brainless defense of free speech is killing us," adding, "if the law says we have to defend the Klan, we have to defend neo-Nazis, we need to resist that law. That is an unjust law. That is not a law that is in line with morality."

Listening to him, I heard echoes of the classic distinction between human and natural law. I heard what he was saying—that we could heed a higher calling. We could protest the very laws we were required to serve.

But what if we lost a case about the rally in court precisely because a judge found that a moral stance was at odds with First Amendment law? What if we handed victories to the white nationalists?

What then?

THE CITY MANAGER, MAURICE JONES, THEN SPOKE. I OFTEN WONdered what the audience thought when they watched him. He was an affable, mild fellow who often would not speak at all during long stretches of council meetings. He could seem almost entirely passive. Yet he was the city's most powerful authority, the one who, unlike the mayor and city council, could pick up the phone and tell any staff member what to do or not do, hire and fire staff, carve out money from agency budgets and spend it—the one who controlled virtually all the levers of the city government's power on a day-to-day-basis.

Jones proceeded to explain the First Amendment laws that the city needed to comply with, showing an unusual degree of personal passion on the subject. He explained that free-speech laws had resulted from important legal cases, and that because of these cases, people like Martin Luther King Jr. had been able to speak. These rulings, he said, had "allowed us—*us*," to speak, referring to African Americans like himself.

He provided a factual account of the events of July 8. He described how the crowd had followed the police to the parking garage and had refused to allow the KKK to leave. He said the law enforcement response was focused on opening the road, and he gave the police department's side of the story in detail. He was repeatedly interrupted with gasps and shouts and guffaws. I spoke out, citing our rules against interruptions. I called several of the audience members to order, saying it was "going to suck" if I had to kick people out.

Jones then got into the matter of the tear gas, asserting, "No one from the city or the Virginia State Police came into the day with the goal of using tear gas." He was interrupted repeatedly by screaming audience members, who also began leaving, shouting about asthma attacks, and chanting "Black Lives Matter." I suspended the meeting for five minutes. Afterward, Jones finished his statement. I led the council to ask Jones for a report and investigation on the use of tear gas, which he agreed to provide. But it never came. And whether it was the fault of the city manager, the Charlottesville police, the state police—or some combination—the failure to provide such an investigation was critical in the collapse of confidence in policing to come.

Jones also discussed the upcoming Unite the Right rally and the crowd's demands that we "revoke the permit": "In terms of keeping folks from speaking in the park, that is not something we can revoke a permit based upon. . . . As awful as that speech may be, you cannot do that. . . . We do not have that power as a municipality." So the city manager's position was clear. I felt it would have been so much better to hear this directly from the police, but Chief Thomas was absent, so we could not hear his perspective or ask him the questions.

Wes Bellamy then read out loud from the ACLU's July 17 letter and said he supported its requests, including the one for an independent investigation. In a phone call the week before the Unite the Right rally, Chief Thomas would tell me how much Bellamy's statement had infuriated the police department. To have the vice-mayor suggest that the police should be investigated by the federal government, he said, was a wound that had not healed. This turn in police morale helped explain why the police resisted any involvement whatsoever from me and the other councilors in their actual planning and execution of August 12 operations.

And it revealed a troubling challenge, which became even more evident in the events to follow: the sheer difficulty of achieving transparency and accountability, of just getting answers, from elected officials, when they themselves might not be in any actual position to provide them due to behind-the-scenes discombobulation.

THE MEETING LEFT ME IN A STATE OF HIGH AGITATION. I RACKED my brain for silver bullets, new ideas, fresh approaches—for answers. I called a retired four-star admiral I knew from the John Edwards presidential campaign to ask him if there were lessons from Iraq and Afghanistan about how to deal with serious civic unrest in an urban location like our Downtown Mall—before it happened. But he didn't have anything to offer that a civilian authority, especially in a position like the mayorship I held, could use.

I then called John Nagl, the author of a celebrated book on counterinsurgency, *Learning to Eat Soup with a Knife*,[7] whom I knew from the Truman National Security Project. After listening to the facts about the Downtown Mall, he agreed that the event was untenable and highly dangerous in the Emancipation Park location. He thought we needed to move heaven and earth to get it to McIntire Park, and advised me to consider a set of logistical measures. We could throttle access to the park by requiring parking permits, for example. That could reduce the crush of attendees enough to prevent the groups from getting into a full-scale clash with each other.

They were promising ideas. But I had a mounting sense of futility as I realized how little chance there was, given my position outside the chain of command, of these ideas working their way into the actual plan.

The next day, July 19, I had a meeting with City Manager Maurice Jones, Assistant City Manager Mike Murphy, and Louis Nelson, vice provost for outreach at UVA, and we talked about UVA helping to create an alternative slate of events on August 12. Perhaps these could draw people away from the coming conflagration. UVA could provide a safe haven of sorts on the "Grounds." I knew that Nelson was enthusiastic about the idea, but at higher levels at UVA, there was the fear that such events could draw the alt-right to the university itself—especially considering that both Jason Kessler and Richard Spencer were UVA alumni.

The day after that, July 20, I launched a blitz of phone calls and emails to find prominent national figures who could come to town to help lead a "calming event" and convince folks from both the left and the right to lay down their arms. The hope—a naïve one, as it turned out, in light of the invasion of multiple armed militias coming to the city—was that we might hold a major event on Friday night that could lower the temperature enough for us to get through the weekend.

From my office, from my car, while walking on the street, I called everyone I could think of who might be able to help provide the city with a preventive dousing to stop us from bursting into flame. I reached out to the Reverend William Barber II, the leader of North Carolina's "Moral Monday" movement (a clergy- and citizen-led weekly gathering meant to challenge socially conservative laws passed in the state), through a friend. I tried Michelle Obama through another friend. I contacted Ohio governor and prominent Trump antagonist John Kasich through his political adviser. I emailed and called Congressman John Lewis (D-GA), the civil rights leader, through another colleague. Governor McAuliffe offered to reach out to Jesse Jackson.

Emily and I still needed to pack, as we were headed north for our annual vacation with Emily's parents in Massachusetts. These week-long summer visits were a nonnegotiable condition of my marriage. But it would hardly be a vacation.

WE ARRIVED IN WELLFLEET, MASSACHUSETTS, A SMALL, REMOTE town on Outer Cape Cod, where my father-in-law had purchased a small, uninsulated, World War II–era cottage thirty years ago. The cottage sits on a dune in the protected Cape Cod National Seashore. With no air-conditioning and an outdoor shower, it was charming but decidedly rustic, essentially unimproved since sailors had stayed there in the early 1940s to look out for German U-boats.

I continued my calls from the cottage. On any given day, I was on the phone three to four hours. I repeatedly talked to my colleagues on the council, trying to convince them to move the event. I tried to get UVA to participate in our programming, but senior officials there, obviously intent on separating the university from the coming melee in the city, were blocking the university's participation in any strategy.

I reached out to a former UVA law professor of mine named Vincent Blasi and laid out the facts to him. Blasi was a genial man with joint appointments at UVA and Columbia. He had taught a treasured First Amendment law seminar I'd taken at UVA, weaving together John Milton's 1644 *Areopagitica*, one of the earliest polemics against censorship and in favor of freedom of speech, and *National Socialist Party of America v. Village of Skokie*. I told him how concerned I was about the prospect of so many angry people jamming against one another right next to the Downtown Mall and said we needed to figure out a new approach. Did he have any ideas?

When we spoke, I was sitting at the kitchen table at the cottage, looking into a cup of coffee, and the whole family was down on the beach. He told me about the high bar of *viewpoint* neutrality in the First Amendment. Viewpoint neutrality meant that the statue protesters could easily claim we were really worried about the costs and the danger of the event because the alt-right's ideas—their viewpoints—were controversial. Their viewpoints were connected to the Lee statue and the broader set of ideas they associated with it, like immigration. And because of that, he said, we would "run into some trouble" if we tried to move the event away from the Lee statue entirely.

He had an idea, though. I carefully took notes while he mused that we could offer the protesters access to the Lee statue for a limited number of people, while requiring the larger crowd to be at McIntire Park. That way, we wouldn't be fencing off the Lee statue. Some people could still get their pictures taken near the statue and "make their point." We would be allowing the expression of viewpoints while addressing the problem created at Emancipation Park by the sheer numbers of protesters downtown.

Blasi suggested that we formally meter access to Emancipation Park with a shuttle from McIntire Park that would allow, say, fifty people into Emancipation Park at a time. We would allow perhaps fifteen minutes for each group. That way, we'd show that we were "bending over backwards not to punish offensive ideas." And then McIntire Park could easily hold the larger group, even if it was a thousand people or more. The more we pushed for such a scheme, he said, the more we'd be able to prove to a court that our approach did not stem from objecting to the alt-right's ideas, but from the physical dangers created by so many people in that kind of space. We would accommodate their desire to protest at the site of their grievance. We could rebut their claim that we were trying to deny *all* of them access.

What were the chances of winning in court? I could almost hear him shaking his head on the other end of the line. "It's not a slam dunk either way," he said. He said it wouldn't surprise him if the case went all the way up to a federal appeals court, or even the US Supreme Court. And he said that, "posed in the starkest form," if a court found that the protesters did have a First Amendment right, the odds were "two out of three" that they would win.

I would go on to push the shuttle idea repeatedly with Maurice Jones, Al Thomas, and my colleagues on the council for the next four weeks, but to no avail. Each time I raised the issue, Jones would turn quizzical and musing. Thomas, by contrast, would become slightly harsh about it and mock the idea. He didn't want to invest in devising a new scheme when the police department had already gone to the expense of developing a different strategy for August 12.

The entire staff was skeptical about doing anything other than plowing ahead on their existing strategy for Unite the Right in Emancipation Park. Maurice Jones forwarded a memo on the relocation option from our counsel's office to the city council. It had been written on July 14—just six days after the KKK event—and essentially, it laid out an argument for keeping the decision about the permit an administrative decision, to be controlled solely by the city manager and the staff members who reported to him, and leaving elected officials like me out of it. I knew this meant that my ideas about using relocation and shuttle buses to avoid a catastrophe were going to be rejected. Upon first reading it, I sighed deeply. It was just so frustrating, so confounding, having to fight uphill with our own lawyers. But the fact was that the city attorney had two masters in our unique system. In most Virginia cities and counties, the city attorney reports to the city council alone. But in Charlottesville, the city attorney reported to *both* the city council *and* the city manager. That one seemingly small fact, I realized, could have profound effects in a time of crisis.

The blurred organizational charts would complicate rather than simplify the situation in which we now found ourselves.

An attorney has an ethical duty to "zealously represent" the interests of his or her client. When representing one party whose interests are against those of another party, the attorney generally cannot represent both parties.[8] So what do you do when the government itself requires the attorney to represent two parties—the city manager and the council—who have different and opposing interests?

That was the predicament. I wanted the office of the city attorney to do one thing; the city manager and chief of police wanted it to do something else. Our lawyers were caught in a terrible bind. And if I was going to make headway, it was going to require running roughshod over some of those organizational lines.

THE JULY 14 MEMO FROM THE CITY ATTORNEY'S OFFICE THREW down a clear gauntlet. It began by asserting a technical but crucial foundational issue: that the decision on the Unite the Right permit be made administratively, not politically, to insulate the decision from challenge. The staff attorney wrote, "I must reiterate that the decision on whether or not to issue a permit for a demonstration is primarily for logistical and planning purposes, and the City's Events Coordinator must make the final decision on the requested permit, in accordance with the City's special events regulations."

The memo then presented a startling series of firm legal conclusions that would have dramatic consequences for our ability to deal with the Unite the Right rally. It said that the Supreme Court had expressly declared that a "restrictive regulation imposed upon a proposed demonstration, rally, parade, etc., if motivated by anticipated listener reaction to the content of the event, is a content-based regulation." It then unequivocally stated that violence was a form of listener reaction and that content-based regulations are presumptively invalid.

The attorney explained that strict scrutiny would be applied by a court in the case of any decision by the city to change the venue, and that we would need to articulate a compelling state interest. But that compelling state interest was extremely narrowly defined. A "generalized concern about public safety" would not survive review by a court, our attorney said, even if the concern was legitimate. Our staff officials (remember, not elected officials) would need instead to present compelling factual evidence, admissible in court, of clearly defined, specific threats to the safety and security of city officials, city police, counterprotesters, rally participants, and traffic and pedestrians; evidence that the threats were real and substantial; and evidence that the threatened violence would be beyond reasonable control by police.

In terms of gathering that information, the memo explained, "rumors are not helpful." Nor were "assumptions" or "social media postings." What we needed instead was "information as to individuals' and groups' specific intentions for this event." That was the only type of information that would give a decision "any chance of surviving strict scrutiny by a court."

The memo did note a window of opportunity that, unfortunately, was never opened. After mentioning a strong preference in the courts for free-speech events to be proximate to a location like the Lee statue "when the location had special relationship to the key message of the permit applicant," it continued: "However, if the police department can establish, objectively, that it is not possible to manage a real and substantial threat of violence at the requested location, but the threat could be managed at a different location, then please let me know that as soon as possible."

In retrospect, this was the real failing. If our government had presented credible evidence to a court that we would be *unable to manage* the rally safely at Emancipation Park, our chances of winning would have been higher—according to our attorney.

However, our staff did not seem to want to concede that the strategy already in place might not succeed. That would have required both specificity of evidence and humility in approach. Whatever the cause, our government resisted until the bitter end any movement away from the strategy we kept hearing about—which, as it would turn out, was fatally flawed. The police specifically balked at the work that would have been required to bolster the legal battle to relocate the rally. Instead, they actively opposed the idea that they could not safely manage the rally downtown. That put the city—and me, as the leader of the relocation charge—in a double bind. We were damned if we didn't, and damned if we did.

Meanwhile, the memo offered a final ominous dimension. City councilors, it said, should defer to "city staff's concerns and planning." Our attorney explained that "if any individual Councilor goes too far out on a limb and appears to be orchestrating decisions, or if Council as a whole steps in to become the event planner, there is a substantial risk of liability to individual Councilors as well as the City Council as a public body, in a lawsuit alleging violations of civil rights."

In other words, our own City Attorney's Office was arguing that if we on the council interfered with the decisions of the city manager and the police chief, we could be held *personally liable*. That possibility threatened the standard "sovereign immunity" elected officials normally enjoy when making decisions like this. It was the first time I would be threatened with personal financial liability for trying to protect the public by pushing the boundaries of the possible. But it would not be the last.

During my last days in Wellfleet, I talked to Chief Thomas again, who again told me the police department had a strategy in place. He said he opposed any effort to move the rally to McIntire Park. If it was weeks ago, he said, maybe he would have supported it—but not now. Too many resources had gone into the existing plan.

Meanwhile, I was spending hours at a time looking at the buildup on social media among the alt-right for the rally and was frightened by their avidity and malice. Bellamy had been right when he had intoned that "these guys are serious." There were contests among them to design a Unite the Right logo, and they were openly employing neo-Nazi iconography like eagles and fists. There seemed to be no question there would be a violent collision. How the hell could this thing be happening at all, I found myself asking, over and over.

I had already been pushing the boundaries of the mayorship in our system, but I pushed harder, ruffling our staff's feathers even more. In another memo, our City Attorney's Office said it had been unable to find case law supporting a "decision to move an event when the proposed location was important to the organizers." But I had, in fact, found one: a 2004 New York Supreme Court case that seemed on point. It was *United for Peace and Justice v. Bloomberg*, where a liberal group called United for Peace and Justice had planned a large rally for the eve of the 2004 Republican National Convention.[9]

After months of unsuccessful negotiation with New York City officials to secure Central Park for the location of the rally, the group sued with the help of the New York ACLU. The city had responded that it would allow the rally to take place only on the West Side Highway, a site that would leave participants three miles from the rally stage, on the fringe of Manhattan.

The lawsuit alleged that the city was unconstitutionally barring large political rallies from Central Park, and that the refusal to accommodate the rally at any location other than the West Side Highway was an unconstitutional restriction on the group's free-speech rights. But the New York State Supreme Court ruled for the city, holding that in denying the permit application for Central Park, the city had not burdened the group's right to free speech. The court found that the city's offer of the West Side Highway had been an adequate site to hold the numbers of people expected at the rally.

It seemed to me the court's logic could be readily applied to our situation. In New York, the protesters had wanted to be in Central Park because the location was connected to their speech, but the city had said the safety of the West Side Highway location was more important than their desires. So, too, we could argue in Charlottesville that even though the Lee statue was central to Unite the Right's speech rights, public safety concerns were more important. They could have their speech, but they would need to do it at McIntire Park.

I brought the case up repeatedly with our City Attorney's Office, but it had no effect on their position. With decisions like this out there clearly showing that it was at least possible to win in court if we decided to relocate the rally, I concluded that we needed more aggressive lawyers.

Toward the end of the week at the beach, I got all four of the other councilors to agree to at least discuss how to force the relocation of the event—with outside legal counsel, if necessary. We were heading into August, when lawyers, especially in Washington and New York, go on vacation. Working on my own from the beach through friends and colleagues, I found only one possibility: a senior partner at a major law firm called Boies Schiller. He was experienced in constitutional cases, and he was available to help. But there was a catch: it would cost real dollars, and we'd need to be able to defend the expenditure to the public. I thought $25,000 was probably the most we could defend. He agreed to a cap of $30,000—but only for one weekend of work, culminating in a letter to Kessler. They would not be able to help us with litigation, if it came to that.

In a text on Saturday, July 29, I told Chief Thomas, "I will be moving forward with the McIntire option from Council in coming days. Stay tuned." But I would need to be present physically in any closed meeting with lawyers where we would make the tough call to insert ourselves into the permitting decision. I set the meeting for Wednesday, August 2. To get there, I left the beach early, driving the twelve hours back to Charlottesville by myself. Emily and the boys would fly back a few days later. I walked into the stale August air of our small house alone. One thing loomed ahead: Unite the Right.

Relocating the rally would require a set of events to happen quickly. We first needed to have a closed session to hire the outside law firm. We would need to overcome the obstacle of the memorandum from the City Attorney's Office stating that the intelligence wasn't sufficient to move the event. Maurice Jones arranged for the Virginia State Police to meet with us in the closed session to give us information on the actual nature of the threats.

Unite the Right was ten days away.

PART IV | FIRESTORM

21

DOMESTIC TERRORISM

| AUGUST 2017 |

M Y LONG DRIVE HOME HAD ENDED IN THE WEE HOURS OF THE morning. A little bleary, I was holding a cup of coffee and pacing in my kitchen in the late morning, August light streaming through the windows, when Governor Terry McAuliffe called me. The closed session was scheduled for that afternoon. It was a very strange call, and it felt staged somehow. (I learned later that the governor was reading from an outline that had been prepared for him by the state secretary of public safety, Brian Moran.) He said he had just received a briefing. There was an unusual tremor in his voice, and he said they were "very worried" in his office that the Unite the Right rally could be really dangerous. He told me what I already knew, that the UVA Hospital had canceled all elective surgeries.

The governor said his office would be recommending several changes for the event. Among others, they wanted backpacks prohibited, the time of the rally reduced, and firearms prohibited at the event.

We talked a little more about the idea of relocating the rally. McAuliffe was very complimentary about my approach and said we should do whatever it took to put the protection of life and property first. I thanked him, and we ended the call.

The call was odd for two reasons. The first was that Virginia law clearly prevented the city from banning firearms at the event, which the governor and his advisers surely knew. So why would they be asking us to do something that we could not in fact do?

The second was that I should not have been receiving the call. It should have been the city manager, who was our "emergency manager" under Virginia law. I could not implement such changes on my own. Given how quickly things were happening, I wasn't even sure if I could get them communicated in the right way to the officials who could—the city manager and the chief of police. We needed a formal written communication spelling out the specific requests, the facts they were based on, and the legal authorities they relied on, sent to our emergency manager. I called the city manager right after the call and tried as best as I could to recall what had been said in the oral conversation with the governor. He said he would "keep an eye out" for a letter from the governor.

No written letter was ever sent from the Governor's Office to the city manager, and so the city manager and the police chief never received the actual requests from the governor. To make matters stranger, the requests were not reiterated during the meeting we were about to have with three state troopers. Pondering the call later, I would conclude it was made not actually to effect any change, but instead to create a narrative that the Governor's Office—by demanding changes ahead of an impending disaster, whether they were achievable or not—had been in the right, while the city was, by default, in the wrong.

The closed session of the city council began at 3:00 p.m. and went for three and a half hours. It began with a presentation from the three Virginia state troopers—two men and a woman—that lasted under an hour. The female officer was the intelligence expert. She went through a PowerPoint presentation she said they had shown the governor earlier that day, right before he had called me.

The presentation, again strangely, featured barely any intelligence about the alt-right, and nothing at all about the mysterious "requests" the governor had made in his call to me earlier. It said nothing about the possibility of violent, organized militias invading the city. The state troopers did hand out a photo of one dangerous felon from Texas who they thought might be attending the event. But the presentation mostly focused on the far left and the specific threats that violent Antifa members might present to law enforcement. They went into the "black bloc" technique in depth and discussed devices that could be thrown at police. "Black bloc" is a method protesters use in which they cover their faces with black scarves and other items, such as motorcycle helmets or sunglasses; it makes it difficult for them to be distinguished from each other and prosecuted, and to some extent protects them from tear gas. The troopers also cited prior conflicts between Antifa and police in Berkeley and Portland.

After they left, we had an animated discussion about our fears about the event happening downtown. Al Thomas asked the councilors whether we had heard "evidence of a credible threat." We were forced to say no. Despite their PowerPoint, and despite the fact that they had led the governor to call me, the three troopers had not presented a single piece of evidence that would rise to the level of a specific, imminent threat of violence from someone likely to attend the rally. I pressed Thomas again about why he could not support a plan for McIntire Park. He again responded that if he had received the request six weeks earlier, it would be a different story, but now too many resources had gone into the strategy they'd decided to use. Bob Fenwick shook his head and said, "It just can't happen downtown." Chief Thomas said, "I'm going to ask you again: Did you hear evidence of a 'credible threat'?" Again, going around the table, we each said no.

Frustrated, Bellamy and I looked at each other and then both made the same point to Thomas: What if we had *just* learned about the rally? Wouldn't he have needed to design a new strategy then? If he *could* do it on such short notice, then why *wouldn't* he? He reiterated that they had a plan in place, and it was too late to come up with a new one. It felt like bureaucratic stubbornness in the face of a coming apocalypse. It felt crazy.

The city council then had a discussion alone with our city attorney, Craig Brown, and a visiting expert on free speech, Joshua Wheeler of the Thomas Jefferson Center for Free Expression. This illuminated the difficulty of the issue, and how little discretion the Supreme Court's jurisprudence gave to city officials, going back to *Terminiello*. We then got the Boies Schiller lawyers on the phone. The senior partner there also didn't sugarcoat our chances. It would be a difficult case to win. His advice was that we should focus narrowly on the most content-neutral grounds possible for relocating the rally, which was crowd size.

After we got off the phone, we talked some more. Fenwick, Bellamy, and I said that we absolutely wanted the rally moved to McIntire Park. Szakos wanted more support from Thomas first, but also said she wanted it at McIntire. Galvin was opposed to moving the event entirely and became quite frustrated, saying she thought that Thomas was telling us that the rally would be safer where it was. I didn't agree. I thought he was saying instead that it was just too much of a hassle to scrap the investment in the current plan and replace it with a new one.

In my view, the problem went back to the KKK rally, the lack of accountability for the tear gas decision, and the unanswered protests that followed, which had together led to a severe lack of trust. If the combined forces of the city and state police had experienced such problems during the KKK event, how could they handle this influx of certain violence downtown? Thomas and Jones were saying they had a strategy for downtown—but why were they resisting another strategy so intensely in the face of evidence that it could be a bloodbath? The social media posts alone, the mounting cycles of fury and threats to employ violence (always, of course, framed in self-defense) on both the right and the left, was beyond alarming.

But we still had to formally stay out of the decision to pass legal muster. In other words, the attorneys were united in advising us that we could not actually *make* the decision. We could just tell Jones it was the decision we wanted *him* to make. So at the conclusion of our meeting we charged Jones with telling us his decision the next morning. He was unhappy. He sighed heavily and said he would get his decision to us in twelve hours.

As I left the closed session, I was mobbed by a small crowd of reporters. I said it was taking a long time because we were being careful.

I went to a burger restaurant on the Downtown Mall that night by myself and sat at the bar with their specialty, a thick grass-fed hamburger topped with blackened onions and a fried pickle. I tried to calm down. Thomas called me at 10:30 p.m. while I was digging into my burger, and we talked for nearly an hour. He described the police force's fury at Bellamy for signing onto the ACLU letter. He told me about his fear that he might not be in his job for much longer (he said he had already canceled a contract on a house, losing a $5,000 deposit, for this reason). Once more, I pitched him the idea of giving rotating access to Emancipation Park rather than either shutting it down or giving unfettered access. He conceded that the logic of the idea was good and said they *could* make it work. But it clearly was not going to happen.

I asked him how I could help. He said I could do one thing—try and get both UVA and Albemarle County to dedicate more police and resources to our effort. After we got off the phone, I immediately called Pat Hogan, UVA's chief operations officer. He said he would look into the possibility by calling UVA's chief of police.

Later that night, I emailed all the city councilors polling their opinion on Professor Blasi's strategy of using the shuttle and metered access to the park. City Attorney Craig Brown, who also received the email, responded, "I think at some point Council needs to step back from this and let staff exercise its independent judgment on the operational details." He said that even though this was a "a poll and not a directive . . . I'm concerned about how it gets portrayed." That email led Kathy Galvin to decline even to participate in the poll.

The idea effectively died that night.

THAT FRIDAY, THE PROVOST OF UVA, TOM KATSOULEAS, CALLED ME from vacation in Greece. He wondered why we couldn't do a single "unifying event." When I explained how complex and cross-cutting the different factions were, he pretty quickly understood that it wasn't possible. When I had been looking at a large community "calming event," I'd discussed it with Vice Provost Louis Nelson, suggesting that we try having a large community event at UVA featuring someone like Michelle Obama. But I'd learned from him that the university was so fearful of the alt-right disrupting such a large event that it was a nonstarter. Instead, we'd come up with the idea of holding smaller workshops with various faculty members leading them at the same time, called "Community Dialogue" rather than "unity" events. Senior UVA officials even put the kibosh on the idea of a press release that would describe UVA's efforts as part of the city's strategy. They didn't want to be linked to us in any way.

We were being held at arm's length. That would turn out not to be the best choice for UVA.

On Friday night, August 4, eight days away from the rally, I tried to decompress by taking in two movies in a row at home, *Lady Macbeth* and *Detroit*. In retrospect, these pictures—respectively, haunting and terrifying—were not really the best choices to lighten one's mood. But I was probably working from a subconscious sense of impending doom. *Detroit*, in particular, was deeply unsettling, a searing depiction of the historic roots of today's rage against police brutality. It was very difficult to watch. I had my laptop open the whole time for developments, in any event.

At 10:39 p.m., I emailed the attorneys at Boies Schiller asking them to address the problem we faced of providing "ample research of the facts establishing content-neutral reasons for the venue change." I wrote about several facts that had recently come to light: the cancelation of all elective surgeries at UVA Hospital due to predicted emergency injuries from the rally; the fact that several important physical locations in the Downtown Mall, such as the library and a church, would be closed to the police; the mounting number of groups from around the country planning to converge on the Downtown Mall; and the planned closure of dozens of businesses on the Downtown Mall on that day. I knew that post-9/11 "fusion centers" had been set up within the state to handle intelligence, in part because small cities like Charlottesville could not do the job alone. The purpose of the centers was to fuse intelligence resources among federal, state, and local agencies. So I wrote, "The State Police's intelligence operation could readily give you a brief on this, I would imagine."

I concluded, "Those are all content-neutral. They would apply to any gathering that threatened disorder at this level."

On Saturday, I had lunch with a former UVA law professor who was a white member of the local chapter of Black Lives Matter. She had been sent on a mysterious delegation by the organization to ask me if I would publicly sympathize with their concerns and their approach in any public remarks I would make during the next week. She said they would appreciate me being more vocal in my sympathy with counterprotesters, and hoped I would expressly talk about the history of racism in Charlottesville in public comments. She said I was in a unique position to connect the dots—to make them feel heard.

The bitter irony was that I could not do this any longer because the Boies Schiller lawyers had given us strict instructions, as we headed into a showdown with Kessler and an almost certain lawsuit, not to reference content in our remarks. So that meant no discussion of white supremacy, neo-Nazis, bigotry, or even racial and social justice. Any mentions of content could undermine our position in litigation the following week. I told her this. She seemed crestfallen but I thought she understood.

This exchange was yet another example of the bind I would find myself in by the convergence of the First Amendment, our legal strategy, and our form of government, as havoc descended.

On Saturday night, I attended a dinner at a friend's house, where I met two women who had started a small opera company in Charlottesville. It's a measure of how hopeful I still was that I brainstormed with them about performing opera on the sidewalk near Emancipation Park. Such performances, I reasoned, could provide the national media—which would inevitably camp out in town—with something else to cover besides the alt-right. It could create a different set of stories about Charlottesville while we were in the national eye.

I still held out hope that we could create a narrative of unity. It was a futile hope, given what was about to hit us.

Six days out, the velocity of events significantly increased. On Sunday morning, August 6, I went to Mount Zion First African Baptist Church to take in some preaching from former mayor Alvin Edwards. Pastor Edwards recognized the trepidation among his congregation amid the trauma of the year so far. But he promised them that love would conquer hate.

I was the only councilor asked to join a conference call at 10:00 p.m. with our Boies Schiller attorneys to talk about the next day. The crucial question was whether Kessler would follow whatever the city required in the permit (which had not yet actually been issued). It was possible that he and his people would essentially engage in civil disobedience if the permit required them to go to Emancipation Park—as he was already publicly threatening to do.

After the KKK tear gas debacle, the ACLU's pressure campaign for a federal investigation into the police response, and Bellamy's support for that investigation, it seemed the police wouldn't want to arrest hundreds of people engaged in civil disobedience. They would be too concerned about the likelihood of violent arrests, the footage that would follow, and the logistics of implementing mass arrests. I guessed they would probably instead just declare an "unlawful assembly"—the mechanism in Virginia law for disbanding an event after it starts on the grounds that it has become impossible to continue safely. But the question was what would happen then. Where would so many angry and frustrated people go once they were dispersed?

In the call with the attorneys, we discussed the plan: Jones would meet with Kessler at 11:00 a.m. to give him the letter we'd spent $30,000 for, and he would ask him to move the event to McIntire. We planned a press conference at 3:00 p.m. to announce these developments. Later that night and early Monday morning, I word-smithed a statement I would read on behalf of the city council that navigated the narrow path between public safety and freedom of speech.

Through all of this, I was playing a far more active role than prescribed in my formal job description. I was directing legal calls, weighing in on legal and political strategy, and forming strategies myself. It almost felt like I was becoming, at times, a strong mayor in our weak mayor system. Recalling this sleep-deprived time, coffee metaphors naturally come to mind: like a triple shot of espresso, these extra duties were at once energizing and agitating. I could have left more up to others. I was certainly coloring way outside the lines of my official job description. But I felt that if there was any possibility—any possibility at all—of reducing the chance of disaster, I had to take it—and I had to make it happen.

ON MONDAY MORNING—FIVE DAYS BEFORE THE UNITE THE RIGHT rally—we had another call with our First Amendment attorneys at Boies Schiller at 8:00 a.m. We talked about what would happen if Kessler chose to ignore the permit denial. I convinced everyone to edit the letter to lead with language about how we were granting the permit for a different location, rather than by saying we were denying the request. I thought this would be stronger in court. At 9:08 a.m., I sent an email to each councilor with the remarks I would deliver at the press conference. I explained that the "bottom line is that there is grave concern from both outside and inside counsel about what I and any elected officials might say when asked any questions at all by the press." The guidance: "We may not say anything that refers to the content or even the controversiality of the speech at issue. The only thing that we may refer to publicly or privately is the size of the proposed rally. Any side or stray comments, however well-intentioned, about anything else could hurt us in court."

Jones met with Kessler at 11:00 a.m. Afterward, he informed me and other councilors that Kessler was hell-bent on Emancipation Park—formerly Lee Park. That meant announcing that the permit was being granted only for McIntire Park was a go. I then had to wrestle with the other councilors, particularly Fenwick and Galvin, to convince them not to say anything about the rally because of the dangers, with litigation likely, of being seen as focused on the content of the alt-right's speech.

Walking into the press conference, and seeing the welter of cameras and microphones filling our small chambers, I reflected darkly on the perverse irony of practicing what I was preaching—I was a Jewish mayor, speaking before neo-Nazis came to town, but not even able to mention them being neo-Nazis. We held the press conference quickly and dryly.

The statement I had planned out reveals, in awful intricacy, how delicate the task was. I said there was no more sacred duty of government than to protect life and property, and then said: "We have spent countless hours in recent weeks carefully considering legal issues surrounding this event. I have spoken with several First Amendment experts from around the country. I also have conferred with other Mayors who have faced similar challenges in reconciling public safety and free speech in a turbulent time."

The most carefully worked section was as follows: "As much as I would like to, I have been advised by counsel not to share my personal opinions about the content of the speech we will hear on August 12 or its controversiality. What I can say is that we on City Council whole-heartedly support the City Manager's decision to move the Unite the Right event to McIntire Park because of the ballooning size of the event's attendance."

These words represented the careful dance that cases like *Termi-niello v. Chicago* dictated in 1949, and that Justice Robert H. Jackson had so feared. The decision had to come from the administrative staff, not elected officials. It could not address the danger of public safety, because that could be a proxy for a heckler's veto. It could not talk about neo-Nazism. It could only talk about the most content-neutral reason for what constitutional law refers to as permissible "time, place, and man-ner" restrictions that governments can place on free-speech events: the ballooning size of the event, and the fact that we didn't believe so many rally participants could safely fit into Emancipation Park.

The press conference was incredibly quick, as we didn't take ques-tions. We were back in the office, lickety-split. We shared a burst of laughter at how much planning had gone into something so short.

But the laughter was short-lived. Hundreds, even thousands, of an-gry extremists on the left and right were coming to the city—bent, we knew from the KKK experience, on conflict with each other and, in all likelihood, with the police. The flyers and graphics alone circulating on-line, with the hashtag #unitetheright, felt militaristic, like the city would be under siege. It felt frightening and uncertain, as if we were planning to go into battle blindfolded. Not only did I not know what the battle plan was, I knew that no battle plan survives contact with the enemy.

THAT SAME MONDAY, I STARTED TALKING WITH POWELL TATE, the DC-based public relations firm we'd hired with the help of $5,000 from the Thomas Jefferson Foundation. This was a relief. So far that awful summer, any public relations from the city had been halting, in-complete, and unpersuasive. For instance, the previous week, the city manager had promised the council that staff would be holding daily press briefings during the crucial week preceding the rally to tell the public what they needed to know about the city's preparations and about what they should be doing. But these had not happened. From the average citizen's perspective, we were staying silent while a firestorm approached.

From the first minute of our conversation, it was clear that our PR team was made up of professionals. They had done crisis management before, and we were in good hands.

After our press conference, Jason Kessler was up on Facebook Live within an hour. He was broadcasting from the roof of our parking deck on Market Street, pacing edgily, gesticulating angrily, proclaiming defiantly that he would hold the rally in Emancipation Park anyway, that the city couldn't stop him. He seemed more shrill than usual and a little desperate.

As predicted, he was also saying he was going to sue the city. To the extent I had allowed myself a smidgen of optimism in thinking he might actually follow the city's plan, my heart sank. In terms of litigation, we would now be on our own, because we'd run out of money for Boies Schiller. The city manager had already told me he was very worried about our City Attorney's Office being overwhelmed. In fact, when Governor McAuliffe had asked me a few days previously how he could help, I had specifically cited the need for extra legal help. He had promised to have his counsel get back to me, but I hadn't heard from him yet.

Late that night, I methodically analyzed every possible scenario. The best case would be that the bulk of Kessler's supporters would go to McIntire Park, with the counterprotesters following them there. The next-best outcome would be that our strategy would divide and confuse them, causing Kessler's event to lose legitimacy, with some supporters going to Emancipation Park and some to McIntire Park. In this scenario, fewer people might actually come because of the confusion that was being sowed. The park would not become overwhelmed with people, and we could claim credit for reducing the size of the rally. In that scenario, the protesters and counterprotesters would be spread thin, and the police would not have to disband the rally.

However, there was also another possible scenario where a large but not huge number of people would go to Emancipation Park, and the police would arrest a couple dozen alt-right demonstrators and counterprotesters, but the rally would not be stopped through the unlawful assembly mechanism. The city would end up getting credit for a day that exceeded expectations, even if it wasn't pleasant.

Finally, I got to the worst scenario, where Kessler would get everyone in his protest to go to Emancipation Park, and the police would not even allow the rally to proceed. The police would be forced to arrest perhaps a hundred people. If that happened, Kessler could become a cause célèbre, and the city would look painfully inept for not being able to stop the rally.

MEANWHILE, I WAS STILL TRYING TO GET UVA ON THE SAME PAGE as the city council. I had tried several times to get higher-ups there to help pitch in for fees for the professional PR firm, and thereby join the stakeholder circle planning the city's broader crisis response. But they again said no—again, trying to hold our chaotic city at arm's length.

At the same time, I learned that the eminent Harvard philosophy professor and social critic and activist Cornel West was coming to the city to lead an early morning prayer service on Saturday. West had been one of my professors at Princeton. He had been incredibly helpful to me in one meeting in particular at a time when I was grappling with whether to pursue a PhD in political theory, giving me trenchant advice on the strengths and weaknesses of the field. When I called him about the rally, I gave him the best background information I could about what had brought us to this point in Charlottesville. He was friendly, curious, and sympathetic about what he was walking into.

Maurice Jones had agreed to my request that he talk with the Community Relations Service of the US Department of Justice about our strategy for after the rally. I'd been referred to this little-known federal department by an academic center focused on counseling post-conflict cities. The Community Relations Service had been in operation for decades under the Civil Rights Act. Its staff had worked in places like Baltimore and Ferguson, Missouri, after the unrest in those cities, and they were supposed to be experts at designing strategies for community reconciliation. If we had a secret weapon in our pocket for after Unite the Right, I was hoping they were it.

Then, the lit match I'd been fearing appeared in my inbox.

ON TUESDAY, AUGUST 8, THE DAY AFTER THE PRESS CONFERENCE announcing the decision on Kessler's permit, I received an email from the Virginia ACLU and the Rutherford Institute demanding a retraction of Jones's decision by noon the next day. The letter intimated, not very subtly, that if we did not comply, they would sue us on Kessler's behalf. The letter claimed the relocation showed a "callous disrespect for the rights of free speech and assembly." It said the decision was "an attempt to undermine the ability of demonstrators to effectively communicate their message." It asserted that the focus on crowd size was just a "pretext for silencing the 'Unite the Right' demonstration." The email also stated that a concern about violence from the counterprotesters—the concern we'd heard so loud and clear in the briefing from the Virginia state troopers—would constitute an "unconstitutional 'hecklers' veto." It concluded: "At the very least, the City must explain in more than just generalities its reasons for concluding that the demonstration cannot safely be held in Emancipation Park."

Without the help of the police in providing that proof, we were headed to court.

There was some good news, however. Several downtown businesses were already working with a local law firm on a brief in support of the city's position. Meanwhile, the city manager told me about his conversation with the DOJ's Community Relations Service, and it didn't sound like they had anything earthshaking up their sleeves. After the event, they would hold a community meeting and create a community stakeholder group. Fine.

We also talked for a bit about what would happen if and when an unlawful assembly was declared. I speculated that the alt-right might then go to McIntire Park after all, and suggested we should plan for that—effectively, a second wave of the event.

Meanwhile, on Wednesday, August 9, just as we headed to court, the US Department of Homeland Security (DHS) produced a stunning confidential memorandum.

THE MEMO WAS TITLED "DOMESTIC TERRORIST VIOLENCE AT Lawfully Permitted White Supremacist Rallies Likely to Continue."

Below this bold headline, in italic type that might as well have been screaming out for attention, the memo read:

> *This article highlights violent confrontations between probable an-*
> *archist extremists and probable white supremacist extremists, and*
> *identifies factors increasing the potential for violence. Our analysis*
> *is based primarily on our review of the six incidents since February*
> *2016 where both groups clashed at lawfully permitted white suprem-*
> *acist rallies. This article is intended to alert law enforcement to the*
> *potential for violence at future white supremacist rallies, including*
> *one planned for 12 August 2017 in Charlottesville, Virginia.*

The report went on to explain, "We assess that a heavily promoted white supremacist rally planned for 12 August 2017 in Charlottesville, Virginia, could be among the most violent to date." This judgment was "based on the planned attendance of numerous prominent white supremacists and on the growing importance of the location for white supremacist extremists and anarchist extremists since two white supremacist rallies were held there this year."[1]

The memo concluded with what seemed like a threat that was more specific, and more imminent, than everything so far that had fallen short of the "credible threat" standard: "Anarchist extremists and white supremacist extremists online are calling for supporters to be prepared for or to instigate violence at the 12 August rally. For instance, a probable white supremacist posted online a ' . . . call to arms . . . antifa must be destroyed,' according to DHS open source reporting."[2]

The memo put me in mind of a similar occurrence at a much higher level: the famous memo the CIA sent to the White House a month before 9/11, which was titled, "Bin Laden Determined to Strike In the U.S."[3] That was also ignored. The painful irony is that the August 9 memo was from one of the state-based fusion centers set up after 9/11 for the precise goal of combining intelligence resources among agencies, to ensure that we were not surprised again. Yet here we were, history repeating itself.

Here's the fact that still astounds me as I write these words: I *first saw* this report over six months later, in March 2018, after a journalist subpoenaed it.[4] The memo doesn't even appear in the independent investigation the city council commissioned (more on this later), which was provided to us in December 2017. During the week before the Unite the Right rally, we were starving for specific evidence of planned violence that would meet the Supreme Court's "credible threat" standard, as laid out by our police chief. We were also starving for *authority* that could help a small city win its case in court. Here was an effort that plainly was trying to give us both things, in no uncertain terms urging preemptive action from the state and local governments most directly affected.

It boggles the mind to think that the report was evidently not communicated through the right channels to be translated into effective action to stop the event. It is equally stunning to think that it was not introduced as evidence in the active court case to prove to the court that the event would be too dangerous for us to allow it to occur.

But that's what happened.

OUR OUTSIDE PR FIRM FINALLY ARRIVED AT OUR OFFICES, READY to help. Given the chaos that had followed the KKK event, I was excited to have experts helping the city. But a problem quickly developed. I learned from the PR people that the city's communications director was refusing to meet with them. The city would not include them in its plans for a "command center," where the most critical officials would be working together. When I confronted the communications director, she said that because the council had approved the $5,000 to get the firm on board, they were there only to help the council—not the staff, and not the city. She said that she and her team had sufficient expertise to handle a crisis and did not need, and would not accept, this outside help.

This was a perfect example of the crazy-making divide between elected officials and staff (which was about to get much worse). A staff member had unilaterally decided to defy a council decision regarding the city's communications strategy in a coming crisis and go her own way—and there was nothing the elected officials could do about it.

I wrote a frustrated email to Maurice Jones immediately afterward, saying that this was "tantamount to insubordination." I felt the council's decision to hire the firm had been a clear policy directive—we wanted professional crisis communications help. But Jones did not require the city staff to work with the PR team. In a day and age when we knew how hysteria could sweep across social media during civic unrest events, with a firestorm racing toward the city, we were not just unprepared. We were about to go dark.

THEN THERE WAS THE MATTER OF POSSIBLE VIOLENCE AGAINST Charlottesville's Jewish population. On Thursday, August 10, two days out from the rally, Rabbi Tom Gutherz called me regarding a worrisome email from Kathryn Mawyer, the synagogue's executive director, about the anti-Semitism in a lot of the alt-right's messaging. I swiftly typed out an email to the city manager, the chief of police, the deputy city manager, and the deputy chief of police, telling them that the synagogue would only have a single security guard outside on Friday night and during the day on Saturday. They would hold services as usual on Friday night and Saturday morning, and they were "obviously right next to Emancipation Park."

I referenced the intense anti-Semitic rhetoric on online sites. Posts on The Daily Stormer about the rally read, "Next stop: Charlottesville, VA. Final stop: Auschwitz," and, "The cops are siding with us over the evil Jew Mayor Michael Signer and his Negroid Deputy Wes Bellamy. We have it on good authority that the Chief of police is going to ensure that the protest goes through as planned, regardless of what the ruling kike/Negroid powers are attempting." I'd listened to a podcast the previous day with two of the Unite the Right organizers. They had referred sneeringly to Charlottesville's Jews, while noting the fact that the synagogue was "two blocks away" from the rally.

I wrote in my email, "Given all of these variables I feel it would be prudent for us to have a more overt police presence near [Congregation Beth Israel]. Rabbi Gutherz suggested a car stationed in front of the building, and an officer nearby, which is the customary practice during High Holidays services." I concluded by pleading for some action: "I would be grateful," I wrote, if the police department would connect with the temple's leadership.

The next morning, I received an email from a lieutenant in the police department offering to talk with the leadership of the synagogue.

But after that conversation occurred, I received an alarming email from the executive director of the synagogue. She had just spoken with the lieutenant and, "though he would like to be able to do so, has let me know that there is no way a CPD officer can be assigned at CBI." She wrote, "I expressed my fear that it only takes one troll with a molotov cocktail to burn down a building which has a history dating from 1882 and is the only synagogue in Central Virginia. He promised that he would make sure that the shift commanders through the weekend will be reminded of the presence of CBI so close to downtown and to the park, and would be encouraged to increase, as resources allow, patrol around CBI." She expressed sympathy with the "difficult circumstances" for first responders and law enforcement and stated the specific hours she still would like help.

She closed on a plaintive note: "I pray for safety for all who will be doing their best to keep order and peace over the coming weekend."

That night, the temple's congregants would remove two Holocaust-era Torahs from the CBI building to a safer place. On Saturday, after morning services, forty people would barricade themselves inside the synagogue while neo-Nazis paraded outside.[5] After the event, the city manager would explain that the city's security plan included measures to protect the area surrounding the synagogue, if not the synagogue itself, such as an officer on the corner of the block where the synagogue is located, snipers on a nearby rooftop, and Virginia State Police officers walking a route that passed the synagogue several times during the day.[6] However, the refusal to provide the car and dedicated officer would leave a wound that proved difficult to heal, especially after the swastikas came out.

I HAD MY FIRST, AND ONLY, FORMAL SECURITY BRIEFING. IT WAS run by the fire chief, Andrew Baxter. City Manager Jones and Chief Thomas from the police department were there as well. The meeting focused on emergency management and the contingency plans we had in the event of open violence, casualties, and deaths. Baxter told me there would be two different locations for personnel—the command center, which would be in the Wells Fargo building overlooking Emancipation

Park, and an emergency operations center, which would be a couple of miles away at UVA's Zehmer Hall.

On homeland security and emergency management policy, my understanding was that the best practice in council-manager governments was to have elected officials on the same page as administrative staff. I asked if I could be in the command center, as I had been during the KKK event.

They looked around at each other uncomfortably before Jones responded, "We'd prefer for you to be at the emergency operations center." I was taken aback. Given what was coming, it seemed urgent that we all be informed—staff and elected officials. I responded that I believed it was really important that I as the mayor be present, especially given the disastrous communications that had followed the KKK event. I said I would not interfere in any way. More uncomfortable look-arounds followed. Jones said, again, "We'd prefer for you to be at Zehmer Hall."

Giving up, I asked Chief Thomas what I could do, as the mayor, to help. "Stay out of my way," he said with a bemused grimace. There was more uncomfortable laughter.

The fire chief, Baxter, said they expected that an unlawful assembly would be declared, and that afterward, the protesters would disperse into the neighborhoods. Borrowing from his firefighter's lexicon, he said they would "be like brushfires throughout the city."

Meanwhile, on the heels of the Richard Spencer torch-lit rally in May, the KKK event in July, and the fracas and controversy surrounding the statues, the national media, and even the international media, knew they had a hit on their hands. Walking the Downtown Mall between meetings, I saw dozens of satellite trucks driving down our streets, parking alongside Market Street and Water Street. Reporters, producers, and photographers were booking hotel rooms by the week, restaurants were filling up, and there was a buzzy feeling in the air.

FRIDAY, AUGUST 11, BEGAN FOR ME WITH INTERVIEWS WITH THE *New York Times*, the *Huffington Post*, *USA Today*, and CNN. Katie Couric met me at the office for a documentary she was working on for National Geographic. She and her team had wanted to film in front of the statues, but I said I would only do the interview at the Daughters of Zion Cemetery. The council's $80,000 investment in the successful renovation was the story I wanted national voices like Couric to know—how we were *actually* changing the narrative. She walked around the cemetery with me and seemed genuinely moved by the low-intensity but profound story told by the renovated headstones that surrounded us and by the work we had done to stop the erosion around the cemetery's edges. I said that the African American men and women buried there were just as much founding fathers and mothers of Charlottesville as Thomas Jefferson, James Madison, and James Monroe. She nodded.

We held a press conference at 4:30 p.m. with Maurice Jones, Al Thomas, and Andrew Baxter. UVA had again chosen an arm's-length approach and was not there. A reporter called out a startling question: Would there be, as he had heard, a torch-lit procession that night? In an exchange that would be studied by investigators and journalists for months, Chief Thomas said he would like to know where that information came from. He didn't seem to know anything about it. And UVA was not there to confirm or deny the rumor.

Emily had gotten word earlier that day from faculty members in Showing Up for Racial Justice that something alarming was planned for that evening. Their decision to reach out to her stemmed from the ill-fated effort by the police to visit the homes of Antifa activists weeks earlier, and Antifa's subsequent decision to forswear communication with the police. So now, just when the far left most needed a line of communication to the city staff and the police, SURJ members were attempting to create a back-door channel to the government through the mayor's wife. She had quickly relayed their request to the police chief's assistant—what I'd been advised to do—but it seemed the information hadn't gotten through. Needless to say, this didn't bode well for how Antifa and the police would communicate on the day of the event.

A NERVOUS ENERGY WAS CRACKLING THROUGHOUT THE TOWN, like electricity before a lightning storm. We got reports of white supremacist flyers being distributed around the Downtown Mall via an email with an eerie subject line: "They're here." When I met Emily at home, she looked at me and said, "I'm not letting the boys sleep in our house."

I wanted to argue with her, to say she was exaggerating, that we hadn't seen any specific threats like the FBI had told us to watch out for back in May.

But there was a gravity in her words that shut me up. I knew she was right.

She'd already made arrangements. We packed everything up and headed out. We got the boys situated on a mattress on the floor at a friend's house in the Belmont neighborhood, about a mile away. They were happily bouncing around, unaware of potential danger.

We headed to the clergy prayer service featuring Cornel West at St. Paul's, a block from UVA's landmark Rotunda. We were searched before entering. It was crowded, and the feeling was edgy and defiant. I saw some friendly faces and got some hugs. The service was searing, full of prayer and anger and love. It's a measure of the paranoia we all felt that when I saw four young men with tattoos and overgrown beards, I worried they were alt-right members who had infiltrated the event and were planning violence. I texted my concern to the city manager and the police chief.

At about 8:30 p.m., I got word on my phone from our city attorney that we had just lost the case in federal court against the ACLU, the Rutherford Institute, and Jason Kessler. I felt deflated. Any hope, any connection with the power of the prayers in the room, the raised voices, the songs, the pageantry of defiance against hate, disappeared like the air from a punctured balloon. Reading the judge's decision in tiny print on my phone, I saw that it turned on the fact that the city had not also sought to move the counterprotests to McIntire Park—that we had moved Kessler alone proved, he said, that our decision was content-based.

Sitting there in the church, I wanted to howl in protest. Our outside attorneys had advised us to focus exclusively on crowd size. We had concentrated on Unite the Right because, from the social media chatter alone, *we knew there would be a large crowd there*. The city manager had specifically observed that there were RSVPs on Facebook in the mere dozens for a left-wing protest planned at a nearby park. We had excluded the counterprotests precisely because we knew there would be so few people there.

Another jolt came from my phone as I saw that Richard Spencer had put up a tweet aimed at me, crowing, "I told you we'd defeat you days ago. Why didn't you just give in?" That was exactly what I'd feared the most, and hated the most: giving these forces of darkness more legitimacy through the courts.

Emily and I went home so I could figure out a response to the court ruling. We left just before an anonymous male called the police, at 8:43 p.m., claiming to have an AR-15 and threatening to open fire inside the church in five minutes. The police put the church on lock-down. From home, I got word that the rumored torch rally was actually occurring. Online, I watched a horrific video of hundreds of people with tiki torches—clearly white supremacists—walking down the lawn at UVA. I called Pat Hogan, UVA's chief operations officer, and told him what I was watching. He said he was online and didn't see any violence. I told him to look at the *Daily Progress* website, as I was. He did so. He abruptly said that he was going to call UVA's chief of police. And then he was off the line.

I continued to watch events unfold with a growing sense of fury. I couldn't hear what they were saying, exactly, but learned later that these hundreds of torch-carrying white people were chanting, "You will not replace us! Jews will not replace us!" They were also chanting the Nazi slogan "Blood and soil." A group of students courageously linked arms around the Thomas Jefferson statue. They were assailed by the alt-right. There were brutal beatings. Pepper spray. A kindly, middle-aged UVA dean was thrown to the ground as he tried to defend the students. There were screams of terror and rage.

After what seemed a long time, the university police finally declared an unlawful assembly and dispersed everyone. I could not get the anguished cries of the traumatized students out of my head. I poured my anger and concern into a quickly drafted statement on Facebook:

I have seen tonight the images of torches on the Grounds of the University of Virginia. When I think of torches, I want to think of the Statue of Liberty. When I think of candlelight, I want to think of prayer vigils. Today, in 2017, we are instead seeing a cowardly parade of hatred, bigotry, racism, and intolerance march down the lawns of the architect of our Bill of Rights. Everyone has a right under the First Amendment to express their opinion peaceably, so here's mine: not only as the Mayor of Charlottesville, but as a UVA faculty member and alumnus, I am beyond disgusted by this unsanctioned and despicable display of visual intimidation on a college campus.

The night was just getting started.

A LITTLE WHILE LATER, I LOOKED DOWN AT MY PHONE TO SEE A text from UVA president Terry Sullivan. She said we should file a "motion for reconsideration based on new evidence." I called her and asked what she was talking about. She said that based on the violence, we could get the judge to reconsider his ruling. I called our city manager and left a message. I then called our city attorney. He sounded exhausted and dispirited. He didn't think he could get the case in front of a federal judge in time, as the rally was scheduled to begin at noon.

There was nothing else I could do on my own. It was 11:00 p.m. I could not require our attorney to call a judge at home. I could not direct that we file an emergency injunction with the court. However, maybe I could get the state involved, specifically the state attorney general. In Virginia, the attorney general represents all public agencies, including public universities like UVA, so perhaps they could get involved on behalf of the university. In short order, I called City Manager Jones and left a message describing Sullivan's request. I texted Governor McAuliffe:

> Terry Sullivan wants us to move for reconsideration based on new evidence because of what happened tonight. Can't happen thru our general counsel. Think maybe the AG could intervene thru uva. Need chops to get federal judge in a hearing tomorrow morning.

I did not hear back from McAuliffe. I called Attorney General Mark Herring and left a message about Sullivan's request. I then called the chief deputy attorney general, Cynthia Hudson—the number-two in the Office of the Attorney General. She picked up. She had seen the news of that night and was horrified. I asked if she could try and get the rally stopped, with UVA as her office's client.

She was interested in trying to help, but emphasized that she would need to talk with UVA first, as they would be her client, not the city. I then talked to Sullivan again, who said she would talk with Hudson. But she confessed she was losing her enthusiasm for the daunting approach. In the end, nothing came of this angle.

It already felt like we were under siege. I couldn't sleep. That night, I guessed there would be so much conflict that an unlawful assembly would be declared after about twenty minutes the next day, that there would then be some mayhem, and then a day of brushfires around the city, just as Baxter predicted. I feared there would be rioting. It would be a rough, stomach-churning day. The alt-right felt similar to ISIS, dedicated to spectacular, violent propaganda, striking where it was least expected and would make the most impact.

I feared our missteps were playing right into Spencer's strike zone—that the event had now been effectively set up for him and his ilk to achieve maximum impact, intimidation, and terror.

This was almost right. It just didn't predict that a terrorist would also weaponize a car.

It was strange to wake up that morning without the boys there. Early on Saturday morning, edgy from coffee and a bad night's sleep, I decided not to head to the emergency operations center at UVA's Zehmer Hall, the sole place where Maurice Jones and his team had said I could be. That was about two miles from the ground zero of Emancipation Park, and I just wasn't going there. I had repeatedly asked Al Thomas whether I could be accompanied by an officer to go onsite to the counterprotest, and he had repeatedly said he could not spare any. It was plainly not safe to go there on my own, so I went to my office at City Hall instead, just a couple of blocks from Emancipation Park. It was an odd feeling. Except for the two folks from the PR firm—who, like me, had been denied entry to the command center—I was alone.

As we sat there, hundreds of right-wing militia members were unloading from buses at McIntire Park and around downtown Charlottesville.

Others were parking their cars in the Market Street Parking Garage, which was located twenty feet from the Charlottesville Police Department's headquarters, adjacent to City Hall. They were dressed for battle. They had a variety of homemade shields and helmets as well as body armor. They had flagpoles they'd fashioned into weapons with extruding screws. There were signs and T-shirts featuring white power insignia. There were bright red "Make America Great Again" baseball caps. And there were weapons, hundreds of them, sidearms strapped to waists and AR-15s being openly brandished.

Meanwhile, hundreds of Antifa members and community members, whether progressives, Black Lives Matter members, or people from the Clergy Collective, had also made their way downtown. They were dressed in protest garb, with T-shirts and signs proclaiming allegiance to various progressive causes, and oftentimes profanity toward the alt-right. There were bandannas and tattoos, and also pepper spray, lighters, spray cans, and plastic bottles full of urine. There were "medics"—that is, counterprotesters volunteering as medics—ready with containers of milk to wash down the faces of anyone who was pepper-sprayed or tear-gassed. The members of a group called Redneck Revolt, headed by a liberal college professor from North Carolina, were dressed in fatigues and holding AR-15s. They were there, they said, to protect the city.

It was a warm, clear August day. Councilors were receiving updates via email from Maurice Jones about the increasing violence at the park. I called him to again request that I be in the command center. He said, tensely and tersely, that they were about to call an unlawful assembly.

At about 11:00 a.m., with the rally scheduled to begin at noon, I watched video of alt-right members bearing Confederate and neo-fascist flags beating up counterprotesters on Market Street, in open view of hundreds. It was nauseating. There was a degree of premeditation and monstrous bigotry that made it seem worse than even the average street riot, more like *Kristallnacht*. At 11:03 a.m., the ACLU of Virginia put up an alarming tweet: "Clash between protesters and counter protesters. Police say 'We'll not intervene until given command to do so.' #Charlottesville." This gave the decided impression that the police were refusing to stop the violence.

All hell was clearly about to break loose. The police were supposed to have provided clear lanes of entry for the rally attendees, but that plan had begun to fall apart when some protesters and counterprotesters parked in the same parking garage, mingling and conflicting even as they proceeded to Emancipation Park. Months later, Vegas Tenold, a journalist who had been embedded during the rally with the alt-right leader Matthew Heimbach and his Traditionalist Workers Party, told me the chaos had its roots in the prior night. According to Tenold, the faction calling itself the "hard right"—including the Traditionalist Workers Party, the League of the South, and the Hammerskins—clashed with Richard Spencer and Jason Kessler over their plans to hold the tiki torch march at UVA without a permit, fearing it could lead to arrests. The next morning, those groups decided to march to the rally separately from Spencer and Kessler. Heimbach said he tried to reach the police for advice on an alternative route to the park but could not get through. They parked in the lot on Market Street—where many counterprotesters were also parked—and walked to the rally on their own, mingling and clashing with counterprotesters along the way.[7]

That was just the start of the havoc. Around Emancipation Park, waves of hundreds of protesters and counterprotesters surged against and into each other before the rally could even start. Officers stood nearby, many behind barricades, not intervening. People were beaten with flagpoles and kicked in the street. There were screams and pepper spray. The volunteer medics rushed to alleviate the pain of pepper spray by pouring milk on people's faces. Residents came up to the police to scream at them in shock and agony. A shocked nation was glued to their television screens, watching the mayhem unfold.

The event, scheduled for noon, hadn't even begun yet. I was sitting at City Hall, in the same room I had converted into a working office nineteen months earlier. My inbox was being flooded with requests from representatives of the media and citizens who wanted to know what was happening. I had no answers. There was nothing happening at City Hall. I felt utterly cut off from the city's government. At 11:19 a.m., I sent Jones a text saying, "I need to come up at Wells Fargo. Won't be in the way but I need to be here." He responded, "I'm concerned about your safety getting here." Chaos was taking over in the streets, and our government was silent. At 11:40 a.m., I responded to Maurice Jones: "Al works for you. You have barred me from the center. We are not together. I don't know what's happening. We are not unified. We can't say no comment or it has to wait. I'm at city hall." Two minutes later, Jones responded, "It has to wait. We have to let this play out for a bit before going in front of the cameras."

Isolated from the nerve center, I felt unable to do my job as the city's titular leader and public face. I looked down at my desk, said, "Fuck it," and went over to the command center. The officer at the front called up to Jones, and after a pause, looked at me and said, "You can go up to the eighth floor." I knew nothing was on the eighth floor except a conference room. I was infuriated. I called Jones, and we had a tense exchange. I briefly lost my temper: he and the police chief worked for me (as a member of the council), I snapped, not the other way around. Twenty minutes later, he wrote, "Mr. Mayor, we are not disorganized. This is a hyper fluid situation. We need to let this play out. And the media can wait for an hour or so." I responded, "Elected officials like me can't [be] barred from necessary information and how to talk about it. That's disorganized. I'm headed to Zehmer [Hall] now."

I left and headed over to the emergency operations center at Zehmer Hall. When I arrived, it was a combination of placid and distracted. A conference room with cold cuts and snacks was to the left of the main door. To the right, down a hall, was a large room with a huge semicircular table. Our fire chief, Baxter, and various officials from Albemarle County and UVA were seated there, watching events unfold on laptops. A large screen in front of the room played different video streams, some sourced from social media.

Emily came and met me and the Powell Tate staff at Zehmer Hall. We sat in a small conference room down the hall from this larger room. The brushfires Baxter had predicted were already occurring, as dispersed militia disbanded to the Downtown Mall, McIntire Park, and other locations around the city. The city still hadn't put out a press release, even in the face of mounting public hysteria about what had happened that morning and what might happen later on. We monitored social media, the news feeds, and my own phone.

Richard Spencer and his followers had decamped to McIntire Park. "Little Mayor Signer—SEE-NER—how do you pronounce this little creep's name?" he asked the rowdy crowd. Some shouted out, "Jew, Jew, Jew, Jew," while others burst out in laughter. Spencer continued: "The idea that I'd ever back down to such a little creep like Mayor Signer. . . . They don't understand what's in my heart, they don't understand the 'alt-right.'"[8]

Just before 2:00 p.m., I received a forward of a Daily Stormer post that said, "It's time to torch these jewish monsters lets go 3 pm." I called Maurice Jones, texted Al Thomas, and texted Brian Moran, the state secretary of public safety, who replied, "Address?" When I sent it to him, he replied, "On it."

I then called Rabbi Tom Gutherz, who told me the congregation was okay. The building was empty. He thanked me for the call. I felt like weeping but could not.

Then, from the small conference room, I heard a cry of shock come from the large room. I rushed in, and someone told me, "There's been a car accident."

THE "CAR ACCIDENT" TURNED OUT TO BE AN ACT OF TERRORISM, but we didn't know that yet. Over the next agonizing hour, we learned that nineteen people had been hit on a lively street I knew intimately. I put up a tweet calling it an accident. I received a few angry messages saying that it was not an accident, it was intentional—it was terrorism. I could not wrap my mind around that possibility. Maybe the driver had had a seizure. Maybe he or she was elderly and had hit the accelerator accidentally. But then I was able to watch the video more carefully, and I saw how the driver had aimed at a crowd of counterprotesters, with their signs and banners and T-shirts for progressive causes. He then slammed his car into the crowd, methodically backed up the long street, and drove away, trying to escape.

We would soon learn that there had been one fatality: Heather Heyer, a thirty-two-year-old anti-racist activist who worked at a law firm in town, who had chosen to counterprotest with friends, while, ironically, avoiding the center of the action. She had been mowed to the ground and died at UVA Hospital soon after, before her mother, Susan Bro, could arrive.

Chaos and silence followed. The city still wasn't communicating. People were going crazy on social media, demanding to know what was happening, why we were silent. A colleague from the county looked at me, frantic. *"What are we doing?"* she gasped, in reference to our seeming inability to put up a tweet, send out a press release. "This is crazy!" "I know," I told her. "I can't believe it either." There were hourly meetings, run by Fire Chief Baxter. At the 3:00 p.m. meeting, our lead consultant from the PR firm, Emil Hill, spoke. "There needs to be a press conference," he said. "Today. Not tomorrow. It has to be today. Everyone should be represented there. The public needs to hear from us." We determined it should be the city manager, the police chief, and myself. Heads nodded. At last the public would hear from us.

Hill and I headed over to City Hall to press the request directly with the city manager. There was a sense that we needed to fight for this—that the city was so afraid of stepping out in front of the public that we might delay any statement at all until the next day, leaving a frantic public bereft and rudderless. Rumors were spreading that the dispersed white supremacists were lying in wait, and that they would be back that evening to terrorize the city again. If my position as mayor meant anything, I felt it should be to speak to the public now, when it mattered most, and let them know what had happened, what we were doing about it, and what they could expect next.

At 4:09 p.m., I sent Jones a text: "We are headed to command center now. Conclusion of principals and policy group was we needed to be onsite to develop message and framing. Obviously will need to be able to come in." He responded, "There is plenty of space in the 8th floor conference room." We got word that Governor McAuliffe was coming to town. He would obviously lead the press conference.

I met with Maurice Jones and Al Thomas in that conference room at about 4:45 p.m. Thomas did not want to be there. He was visibly frustrated to have been required to be at a meeting about a press conference. While we were sitting around the conference table, he looked down at his phone. His face went blank. Tersely, he said, "A helicopter has just gone down. I have to go." We found out later that two Virginia state troopers, Jay Cullen and Berke Bates, were killed in the crash. After Thomas left, we talked about messaging and the structure of the press conference a bit, and Jones left quickly, too.

Jones then sent the city councilors an update telling us that three arrests had been made. *Three arrests?* I thought. How was that even possible, when there had been near-riots in the street, when gangs had been assaulting each other, when hundreds of clear assaults had occurred in view of thousands of officers?

Of course, one of those arrests included James Alex Fields Jr., the young neo-Nazi who had driven his Dodge Challenger around a wooden sawhorse blocking Fourth Street, aimed his car at a group of counterprotesters gathered there, and sped across the Downtown Mall's pedestrian crossing, plowing into the people, tossing bodies in the air, and killing Heather Heyer. He had then backed up back across the Downtown Mall at a furious speed, turning back out onto Market Street, before fleeing under the eye of helicopters overhead. He was arrested on a neighborhood street minutes later.

RICHARD SPENCER, SHIRTLESS, HIS SKIN RED AND SPLOTCHY, PUT up a video from a room somewhere. Defiant and agitated, he bragged about being maced by the police. He crowed about the ACLU taking their side in the court battle earlier in the week. He said, "We are going to make Charlottesville the center of the universe. . . . Your head is going to spin." He taunted me and the city's leadership: "You looked like stupid little provincial tyrants who don't understand the law." He concluded: "This was a propaganda victory, a moral victory. I'm proud of everyone."

That afternoon, I also learned that, in making his first public comments about what had happened that day in Charlottesville, Donald Trump had condemned the "hatred, bigotry and violence on many sides," repeating "many sides." I watched the video on my phone, disgusted. How could he have *said* that? It didn't make any sense. I had been a target of the far left's anger and had been frustrated and bruised by the experience. But they were not the initiators here. They were not *at fault*. The people at fault were the neo-Nazis and white supremacists who had come to the city with brickbats, looking for a fight, who wanted to threaten, to intimidate, and even to murder. There was no equivalence. It was dastardly and dangerous, and I wanted to call it out.

The press conference with the governor was scheduled. There was a harried, ragged feel to all of the proceedings. The governor swept in with his entourage. We chatted briefly. I had inquired about the possibility of declaring a curfew that evening. We were advised by the city manager and city attorney that I would need to call an emergency meeting of the council after the press conference in order to do that. We couldn't call a curfew ourselves directly—yet another curlicue in our baroque form of government. We would have to pass an ordinance enabling the police chief to do it.

McAuliffe made a brief but powerful speech, telling the alt-right to "go home." He then introduced me. Here's what I said:

This is one of the world's truly great cities. We have been the home of a lot of history. We have overcome a lot in our democracy. We've overcome McCarthyism, we've overcome segregation. And we're going to overcome this. This tide of hatred and of intolerance and of bigotry that has come to us and that has marched down with torches the lawn of one of the founders of democracy. It is brought here by outsiders and by people who belong in the trash heap of history with these ideas. This day will not define us. We will define this day by the story that we continue to tell tomorrow, and the tomorrow after that, and the week after that and the year after that.

There is a very sad and regrettable coarseness in our politics that we've all seen too much of today. Our opponents have become our enemies. Debate has become intimidation. What democracy is about, and we know this here, because we're the birthplace of democracy. It's about deliberation, it's about action, it's about progress, it's about working together. And it's about, at the end of the day, if you disagree with somebody, you don't try to take them down, you agree to move forward. These folks do not want that. They do not agree with the rules of democracy. And they are on the losing side of history.

The work of rebuilding and of healing is just beginning today. Tomorrow will come, and we will emerge, I can promise you, stronger than ever.

I expressed two other thoughts that day. First, I told the Associated Press, "I'm not going to make any bones about it. I place the blame for a lot of what you're seeing in America today right at the doorstep of the White House and the people around the president."[9] On the same note, I told the *New York Times*, referring to Trump's inclusion of white nationalists in his political coalition, "I do hope that he looks himself in the mirror and thinks very deeply about who he consorted with during his campaign."[10] Second, I responded to a tweet from former attorney general Eric Holder, which had said, "If ISIS rammed a car into a crowd this would be labeled quickly & logically. Charlottesville—call it what it is—domestic terrorism." At 11:41 p.m., I tweeted, "It was domestic terrorism, General. Full-stop."

Immediately after the press conference, we announced an emergency session, cleared the chamber, and swiftly passed the measure to allow our police chief to declare a curfew. We had suffered a terrorist attack, and the curfew was designed to keep people in their homes so they would be safe. But the public would never hear about this decision. The city's email, through which we sent out press releases and corresponded with our clerk of council and communications director, had stopped working, because our computer system was under attack. At 7:49 p.m., Jones sent a text: "Mr. Mayor, the City's computer network is down right now. Best way to communicate is text or phone." Two days after August 12, Jones texted me that the city had "received a flood of hits in what we believe is an attack on the system so we took it down." The hacking would continue to be a problem for days.[11]

Meanwhile, we received a blizzard of media inquiries. By late Saturday night, I had been rapidly booked on *Meet the Press*, *Face the Nation*, *State of the Union*, and *The Today Show*.

I ASKED MAURICE JONES FOR HELP WITH TALKING POINTS. HE sent me back a few bullet points emphasizing that the police had done a good job. I knew I'd only have a few minutes to speak, and I didn't think it was the right time to get into the debate about policing. There were larger points I thought needed to be made—about tolerance and the diversity of Charlottesville; the resilience of American democracy; the dangers of Trump's winking and nodding to white nationalism; and the need to stand strong against extremism, hate, and terrorism.

When I was on my way to one of the TV studios, Trump's homeland security adviser in the White House, Tom Bossert, called me. He was friendly, complimentary, and sympathetic. He offered some bland gener-alities and said a call from the president might be forthcoming. Yet there was no call from Trump. My frustration and fury at his statements, and the aid and comfort that the modern Republican Party and the Trump campaign had given to forces previously unmentionable in American po-litical life, only grew.

On television that morning, I talked about how Charlottesville had become a target for white nationalist extremists precisely by being progressive and seeking to tell the whole truth about race. I described the car attack as domestic terrorism. I did my level best to defend the police, saying that we'd had the largest assembly of law enforcement in Virginia since 9/11. And I did my best to call out the dangers within Trumpism. Early that morning, the phrase "dance with the devil" had come into my head. Googling, I found the full saying: "When you dance with the devil, you don't change the devil, the devil changes you." On *Meet the Press*, I said we'd seen a "terrorist attack with a car used as a weapon," adding, "When you dance with the devil, the devil changes you. And I think they made a choice in that campaign, a very regrettable one, to really go to people's prejudices, to go to the gutter."[12] On *State of the Union*, in response to a question about why the prior day I'd placed blame "right at the doorstep of the White House," I said, "Well, look at the campaign he ran. I mean, look at the intentional courting both on the one hand of all these white suprem-acists, white nationalists, groups like that, anti-Semitic groups. And look on the other hand at the repeated failure to step up, condemn, denounce, silence, put to bed, all those different efforts, just like we saw yesterday."[13]

This early judgment was validated by an interview *The Atlantic* did months later with Richard Spencer, released in 2019 as part of an "oral history of Trump's bigotry." Here is Spencer in his own words: "There is no question that Charlottesville wouldn't have occurred without Trump. It really was because of his campaign and this new potential for a nationalist candidate who was resonating with the public in a very intense way. The alt-right found something in Trump. He changed the paradigm and made this kind of public presence of the alt-right possible."[14]

It seemed even then to be an open-and-shut case, and by now it is plain. Through ideas like the Muslim ban, or the wall with Mexico, and through its embrace of the neo-Confederate cause, Trumpism has openly stoked the fears of many in white America of threats posed by "others"—whether African Americans, Muslims, or immigrants. When the former KKK grand wizard David Duke embraced Trump during the presidential campaign, Trump refused to condemn him, sending a strong signal that Duke and his followers were welcome in his coalition.[15] In the process, Trumpism opened the door for the alt-right's violent white nationalism.

By that Sunday afternoon, the *Washington Post* had put an article online with the headline (alluding to my response on *State of the Union*): "'Look at the Campaign He Ran': Charlottesville Mayor Is Becoming One of Trump's Strongest Critics."[16] I couldn't help but think that my strong condemnation of Trumpism was linked to a phenomenon that started that same day. I started to see bizarre Twitter traffic with the apparent aim of character assassination—toward me. A parody account named @RepStevenSmith, purporting to belong to a (fictitious) Republican representative of Georgia's 15th congressional district, put up this tweet, at 12:07 p.m. on August 13: "#Charlottesville Mayor who wanted electoral college coup against Trump allowed Antifa and KKK to walk right into each other—no police."

Then there were vile, psychologically insidious messages like this one from a "Brian Riley":

> It's a goddamn shame that you and your ugly fucking wife and kids were not ran the fuck over you motherfucking socialist cunt. You allowed the police to stand back and that permitted the niggers and white socialist CUCKS to begin the battle. 90 million armed citizens against your socialist limp wrristed Twink cocksucking party. . . . The king nigger started this. We will finish it. Buckle your faggot ass up. It's coming. Allow the sand Niggers to overrun your cesspool city. I'm sure your nasty fucking wife will enjoy being raped and left for dead. Fucking rot.

These were the first licks of flame in an act of arson directed squarely at me and my family.

WHITE SATELLITE TRUCKS WERE CAMPED OUT ALONG THE DOWN-town Mall, reporters hanging out around the spidery structures of TV lights and cameras, thick black television cables sprawling across the mall like snakes. The next day, August 14, I was on *Morning Joe, New Day, Anderson Cooper 360,* and *The Rachel Maddow Show.* It was an adrenaline-fueled blur. I continued responding to questions about the policing by saying we had "set the conditions for peaceable assembly," repeatedly employing a statistic from Fire Chief Baxter, who had said that we had "the largest assembly of emergency responders since 9/11." As much as possible, I pivoted back to Charlottesville—that it was, and would continue to be, an amazing city (with the hosts usually agreeing it was).

But we started seeing shocking video of several white men brutally beating a young black man in the Market Street Parking Garage, which was just a few paces from the Charlottesville Police Department's head-quarters. The video was hard to look at, or to accept. It seemed that abom-inable abuses had taken place in the center of Charlottesville, right under the noses of the police.

I did not realize that in talking about the greatness of Charlottesville and in defending the police, I would be exposing myself to more attacks as the true impact of the policing failures would set in.

I WAS ONLY A PART-TIME MAYOR, AND MUCH OF WHAT I DID FELL into a gray area between what I had to do—my actual prescribed duties—and what I felt compelled to do as the figurehead of the city. I had always been more active than many "weak" mayors of small cities, and now the days became a blur. On Monday, as hard as I tried, I couldn't rip my thoughts away from the churn of the city to concentrate on negotiating contracts or looking over leases. As I began to field hundreds of calls, emails, requests, and demands, I realized I would not be able to perform the most basic duties of my day job as the general counsel of a technology firm. On Tuesday, I was on the phone for nine straight hours, including an hour trying to figure out what our tourism strategy would be. I called my boss and said I would need the rest of the week off, and he readily agreed.

The news from the Trump White House continued. In protest of his comments on the day of the rally, several national leaders had resigned from advisory councils on the arts and business. On Tuesday, August 15, Trump held a press conference, apparently intended to walk back his Saturday remarks, but instead he did the opposite, repeatedly expressing sympathy with neo-Confederates. Interrupting a reporter to describe the Unite the Right attendees, he said:

> Excuse me, they didn't put themselves down as neo-Nazis, and you had some very bad people in that group. But you also had people that were very fine people on both sides. You had people in that group—excuse me, excuse me. I saw the same pictures as you did. You had people in that group that were there to protest the taking down, of to them, a very, very important statue and the renaming of a park from Robert E. Lee to another name.[17]

Trump would repeat this canard in April 2019, when former vice president Joe Biden launched his campaign for president with a video focused on Trump's "both sides" comment. Trump said, "I was talking about people that went because they felt very strongly about the monument to Robert E. Lee, a great general."[18]

But this was false. While Confederate history enthusiasts had certainly played a role in the early stages of the Charlottesville story—

for instance, the "flaggers" who had protested at the press conference Wes Bellamy and Kristin Szakos held at the Lee statue back in March 2016, or at the city council meetings since then—they had no role in the Unite the Right rally. August 11 and 12, 2017, were not events by, about, or for Confederate history enthusiasts. They were instead a coordinated invasion of the city by white nationalist paramilitary groups like the Pennsylvania Light Foot Militia, the New York Light Foot Militia, and the Three Percenters militia from Maryland. They had been trumpeted by The Daily Stormer, and they were built around a campaign of intimidation (those shouts of "Jews will not replace us"). And the turmoil had concluded with the terrorist attack by James Alex Fields Jr.

There was a silver lining in Trump's mangled response, however. In that same August 15 press conference, Trump was asked about Steve Bannon, a principal architect of Trump's strategy to include white nationalists in his political coalition, amid rumors he would be forced out of the White House as a result of the scandal over Trump's comments. Trump defended Bannon, saying, "He is a good man. He is not a racist—I can tell you that."[19] But he would fire Bannon just three days later in the wake of the renewed uproar stoked by the second press conference.

That week, I would appear on more national TV shows in the mornings and evenings from the Downtown Mall. I was virtually the only one taking on this role on behalf of the city. Our communications director was out of the office, the police chief was not returning calls, and the city manager seemed to be in a bunker. It was a lot of media, and a lot of stimulation for my ego, but it also felt perilous. There were too many representatives from the media in town, with too little to do. And the videos of shocking assaults on the street kept coming. Every day, the ceremonial mantle of the mayorship was growing at once lusher and heavier, like an ermine about to strangle me.

We then heard that both Governor McAuliffe and Lieutenant Governor Ralph Northam—who was running for governor—had changed their position on Charlottesville's statues. The mayor of Richmond, Levar Stoney, followed suit. I talked with Northam and was struck that he had moved beyond Governor McAuliffe's position—the standard one—of giving localities the right to decide what to do with their monuments.

Northam had said that all Confederate monuments should be moved to museums or battlefields.

In the wake of the terrorist attack, I admired the seriousness of his proposal. There was undeniable moral power—deontological force—in Northam's position. It was the same thing I'd seen in Mitch Landrieu's speech. But I also felt that his position was not really a serious path forward: it did not address how to resolve the state law, or the cost of taking down or moving statues, or the logistics and politics of where they could be put instead. It was yet another symbolic effort.

I felt torn about what to do, committed as I was to the advice we'd been given by the Blue Ribbon Commission.

That split feeling about the statues persisted as I went to the memorial service for Heather Heyer on Wednesday morning, August 16. Senator Tim Kaine came to my office with his wife, Anne Holton, as did Emily, and we all walked over together, a press entourage following us. At the impromptu memorial for Heather, we took in the flowers, chalk drawings, mementos, and burning candles. We all said prayers. When Heather's father spoke, he came back and sat by himself a few seats down from us. Emily looked at me and said she had to go to him, and she did, sitting next to him and embracing him, just one human to another. I moved next to her.

We then went back to my office and did an interview with Vice News. I shook hands with Elle Reeve, a reporter who had done an extraordinary report on the event. It had featured profound footage and interviews with the organizers, and her evident disgust in interviewing alt-right leaders like Christopher Cantwell had become a major part of the national narrative. The camera focused on a copy of my book *Demagogue: The Fight to Save Democracy from Its Worst Enemies* in my office, and Reeve asked me whether I thought Donald Trump was a demagogue. I said of course, and that an active democracy's job was to repudiate the demagogue with constitutionalism. This was the very idea of agonism, that democracy's victory over its own worst demons would only emerge through contestation, but that those muscles, when tested and tried and exercised, could outmatch the ancient foe.

Something clicked, hard. As I reflected on Susan Bro's call to magnify Heather's voice, as I considered the problem of demagoguery and the passions in light of what the alt-right thought they were doing in invading our city, and about how the statues had functioned during all of this, I realized that my position on the statues, and the Blue Ribbon Commission's position, was no longer tenable. The terrorist attack had changed everything. I resolved to support the removal of the statues from downtown Charlottesville.

That night there was a candlelight vigil at UVA. The provost had called me for advice a couple of days earlier, and I had talked him through how I thought they could avoid trolling by the alt-right. Don't publicize it much in advance. Have a few trusted students and faculty spread the word. Have a program planned out in advance. It went off beautifully. We were there with our boys, who were exhausted but enchanted by the candlelight. Thousands of students and community members, cradling the candles in paper holders, embraced each other and sang hymns and other songs. People were gracious and kind. It felt restorative and calming.

With the grace of that evening, I felt hopeful that, despite the slow-rolling disaster at the White House, the legacy of Charlottesville would be unity. Perhaps it could put an end to this horrific chapter of our history, where violent nationalists had been invited into a major political party.

LATER THAT EVENING, I PUT IN CALLS ABOUT MY POSITION ON THE statues to Lieutenant Governor Northam; our state senator, Creigh Deeds; and our state delegate, David Toscano. I talked with Governor McAuliffe the next morning, and then I worked frantically on a draft of a statement, which I sent around to the other councilors. In the statement, I recalled how Susan Bro had said, "Let's channel that anger not into hate but into righteous action." I said that the new developments now translated into a call to action on the statues. We had to do better at reconciling public safety and the First Amendment, I said, and we had to honor Heather's memory in the city.

I told the story of how I had realized at the memorial service that the meaning of the statues had been changed forever. It would never again be possible for the Lee and Jackson statues to only tell the story of what had happened here during the Civil War and Jim Crow eras. The meaning now, and forevermore, would be linked with August 12, 2017, and they would be a magnet for terrorism. With the terrorist attack, the monuments had been transformed from equestrian statues into lightning rods. We needed to deny the Nazis and the KKK and the alt-right "the twisted totem they seek."

I called for the removal of both the Lee and Jackson statues from downtown Charlottesville. I thanked Governor McAuliffe for his call for the General Assembly to act. And I went the additional step of requesting that he and the General Assembly come together in a special session so the legislature could swiftly change the existing law. Local governments should be able to determine the fates of the monuments within their borders.

On Friday morning, *The Atlantic* published an embargoed copy of the statement. After it was made public, several national television shows interviewed me. All in all, I felt like the statement was well received. I had not reckoned, however, on how controversial one item would be.

It turned out that Governor McAuliffe did not want to call a special session of the legislature to change the law. Admittedly, that would have created a huge headache for him, and the outcome would have been uncertain. His spokesperson put out a crisp rejection, saying, "The governor hopes the court will rule in the city's favor soon and encourages Mayor Signer to focus on that important litigation rather than a redundant emergency session." This was a political pirouette away from the issue most directly at hand, as the litigation was doomed to months, if not years, of further purgatory. But there was no sense in getting into a battle with the governor and his allies, so I accepted his position and stopped talking about a special session.

The next day, the *New York Times* published an op-ed I had drafted earlier that week at their request. In this piece, I argued for the thesis that had buoyed me all along: that extremism was a threat that had emerged from within democracy, but that democratic norms and institutions, reinvigorated for this new challenge, were equipped to deal with it. I called for action from our colleges and universities, our governments, our media, and our private sector, all critical institutions of a free republic. It was a public argument for agonism, for the productive, creative role of struggle in how democracy can realize our principles—for the notion that Charlottesville, wrenching and violent though it had been, would end up serving a higher purpose.

In other words, the agony we were undergoing would be a means to an end. But there was a problem: it wasn't done with us yet. It was only just getting started.

For as the public really started to digest the violence that had been enabled by the failure of the police to intervene in hundreds of assaults around town, as the horror of a car attack plowing across a pedestrian mall into a crowd of people mounted, the brushfire of accountability was about to burn up the town.

ACCOUNTABILITY HAS BEEN A DEMAND FOR GOVERNMENT FOR centuries. But there is a fundamental logical problem with the demand for accountability. We must account for mistakes with the benefit of hindsight—we will always know more after a disaster, by the very fact that it happened, than we did before it happened.[20] In other words, hindsight is 20/20, and we often have blurry vision when making the very decisions we later feel the need to account for.

We blame. We imagine decisions to have been easier than they were. We want to judge mistakes yesterday by what we know today. It's a human need. But it's not always what is good for us. It's not how we can actually move forward.

Reform advocates are particularly notorious for imagining that they can come up with solutions that could have been inserted into the mix before the disaster occurred. Scholars have argued that this fallacy can become a "source of problems and dysfunctions even greater than those they were designed to tackle."[21]

But this was all just academic for a public hungry for accountability. A new brushfire was racing toward us. At the time, it was almost impossible to parse what was happening, or when and how any one scandal became dominant. But much of the mayhem we were about to experience all went back to a false rumor.

In fact, the rumor became a conspiracy theory: that I had ordered the police to "stand down."

IT ALL STARTED WITH THE ACLU OF VIRGINIA'S TWEET ABOUT AN anonymous officer saying, "We'll not intervene until given command to do so." That tweet had a profound effect. As outrage over August 12 burned, a Fox News correspondent, Doug McKelway, reported:

> I know for a fact that we have heard from a senior law enforcement from another county nearby this one, nearby Albemarle County, who that says that some of his underlings who attended a briefing here conducted by the city of Charlottesville and the police department of Charlottesville and the Mayor's office of Charlottesville before Saturday morning's riot happened, that they were not to make arrests without the explicit approval of the Charlottesville Mayor.[22]

McKelway went on to say that Chief Thomas had rejected this assertion and said he would like to know which officer had said it. But I felt the report still left the impression that the "fact" McKelway was reporting was not only the officer's supposed report, but the "explicit approval" I supposedly could have given for any arrests. I knew all too well that the Charlottesville mayor has no role in arrests whatsoever.

But I watched, aghast, as the fake news metastasized. The next day, a site called Your News Wire cited McKelway's reporting in a story titled "Police: Charlottesville Was 'Inside Job' to Ignite Race War," which stated that I had "ordered police to stand down during the most chaotic and destructive period of the protests." The piece said I was a Democratic activist with ties to John Podesta and George Soros who was working with the "New World Order" to send crowds of "paid protestors and useful psychopaths" to "sour the mood of the nation and further divide us all." The piece included the following quote from a supposed Charlottesville police officer:

> We were ordered to bring the rival groups together. As soon as they were in contact with each other, we were told to stand down. It was outrageous. We weren't allowed to arrest anyone without asking the Mayor first. We weren't even allowed to stop the driver as he sped away. The event was being set up as far back as at least

May and it went like clockwork. We wanted to do our job and keep the peace. But these mother******s in charge really want to destroy America.[23]

Read that out loud to yourself. Does that even *sound* like a real officer speaking in a real officer's voice? No. It sounds like someone who wanted to *make up* a real officer *saying something outrageous on its face* that would then warp and twist and make the news. It sounds like a lot of trolling from bots. It sounds like a lot of the news that's manufactured by troll farms.

Your News Wire is published by Sean Adl-Tabatabai, a former MTV producer, and another man, Sinclair Treadway. The UK *Evening Standard* published a piece about Adl-Tabatabai marveling that "he actually seems to believe the stuff his site publishes—or at least, to relish its textures and its tremors, like a teenager who's got a little lost inside a role-playing game."[24] In 2018, the Poynter Institute published an article describing the site as one of the most popular fake news publishers in the world. It "regularly pumps out hoaxes and conspiracy theories." Its articles had been debunked least eighty times, and its posts fact-checked as false, through Facebook's fact-checking partnership, at least forty-five times. But at the time, its content was still available on Facebook.[25]

I started receiving hundreds of messages calling me a murderer. This is just one example:

> *To Whom It May Concern,*
>
> *Looking forward to Signer accomplices being CHARGED, TRIED AND CONVICTED for aiding and abetting the violent leftist terrorists. Racism is repugnant, but you cannot characterize a whole bunch of peaceful conservative protesters as racists just because a few racists showed up as well. The vicious attack by ANTIFA, BLM and other deluded thugs, not to mention deep state provocateurs, has been overlooked and covered up by the mainstream propaganda media.*

Your Mayor needs to APOLOGIZE on the national stage. Focusing on Trump would be a laughable ploy were it not too serious to laugh at, in the midst of deep state calls for his ouster or murder. So, it is past time for traitors to see justice. Now it seems your Mayor has joined their seditious ranks. Let's hope that justice will prevail and he will receive what is due. Let Signer know: Everyone who is not brainwashed by the propaganda mainstream media SEES WHAT IS HAPPENING. If our justice system were not totally broken, he and Soros and whomever else is involved would undergo Nuremburg like trials and hang as they should. One can hope.

Please push for his immediate ouster.

Sincerely,
A sickened onetime (long ago)
C-ville resident and UVA grad

There were hundreds more concise attacks on Twitter. "Teddy," using @TeddyFlorida, wrote: "#ArrestMayorSigner Mayor @MikeSigner told police to stand down, he's responsible for the death of Heather Heyer." "Deplorable Covfefe," using the handle @sparks1017, wrote: "Of course they did. Mayor Signer had them funnel the 2 groups to each other then STAND down. #ArrestMayorSigner @CvilleCityHall."

Later that next week, someone told me that the conspiracy theorist Alex Jones, founder of the website Infowars, had done a show about me. I only watched it months later. The video was later deleted from YouTube along with Jones's entire account, all in connection with a defamation lawsuit against him. However, a few remnants of it remain online in discussions about it. According to TruthOut.com, the piece was titled, "Confirmed: Mayor Ordered Police Stand Down/Caused Death in Charlottesville, VA."[26] In it, Jones said that "people playing in this whole white nationalist thing are morons." He expanded: "In my view, marching out there in the middle of this, you know you're going to give George Soros and the media the target they need. Especially in a Democratic-controlled city where police are going to stand down. And then you're going to be attacked, and then the media is going to say that you attacked." Later in the show, Jones said that I was responsible for the death of Heather Heyer—and that I should be given the death penalty for it.

It was surreal. Up to this point, although I had experienced it just a little in my position as mayor, I had mostly watched the insanity of social media conspiracy theories from afar. Now a full-on character assassination campaign was taking hold with me in its sights.

The theory was in that first Your News Wire piece: The first video of the attack that went viral had been filmed by a guy named Brennan Gilmore, who had served as former congressman Tom Perriello's (D-VA) chief of staff. That much was true. Gilmore was also a casual friend of mine through Perriello. Perriello and I had both worked at the Center for American Progress (though not at the same time), which received funding from the left-wing financier and philanthropist George Soros. So the conspiracy theory was that all three of us had therefore conspired, with Soros's money, in a scheme to lure the far right to Charlottesville, so they could be beat up by far-left protesters, who were actually Jewish actors we had hired with Soros's money.

I watched as this madness spread further. I was gobsmacked when I was asked live and on prime-time national television about the "stand-down" idea. This happened with Anderson Cooper of CNN and Chuck Todd of NBC News. Each time, I gave the simple truth: in our form of government, I couldn't have ordered a stand-down if I'd wanted to. But in the brutal new might-make-right ecosystem where sensational lies could dominate the public consciousness by their sheer muscle (an art obviously perfected by Donald Trump), I felt that I was shouting into the wind. I knew the truth would ultimately win out. But I also felt like the gears of rumor and the passions and the quest for immediate accountability were spinning wildly out of control while the large gear of rationality was lagging lazily behind.

There was a second problem as well: the horrifying video of the brutal beating of the young black man in the Market Street Parking

Garage. It went viral, and horrifically, it was not fake news: it had actually happened.

DeAndre Harris had received severe head lacerations requiring stitches, as well as a broken arm and a spinal injury. The viciousness of the attack in the video transfixed the nation. One activist, Shaun King, launched a national online crusade to find and punish the assailants. On August 18, he sent out an email stating that he had found one of the men who beat Harris. This man, he said, was in Marietta, Georgia—but the Charlottesville police had not issued an arrest warrant. "Police still refuse to move," he wrote. "It makes no sense. With each day that passes, they are literally teaching the nation that Nazis and white supremacists can violently assault a man without consequence. You and I both know that if the roles were reversed, and black men were mauling a white man like this, heads would roll."

He continued: "We need you to contact the powers that be. Forward them this email. Give them the evidence. Ask them why they have not moved on this case yet." He explicitly asked people to contact me, the mayor.

I began receiving hundreds of outraged emails from people around the country demanding that we lock up and prosecute the white men who had savagely beaten and kicked Harris in the Market Street Garage. One person wrote: "Mayor, Why no arrest made of the identified criminal who brutally beat DeAndre Harris? Is it because DeAndre Harris is not a relative of yours, or maybe you thought he deserved it. Continuing to let this crime go unpunished is letting the racist know that they have friends in your office. This is a Shame and a Disgrace to Real Americans. God is Looking."

In Charlottesville, we had added a half-time position to help with administrative overhead, but that meant we still only had one and a half staff members. It was simply impossible to respond to these emails; it wasn't even possible to acknowledge them. They just landed in my inbox, like soft, rotten tomatoes. I plaintively informed King by a Twitter message that Charlottesville had a separately elected commonwealth's attorney who served as the prosecutor, and that the city council had no power over the investigation or prosecution. He promptly acknowledged the response and thanked me for the information. But that didn't stop hundreds of angry people from lashing out via social media and email.

Meanwhile, based on a report by one of his assailants, Harris was himself investigated by the Charlottesville Police Department and charged with misdemeanor assault by the commonwealth's attorney. He was ultimately acquitted of the charge, but not before these events set off another chain reaction of outrage from activists, which again landed in my inbox.

Then there was a third problem: a looming economic catastrophe.

DAYS AFTER UNITE THE RIGHT, I WAS ALREADY HEARING THAT downtown businesses had suffered a crushing decline in revenue. So little business was coming in the doors that several restaurants had maxed out their lines of credit to pay their staffs. The Virginia Tourism Corporation volunteered to help. We had also received a pro bono offer from a large international PR firm, which had sent two lead staffers to Charlottesville to help.

Following the famous "Virginia is for Lovers" slogan pioneered decades earlier, an enormous "LOVE" sign had been erected on the Downtown Mall. But that was all, so far. The week after Unite the Right, I would schedule a meeting with the Virginia Tourism Corporation to discuss an expanded "Cville Stands with Love" campaign. City Manager Maurice Jones, Wes Bellamy, and several other community leaders were there. I had brainstormed a strategy that would focus on reconciliation and rebuilding, and the PR firm had come in with a mockup for a new brand for the city—"CvilleStandsforLove."

But the meeting declined quickly. Bellamy attacked the idea of love, saying that equity needed to be the city's focus. It was confusing—why could we not do both? But Bellamy argued that we could not pursue unity and equity at the same time, because they were in conflict. We ended the meeting with no clear steps forward. The international PR firm, dismayed by their client's disarray, terminated their pro bono engagement with us the next day. We were on our own, with no message to offer our public, no strategy for our ailing businesses, and no narrative for a nation and a world that now, when they Googled "Charlottesville," would see images of bloodied neo-Nazis in helmets and shields, swinging flagpoles and clubs on our supposedly bucolic streets.

And that was not all. The fourth and final problem racing toward us was the need for an investigation into just what had happened to make things go so wrong.

ON SUNDAY, AUGUST 13, THE DAY AFTER UNITE THE RIGHT, TIM Heaphy, the former United States Attorney for the Western District of Virginia, had emailed me and Maurice Jones suggesting an independent investigation into what had happened. Heaphy was now a partner at the law firm of Hunton & Williams. I knew him well through Democratic and social circles and liked him. But I was concerned about having a law firm do the investigation, for several reasons. First, it could be expensive. Second, it could be, by default, attorney-client privileged. Third, it would be interpreted only through the narrow lens of a few lawyers rather than citizen leaders.

I thought a blue ribbon commission could instead investigate what had gone wrong. On August 18, I texted Maurice Jones suggesting that such a commission would be "far better and a great pivot and reframe." As members, I suggested former mayor Alvin Edwards, former UVA president John T. Casteen III, UVA law professor and Black Lives Matter member Anne Coughlin, and former Virginia Supreme Court chief justice John Henry Thomas. And that Heaphy could be the outside counsel. I received no response.

I mentioned the idea again in a phone call. I mentioned it to my colleagues, who were generally supportive. The idea got no traction and died. It was difficult to get any consensus from city councilors, let alone staff, on how to proceed. But we needed to move ahead. This was the only offer we had, and so it was the only one we would ultimately accept. We would end up repeating the same problem we had with our City Attorney's Office, but now, we would be hiring a law firm that would have several clients: the city manager, the city attorney, and the city council. The final report, when it ultimately emerged, would reflect that problematic arrangement.

ON TOP OF THOSE FOUR MAJOR PROBLEMS, SURFACING JUST during the first week after the rally, I was experiencing a witches' brew of anxiety and stress. I was receiving a blizzard of emails, Twitter messages, and old-fashioned letters, a combination of praise and hatred. I found myself tossing and turning in this cyclone of uplift and downdraft.

One day, a package of hole-punched, hand-cut doves bearing hand-written messages of support to Charlottesville arrived, threaded together with a slender purple ribbon. It was from Temple Beth-El Mekor Chayim in Cranford, New Jersey. The folded note said, "We hope that [the doves] are a source of comfort in the midst of ugliness. May your community find healing and a way forward. I can't imagine the personal toll this has taken on you and I hope you too find healing." I also received over a hundred supportive postcards from around the country. One, from Battleboro, Vermont, read simply, "Keep the faith. We have weathered many storms and know that love wins over hate." It was signed, "Local Love Brigade."

One woman sent me a package with a 1961 hardcover copy of John F. Kennedy's *Profiles in Courage* with a folded, handwritten note taped to the outside: "I would be hard pressed to find any one more deserving of this book than you. You epitomize what a true American speaks like and act [sic] like. Thank you for standing up what [sic] you and true Americans believe in. Stay strong." Emily and I were moved to tears and clung to the book like an amulet.

But there were all the other messages as well, which seemed designed, like implements of torture, to hurt as much as possible.

ON AUGUST 13, ON FACEBOOK: "CONGRATS ON YESTERDAY. IF YOU had not violated the 1st amendment and forcibly shut down a lawful event all the violence and loss of life would never have happened. You will be investigated for this and I truly hope you are convicted qnd [sic] locked up." On August 15, again on Facebook: "Don't blame President Trump . . . you're at fault here and I blame YOU for the death and chaos in C'ville." On August 17, Facebook: "Mayor Signer, you should be in prison. You have blood on your hands, and you are a murderer. . . . You may not like the ideology of the group that LEGALLY obtained a permit to demonstrate. . . . [S]ince no order was being established, Antifa and BLM who are hate groups were permitted to attack the people that were there to demonstrate peacefully. YOU HAVE BLOOD ON YOUR HANDS. YOU ARE RESPONSIBLE FOR THE DEATH OF THAT WOMAN."

SIX DAYS AFTER THE RALLY, WE WENT TO SERVICES AT CONGREGA-tion Beth Israel with the boys. As I was holding one of them and listening to the music, the horror of it all started to sink in. I quietly wept almost all the way through. It was amid this storm of high and low emotions, of intense hope and entangling fear, that I felt the need to play a cheer-leader role for the city. At City Hall, a member of the communications staff asked me if he could take a photo of me in front of the "LOVE" sign on the Downtown Mall for the city's Twitter feed. "Sure," I said. When we arrived at the sign, I decided it would be a good idea to try and inspire confidence through a physical embodiment of the "Cville stands for love" message by leaping up into the air in front of it while smiling. I sent the resulting picture out on Twitter with the message: "After a hard week, Cville is back on our feet, and we'll be stronger than ever. Love conquers hate! @virginiaisforlovers!"

I was trying my hardest—and too hard. The "leap" rang as tone-deaf to a city aching with trauma and unresolved calls for accountability. While it was a well-intentioned attempt to improve the city's damaged image for the outside world, I realized later why the picture was such a mistake inside the city. It was too much, too soon. We were still grieving. We were still seeking accountability. We were not, in fact, back on our feet yet.

BELLAMY AND I TALKED AROUND THIS TIME. HE SAID WE SHOULD do a town hall for residents to get their feelings off their chest; in the same meeting, the police could directly answer people's questions. Bel-lamy thought it was especially important to do this before the next city council meeting, and I completely agreed. I called Maurice Jones and asked for a town hall, saying that the vice-mayor and I wanted it. He said he would get back to me. Our staff seemed to have almost completely collapsed at this point. Our communications director was out of the office. Police Chief Thomas was not returning calls. Jones had been under unyielding pressure for weeks. The next council meeting would be on August 21, and as the days ticked by, I asked again and again about holding a town hall. It became achingly clear that it would not come together—that the boil of rage, infected and swelling fast, would not be lanced, and it would explode on August 21.

August 21 wasn't just the date of the next council meeting. It was also the day of a total solar eclipse that would be visible across the entire contiguous United States. At the appointed time, Emily and I gathered with friends on a deck overlooking the Downtown Mall with the Blue Ridge Mountains in the distance, solar glasses in hand. Masses of clouds were crowding the sky and threatening to obscure the eclipse, but at the last minute, through wisps of clouds, we were able to glimpse the moon overtaking the sun. To see light extinguished, even momentarily, and then return in blazing brilliance seemed fraught with meaning. Watching the knife-edge between darkness and illumination, I felt a commingled sense of foreboding and fascination.

That mood lingered as I walked into the crowded, raucous chambers that night. Little did I know that photos and videos from the meeting would soon literally travel around the world, ending up at the *New York Times*, CNN, and the *Washington Post*. I did not know that a "takeover" had been planned for days: someone took a photo of an image on Reddit with a graphic of a polar bear wearing a steel helmet that said "MAYOR SIGNER: READY FOR AUG 21 CITY COUNCIL MTG." An Instagram account named "memesofthehook" posted on August 22, "On Sunday we force Cowardly @mikeSigner to resign. #DefendCville."

What I did know, walking through the narrow aisle up to the dais, past angry sidelong glances and bristling signs, was that hundreds of restive citizens were in the audience. They were spilling into the aisles and into the hallways. The media was there, too, more cameras than I could count. The national media's satellite trucks were still parked on our streets, because many of the reporters had decided to stay for another week. They would approach random passersby on the Downtown Mall and ask for interviews at every chance they got.

I started our regular business with a statement about August 12. We had a moment of silence for Heather Heyer and the two state troopers who had died, Jay Cullen and Berke Bates. I read a statement about changing my position on the Lee and Jackson statues, and I reemphasized my call for Governor McAuliffe and the General Assembly to come together to enable local governments to determine the fate of Confederate monuments. I reiterated the urgent call for a change in state law to prevent either the open-carry or concealed-carry of firearms at an event of the sort we had seen the previous weekend.

I promised to work with my colleagues on the city council and on our staff to launch a comprehensive review of our permitting process. I hoped that such a review would result in real changes, maximizing the city's ability to prioritize public safety in such situations. I said we should be permitted to limit the size of events, and the "credible threat" legal standard needed to be updated in light of what had happened. Given the growth of extremism, we needed a new approach that could address the threat of the intentional creation of mayhem before it happened.

Returning to our continuing First Amendment dilemmas, I said we needed to refine our approach to account for the devious developments we were seeing among today's bigots and alt-right proponents. The alt-right protesters had often framed their provocations, the weapons they carried, and their uniforms as self-defense—but it became clear once they arrived that these were all preparations to draw others into conflict.

It had become crystal clear that government needed new tools under the First Amendment to protect the public from such intentional mayhem, I argued. The meaning of the Constitution has changed over time, and governments have always needed to strike a balance between free speech and public safety. In our review and in the actions to follow, I said we should consult with leading First Amendment scholars so that our new rules would meet the spirit of the Constitution.

I talked about how Heather Heyer had become a martyr in what Senator John McCain had recently described, referring to Charlottesville, as a battle "between our better angels and our worst demons." We needed to take concrete steps to memorialize her name and legacy. The launching of the Heal Charlottesville Fund, soliciting community donations, would be one step toward that goal.

I closed with thoughts on transparency and accountability regarding August 12, which many were now calling simply "A12" or "8/12."

Law enforcement would need time to investigate and prosecute crimes. We were in the process of forming an independent review of the planning, execution, and post-reporting process for the city's response to Unite the Right.

My ending was hopeful. Beckoning to the agonistic idea, I said that democracy itself was under attack on 8/12, but that we would get through this. The people who visited terror on us were using the mechanics of the Constitution—freedom of speech, freedom of assembly—to attack the soul of democracy, to set fire to the pillars of civility, deliberation, compromise, tolerance, and reconciliation that underwrite our system of government. Ultimately, I predicted their strategy would backfire. Our democracy had overcome "stress tests" like McCarthyism, and we would also overcome this wave of nihilism, beginning in places like Charlottesville's city council.

I urged everyone that night to "please, be civil, and please follow the rules."

But that was not to be.

PEOPLE THEN BEGAN SHOUTING, AND I EXPLAINED I WOULD HAVE to eject people from the meeting if they kept interrupting. I called several people to order. I said, "Look, we're going to have to remove you from the chamber." With one woman, I said, "Listen, listen, listen— ma'am, you've been called to order." I gave people one chance after they were called to order. They screamed some more. I pleaded, "What's the alternative, for everyone to just shout and scream?" Folks still shouted. I said, "But those aren't the rules." A well-known antagonist to the council continued screaming at us. I then asked the officers to remove her.

She allegedly resisted, while being aided by other protesters. The police officers on the scene then decided to arrest her and two other people. The officers physically removed them, while many in the crowd shouted and screamed.

Two people then took over the dais with a large banner that said, in huge black block letters, "BLOOD ON YOUR HANDS," decorated with dripping red handprints. I suspended the meeting, and we were escorted by police officers into the back room, where the city's media staff produced the video of council meetings running live on our public-access television station. A woman I didn't know was there as well, watching the scene unfold on a screen showing the live feed with both hands over her mouth. Maurice Jones was angry, which was unusual for him. "If they're going to behave like this," he snapped, "we're going to cancel the meeting." The police officers also thought we should cancel the meeting.

It was a hectic scene, but I felt strangely calm. I talked with each of the other councilors. Galvin, Szakos, and Fenwick all thought we should cancel the meeting; Bellamy argued for us to continue. I decided, at some tipping point, that the business of government needed to go on. Bellamy and I agreed that we would try and hold basically an impromptu public hearing with one minute given to each speaker. We returned to the dais, one by one.

The speakers were extremely agitated. One man said, "You let citizens get murdered. I knew that girl. You let her get murdered." There were loud chants from dozens of people saying, "Signer must go."

Emily was texting me frequently. She had gotten word separately from city staff in the room that the police were worried about our safety. They had advised there were ex-offenders in the room who could turn violent toward us at any moment. The dais was not bulletproofed; there was no barrier between us and the crowd, except for the particle board front of the desk.

An ex-convict with a tattooed face came up to the podium, wearing sunglasses. He took them off, then began shouting at me directly from behind the microphone: "I see that fucking smirk on your goddamned face. You ain't doing a motherfucking thing, it's going in one ear and out the other. I should know, I used to do that when I was a kid. But I got smart. What we need, you don't do. So if you want us to take over, then we will. Because we sure the fuck don't need you." He continued: "With that goddamned smirk on your face, you should go outside and kick yourself in your ass." Was this a threat? It *felt* like one.

With Emily's fears in mind, and our rules against threats, I told him, "That's a threat," and I said, "Colleagues, I'm canceling this meeting." The man began shouting from the crowd, "I grew up on the motherfucking streets." I protested, "We do have kids watching." I said we had a town hall meeting coming up on Thursday night. John Heyden, the conservative speaker who had appeared before, then spoke. He was repeatedly harassed after his speech with profanity. So many people were standing up and shouting that it seemed likely to me that the crowd could break into violence.

It seemed untenable. I said I was canceling the meeting, referring again and again to the town hall coming up on Thursday night. I said, plaintively, "We have rules." People were shouting at Wes Bellamy, and he was shouting back. I got up and walked out to find Emily, who had driven down to meet me. I walked quickly toward her, alone except for the three officers flanking me. They were acting as if I could be attacked from any angle. I found Emily sitting two blocks away in our Ford Escape, shaken. I learned from a friend that after I left, Bellamy had taken my seat in the center of the dais. As I comforted Emily, I also realized that I had to go back.

I walked back to City Hall as quickly as I could, entered from behind the dais, and tapped Bellamy on the shoulder. He first looked up at me with annoyance, then yielded the seat and returned to his. I sat down, but I asked Bellamy to run the public hearing. He had the emotional intelligence and the rapport with the crowd to manage it. He started with one minute for everyone, but after that collapsed, he—and the rest of us—just let everyone else talk.

During all of this, the city manager was silent, for the most part. Citizens rained their fury down on me—even though I didn't know the answers to most of their questions.

At one point, an agonized woman with long hair confronted me directly: "You led me down the primrose path that you were in a position to protect us," she charged. "My question, then, who is actually in charge of Charlottesville?" Trying to answer her question as best as I could in light of the handling of the rally, and the council-manager form of government making the city manager the CEO, I simply answered, "The city manager." She replied, "Then why is it so confusing? It shouldn't be this confusing!" I agreed with her. It *was* confusing. Technically, in our council-manager form of government, the council was "in charge" of the city, as we passed the policies the city manager was supposed to implement. He reported to us, we had hired him, and we could fire him.

But the city manager was the CEO; he, not council, had exclusive authority over every "operational" decision. He could order the police chief to design a new security plan. He could order a permit denied. He could fire staff members who failed in their jobs. Not us. This was especially the case in a crisis, where the minute-to-minute decisions—where to send forces, how to communicate with the public, what to tell the state police, were *all* operational. The city manager, and the staff reporting to him, *had* been in charge.

To make matters worse, the chief of police was still not present. Leading up to the meeting, I had asked City Manager Jones several times whether Chief Thomas would be there. He punted each time. That day, Jones said that Thomas had left town "for personal reasons." He was not at the meeting at the very time when we needed him most, when he could have answered questions that only he, presumably, could answer.

Very gradually, the venting started to turn into anguish, and then sadness, and then grieving, and finally we got to a stage in the meeting, late at night, where Jones was able to answer some questions. He explained how Dillon's Rule had so severely constrained the city from preventing firearms at the rally (because the state statute prohibited the city from doing so), and how the First Amendment had tied our hands in terms of stopping the event entirely. But he did not provide answers to the questions about why the police had not stopped the street fights.

We voted to shroud both statues in memory of Heather Heyer, and we agreed to then remove them. We talked about a thorough review of the permitting process. Toward the end, the meeting became productive, in a policy sense. But people would only remember the beginning.

It was a horrific experience emotionally, the most bruising of my time in public life. I was shaken to my core, but strangely, as awful as it was for everyone else to watch and to experience, I also was able to keep a sense of perspective. I thought that by comparison, almost anything that could come next would seem reasonable. And as awful as it had been, I believed that the agony could become part of a productive cycle for the city.

In the coming days, I said we were seeing the beginning of catharsis. I was intentionally using the ancient Greek term referring to the purging of repressed emotion. And I meant it. After the meeting, a neighborhood leader I knew a little, but not personally, sent me a note on Facebook: "Mike: I haven't agreed with everything you've done,—we're all human, right? I want you to know that what you saw tonight was the voice of pain. They were yelling at the title (Mayor) in front of your name—as well as many dynamics that have little to do with your worth as a person. Hang in there and keep doing good work."

Such sentiments helped. But that didn't mean it wouldn't get worse before it got better. The accountability brushfire was about to intensify.

On Tuesday, August 22, Wes Bellamy called me. I was at my day job, where we had an open office plan, so I retreated into a small cubby reserved for private conversations and asked him what was up. He said he thought both Maurice Jones and Al Thomas should be fired and asked me whether I agreed. I said, "Okay, wow." I asked him how he would address the fact that both officials were African American. He scoffed and said that if you screw up on the job, it shouldn't matter what race you are. I told him I would talk with Kathy Galvin the next day.

Considering Bellamy's words, I also thought about our form of government. Our charter had required the city manager to consult with the city council on the hiring of the police chief. But after his hiring, the city manager alone had authority to fire him. The city council could fire the city manager, but we'd need to be exceptionally careful to establish that he was being fired for cause. It seemed like the most prudent course would be to start with demanding accountability from the city manager for the police chief's obviously deficient security plan. Working late Tuesday night and Wednesday morning before the boys woke up, I drafted a letter to Maurice Jones asking for Al Thomas's resignation, detailing several pages' worth of problems and questions. I finished it just in time for a 10:00 a.m. meeting with Galvin and printed it out. When we met, I gave it to her and left her to read it.

I came back a few minutes later, and she said she was particularly shaken by a part describing the failure to meet the synagogue's requests. She said there were a couple of things she wanted to add to the list of problems, but she wasn't willing to ask for anyone's firing yet. She said she wanted a process instead—to go through the proper channels. Since Jones was the CEO of our government, she suggested having a personnel meeting where we would ask questions.

All prospects of swift accountability began dying with that word, "process." So that meant only Bellamy and I would support outright terminations. I doubted that Szakos would support telling Jones to fire Thomas. She had championed hiring Jones and had been his strongest political supporter on the council for years. Meanwhile, in the prior weeks, Fenwick had been publicly expressing staunch support for the police and Jones.

I reluctantly agreed to revise the letter as a memo asking for a meeting instead to demand answers (and, I hoped, accountability) for the government's obvious failures. It would include new information suggested by Galvin regarding threats that had been posed to low-income housing sites near the Downtown Mall. I then called Szakos. I was surprised when she largely agreed with the course Galvin had suggested. She used the word "hubris" to describe Thomas's approach. It sounded like she might want him to be terminated by Jones. But she, too, wanted a "process," and she requested that I add a couple of items of her own—including a reference to a long email she had written asking hard questions about why the police hadn't interfered in street fights. She said she had never gotten a response from the chief. Later, she would add some additional edits to the letter.

While I was still drafting the letter, Jones suddenly informed the council via email that he had directed the Parks and Recreation Department to shroud the two monuments. I headed over to Justice Park, and I discovered that the monuments had already been covered with a sort of plastic-looking black tarp. The shrouds looked awkward and ungainly. Others would say the covers looked like Hefty trash bags, and they did. I was swarmed by cameras and made some points about the need for catharsis and mourning and healing.

The next day, Thursday, August 24, was the date of our closed session. I woke up very early and saw my inbox and social media filled yet again with hysterical falsehoods about my directing a stand-down, along with more cites to "BLOOD ON YOUR HANDS." I was strung-out. We were to meet with Jones at 10:00 a.m. I had worked late into the night drafting a Facebook post that I hoped would at last provide a series of answers for a public crying out for information and accountability while rebutting, once and for all, the metastasizing falsehoods.

In the morning, I put the post up. It made a series of points, all at once. We needed accountability, I said, for a public crying out for answers. We had a city manager form of government, with roots in the Progressive era. The police chief reported to the city manager, who had operational authority over the city's response to rallies. The mayor and the council did not have an operational role.

I explained that we had not even been given the security plan for August 12. When I had asked what I could do to be helpful during my one and only security briefing on August 10, Chief Thomas had answered, "Stay out of my way." I had been refused entry to the command center during the firestorm despite repeated requests. As for the conspiracy theory that I had ordered a stand-down, I wrote that I couldn't have ordered one if I'd wanted to.

I said in the post how we'd worked hard on the council to relocate the event, spending dozens of hours conferring with lawyers, law professors, staff, other mayors, security professionals, and other experts to develop another option. I said we'd ultimately arrived at the "green field" option of McIntire Park. We'd hired an outside law firm to "advise the City Manager and Police Chief" on "how such a plan could be developed on the strongest legal grounds." Even then, however, I was concerned about saying what had really happened—that we'd actually overruled both Jones and Thomas on the issue of relocating Unite the Right to McIntire Park.

I explained that the city council had been under firm instructions not to speak about the rally at all, except to refer to its expected size. This was very frustrating for a public looking for condemnation of groups like the KKK and neo-Nazis. It had been frustrating for me, too. But I said that if we had spoken out against the content of the speech that was coming to Charlottesville—against its bigotry and hatred—it would have made it even more likely that a judge would have found the removal decision to be "content-based."

I explained that all of this was why we had called for an independent review of all the decisions that had been made—not only about August 12, but about the July 8 KKK rally and the prior torch-lit rally at Emancipation Park as well. This was also why the city council had deemed it necessary to hold an emergency closed session with the city manager: we would be discussing personnel matters. The events of August 12 had raised "serious questions about the City's handling of security, communications, and governance." Those were the questions the council needed to ask, I said, because we did have authority, in our form of government, over employment of the city manager. We were starting that process, I said, that very day.

I thought the public deserved to know what we were meeting about and the fact that we took their concerns seriously. But under the sway of that week's adrenaline and sleeplessness, fury and frustration, the demands for my resignation, the trolling, the fake news attack that I had issued a "stand-down" order, and the fears Emily and I had about our family's safety, I didn't realize just how big a target I was now putting on my back. Describing the search for accountability in a closed session regarding personnel matters on Facebook wasn't the best idea. In Virginia, such meetings are exempt from "open meeting" laws, and there is a general expectation that elected officials will keep those matters confidential—though no law formally bars a councilor from describing what happens in a closed session. (Indeed, I believe I owe a duty to the public and to history to recount the discussions we had in closed meetings.)

Nor did I realize the risk of associating myself so publicly with Bellamy's call for consequences for our professional staff. Although he would make that call privately with me, it was a banner he would swiftly drop once I took it up.

I REMEMBER PUTTING THE POST UP WITH SOME TREPIDATION, BUT some enthusiasm as well. In a week of staggering irrationality, at last I could start setting the record straight.

We settled into our seats in the closed session. Maurice Jones entered carrying a printed outline in his hands. He began by reading a prepared set of talking points explaining, but not critically analyzing, the two dozen questions from my memo, which he'd been given the day before. He had an answer, it seemed, for everything. I watched as Galvin retreated from any interest in demanding imminent accountability.

After his presentation, I pressed Jones hard on the central point: Why had the police not arrested more people? Why were people allowed to beat each other in the streets? He then recounted the concern he and the police shared about "images" of police using batons, or even weapons, against the violence. I gasped audibly before heatedly challenging him. How could our status quo—multiple black eyes for poor performance in the world press and pictures of so many bloody people—possibly be better than those "images," I demanded? Didn't someone have to be held accountable? He did not answer.

I then pressed him on the matter of the synagogue's unmet requests for an officer to be present. Jones said, "We're going to have to look more into that."

He did concede that there had been an utter breakdown in communications. He was unable to describe what the communications office had done over the past two weeks. And he intimated that the communications director I had accused of insubordination would be fired. But there was little more than that in terms of accountability.

He left the room so we could talk among ourselves. I was stunned. Bellamy led by asking whether we felt "that" deserved accountability. I loudly said, "*Yes!*" Fenwick said no. During the meeting, he had been with Jones all along, telling stories about being in fights when he was young and saying it was no big deal. Galvin was wishy-washy, looking down at the desk, essentially subtracting herself from the accountability equation. Szakos, who had played a major role in hiring Jones for the city manager position in the first place, had always been his strongest defender. Unsurprisingly, she did not support any discipline.

Depressed at where this was going, I asked our city attorney for the range of disciplinary actions available to us. He said it went from termination to a reprimand to other measures, including probation. Szakos piped up: "How about a letter of concern, with an improvement plan?" She emphasized that this would only be in his "personnel file." I sighed, reading the votes in the room, and agreed. Bellamy also appeared reluctant, also sighed, but said, "Okay."

I went back to work that day with a bad feeling. I had a meeting with a local attorney at the large law firm K&L Gates who had reached out to me a few weeks earlier to offer pro bono help on the city's First Amendment challenges. The meeting went great; I thought they could really help us with revising our permitting procedures to enhance public safety.

I came home. We made dinner. I read to the boys and put them bed. I was unaware of the storm about to hit.

THE NEXT MORNING, KATHY GALVIN CALLED ME. SHE COMPLAINED that my Facebook post had "damaged the reputations" of Maurice Jones and Al Thomas. Szakos called and demanded I put up an apology and retraction on Facebook, going so far as to send me language she thought I could use.[27] I then called Bellamy. He said I should talk to the others to figure out a way forward. He thought I should do the Facebook apology they were requesting.

Meanwhile, we learned that the memo to Jones we'd prepared for the meeting was in the hands of at least two reporters. I called and emailed Jones expressing my alarm and concern about what was apparently either a leak or a hack. I changed my council email password, as I knew we'd been under sustained cyberattacks since the rally.

I taught at UVA on Friday afternoons, and classes were just beginning for the new school year. I put together my final syllabus before racing over to the university. During a break in classes, I got a call from the editor of the local NBC station and a reporter about a story they were going to put up that night. The lead was that people were "questioning my fitness to be mayor."

Things were whipsawing. I asked Emily what she thought about it all. She said I was on the right side of history, that the stories to come were going to show how horribly things had been run. She thought we were going to have to endure a rough patch, but that it would get better. This broader perspective helped. I had to focus on what the struggle would ultimately produce. We picked up our boys. It was a beautiful day, not humid for once, and we walked with them up to the pizza shop, where we dropped them off with a sitter. We went to a service at the synagogue, where a singer named Judy Silver was visiting from Washington, DC. The lovely service was flowing and musical, with startlingly simple and pure moments about healing and listening. Dozens of people came up to me and embraced me and thanked me, most of them referencing my appearances on behalf of C'ville during the awful week. They were gracious, and it was healing.

While listening to the music, I considered whether I should resign in protest of the government's apparent unwillingness to hold anyone accountable for the mistakes of 8/12. Should I go public with the unbelievable admission from Jones in the closed-session meeting that people were allowed to beat each other up so that there weren't "images" of officers using batons and force? I fantasized that by resigning I could bring moral clarity to the situation. Perhaps it would shock people into a greater understanding of my actions and the entire situation.

But I also realized that I was now out on a limb alone.

THAT NIGHT, I WENT TO A SERVICE WITH THE CLERGY COLLECTIVE and the Reverend William Barber II, from the Moral Monday movement. I walked up to him and he embraced me—he was a bearish, magnetic man who walks with obvious difficulty from painful spine issues. He told me that the situation was like a cut where the infection had to be removed from the inside. He said he appreciated my focus on policy. I hugged him back and said we needed healing—especially within the government.

The next day, a devastating *Washington Post* piece appeared on the paper's front page. It described the entire event, revealing a clear dereliction of duty by the planners and attributing the catastrophe to negligence or worse.[28] The piece made crystal clear that I had no role in the events, explaining that I was "frantic" about the threat to the synagogue, but had been pushed away from the planning.

But could the truth matter?

SUNDAY, AUGUST 27, SIX DAYS AFTER THE "BLOOD ON YOUR HANDS" council meeting, was the day for the town hall meeting, which would be led by the Community Relations Service of the US Department of Justice (DOJ). That morning, I went with my mother-in-law, Stef, Emily, and our twin boys, dressed in their Sunday best, to the morning service at Ebenezer Baptist Church. It was a small, historic African American church in our neighborhood where I had many friends. I hadn't been sure what to expect. I was bruised from the prior two weeks and was so nervous about the town hall coming up that afternoon that my stomach was hurting.

After the opening prayer and songs, the pastor, Ken Edwards, saw me in the back row. He quieted the congregation and said, "Our mayor is here with us today." Heads turned to look at me with my boys and mother-in-law, standing in the back. I looked back. I didn't know what to say, or whether to say anything. After a pregnant pause, he said, "We love you. We stand by you." He asked me to come up to the front and say a few words. I walked up the aisle, my legs shaking, and looked out at the crowd. We had been through so much together. *They* had been through so much together.

I can't remember exactly what I said next, except I know it was on the theme of community and how we were stronger than hate. I had been there many times. I *knew* them, and they knew me. I thanked them for their compassion. My heart was overflowing. By the end, my cheeks were wet with tears. The pastor invited the entire congregation to come to the front and gather around me. As we held each other's hands and shoulders, we all prayed together.

My family watched from the back as I wept in the front, the pianist playing soft piano music in the background. Beams of light streamed through the old stained-glass windows. The love was a force so powerful I felt the room almost quaking with it.

THE TOWN HALL WAS SCHEDULED FOR 3:00 P.M. AT CHARLOTTES-ville High School. We spent some time in the early afternoon rallying supporters. In the event there were calls for my resignation, we planned on having dozens of vocal supporters shouting back. My mom, Marj, came from Arlington, my sister Mira from Richmond, my sister Becky from Falls Church. Dear friends called and said, in no uncertain terms, that they were going to drive us there.

The town hall was a mess. The DOJ facilitators seemed ill-prepared, like they were winging it. The staffer taking minutes on a projector kept falling behind and making mistakes. Commenters were allowed to go on too long, and there was no real moderation. Meanwhile, Maurice Jones was there with Al Thomas sitting right next to him—hardly an image for accountability. Instead, it seemed like the city's professional staff was circling its own wagons.

There were hundreds of people in the room. One young bearded man was holding a small, bright yellow sign to his chest: it read, "SIGNER RESIGN."

Only one clear point emerged through dozens of fractious comments: we needed to do more for poor people in the city. The attack had particularly wounded the underrepresented—white supremacy being wielded in such a violent way was experienced most violently by those with the least power. There was significant discussion about affordable housing. We were collectively lighting a fifth and final brushfire, a new drive for equity in a town that had previously avoided fuliminating more directly about the dark nexus between its own systemic racism and history of oppression, especially toward low-income African Americans, who had been disenfranchised for generations.

Of all the brushfires of our unique firestorm, I instinctively felt this one could be positive for the city. In the same sense that slash-and-burn agriculture can nurture charred soil with ash for new growth, talking about racism and inequity could lead to growth and change. But this brushfire, like the others, was unruly and eager for new tinder. On August 20, the day before the "Blood on Your Hands" council meeting, an article had appeared in *Salon* titled, satirically, "Charlottesville, 'Happiest City in America'—But for Whom?" The subtitle was: "When a city with a white supremacist presence and marginalized black working class is run by genteel 'progressives.'" The author quoted Tanesha Hudson, a local African American woman who frequently appeared at council meetings, often interrupting and shouting from the audience. "There's a rich set of people in the city and there's a poor set of people in the city," she said. "It took this rally and someone dying for people to be willing to talk about it."

The author cited the ACLU's critique of the city's litigation technique, asserting that it was white supremacy rather than the law or the facts that had led the city to lose the lawsuit against the ACLU. Because the statement I issued afterward stated that the city was disappointed with the ruling, but would comply with it, the article said I had "skirted away from condemning white supremacy." The author said that "moderation and gentility, which often characterizes a 'progressive' political stance . . . may be an insidious culprit in keeping poor people and people of color second-class citizens in Charlottesville."[29]

It felt horribly unfair, but I saw the appeal of that story. The politics of symbolism is seductive, and surface impressions are easier to comprehend than underlying complexity. The police had not intervened. The statues had not been removed. The city had not denied the permit. No other facts mattered—nothing that had been done or tried. It was all white supremacy. It was all a power structure defending itself and the corruptions of the ruling world.

Nothing made this symbolic story more vivid, and more seductive, than the general anguish about one thing in particular: accountability.

ACCOUNTABILITY IS AT ONCE SEDUCTIVE AND ELUSIVE. IN THE Book of Leviticus, a goat is sent into the wilderness after the Jewish chief priest symbolically lays "the sins of the people upon it."[30] The scapegoats that emerged for the events in Charlottesville provided an escape for others from the trauma and grief of what had happened. Governor McAuliffe, for instance, himself under the gun for the failures of the Virginia State Police, attempted to shift the blame to me and the city. That was evident when he told our local NBC affiliate, in December 2017, "I'm still outraged that [the rally] was put in Emancipation Park in the middle of downtown Charlottesville. I had called and told the Mayor way in advance you need to get this out of downtown."[31] In fact, it was I who had called the governor, just a few days after the KKK event, to ask him what he thought about moving the rally. He had responded that it was a good idea. I had asked him for legal help, citing our under-resourced counsel's office. I had followed up on that request the next week, and he had volunteered that his counsel could help us. On August 2—ten days before Unite the Right—I sent him a text wrapping all this together, pleading again for help. I wrote:

> Governor, our City Manager made the decision to relocate the rally. This will be announced Monday. Confidential till then. I did not hear from Carlos [Hopkins, the governor's counsel]. We are working with Boies Schiller but it's prohibitively expensive. $200k to litigate two levels (district court and appeal). We are agreeing to $30k as first cut for help with doctrine and advice. Doubt AG will involve himself in local govt representation. If you can provide help with litigation through your office or a pro bono of counsel firm of [sic] discounted VA firm who can work on 1st Amendment issues on short notice, that is one help we need. Thank you.

He had responded:

> OK. On it.

So how could he now be claiming to be "outraged" at me that the rally hadn't been relocated—when he himself had committed to helping us try and relocate it?

The answer was simple. He could not.

The blame game would continue in a short book McAuliffe published, *Beyond Charlottesville: Taking a Stand Against White Nationalism*, which took pains to state that "recommendations communicated by the state to the City of Charlottesville were not accepted, including industry best practices for handling violent events." The book spent several pages on the phone call he had made to me on August 1 that had felt so odd, including reprinting the "talking points" memo for the call in full. This was the call where he had requested we ban firearms from the event, which we could not do under Virginia law; the one where the letter containing the specific requests was never later sent, as promised; and the one immediately followed by a ninety-minute meeting with the three state troopers, who did not reference even one of the supposedly critical security requests. The book also contained a significant error about the city's permitting process. It called the permitting process "pathetic" and said that according to the city's rules, a permit would be automatically granted if it was not approved or rejected within ten days. The book stated, "Charlottesville authorities had boxed themselves into a corner and let Jason Kessler's permit be approved automatically, with no restrictions whatsoever. That should never have been allowed to happen. Next time would be different." But this is false. There was no "automatic" approval of the permit. In the months leading up to the rally, the city's permitting office had always deemed Jason Kessler's permit application to be "incomplete." The city never actually granted a permit to Kessler until August 7—the Monday before the Unite the Right rally—on the condition that the rally be held in McIntire Park, where the groups could be safely separated.[32]

But I, too, sometimes neglected the key accountability problem—the danger of forgetting that hindsight is often 20/20. I could also forget that in a crisis, it's just human beings who are trying to do their best, and that we should give them the benefit of the doubt, and learn from their mistakes, rather than crucify them for them. Yes, I blamed Maurice Jones for letting me hang out to dry during the "Blood on Your Hands" council meeting and for the lack of accountability so far. But I still viewed him as a kind, considerate, and caring man who had put years into the city. The experience had to be just as brutal for him and his family as it was for me and for the rest of us. He probably felt paralyzed. Al Thomas and I were friendly, and I liked him. To be sure, I was frustrated by his errors, and that they had splashed back on me. But did that justify loading the failures of the entire system onto his shoulders? I disagreed with many of Wes Bellamy's choices. But he was inarguably committed to racial and social justice, and he had been the target of vicious racist threats. I couldn't blame him for doubling down on his approach in the face of these assaults.

Terry McAuliffe was a personal friend of mine. He had attended our wedding party in Washington in 2012 by himself for two hours. After he was elected governor, I'd chaired his transition council on homeland security. He was a leader who had taken a clear stand against bigotry and extremism, but he was probably disconnected from the moment-to-moment policing decisions of the state police. He had been blindsided by mistakes in the face of a unique, once-in-a-generation invasion. I couldn't blame him for seeking to escape blame he felt he didn't deserve.

The fallacy in scapegoating is the certainty that whoever you are blaming could have done a better job than they did. We heap our anger and our scorn on them and expect them to carry it away. It's no surprise that we often have heroes at the same time we have scapegoats. But in our case, there was an imbalance on both sides of the scale. There were no easy scapegoats. And there were no heroes. What happened in Charlottesville was like what had happened in Portland and Berkeley, multiplied by a factor of ten. There were no easy and evident solutions, certainly no superheroes, for the godawful, miserable, unique situation in which we found ourselves.

And so when I was scapegoated, just as when I was scapegoating others, I could still see the ancient practice as bearable, given the trauma we'd been through. And it was nothing, really, compared to the cruel blows that had been delivered on the streets on August 11 and 12.

I RECEIVED WORD EARLY MONDAY MORNING, AUGUST 28, THAT Kathy Galvin had requested an emergency closed session of the city council to discuss "disciplinary matters." It would be at 2:00 p.m. that same day. I was not invited to the meeting, because it was me that the other councilors would be meeting to discuss "disciplining."

I blew off steam by drafting a speech where I told the facts exactly as I saw them, placed the blame where I thought it needed to go, demanding accountability in protest of a city where none of the right parties were taking responsibility, even resigning in protest. But I would never deliver it. Talking with old and trusted friends, I heard again and again that Charlottesville was bone-tired, to the breaking point, of fighting. Even if I was telling the truth—whistle-blowing even—could I put the public through such a spectacle, when the city was already so torn apart?

The issues we were experiencing were, I felt, about people and systems and choices we needed to make, both to provide accountability and to prevent a Unite the Right type of rally from ever happening again. They were not about politicians, and they were not about me. I could not take a path that would put me at the center of the drama to come— making *me* both protagonist and antagonist in a new public spectacle.

It would require my constituents, the media, and the other leaders of the city to focus yet more on me. To the trauma the city had already been through, I could not add a drama about whether their mayor was winning or losing.

So I decided to cast my lot with the crucible rather than try and escape it, to embrace the agony and work through to the other side, to fight through the fire. I knew it would be a difficult and costly choice. But as I planned for the meeting, I decided I would probably make the apology for the Facebook post my colleagues had demanded and trudge ahead as best as I could. I would contribute, in whatever way I could, to forging a new unity from the struggle we were experiencing.

I then received news of a startling development that threw more fuel into the red-hot center of the commingled brushfires of law, accountability, and order itself.

THE VIRGINIA MUNICIPAL LEAGUE (VML) PROVIDED THE CITY'S liability insurance. This nonprofit, nonpartisan organization assists city governments in various other realms as well, such as legislative advocacy and research. After my Facebook post, however, the insurance representatives had concerns. They spoke with our city attorney about my promise to provide a "thorough report in two sections," including a "comprehensive factual summary and legal analysis of relevant events." My statement had alarmed them. They wrote the city a letter saying that the VML "strongly recommends that the City rethink its position."

The problem was the insurance coverage. The VML warned that if officials, "through their public comments and actions, prejudice our ability to adequately defend the City," they would "have no choice but to take the extraordinary step of denying coverage to the City and to those individuals responsible for the prejudice." In other words: "City representatives should understand this exposes the City and personally exposes them to the costs associated with defending claims against them and paying any resulting damages awarded."

The VML also complained about any scenario in which the independent review—which would be prepared by the law firm of Hunton &

Williams—would be released to the public. After their phone call with our attorney, the VML reps wrote, they had been "assured this review would be protected by attorney client privilege."

The letter continued, "Should any city representative choose to hire their own counsel, that is entirely at their own expense and will not be paid for by VMLIP [VML Insurance Programs]."

Thus I was put in a virtual straitjacket: I was told in no uncertain terms not to say anything further about the failures that had occurred, lest I expose myself *personally* to the cost of defending claims.

AT THEIR CLOSED SESSION AMONG THEMSELVES ON MONDAY, THE other councilors had agreed to hold another closed session with me on Wednesday, where they would consider how to redress my decision to write the Facebook post criticizing Jones and Thomas. I spent most of the day on Tuesday talking to over a dozen former mayors and councilors, most of whom were appalled by the rush to somehow punish me for stating the obvious, and who volunteered to reach out to some of the other councilors to try and calm things down.

I went into the closed session feeling eerily composed. I sat at the head of the table at their request. Before the closed session began, TV cameras took a few photos. We then read the motion to go into closed session, the photographers filed out, and the doors closed. Kristin Szakos handed me a two-page memo in the distinctive, narrow font that Kathy Galvin often used in emails to her colleagues. It detailed over a dozen instances where I had "overstepped my bounds" as mayor. The threat was that my colleagues would go public with this list in connection with a censure or removal from office.

I looked down at the list and quickly skimmed it. It had obviously been cobbled together. Most of the items were petty or plain false. I was criticized for convening independent groups like the Mayor's Advisory Council on Innovation and Technology without the official permission of council, for holding monthly office hours, and for taking up too much of our clerk's time. I was charged with bringing in outside professionals with whom I had prior relationships (alluding to the PR firm and the law firms), which was false. I was accused of supposedly saying in a meeting that I was the "chief executive" of the government, which I never said. I was charged with putting out a press statement on city letterhead when I changed my position on the statues, which was something other mayors had done in circumstances not that different. I was accused of not seeking the advice of former mayors, which was patently false—in the prior year alone, I had repeatedly conferred with at least six former mayors; I just didn't talk or tweet about it.

These allegations were intended to establish a central offense: that the Facebook post was just a symptom of a broader problem. I had systematically exceeded the traditionally weak mayor role. This was, of course, an open secret. I *had* tried to expand the power of the office, openly so. I *had* pushed into the gray areas, asserting more authority than existed on paper. I hadn't been criticized for this much when I wasn't exposed politically. But now that I had gotten crossways to the city manager and the police chief, now that many were baying for blood in the wake of the scandal of the supposed "stand-down" of the police, my well-known approach to the office was fair game.

I thought it was a slapdash effort that I could easily dispute, both in part and as a whole. But sitting there, given the agony the city was already plainly going through, I could not imagine creating such a spectacle. I repeatedly urged the others to consider whether this was really the right focus at a time when the city needed us to come together and move forward. The former mayors I had talked to the day before had been uniform in their opinion: Why do this *now*? It bordered on insanity to turn on me at such a critical time. It would send a message of disunity and division just when our public most needed confidence and optimism from their elected officials.

At one point, Kathy Galvin said that my Facebook post criticizing Jones and Thomas "approached malfeasance" by me—because of the threat by the VML to lift our insurance coverage in relation to the post. Galvin thought the council could not only censure me, but expel me, under the provision of the City Charter allowing expulsion of a member for malfeasance. This was ridiculous, not least because I knew the legal standard for malfeasance: it requires intent, and it never would have occurred to me that legitimately voicing concerns about decisions by our city manager and police chief could create a legal hazard—and we had never been advised by our lawyer that being critical of our government could expose us to legal hazard.

It was then that I said I might need to get a lawyer.

I was asked to go into a separate small conference room, where I waited for forty-five minutes. As the time wore on, I drafted a defiant statement declaring that this was a show trial. I condemned and refused to accept the entire process. I was then asked to come back in.

Szakos looked at me and said, "You have two options." The first was to apologize and accept some limitations on my authority as mayor. The second was to be censured. I still wrestle with whether I should have walked out and taken my case to the people. But I also could not envision the drama that would then ensue. I could see the headlines: "Mayor Refuses Censure, Takes Case to the People." And what would happen then? Months of headlines about me, and about the internecine war among the councilors. And that would do immense harm to the city.

Considering the matter in the conference room, I had concluded that the true facts could still come to light—the galloping frenzy would eventually yield to the truth. I believed I could still lead the council to commission the independent investigation into policing on 8/12 that was badly needed. I believed things would eventually calm down, and that people would be able to see what I and others had done—and not done. Better, I thought, to view the truth as a marathon than a sprint. And so I chose the first option. For another half-hour, we negotiated the language of an apology. Swallowing my pride, I agreed to make a statement that the Facebook post had been "ill-advised" and that it had "impugned the reputations of our City Manager Maurice Jones and our Chief of Police Al Thomas."

We walked into the chambers, where the cameras were waiting, and arrayed ourselves in front of the podium, facing out toward the seats. I read the apology through what felt like gravel in my mouth. Then Kathy Galvin read the council's acceptance. Szakos read a jarringly different statement, saying we had "recommitted to one another to work as a leadership team," that we were "learning from the events of the day, discovering ways to have a more constructive community dialogue moving forward and, eventually, reemerging as a stronger city." The statement improbably concluded that, "to be successful, we as leaders must be united if we expect our community to be united."[33]

What was happening felt absurd, given the gravity of what had come before and the plain failure of our policing strategy. While the exercise was clearly intended to inflict maximum damage on me as the city's political figurehead, while circling the wagons of the city's staff leaders, it also felt like the most wantonly self-destructive performance imaginable by the city's slate of elected officials at that precise time.

This was all occurring, after all, on the very day that we were supposed to be announcing a new city website that, at long last, would be a one-stop-shop for resources and updates on recovery and healing events. The statement went on to announce the new website, which would be updated on a regular basis. Among other ironies, the website would never be updated again after that day. The deed was done, the message lost. Barely any of the coverage mentioned the new website. Again, we would fail to communicate with the public just when they needed us most. The coverage focused, predictably, on a very divided council.

MY MOM AND SISTERS CALLED: THEY KNEW HOW PAINFUL IT HAD been. Emily picked me up from City Hall, and we went to Toys R Us with the boys. She was outwardly cheerful and supportive, but inwardly, I knew, furious and frustrated. She had opposed the apology, had wanted me to fight, had wanted me to take our family's side against the whole world, if necessary, in light of the facts as we knew them. But what she said was, "That's just who you are." The boys rode around the inside of the store with bikes, and then we bought two of them to take home. We made the boys dinner, and they rode their new bikes around our living room, ecstatically. I read to them and put them to bed. It felt surreal, post-trauma, as if I'd been in a boxing ring without any defenses, pummeled and brutalized. I fell asleep, but woke up at 5:00 a.m. I went outside to get the paper in the dawn light and saw "Signer Apologizes" above the fold.

One psychologist friend later told me, with sympathy, "It would have killed me to do what you did." Another friend in business said, "After going through what you did, you can do anything you want—anything." I couldn't really articulate, at the time, my approach. It felt murky and intuitive, like swimming at night underwater. It was complicated by the terrible feelings I had—the 4:00 a.m. awakenings, the sense of shame and embarrassment, the uncertainty about whether I had made the right choice, and (this might be too much information) my exhausting and frustrating bouts with my first experience of irritable bowel syndrome (IBS).

But I also knew that I had poured my heart and soul into the mayorship and the Summer of Hate while trying to navigate the fraught gray area between public safety and freedom of speech. I had reached out to colleagues and authorities far and wide, led my colleagues to overrule staff when we felt they were not serving the public, hired outside authorities to fill in the gaps, improvised new authority, and, in short, fought tooth and nail, entangled in a web of legal direction, gag orders, and double-binds, all for what I felt were the right reasons. I suspected the events in Charlottesville would mean many things to many people (though I could not know how historic the events would truly become), and thought things would look different the next year, and the year after that. I knew the large, slow, but powerful gear of truth would continue to turn, eventually outmatching the small, furious spinning of rumors and petty politics and social media. I knew struggle would lead to insight, maybe even transcendence.

Several months later, a friend of mine who had served multiple tours of duty in both Iraq and Afghanistan as an army ranger and captain said something that resonated with me. "I was most proud of the apology," he told me. "You put the village in your rucksack." He went on to explain how he and his buddies had used that metaphor in Iraq to described getting out of a tough situation by bearing the burden of the towns for which they were responsible. I held fast to that comforting image in the months ahead.

ANYONE WHO THINKS THEY HAVE TO LIE OR OBFUSCATE ABOUT seeking counseling probably needs more of it. In a time when most professions recommend counseling, including the military and corporate America, not only is there nothing to be ashamed of, but it has become a

best practice for individuals seeking to reckon with difficult pasts and trying presents, or just seeking to achieve wisdom by getting out of their own
way. The experiences and the traumas of the past year were weighing on
me heavily—interrupting my sleep, causing fits of anger and periods of
distraction, not to mention the punishing bouts of IBS. I believe most
therapy should be, and should remain, personal and confidential. But
there was one strand in my experience that is relevant for the account
in this book: my mistakes. As I started sessions with a skilled counselor,
I confessed my fears about where I had gone wrong, yet I was initially
reluctant to admit I had made mistakes. This was precisely because I
was so angry about the treatment I'd received and the double-binds I'd
been put in.

This dam cracked during a later session where I teared up while ad-
mitting that what disappointed me the most was that I hadn't been able
to reassure people—to provide the emotional support they needed in a
time of crisis. I wrote up a list of mistakes to bring to the next session.
It started slow but then tumbled forth: "Being impetuous and willful
in starting everything with the procedures," "Should have created more
allyship with far-left and accepted their positions," "Impetuous decision
to write statement siding with cops on the KKK rally," "Should have explained structure of government to the people and stepped aside."

It was reminiscent of the haunting "Al Chet" prayer during Yom
Kippur, when Jews lightly tap their hearts with their hands as they
quietly chant a litany of sins they committed that year.

In the months ahead, friends would tell me about other instances
they'd heard about where mayors—whether through their own fault or
not—had become caught up in the tangled web of accountability, finding themselves unable to escape. One friend connected me with Dayne
Walling, the former mayor of Flint, Michigan, who was punished by
voters for the water crisis in that city, though he had not made any of the
decisions that had led to the problem. In one notable error, he cheerfully
drank the water to try to show it was safe. He believed what he had
been told, that the water *was* safe. But when the water was shown to be
dangerous, many blamed him. His off-synch effort to cheerlead for his
city reminded me of my ill-timed leap in front of the "LOVE" sign on the
Downtown Mall. In a phone conversation with Walling, I gathered that

his mistakes, if you could call them that, revolved around his inability to resolve public anguish.

It's a simple equation. Public service, particularly elective office, brings risk in proportion to the goals ventured. I'd been very public, whether on the First Amendment or on decrying the alt-right and Trump. I'd taken many risks, I'd made mistakes, and I was suffering the consequences. But I'd also done my best. And I knew from history that such struggle was often essential to growth, that agonies become absorbed in progress as surely as the ashes from a forest fire fertilize new growth.

Most fundamentally, I was aware that this wasn't about me, personally. It was about what I'd come to represent, politically, in the midst of a firestorm. While the experience was not pleasant, it would be short-term and small compared to the real trauma that had occurred. After all, a woman had died and nineteen people had been badly injured by an act of domestic terrorism, and thousands of others had been physically harmed and psychologically traumatized. I would eventually recover; others might never do so. We all needed perspective, which would come in time. My experience, after all, was just part and parcel of a whole city's trauma.

WHEN I GOT MY HEAD OUT OF MY OWN TROUBLES, I WOULD SEE small but unmistakable signs of hope around town. For example, thick burlap wrappers had been tied around trees in town with "CVILLE STRONG" written on them. There was one near my office on Second Street Northeast, another on Main Street next to Ridge Street. They were rough and organic. They seemed almost to have come from the trees themselves. They were not the "LOVE" sign. They weren't the purple "Cville" signs meant to memorialize Heather Heyer. They weren't policy or law.

They were the community rebelling and defying—standing strong.

PART V | AFTERBURN

22

"DONALD TRUMP IS GOD!"

A NEW NORMAL TOOK HOLD—A JITTERY, ONE-DAY-TO-THE-NEXT reality, where different sectors of a traumatized community—all traumatized in different ways—sought to live side by side. It didn't help that onslaughts of hatred continued. A friend working at a local bed and breakfast near the Downtown Mall showed me a handwritten letter the inn's owner had received from a man in South Bend, Indiana, who had the audacity to include his name (or at least a name) on the outside of the envelope. It read, in agitated lowercase letters (with swastikas drawn where I have indicated below):

> Youre [sic] town is a disgrace. Filled with spoiled rotten,
> dirty, lazy snot nosed punk kids—unbelievable un-american,
> anti-american, commie, homo, transgenders, transvestites,
> queer transvesticles and all around punks who still live in
> their mommies basements. [swastika] White Power!!!!!!
> Donald Trump is God!
>
> Kill all nigger loving white traitors to this (our [swastika]
> W.A.R.) country. W.A.R. = "White Aryan Resistance." Kill

263

*all black nigger devils, brown shit-skin cockroach latin spics,
yellow gook, zipperhead dog-eating Asian scum, and every single
white mudperson in this ([swastika] our) country. Kill all jew-
kikes of this ([swastika] our) (and all libtard liberals) Z.O.G.
government. Die!*

*heather heyer is dead in Virginia! Great! The fat skank should
have been at work, or better still minding her own fat ass ugly
business. That is what you get when you fuck with Nazis.*

yeeeeeee-hahaha!!!!!!!!!!!!

Go live in Iran you fucking filthy scumbag Virginia assholes.

W.A.R. [swastika]

It is perhaps telling of my state of mind that I didn't even report this
to the police or the FBI. I understood that the threats would likely be
deemed too fantastical to lead to an investigation. In the legal lexicon I'd
gotten to know all too well, they weren't imminent and specific enough
to be deemed "credible threats."

At our next city council meeting, there were about a dozen "Signer
Resign" signs in the audience and a handful of harsh statements during
the public comment period, which went on for almost three hours. But
it was nothing new, and nothing that really gathered steam as a narrative or dominating event. With one exception. A mild-mannered white
man encouraged us to adopt the "compromise" of recontextualizing the
statues. After he finished, he forgot his hat. Bellamy called out from the
dais: "You left your hat, and when you get your hat, take that compromise
with you."

In that same meeting, Bellamy rose and gave an impromptu Black
Power salute. On his Facebook page, he posted a photo of that moment
with the comment, "It's OUR turn now. I'm tired of 'compromising,' I'm
tired of 'meeting in the middle,' and I'm tired of other people who know
very little about us trying to tell us how we should be or act or conduct
ourselves." Afterward, in an interview with the *C-ville Weekly*, he said

Robert's Rules of Order tries to "shut people up." He expanded, "There are no norms. I don't get why people are in a rush to get back to convention in an unconventional time." The article was titled, "Do Robert's Rules of Order Mask White Supremacism?"[1]

Several of the comments harshly turned toward the inaction by the police. By this point, the city council had quietly authorized Jones to spend $100,000 on the independent review by Tim Heaphy at Hunton & Williams, and that review had started. But we were also still complying with our lawyers' orders to be silent. So we sat there, just absorbing all the anger.

In private, I ruminated. Part of me still wanted to punch back, to be vindicated. The feeling was so powerful I would sometimes wake up at 4:00 a.m. with my heart pounding with it, my mind drafting speeches I would make. But that feeling was always soon countered by another: what really mattered was not my political future, but the city, the victims, their healing and justice, our democratic system, getting the facts right about what had happened, and implementing reforms so it couldn't happen again. A new short-term battle for my reputation would be self-serving and deeply at odds with the still-unfolding citywide *agon*. I knew from studying political history that over the longer run, patterns reveal themselves, perspectives shift, and facts come to light. As you're fighting through it, a firestorm seems to engulf everything. But when you're viewing it from above, you see its edges. When it's over, you can walk through the ashes. The point is, you do walk through it. It will, after all, end.

A COUPLE OF WEEKS LATER, I ATTENDED ROSH HASHANAH SER-vices. People were incredibly gracious. Yet there was a deeper undercurrent of concern about our community as well. An older man told me he was worried we'd be like Birmingham, Alabama, which, fifty years later, was still known for a church bombing. The sermons were all about 8/12, and the fear and sense of intimidation the Jewish community felt. The question of "where had God gone" was raised. A couple of people asked why the police hadn't done more to protect the synagogue. And I told the whole story again, including my own frustration and anger. I wasn't afraid of legal liability, not in a house of worship.

The prayers were more meaningful to me than ever before. The rabbi read a line about how conscience rises above all else: when you are attacked by enemies, you shall respond with silence. But he also prayed that God would destroy the plans of malevolent people. That was the goal now—with conscience as both beacon and compass. A friend said to me that night, "I don't know how you've gone through this." I answered, "I have to be stronger than this bullshit," and he looked at me and nodded.

MEANWHILE, THE INJURIES AND SUFFERING AND TRAUMA IN THE community continued. The Dave Matthews Band planned a massive "Concert for Charlottesville" that would raise money for a fund that had been set up by the Charlottesville Area Community Foundation. Ariana Grande, Justin Timberlake, and Stevie Wonder all performed. It was an incredible show of talent. But it, too, was protested. Solidarity Cville, a far-left group that included many Antifa members, released a manifesto calling for the elimination of Confederate monuments, my removal from office, and the dropping of all charges against the counterprotesters who had been arrested at the July 8 and August 12 rallies. At the concert, Solidarity Cville members arrayed themselves on a small hill in front of a nearby dormitory and called for the community to "rebuke the 'Concert for Charlottesville' as a show of false unity."

The *Daily Progress* responded with an editorial lamenting the protest as a "a sign that our community is further splintering," observing that it "exposes the fact that the community is disunited about the very idea of unity." The protesters were claiming not only that "my unity is better than your unity" but that "my unity is the only unity."[2]

It was at the concert that I met Susan Bro, Heather Heyer's mom, for the first time. We were in an area off to the side of the viewing seats, and she was calm, friendly, and comforting. We agreed to get together later to talk some more, and we did that a couple of months later, when I served her breakfast and coffee at my house.

People were still in the hospital, still wounded. A community of therapists was offering free counseling through the C-ville Wellness Fund. From donations, they raised nearly $5,000.

OTHERS WERE STRUGGLING WITH THE REPERCUSSIONS AND RE-criminations, too. Waldo Jaquith, a Charlottesville resident, resigned from his position on the board of the ACLU of Virginia. Jaquith was a blogger who had run for a seat on the Charlottesville City Council soon after graduating from college. Although the campaign was ultimately unsuccessful, it helped him build a following online. On August 12, he posted a tweet:

 I just resigned from the ACLU of Virginia board.

 What's legal and what's right are sometimes different. I won't be a fig leaf for Nazis.

The *New York Times* published an article titled "After Backing Alt-Right in Charlottesville, A.C.L.U. Wrestles with Its Role," where it reported Jaquith's assertion that the ACLU bore responsibility for reversing the decision to relocate the rally. "If we hadn't intervened, the event would have been held a mile away, far from downtown, and three people would be alive."[3]

Less than a week after 8/12, the national ACLU had announced that it would no longer represent arms-carrying white nationalist groups.[4] Soon after that, protests began against the executive director of the Virginia ACLU chapter when she spoke in public. At the College of William and Mary in early October, protesters carried signs and chanted, "ACLU, free speech for who?" and "The oppressed are not impressed." The college had to cancel the event. On its Facebook page, the William and Mary Black Lives Matter group posted, "In contrast to the ACLU, we want to reaffirm our position of zero tolerance for white supremacy no matter what form it decides to masquerade in."[5]

The *Wall Street Journal* published an internal memorandum from the ACLU's national headquarters that contained an exhaustive new set of criteria the organization would now use to evaluate the cases it took as a result of Charlottesville.

The document laid out a breathtaking new doctrine for the organization that had created the *Skokie* doctrine. In making a decision about taking a case, the first question, according to the new rules, was whether the speaker sought "to engage in or promote violence." The ACLU would now decline to represent speakers who did. Second, because weapons could be "intimidating and inimical to the free exchange of ideas," the ACLU would not take cases from protesters planning to carry arms. Third, because the ACLU's defense of speech "may have a greater or lesser harmful impact on the equality and justice work to which we are also committed," it would consider the "potential effect on marginalized communities" of a potential case and the extent to which the speech may "assist in advancing the goals of white supremacists."

Finally, the ACLU said it would reserve the right to "condemn the views themselves." To enable the ACLU to simultaneously defend a speaker's right to speak and condemn the speaker's views, the ACLU would "seek to preserve that right through ethically appropriate representation agreements." It even reserved to itself the right to require clients to "sign an ethically appropriate advance waiver of potential conflicts arising from our condemnation of their views." They gave themselves the right to denounce their clients' views in press statements, op-eds, and social media and to participate in counterprotests.

The document noted, in a footnote, that "true threats"—statements that communicate a "serious expression of an intent to commit an act of unlawful violence to a particular individual or group of individuals"—are not protected by the First Amendment. The organization's point of view was that "subjective intent to threaten is an essential element of any true threat." The ACLU's position would continue to be that the First Amendment "does protect broadly threatening language not targeted at a particular individual or group of individuals, hyperbolic threats, and speech that it is deeply offensive to particular individuals."[6]

The overall picture I had, after reading this, was of an organization twisting itself into a pretzel entirely of its own making. The ACLU now seemed to want to be situated at the farthest end of the far left, while at the same time still taking on high-publicity clients like Kessler.

Call me crazy, but I think that it just shouldn't take on clients like Kessler in the first place.

23

FLASH MOB

OCTOBER 7, 2017, BROUGHT YET ANOTHER CHAPTER IN OUR MAD drama. Richard Spencer came back to town. He and a couple dozen followers unloaded from a van a few blocks from Emancipation Park. In shaky live-feed video, they filmed themselves walking nervously up Market Street with lit tiki torches, past residents innocently eating at a Thai restaurant's outside tables.

It was pure theater, performed for social media. Next they arranged themselves around the Lee statue and chanted "You. Will Not. Replace Us." They chanted "Blood and Soil." They sang "Dixie." They chanted, "The South will rise again. Russia is our friend. The South will rise again. Woo-hoo! Wooo."

One speaker attacked Charlottesville's very sense of community, shouting: "All of you in this city, your lives are empty. What do you do every night, you go home, you drink box wine, maybe you eat some ice cream, maybe turn on Netflix. You don't have a real community. You don't have a real city. You don't have a real community. You don't know what your neighbor's name is. This is a fake city, a fake community. Your life is consumed by media and what comes up on your screen."[1]

Much white nationalism comes from isolation, from lonely young white men seeking solidarity. I suspect he was projecting from his own life. Because if Charlottesville was anything, it *was* a "real community," where we *did* know our neighbors' names. The white nationalist didn't know us. He was projecting something dark and broken from his own experience onto us. It seemed like he was literally from a different country. And perhaps, effectively, he was.

I responded to all of this with a tweet that cited future legal options: "Another despicable visit by neo-Nazi cowards. You're not welcome here! Go home! Meantime we're looking at all our legal options. Stay tuned." I meant to foreshadow the event that had been scheduled for just five days later, exactly two months after August 12. The city council would convene the next morning to join the Georgetown Law Center in litigation asking for an injunction against the paramilitary groups on the grounds that they violated the "subordination clause" of the Virginia Constitution preventing any militias that aren't overseen by the state.

Spencer tried to bait me, tweeting: "How are we 'cowards'? We came back. Also, you have no authority to ban American citizens from C'ville, doofus." As always, the specter of a legal loss, and what it would become in the hands of these social media terrorists, loomed large. Needless to say, I didn't respond. I didn't need to get into a back and forth with yet another troll. There was real work to do, and we could do it. As I had promised back in August, our norms and institutions were more resilient than this anarchist evil.

THE LAWSUIT I WAS REFERRING TO WENT BACK TO A CALL IN SEPtember from a woman named Mary McCord, who introduced herself as a former national security federal prosecutor now with Georgetown University. We spoke about the possibility of a new effort to sue the people who had invaded us, to stop them from doing it again. She mentioned a novel legal theory that had come out of an article that Philip Zelikow, a UVA history and law professor and former director of the 9/11 Commission, had published in the Lawfare blog just three days after 8/12.[2]

It turned out that Virginia had a provision in its state code that prohibited militias from operating without permission from the civilian government. So did forty-seven other states. These laws had never been enforced, though, because they'd never *needed* to be. But we were entering new territory now. We needed to look to them again as we entered, apparently, a new Wild West. And so I started helping McCord with her lawsuit.

The first thing we needed was as many plaintiffs as possible, including neighborhood associations and businesses. But the most important would be the city itself—to give the suit the greatest force and legitimacy, we needed to get the city council behind the lawsuit, even though it would create the potential for discovery, depositions, and countersuits. We also needed to decide whether we would include not just far-right militias but also far-left ones—like the far-left Redneck Revolt, which had shown up, assault rifles in hand, with the purported goal of defending Antifa from attack.

McCord's advice was that including militias across the ideological spectrum would insulate the lawsuit against attacks that it was content-based. Antifa, of course, would attack us for not supporting their efforts at "community defense." I was willing to take that risk. I couldn't abide sanctioning private armies in our streets. It went against everything I believed about democracy. It was conceding the state itself to the extremes.

After some discussion, the council agreed. Redneck Revolt would stay in.

MEANWHILE, THE GEORGETOWN TEAM HAD UNCOVERED DISturbing research that had been conducted by a website called Unicorn Riot. The left-wing site had investigated the "dark web" where the organizers of Unite the Right had plotted the 8/12 event. One of these dark web platforms was Discord, an online chat site for gamers that the alt-right was subverting to hold more sinister conversations as well. The US Supreme Court ruled in 1982 that "mere advocacy of the use of force or violence does not remove speech from the protection of the First Amendment."[3] That doctrine had protected the social media posts in the Antifa research from July. But these new, hidden conversations crossed the line. It seemed a judge could have readily found they met the "credible threat" standard of specifically planning violence.

One user, named "Americana - MD," described Unite the Right, innocuously enough, as "an event where there will be known hostilities." But then he wrote: "Be better at violence th[a]n they are"; "Attack on all fronts"; and "Get jacked so you can look good when you stab commies with a knife."

Another, "Heinz - MI," urged everyone to "prepare for violence" and described Unite the Right as "a protest/rally where we expect violence." He also "suggest[ed] learning how to actually fight in a shield wall." "Kampfhund VA" wrote, "Violence of action is extremely important!" "PureDureSure" advocated "us[ing] their ammunition against them and return[ing] fire with several times the force." "Requiem" posted pictures of the words "YOU DIE" written underneath an X'ed-out Star of David, along with a hand carrying a knife, captioned, "Fight Until the Last Drop."

There were also explicit descriptions of how they planned to use their flagpoles as weapons. One participant in the discussions, "kristall. night," said "cheaper [flagpoles] won't be very useful to double as spears"; another told the others how "to use [a flagpole] as a club." "Kurt - VA" wrote that "impaling people is always the best option," and told others to "put your own spike on the top of [a flagpole]." "Chris Liguria" wrote, "If you use PVC [for flagpoles] get schedule 80 for thicker thumping," and "Whip them into passivity like their parent[s] should have." "Tyrone" urged others to "have a plan to kill everybody you meet." With respect to flagpoles, he said, "Anything longer is too long to effectively bludgeon someone with," and "You only are going to get 3–6 whacks to something solid before it breaks." He noted, "You want something designed for longitudinal stress." "I'm bringing Mosin-Nagants with bayonets attached," he said. "It will shoot clean through a crowd at least four deep." "First," he added, "I have to kill me a Communist."

The most chilling comments, in light of James Alex Fields Jr.'s terrorist attack on the day of the rally with his Dodge Challenger, were the ones about using vehicles as weapons. "Tyrone" wrote that being able to run over protesters "sure would be nice." He posted a picture captioned, "Introducing John Deere's New Multi-Lane Protester Digestor" and asked the forum, "Is it legal to run over protestors blocking roadways? I'm NOT just shitposting. I would like clarification."

"AltCelt(IL)" posted a truck plowing through a large crowd: "This will be us," he said.[4]

WE ANNOUNCED THE GEORGETOWN LAWSUIT ON THE TWO-MONTH anniversary of 8/12. We held a special vote in council chambers, and then a short press conference.

I wanted to explain in my statement as strongly as I could why the lawsuit was important. I began with the most central point: we were taking a stand against the disintegration of our democracy. We hoped to close this horrible chapter in our democracy where people thought it was acceptable to parade in military outfits in public, to openly threaten violence against other people, to fire weapons into crowds, to beat people in public, and to use a car as a weapon.

I explained that our forebears had, in their wisdom, built our democracy on two pillars. The first was that democracy depends on deliberation. And deliberation, I said, requires some measure of civility. Even if we disagree vehemently with one another, we need to treat others as we would want ourselves to be treated. The second pillar was that the state must have a monopoly on the legitimate use of force. That's why we don't allow private armies in this country. And it's why Article I, Section 13, of the Virginia Constitution guarantees that "in all cases the military should be under strict subordination to, and governed by, the civil power."

I argued that the rogue militias were like arsonists setting fire to these pillars. They were replacing respect with intimidation, and going by a "might makes right" approach that was right out of the Wild West. Cynicism begets nihilism, and nihilism begets terrorism. It was no surprise that the rhetoric and the plans revealed through the extraordinary research in the court filing would lead to attacks on government itself. The emergence of these paramilitary groups in the public sphere was a threat to democracy itself.

After we finished the press conference, we walked the package of papers over to the courthouse, national media scrambling backward in front of us the whole time.

HOWEVER, THERE WAS POSITIVE ENERGY COMING FROM THE OTH-erwise disastrous Department of Justice town hall meeting from a few weeks before: the communal desire for equity-driven programming to rebut the white supremacists' attack on our most vulnerable residents—specifically, through affordable housing. I had been looking for a strategy that would put hard numbers against the long-standing strategy of ensuring that 15 percent of the city's housing stock was affordable. At last count, we were at about 11 percent, and it seemed that percentage might decrease rather than increase, due to the lack of new units and a flood of new residents to the city.

At long last, we now started to move the needle on affordable housing with the funds that had been doubled after my long-ago State of the City address. That fall, we would dedicate almost $2 million to creating sixty-four units of new affordable housing, rehabilitating thirty-five more affordable rental units, and rehabilitating sixty to seventy homes at risk of being sold by low-income owners who could not afford the substantial repairs they needed. This was at least a 500 percent increase over what prior councils had been able to do. As fractured as we were, we could still serve.[5]

But, as before, there was precious little attention paid to this substantive advancement. The city was hesitant to claim too much credit for a progressive victory, so there was little press attention. Social media virtually ignored the package. All the attention remained on the restive far left, whose members were gearing up for more confrontation.

PLANNING COMMISSION MEETINGS ARE USUALLY ABOUT AS EXCITING as a yawning fit. Developers present slide decks with projects they hope will be approved under the zoning code. Neighborhood residents show up to support or oppose. This one, however, was different. The planning commission was scheduled to hear an application for a luxury apartment building proposed for a spot just off the Downtown Mall. The developer wanted to add extra stories to the height allowed by the code. The chambers were mysteriously crowded for a planning commission meeting, with a couple dozen Solidarity Cville members there. They sat quietly together in a few of the rows for the first ninety minutes of the meeting.

When the agenda item for the project was announced, the group started shouting. Two of them rushed down the aisles and took over the dais, standing on top of it and unrolling a large banner that said, "CVILLE IS NOT FOR SALE." I had flashbacks to "BLOOD ON YOUR HANDS." They handed out flyers that declared, "White supremacy in this city manifests in many ways." It linked the assault charges that had been filed against DeAndre Harris (the victim of the vicious beating by several white assailants in the Market Street Parking Garage) with the project under discussion. "This has happened over and over again," the flyer said. "White supremacists either going to the magistrate to press bogus charges against anti-racist activists or going to the Planning Commission to ask for special-use permits to displace residents."[6]

The frazzled chair had to suspend the meeting. An African American woman on the planning commission walked up to the protesters and demanded they stop. "We have business to do here," she said. "I've got a daughter at home and a sitter. We're here to work." I approached one of the organizers, a long-haired white guy with a frizzy beard, and asked him if he thought we were doing a good job with our dramatic recent investment in affordable housing. He looked at me and smiled, "Too little, too late." I expressed astonishment. "But this is political theater!" he told me. He grinned again and told me, "You, of all people, should understand that." I was disturbed by the cynicism underlying the sentiment.

The fracas went on for about half an hour, until Police Chief Thomas arrived in workout gear. He made an abrupt decision to cancel the meeting altogether on public safety grounds. Some of the planning commissioners were disgruntled about their work being stopped.

That event led me to convene a meeting with our city manager and police chief to devise a new security protocol for all the meetings that could conceivably now be taken over in the new political reality in Charlottesville. We developed a flow chart of what would happen so that everyone would be on the same page—especially whoever was chairing the meeting, the police, and the city manager. It walked through what should happen if an attendee refused to leave the meeting after being requested to do so (he or she would be escorted out by a police officer and would not be permitted to return to the meeting). It addressed the kind of scenario where "several attendees [were] disrupting the meeting": "The Chair may call a recess for a period of time in order to allow for the disrupting attendees to be properly dispersed. Microphones and cameras will not broadcast during a recess."

And it explained the "role of the Police": "If an attendee engages in disorderly conduct or illegal activity during the course of a public meeting, a police officer may take action, to include making an arrest if deemed necessary." And if the police determined that a "vast majority of attendees at a public meeting are engaging in disorderly disruption," they could "take necessary steps to clear all attendees from the meeting space."

This is what it had come to. We were far beyond the "civility" debate. We were now determining whether we could govern at all in the wake of the "Summer of Hate."

All that fall and winter, there were similar disruptions in city council meetings, with the anger often expressed toward me. One young African American woman, who sometimes appeared in a beret (and who the next year would heckle Wes Bellamy, leading him to call her out for what he said was posturing as a radical), made a habit of giving me the bird from the left side of the gallery. A transgender white woman, sitting in the front row, interrupted me once to shout, "Fuck you, Signer!" and just sat there, glaring at me. Later, she worked at a local coffee shop. When I bought a cup of coffee there, I tried to be friendly, but she wouldn't make eye contact with me when I paid. It was awkward, to say the least.

Have I mentioned that Charlottesville is a small town?

24

"UNMASK THE ILLUSION"

T HE WEATHER TURNED COOLER, THE LEAVES FELL, THE APPLES
grew crisp on the trees. But the embers from the firestorm were still
as incendiary as ever. The trolling continued, with Facebook messages
like this one from a user on November 23, 2017: "You stupid son-of-a-
bitch. It will always be Lee Park. You kowtowed to the niggers like the
coward you are. Robert E. Lee is sacred. Your political career is over. You
are most likely a closet homosexual."

As trying as the personal angle was, as fractious and infuriating as
the politics were, there was still policy to be made. We still needed to
keep the city safe.

The K&L Gates law firm had put hundreds of pro bono hours into
helping Charlottesville overhaul the way events were handled. In the
process, we had made significant practical adjustments to the balance
we could strike between freedom of speech and public safety.

A big question was how to ban tiki torches, which had now been
used in the city three times—by Richard Spencer and his followers on
May 8, by the Unite the Right marchers on August 11, and by Spencer

again during his "flash mob." Why had we never been able to stop them? It turned out that Charlottesville did have an ordinance prohibiting open flame. But it was unclear who had the authority to enforce it—the fire department or the police department. Even more of a problem was the free-speech question. If we enforced it against tiki torches, why would we not enforce it against, say, a candlelight vigil?

Those were the questions that came up as we sought to prevent tiki torches from being used in our city parks. Would it be all city parks? What about city sidewalks? Should we prohibit anything with a flame, whether a sparkler or a candle?

I asked our city attorney about the idea of exempting wax candles from the open flame part of the new permit regulations, arguing that there would be widespread appeal in allowing candlelit vigils. The Commonwealth of Virginia's own interim regulations for the Lee monument in Richmond (which was on state-owned property), as well as the City of Richmond's new municipal rules, allowed candles during demonstrations and vigils. In the end, we would adopt an ordinance that defined "open flame" as "fire whose flame is supported by a wick, oil or other slow-burning means to sustain itself." The law explained that "open flame" "includes, but is not limited to, flame producing devices such as candles, torches, and juggling or other fire artist equipment; provided, however, that 'open burning and open fire' and 'open flame' shall not include handheld candles when used for ceremonial purposes, provided that they are not held or used in an intimidating, threatening, dangerous or harmful manner."

If the consequences of Richard Spencer's antics, and his tiki torches and flash mobs, weren't so disastrous psychologically, these bureaucratic contraptions would have been worthy of Joseph Heller's *Catch-22*—or a Monty Python episode.

Another question was whether to enforce limits on crowd sizes for rally permits. As I knew from my experience with the Capital of the Resistance event, we didn't enforce the on-paper limit of fifty people before an event had to be permitted days in advance (we had the exception for "press conferences"). The question was, after what had happened, *should* we start enforcing the limit? Our attorney advised us that we should and recommended lowering the limit to twenty-five.[1]

Then there were all the weapons and insignia and uniforms that people had brought to the rally. Again, both First and Second Amendment absolutism loomed. We already knew we could not ban firearms or ammunition from our parks. But could we stop people from wearing military-style uniforms and insignia? From having shields and helmets? From parading as if they were paramilitary organizations or private armies?

The legal advice was that we could, yes—but the law would have to be written carefully. We would have to clearly signal to anyone in the area that these rules were now in place so they had fair warning. They would have to apply equally to everyone, not to particular speakers or followers.

The lawyers suggested it would make more sense to start from scratch, to have a comprehensive new ordinance that addressed all of these questions, and then to begin enforcing it. So we all got to work.

Meanwhile, the governor was preparing his own report on what had happened. But in contrast to the searching, complicated deep-dive that was happening in Charlottesville, it was clear the state's inquiry would be more political. The Governor's Task Force on Public Safety Preparedness and Response to Civil Unrest met a total of four times and seemed more focused on shifting blame to the city and framing reforms going forward (such as the need to adopt established federal emergency management protocols, like the National Incident Command System and Unified Command System, which would prevent the conflicts and disconnects we'd seen in Charlottesville) than on examining what had actually happened. Indeed, the task force resisted Freedom of Information Act requests from our own investigation. They did not even contact me. Their final report contained virtually no criticism of decisions within the Office of the Governor, the Secretary of Public Safety, or the Virginia State Police; it just shifted blame to the City of Charlottesville.

That perhaps shouldn't have been surprising, given the destructive force of the firestorm and the attendant political risks, but it was still disappointing.[2]

WITH ELECTION DAY CAME A HUGE POLITICAL BOMBSHELL THAT spoke volumes to the increasing intensity of the brushfire for equity that had been sparked: Nikuyah Walker won a seat on the council as an independent. Walker was the activist who had sent such scorching emails accusing the city council of being like modern-day slave masters, and who had asked the new council, "Is Mike your daddy?" She received almost eight thousand votes—the largest vote total for any city council candidate in Charlottesville's history. Walker had devised the campaign message "Unmask the Illusion," which she'd emblazoned on yard signs featuring the red, green, and black colors traditionally associated with Africa.

Across the state Virginia experienced a wave of Democratic anti-Trump sentiment in the election, with the Democratic lieutenant governor, Ralph Northam, winning the governorship by nine percentage points. The Democratic candidate Justin Fairfax, an African American former federal prosecutor whom I knew from our time together at WilmerHale in DC, won for lieutenant governor, and the sitting Democratic attorney general, Mark Herring, won his reelection campaign. Seventeen Democratic candidates for the House of Delegates also won, an astonishing development that put that chamber almost within Democratic control.

Meanwhile, I continued working on what had begun as the "Civility Alliance" but, after 8/12, we were now calling the "After Charlottesville Project." In regular conference calls, I connected with new and unlikely bedfellows interested in confronting extremism, like the Charles Koch Institute. The idea now was to convene leaders to generate lessons from Charlottesville with an eye to how innovations like the Georgetown lawsuit could provide a model for other localities trying to fight other firestorms. Jonathan Greenblatt, the CEO of the Anti-Defamation League—which had been founded in 1913 to combat anti-Semitism, but whose mission had now expanded to confront all forms of extremism and bigotry—offered me all the in-kind support we would need to get the project off the ground. We could now do something to help other communities learn from what we'd experienced.

I WENT IN FOR MY LONG-AWAITED INTERVIEW WITH FORMER FEDeral prosecutor Tim Heaphy for the independent investigation with a detailed outline covering my thinking and actions over the past year.

I was the last city official to be interviewed. A few days later, the report was complete, and I had a two-hour briefing on it with Heaphy and Maurice Jones. The full title was "Independent Review of the 2017 Protest Events in Charlottesville, Virginia," but we soon started calling it simply "the Heaphy Report." During the briefing, I realized that the report would be devastating for both the Charlottesville Police Department and the Virginia State Police. One fact struck me in particular: when Heaphy showed me a whiteboard featuring the map of the security plan for 8/12, it was the *first time* I had seen it.

The pictures made abundantly clear how deficient the plan we'd been so skeptical about on the city council had really been. The area where people had openly battled was sliced and diced into small areas, with inconsistent coverage by both state and local police in the different areas, confusion throughout, and no way to address failures or contingencies, like when the protesters and counterprotesters mixed and clashed on the streets before the rally and in the aftermath of the declaration of an unlawful assembly. It was the farthest cry imaginable from the "green space" between the groups that would have been possible at McIntire Park.

25

"LIKE TALKING TO A BRICK WALL"

WHEN IT WAS RELEASED ON DECEMBER 1, 2017, THE HEAPHY Report found failure at many levels in Charlottesville's planning for the event. The report concluded that on 8/12 the Charlottesville Police Department (CPD) had implemented a "flawed operational plan that failed to protect public safety" in several key respects. It noted that the CPD had not sought input from law enforcement personnel experienced in handling similar events. (Indeed, the police had never called the chief of police of Houston, despite Houston mayor Sylvester Turner's offer to me, which I had immediately conveyed to our city manager.) It concluded that the CPD did not provide adequate training or information to its officers leading up to 8/12. It then waited too long to request the assistance of the Virginia Department of Emergency Management. The city didn't provide adequate information to the public about plans for the event. And the city erred in concluding that items that could be used as weapons—such as flagpoles—could not be banned at the event.

The report also faulted the Virginia State Police (VSP). Just as there had been a lack of coordination during the tear gas incident during the

KKK rally, the report observed that the two agencies had not even had a unified command. The two agencies did not have a single all-hands briefing that morning; astonishingly, they had separate briefings. The report found that they weren't even on the same radio frequency. The VSP had not shared its operational plan with the CPD—instead just protecting the areas it had decided to protect. The report discovered the VSP had directed officers to remain behind barriers within Emancipation Park, with devastating consequences: "Their inaction in the face of violence left the City unprepared—and unaware that it was unprepared—to address one of the predictable risks of the event: brief but serious incidents of interpersonal violence and mutual combat." The errors continued after the long-predicted unlawful assembly. The report found that after the declaration of an unlawful assembly, protesters were "pushed directly toward counter-protesters without separation."[1]

The problems in the plan were compounded by the same inflexibility we'd seen when the police resisted the council's request that the rally be relocated to McIntire Park. One captain said that command staff had dismissed some of her concerns as a "worst case scenario" unlikely to happen. A lieutenant said that CPD's leadership had approached August 12 like a concert event, not a potentially violent confrontation. When he offered suggestions regarding the plans to the captain in charge of planning, "it was like talking to a brick wall," he told Heaphy's team.[2] One lieutenant in charge of First Street had instructed his officers to avoid engaging attendees over "every little thing." An officer in that zone said that officers "were not going to go in and break up fights" or enter the crowd to make arrests "unless it was something so serious that someone [would] get killed." A sergeant said the instructions he received were not to "interrupt mutual combat" unless someone was seriously injured.[3]

The errors went on. The plan did not adequately ensure separation between the protesters and counterprotesters. Law enforcement did not intervene in violent disorders and did not respond to requests for assistance. The areas where conflict had predictably occurred were not occupied by officers. Both CPD and VSP personnel were "insufficiently equipped to respond to mass unrest." Riot gear had been stationed several blocks away from the police, so when the violence began, the police were not able to access the gear that would have kept them physically safe. As a result, instead of wading out into the crowds to stop assaults, they stood behind the barricades.[4]

Finally, on the question of what exactly had happened at Fourth Street, where Heather Heyer had been killed, the report concluded that the traffic plan had placed insufficient resources, leaving the mall area "vulnerable to a vehicle used as a weapon." Specifically, a single school resource officer had been placed near a single sawhorse, which she had left after determining she was vulnerable to attack.[5]

The report also addressed the First Amendment crisis around the "credible threat" standard and the misplaced blame on me and city council for not stopping the rally from happening. Despite information that white supremacists were likely to bring bats, batons, knives, and firearms, and that anti-racist militants would respond with soda cans filled with cement, bottles filled with urine or fuel, and pepper spray, the report at last told the plain truth about the legal analysis and direction the elected officials had received about whether the event could be stopped: "Council was told that generalized threats of violence, promises to use violence in self-defense, and information that counter-protesters planned to use violence . . . were insufficient."[6]

THE CITY COUNCIL AND I DID NOT ESCAPE THE BLAST FORCE OF the report's censure, however. The report began its narrative with a critique of my "Capital of the Resistance" rally, quoting a CPD lieutenant who said the event was "tantamount for war rhetoric" and a "recipe for undermining the legitimacy of institutions of government."[7] The report also quoted an assistant city manager saying that the fact that I hadn't gotten a permit for my event made it difficult to cite Richard Spencer for his own unpermitted tiki torch rally at Lee Park.[8]

The second critique made sense to me, and I felt awful that it might have made the city a softer target for predators like Spencer. I had no excuse, just the explanation that I'd understood that we didn't require permits for these sorts of events at the time. This was unquestionably one reason we needed to tighten our permitting ordinance. I was more dismayed at the first critique. At a shallow level, I felt like I was being blamed for continuing the work I'd begun with the Electoral College campaign: challenging a president I felt had been elected only with the overt assistance of a foreign power, and who was already undermining our Constitution with actions like the "Muslim ban."

But I also responded at a deeper level, losing some sleep. *Had* the gathering helped set off a chain of events that had drawn the alt-right to Charlottesville? Kessler, after all, had come to heckle Khizr Khan. Tossing and turning, I asked myself, then again, what was the alternative? While I'd gone to pains to say we were "a," not "the," capital of resistance, I could see how some felt the title was overblown. But it was no less defiant than what Mayor Marty Walsh in Boston had said: "If necessary, we will use City Hall itself to shelter and protect anyone who's targeted unjustly."[9] If white nationalist terrorists had attacked Boston after that declaration, would he have been responsible? I concluded, closing my eyes at last, that these paradoxes are just the lumps of leadership. I never publicly challenged the Heaphy Report on its focus on the resistance rally.

The following summer, however, federal judge Norman Moon seemed to shut the door on a causal link between the resistance rally and the Summer of Hate. In *Sines v. Kessler*, after considering extensive discovery documents and arguments from both sides, he wrote, "The genesis of the Defendants' interest in Charlottesville was the renaming of the park."[10] In other words, evidence reviewed in federal court showed that the alt-right came to Charlottesville in response to naming Lee Park Emancipation Park—not the resistance rally.

The rest of the city council and I were also harshly criticized for "unduly interfering with operational planning" by directing the event to be moved to McIntire Park. There were two grounds for this critique. The first was the council's "lack of deference to law enforcement." The second was the "timing of the decision." Both conclusions, I thought, depended on severe factual errors and illuminated profound problems in the accountability mechanisms that, in turn, went back to the problems of a divided government. The report said the council misconstrued its role:

As elected representatives, Council should respond to public concerns like those expressed in the days before August 12. But rather than micromanage professional staff and second-guess their decisions, Council should have helped the community understand the rules that govern these events. Rather than overruling law enforcement and forcing them to prepare for a more complex event, Council should have helped the community understand the public safety challenge and anticipate the law enforcement response to the event.[11]

This sounded good in theory. It was an easy way to cast blame equally across all members of the city government, essentially throwing a pox on all the houses.

The problem was that it lacked context. From my seat, the variable that explained this decision was the failure of the VSP, the CPD, and the city manager to provide an explanation of the tear gas decision—particularly in light of the accusation that protesters had begun the escalation by releasing pepper gel (which the report itself found to be baseless).[12] It was 20/20 hindsight. The second problem was the failure to reassure the city council that the CPD's "strategy" was manageable in the Downtown Mall area. Indeed, the security plan was precisely what we on the council feared it would be—poorly designed and impossible to execute downtown.

It was a puzzle. The report seemed to be saying that even if we knew we were headed into a disaster, and even though trust had been destroyed, because we were elected officials our duty was to shut up and let things unfold. That still doesn't make any sense to me.

The report also slammed the council for the timing of the decision to relocate the rally. It found the decision was made "much too late":

Despite the ample notice of Mr. Kessler's desire to hold a large gathering of white nationalists in Charlottesville, the violence that had ensued at similar events around the country, and accurate intelligence about the potential for violence here, City leaders waited until just days before the event to act. Waiting until the week before the event to move it away from the location requested by the organizer negatively impacted both planning and communications. Law enforcement officials were suddenly forced to prepare for the possibility of protest activity in both McIntire and Emancipation Parks. Planners were already attempting to prepare for the unpredictable behavior of protestors and counter-protestors; the decision to move the event exacerbated these concerns and created additional uncertainty in the difficult days before August 12.[13]

But again the conclusion ignored crucial facts and contextual factors. In my interview, I had emphasized repeatedly that I first brought the idea of moving the rally to McIntire Park to Jones and Thomas five days after the KKK event. The delay, in other words, was not caused by the elected leaders. It was caused by staff.

Most crucially, however, the report concluded both that the relocation to McIntire Park would, in fact, have made the event safer, and that the police had actually prepared a relocation plan several days *prior to* the council's emergency closed session on August 3 where we resolved, once and for all, to force the decision. The report read:

> When it became clear that City Council was seriously considering attempting to move the event to McIntire Park, Captain Mitchell assigned Lieutenant Durrette responsibility for designing a plan. The large layout reduced most of the complications posed by having a rally in the congested downtown area. Durrette was able to quickly determine that two baseball fields that sat next to each other created convenient areas to corral the Unite The Right demonstrators and opposing counter-protesters. He staged a law enforcement safety zone nearby, and drew up a map showing where additional barriers would need to be placed. He submitted the plan to Captain Mitchell on July 31.[14]

In other words, the police had prepared a relocation plan *four days before* the council met. At that very same meeting, Chief Thomas had protested that it was "too late" to execute another plan, compared with the "strategy" the police already had. Yet the report concluded that the plan the police prepared for McIntire Park, unlike the one for the Downtown

Mall, would have allowed for the separation of the groups and a correct staging area. In other words, the police had prepared a safer plan several days in advance of council's meeting, and yet they still fought back against the council's attempt to relocate the rally. It was painful to read.

The Heaphy Report also contained a final, simple recommendation that was revelatory for me, reminding me of similar lessons from the world of homeland security and preparedness: "Train for contingencies in advance of large protest events, using table top exercises in which all personnel can anticipate and prepare for complex, volatile events."[15] The Charlottesville Police Department had not used either table-top exercises or field exercises as tools where all the stakeholders could walk through anticipated events, prepare for contingencies, brainstorm, and learn how to work together. Not with the council, and not without the council, either. We hadn't practiced working together, even with a massive crisis bearing down on us.[16]

When Heaphy appeared before us in the council chambers at our first meeting in December to answer questions about the report—amid jeers, heckling, and shouts from the crowd—it was tough to get a word in edgewise. I asked a single question for the record: His report found, did it not, that the police officers who had prepared the contingency plan for McIntire Park had concluded that it would have been safer than downtown?

Yes, he conceded, that was true. But he quickly added that it had been "too late."

His own report showed that lateness was not council's fault. But there didn't seem to be any way to get to the truth in the charged environment of that meeting. For the time being, the facts in the report would have to do.

In the late autumn, as my mayorship began to draw to a close, I began to take stock of a roller-coaster two years. I had lost ten pounds from the miserable, months-long bout with IBS. Our meetings were still chaotic and upsetting. And we'd still accomplished almost everything I had set out to do. We had increased the level of affordable housing, supported our public schools, improved city infrastructure, and created regional governance with the neighboring county. We had improved voting rights, strengthened our creative economy, enhanced transparency through my "open data" initiative, protected immigrants and refugees, rehabilitated the Daughters of Zion Cemetery, and fought gentrification. We had even overhauled event permitting and collaborated with Georgetown to sue the militias. It was a good list of actual results, and I was proud of it.

I traveled back to my alma mater, Princeton, to deliver a lecture on what Charlottesville meant for democracy. I spoke about my belief that American constitutionalism would ultimately be strengthened by and through these trials. The next day, I was asked to visit with a graduate school class on public policy. I steeled myself for questions about statues, racism, and government accountability. Instead, the first question was from a student who said, "I was reading about your Open Data Policy. How did you get that passed? What's the story?"

I laughed for a moment and then talked about the values of innovation, governance, and accountability that had led me to take up this charge. I described all the steps involved: creating a stakeholder group, researching policies around the country, working with staff on successive resolutions, and implementation.

It was a relief to talk about things we had gotten done, rather than fights we'd had or symbolic victories and failures. It was refreshing to get out of our fishbowl for a little while and see the work of government with clear eyes.

THE SECOND MEETING OF DECEMBER WAS MY LAST AS MAYOR. WE officially voted for the new permitting procedures. But the rest of the meeting was chaotic. I was crushed when the equity brushfire took a sudden turn against the complicated package I'd negotiated over the course of a year to redevelop the long-abandoned Landmark Hotel on the Downtown Mall into a mixed-use project including a five-star hotel. To address the building's lack of parking and the realities of construction finance in the Charlottesville market, we had negotiated a performance agreement involving tax credits and a discounted parking program, as well as special zoning approvals to allow an extra story with more rooms. The deal would have invested $1 million in tax credits in exchange for $10 million in tax revenues over the next decade, which could be spent on priorities like affordable housing, the schools, and other equity initiatives.

But activists at the meeting loudly protested that it was a giveaway to a wealthy developer. One told a local TV station that the project "sends a message that City Council is just disconnected with what the community needs right now."[17] At the meeting, activists said the city should condemn the property and turn it into affordable housing—not understanding that a condemnation would require us to pay the owner fair market value, probably $10 million, and that any redevelopment would cost tens of millions of dollars more. But suddenly, Bellamy and Fenwick, who had previously supported the deal, voted against it. The audience erupted in cheers. In 2019, Bellamy told me in private, and then publicly stated, that he had made a mistake, but it was too late. With mounting construction costs and decreased confidence in the city's participation, the developer had scrapped his plans for a new hotel. As of this writing, the building is still vacant—a symbol of the barrenness of the politics of symbolism.

During a discussion of accountability for August 12, the crowd erupted in jeers. Kristin Szakos attempted to speak several times but was harshly heckled. This was her last council meeting. She was slated to receive a plaque that night for her service, along with Bob Fenwick. But we couldn't give them their plaques because the environment was so volatile and hostile. At the break, Szakos was crying. Kathy Galvin was crying at the end of the meeting.

Jim Hingeley, a public defender who had served the city for years, made a speech about civility during the public comments. A young audience member held a small whiteboard with "FUCK CIVILITY" written on it.

Emily had been watching the livestream the whole time. When I came home, we basically collapsed into bed and stared at the ceiling. It had been a hell of a year.

26

THE CRUCIBLE

| 2018 |

THE TWO-YEAR JOURNEY THROUGH THE FIRESTORM WAS ALMOST over. Charlottesville mayors usually served for just a single term, and before the meeting I announced that I would be adhering to that tradition. Even if I could have gotten the two votes needed for another term, the truth is Emily and I needed a break. It was someone else's turn. At the first city council meeting in January 2018, I seconded the motion for Nikuyah Walker to become mayor. I had thought long and hard about this choice. Despite her attacks on me and the difficulties she'd presented in our meetings, I thought having an African American woman as leader would be a positive thing after the Summer of Hate. And I felt that giving establishment power to the antiestablishment movement she represented would require its members to address the realities of government rather than railing at it.

In the minutes after Walker was selected, I felt a wave of relief and lightness sweep over me. It was a slightly surreal experience. The ceremonial mantle had passed from my shoulders. One moment I was wearing it, the next I wasn't. I felt a hundred pounds lighter.

WITH THE SPOTLIGHT OFF ME, I HAD MORE TIME AND SPACE TO
reflect on the year and to try to understand how Charlottesville had
become such a microcosm for the nation in a troubled time. There had
been no silver bullets, no easy answers, no black-and-whites here. Instead, we just had a crazy quilt of contradictions, a messy reality that
mirrored a nation in a constant state of struggle.

The past year had included internal struggles for many, but it had
also been a struggle about Charlottesville—how to define it, how to
frame it, and how to tell the story about where it stood in the nation's
predicament. In a sense, the rallies reflected the explosion of an all-out
battle to claim the past and define that narrative.

In contrast to those who felt that Antifa's intentional and violent aggression had played into the alt-right's hands, and actually made things
worse, there was an active effort to say instead that the left had effectively
defended the city. A prominent voice for this view was Jalane Schmidt,
the UVA religion professor and Black Lives Matter chapter cofounder.
Schmidt frequently argued that the establishment matched the alt-right
in nefariousness because it was passive and therefore complicit with white
supremacy. A few weeks after 8/12, she wrote a piece that said the "Don't
Take the Bait" message during the KKK rally was actually "Ignore them."

She argued that Charlottesville was so deeply imbued with white
supremacy that the threat was actually from within, not from without.
She noted that the KKK had risen in Charlottesville in the 1920s, just
when the Confederate statues were being installed. At that time, she
said, "KKK parades filled the streets, Klansmen occupied positions of
influence (e.g., the sheriff), and visiting Klan figures held 'free speech'
presentations inside the Albemarle County Courthouse beside the
Stonewall Jackson monument."

Likening Charlottesville to Weimar Germany, Schmidt wrote, "We've
seen what happens in history when the growth of fascism is ignored and
its threat is not taken seriously." She added: "To be clear: I am not calling
for violence. What I am calling for is physical presence and vocal resistance. And if physical or emotional vulnerability make it difficult for you
to engage in direct action, don't go."[1]

When Richard Spencer canceled the rest of his college speaking tour in March 2018, due to Antifa's violent confrontations during his events, it seemed to bolster Antifa's argument. Some of the universities canceled his events or said no in the first place to his requests to come; others insisted he speak in venues situated far from their main campuses or during school breaks. Some required him to pay security deposits or insurance fees. They were all looking for ways to minimize the conflict his visits would bring, and they were largely successful—the sizes of his audiences were declining. Antifa itself claimed credit, and even Spencer complained that "Antifa was winning."[2]

I disagreed that Antifa deserved the credit, however. I felt Spencer was collapsing in part because of the violence of his own movement, and especially because of the murder of Heather Heyer. In Charlottesville, its malevolence had been fully exposed before a national audience, much as when Bull Connor, the commissioner of public safety in Birmingham, Alabama, in 1963, brutally ordered his firefighters to turn fire hoses on peaceful protesters, thus exposing the violence of segregation for a national audience and turning the nation against segregation.[3] So while I appreciated nonviolent activism, I felt that Antifa-led violence, and much "direct action," had not helped the counterprotesters' cause; instead, it had intensified the cycle of antagonism.

But that was just my view, and I will readily admit I could be wrong. There is no way definitively to answer the chicken-and-egg question of what caused what. In any case, the battle to frame the narrative showed that the past itself was contestable: it was an issue not so much about what had actually happened in history as about defining and claiming that history for both the present and future.

The battle over history surfaced a deeper ongoing cataclysm, a collision between radically opposed ideas about order and civility—about how to best address the threat of violent white nationalism in the United States. Should we do it within the nonviolent system we have, through our laws and institutions, and through nonviolent means as described by Martin Luther King Jr. in his first book, *Stride Toward Freedom*?[4] Or should we employ extralegal tools, including vigilante violence?

THE RACE AND HISTORY BRUSHFIRES SMOLDERED ON. AS OF THIS writing in the spring of 2019, the statues remain in Charlottesville's parks. Circuit Court Judge Richard E. Moore ordered the tarps removed after six months, saying that as war memorials, they were protected by state law.[5] That spring, Mary Carey, a local African American activist, began a petition protesting the parks' new names, which she said were still linked to slavery. A round of surveys confirmed that the public wanted more innocuous local names, and the city council renamed Emancipation and Justice Parks as Market Street and Court Square Parks, respectively.

Because of the court rulings, we had been advised by staff and counsel to stop any forward movement on the original "recontextualization" project to transform the parks by adding new design elements and monuments for context. We had already issued a request for proposals and received several bids. But under the state statute, this work, too, could now be seen as "interfering" with the statues. And so that work was stopped.

Apart from the parks being renamed, the only material result from the push to move the statues was that the plaque describing Lee as a Confederate hero had been removed. Other than winning the lawsuit—which will doubtless be appealed in years to come to the Virginia Supreme Court—the only way to resolve the situation is for the Virginia legislature to repeal the law. But despite repeated attempts, those bills keep on being killed in committee by the General Assembly.

Another way forward began through the city council's donation of $50,000 for a pilgrimage related to John Henry James, the victim of an 1898 lynching in the Charlottesville area. Community members gathered soil to be transported to the National Memorial for Peace and Justice in Montgomery, Alabama, established by the Equal Justice Initiative, founded by Bryan Stevenson, in 2018. Localities from around the country could contribute soil samples to the Montgomery memorial from their own lynching sites in exchange for memorials they would bring back to their communities. The museum's ultimate goal in memorializing the 4,400 victims of such racial terror was to help the country heal. According to the museum's website, "a history of racial injustice must be acknowledged, and mass atrocities and abuse must be recognized and remembered, before a society can recover from mass violence."[6] A group

THE CRUCIBLE | 295

from Charlottesville boarded two buses bound for Montgomery in July 2018. Along the way, they made stops in historic locations to learn about systemic racism and racial justice.

A year later, in July 2019, I watched from the audience on a warm July day as a plaque to John Henry James was installed on the lawn near the Albemarle County Courthouse, just steps from a plaque celebrating Thomas Jefferson and Monticello, and just across the road from the slave auction block embedded in the sidewalk. During the gentle, moving ceremony, two pastors (one black, one white) and a rabbi led the crowd in chanting, "We struggle for the possibility of a just world."[7]

Meanwhile, Charlottesville continued to earn notoriety for the particularly Manichaean way in which equity was being framed and pursued. In October 2018, the *New York Times* published a ProPublica exposé on the dramatic race and class disparities in Charlottesville's public school system (though such differences are shared by most cities in America, and certainly by almost all of them in the South). In an interview for the article, Mayor Nikuyah Walker said Charlottesville was "beautiful physically and aesthetically pleasing, but a very ugly-in-the-soul place."[8] The assertion exploded across social media. There were concerns that UVA would have even more trouble attracting African American students and faculty.

And throughout the charged year of 2018, the topic of Confederate statues continued to percolate around the country.

THE CITY OF RICHMOND HAS FIVE MASSIVE STATUES OF CONFEDerate generals—Robert E. Lee, J. E. B. Stuart, Jefferson Davis, Stonewall Jackson, and Matthew Fontaine Maury—along a grand promenade. In 1996, it had chosen to install a new statue of the city's local hero Arthur Ashe, tennis racket in hand, on the end of the promenade.

In July 2018, the Monument Avenue Commission that Richmond mayor Levar Stoney had put together released its report. It echoed the nuanced approach we had originally pursued in Charlottesville. Hundreds of Richmonders engaged with the commission, which dated back before August 12, 2017. At times, the meetings were fractious. Over five hundred people attended an August 9 meeting, and several hundred more were turned away for lack of space. The meeting devolved into a "shouting match between those with opposing points of view of 'leave them alone' or 'take them down.'"[9] In a city poll the following spring, about 18 percent of respondents wanted the monuments kept as they were with no changes; about 44 percent wanted them kept, but with context and/or new monuments; about 12 percent wanted them relocated to a different place; and about 22 percent wanted them removed from Monument Avenue altogether. The remainder of the respondents were unsure.[10]

The commission ended up recommending that the Jefferson Davis statue be relocated, "pending litigation or changes in state law which the City may choose to initiate or support," but that the other statues remain.[11] In a striking echo of the initial approach in Charlottesville, they also recommended "changing the face of Monument Avenue by adding new monuments that would reflect a broader, more inclusive story of our history."[12]

In 2019, the city began doing just that. In March, the Richmond City Council voted to rename a major thoroughfare through the city after Arthur Ashe, the city's African American tennis star, who already had a statue alongside the Confederate generals on Monument Avenue. In July, the Virginia Museum of Fine Arts announced that a massive statue by the noted African American artist Kehinde Wiley would be permanently placed outside the museum along the new Arthur Ashe Boulevard. The thirty-foot bronze sculpture features a young African American man riding a horse.

According to the museum, Wiley was inspired to create the statue after a visit to Richmond, where he encountered the massive equestrian monument to the Confederate general J. E. B. Stuart. The new statue was his "direct response" to the Confederate monuments. The new statue, a museum spokesperson said, would present a "powerful visual repositioning of young black men in our public consciousness while directly engaging the national conversation around controversial monuments and their role in perpetuating incomplete narratives and contemporary inequities."[13] For anyone looking for an example of what "recontextualization" would mean—this was it.

The University of Virginia broke ground on its own recontextualization project—a massive circular memorial to enslaved laborers that gently rises out of the ground—in December 2018. It is meant to echo a link in a slave's shackle and will be inscribed with the names of the enslaved men and women who served UVA but went unrecognized for so long.[14]

At the same time, in some places the absolutist approach gained momentum. With little fanfare, the UVA Board of Visitors voted to remove a plaque to Confederate soldiers from the outside of the Rotunda in September 2017. In Durham, North Carolina, activists tore down the controversial statue to Silent Sam, leaving the stone pedestal up, in August 2018. The president of the University of North Carolina tried to come up with a nuanced approach, where the statue would have been relocated to an expensive new museum, but the university's board of visitors rejected that approach. In the end, the university president ordered the pedestal itself removed, while at the same time announcing her resignation.

The mayor of Birmingham had ordered a Confederate statue to be wrapped in plastic and surrounded by plywood in August 2017. Alabama had a statute regarding Confederate monuments that was similar to Virginia's, but with an important difference: theirs had been passed by the legislature on May 20, 2017, just after Charlottesville's movement got underway. In January 2019, an Alabama judge struck down the state statute on freedom-of-speech grounds, ruling that the city "has a right to speak for itself, to say what it wishes, and to select the views that it wants to express"—and that the state's attempt to prohibit removal of the statue was "impermissibly content-based."[15]

Meanwhile, Charlottesville's narrative continued to evolve, many of us (myself included) along with it. In our council meeting on July 1, 2019, Mayor Walker and Wes Bellamy proposed that the city replace the annual city holiday for Thomas Jefferson's birthday with a new holiday to recognize the freeing of slaves. I had nursed a longtime beef about Jefferson. One reason I wrote *Becoming Madison* was to correct our longtime seduction by Jefferson's poetry around constitutional rights, instead of the prose of Madison's ideas of statesmanship. I had been deeply troubled by Charlottesville historian Henry Wiencek's portrait of Jefferson avidly calculating the value of his children slaves in *Master of the Mountain*.[16] However, I was reluctant to vote for the measure. I thought we could instead recontextualize the holiday.

As debate began behind the dais, however, my opinion shifted. I heard the voices of the citizens who spoke at the meeting, and then Mayor Walker and Bellamy as they voiced their frustration and fury at the unqualified, singular veneration of the slave-holding Jefferson. Indeed, Jefferson had written that blacks were "inferior to the whites in the endowments both of body and mind."[17] As I listened, I realized that Jefferson was the only individual (other than Martin Luther King Jr.) recognized with a holiday in Charlottesville. On the city's website, I learned that the holiday was added only in the 1940s, and I reflected on how Democratic committees around the country had been replacing their "Jefferson-Jackson Day" annual fundraising dinners with new, more inclusive names.

And I changed my mind. In a tentative voice (for once, I was not sure what I would say ahead of time), I talked about how I'd been moved by my colleagues' testimonials, and said I would support the holiday changes. But despite these changes, the Virginia statute remained, as impassive as Lee and Jackson on their bronze horses and stone pedestals. It also contained a real threat to me and to the other councilors who had voted to sell the Lee statue.

THE COUNCILORS WHO HAD VOTED TO REMOVE THE STATUE AND to install the tarps in 2017—initially, Kristin Szakos, Wes Bellamy, and Bob Fenwick, and then later myself and Kathy Galvin—had been sued under the 1987 Virginia statute preventing the "disturbance or removal" of war memorials. A 2000 addition to the statute included a provision requiring the losing party to pay the winning party's attorneys' fees.

That 2000 provision ran so far afoul of traditional rules giving legislators immunity for liability on their legislative acts that our attorneys in the City Attorney's Office hadn't even mentioned it. They had not advised us that by voting for removal and the tarps, we—as legislators—could be swept into its ambit. It was outlandish, unthinkable. In 2016, the Virginia Supreme Court had refused to strike down the decision by a Danville, Virginia, judge allowing that city to remove a Confederate flag from its courthouse, and that decision seemed to call the entire state war memorials statute into question. Less than two weeks after Unite the Right, Attorney General Mark Herring had issued an opinion affirming the Danville judge's conclusion that the law did not apply to monuments constructed prior to 1997.[18]

Yet Judge Moore issued a letter opinion on June 15, 2018, suggesting that we could be held responsible for legal expenses under the statute.

Whether the legislature could penalize legislators in such a way—whether it could impose penalties on city councilors for voting in a certain way—got to the heart of the hot national "preemption" debate. And it had vast consequences. We had to bring on lawyers (Jones Day, a major international law firm, agreed to represent us pro bono). We had to subject our emails and files to discovery. We had to have our legislating activity under the thumb of court scrutiny. We had to feel like we had done something that might be illegal just by taking a vote.

Richard Schragger, a noted expert on local and state government law, wrote an editorial in the *Daily Progress* about the ominous consequences of the litigation. If the courts allowed elected officials to be held personally liable for their votes, he argued, "very few people would take the risk of becoming a city councilor or a member of a school board or a member of any local government body." He observed, "Constituents who disagree with legislators' votes would harass them with endless lawsuits. . . . [T]he Charlottesville case is exactly why immunity is needed."[19]

It was with a huge sigh of relief that I learned in July 2019 that the judge had ruled in our favor. We were, he ruled, entitled to absolute legislative immunity under Virginia law. While the decision was welcome, I was angry that the attempt to silence and punish elected officials had gotten as far as it did.

AT THE SAME TIME, THE FIRST AMENDMENT WAS EVOLVING BEfore our very eyes. In late 2017, the City of Charlottesville, through our professional staff and our City Attorney's Office—without consulting the city council, and without even advising us of this action ahead of time—denied Jason Kessler a permit for a one-year anniversary rally of Unite the Right. I was upset about not being informed but strongly supportive of the approach and the decision.

The city's decision, announced on December 11, 2017, stated flatly that "the proposed demonstration or special event will present a danger to public safety, and cannot be accommodated within the area applied for, or within a reasonable allocation of City funds and/or police resources." It said that Kessler "likely underestimates the number of participants," and that he had requested that the police separate the two sides, but that "the city does not have the ability to determine or sort individuals according to what 'side' they are on, and no reasonable allocation of City funds or resources can guarantee that event participants will be free of any 'threat of violence.'"

Compared to the prior approach, this was an abrupt departure for the city. The statement of facts, legal analysis, and strategy were all different from what we had said before. That showed how much things were changing. On the basis of the disaster that had come to pass during the August 2017 rally, our attorneys felt confident in making bolder claims and taking more risks. In contrast with the hubris demonstrated earlier by Chief Thomas, and his overconfident reliance on his "strategy," the city now admitted that it didn't have the "ability" to estimate how many people would come. Instead of accepting the duty to manage public safety, it flatly said that the standard should be whether the city could "guarantee" safety—and admitted it could not.

The decision was a window into how the law works in a common-law system. It evolves organically around practical developments. In this case, the city took a calculated risk that public safety and cost now *could* be cited to deny the permit. The city's attorneys thought that a judge would now give the city, rather than bright-line rules, the benefit of the doubt. Kessler, as expected, sued the city a few weeks later, citing a violation of his First Amendment rights. But as we went into court, the circuit court judge, Richard Moore—the same judge presiding over the statues case—was notably skeptical of Kessler's claims. While there was ultimately no court decision due to Kessler's withdrawal of the permit application, the combination of events set one more precedent for other cities seeking to cite public safety and expense as reasons not to allow an event they reasonably believed would be too dangerous.

On July 9, 2018, Kessler and many of the other defendants from 8/12 were delivered a punishing blow in federal court by none other than Judge Norman Moon—the same judge who had ruled against our city council defamation rules when Joe Draego had sued us, way back in the fall of 2016. Through the organization Integrity First for America, led by the noted attorneys Roberta Kaplan and Karen Dunn, ten Charlottesville residents had filed a civil suit seeking monetary damages from the defendants. In the case, *Sines v. Kessler*, Judge Moon ruled against the defendants' motion to dismiss; in doing so, he issued a legally sweeping, factually nuanced opinion that worked through a full range of offenses on constitutional grounds, including allegations that the defendants had engaged in a conspiracy of violence against racial minorities in violation of the 1872 congressional act preventing organized terrorism in the Reconstruction South by none other than the Ku Klux Klan.

The decision made for powerful reading as a survey of the stunning violence of the Unite the Right rally. It also directly confronted otherwise abstract First Amendment issues through the lens of specifics. Noting that the defendants would indeed be protected by the First Amendment if they had "only engaged in 'abstract' advocacy of violence,"[20] the judge found instead the opposite:

> The complaint, though, is replete with specific allegations that extend beyond mere "abstract" advocacy. The allegations of physical assault are "not by any stretch of the imagination expressive conduct protected by the First Amendment." And even many of those allegations that do concern expressive conduct, which the Court included in its above analysis, fall into three main categories of speech that extend beyond the First Amendment's protections for advocacy.[21]

The judge also found sufficient cause to consider violations of Virginia's hate crimes statute, which prevents "intimidation or harassment or . . . violence directed against [a victim's] person . . . where such acts are motivated by racial, religious, or ethnic animosity."[22]

On August 2, 2018—ten days away from the one-year anniversary of Unite the Right—Kessler delivered the coup de grace and dropped his lawsuit.

WHAT WAS HAPPENING? THAT WINTER, AN ARTICLE HAD APPEARED in *Virginia*, the UVA alumni magazine, by Fred Schauer, a preeminent professor of First Amendment law at UVA. He elliptically suggested that the First Amendment could—and would—change. While "the opposing parties hurl hackneyed slogans at each other," he bemoaned, "we find little serious public thought about the values of freedom of speech and the qualifications that should be imposed on it." Noting the "all-too-frequent failure to distinguish what the law is from what it should be," he went on to argue "that just because the law is the law doesn't make it immune from criticism or change."[23]

In 2019, Schauer expanded on these insights in an article for the *Notre Dame Law Review*, where he argued that, in both actuality and in practice, First Amendment law is far less absolute than the First Amendment absolutists claim—particularly as regards the "hostile audience" issue that led to the "heckler's veto" concern preventing Charlottesville from canceling the rally due to public safety concerns.[24] There were actually "substantial and increasingly salient questions unanswered" in the doctrine, he said, including the fact that many Supreme Court decisions depended on critiques of vague governing standards (such as the "breach of peace" ordinance in *Terminiello*) rather than setting out specific standards for better rules. The "worry," he wrote, had always been that "such vagueness will allow excess official discretion, a discretion that would create an undue risk of impermissible content-based . . . discrimination against demonstrators." But "as a consequence, we know less than we might—here and elsewhere—about just what kinds of specific, nonvague standards would be permissible, or just how specific the standard must be to avoid invalidation on vagueness grounds."[25] But there's a positive side to this ambiguity in the wake of events like Charlottesville. It offers fertile ground for moving the line separating freedom of speech from public safety closer toward public safety. The ambiguity was one reason why the City of Charlottesville was able to deny Kessler's permit the second time around.

Schauer noted an area, which was evolving in the wake of Charlottesville, where the law might also permit cities to adopt Justice Jackson's original argument in his *Terminiello* dissent for more deference to local authorities: cost and practicality. He noted that the Supreme Court has not really addressed the issues that became so critical to Charlottesville and to Berkeley. While the Supreme Court used to assume that the "expense of providing protection" was "prone to be exaggerated by state and local officials eager to prevent the speech in the first place," he wrote, ". . . today such suspicions rest on a flimsier basis."[26] In real numbers from real events, we could now see how expensive these events really are. Indeed, in the Charlottesville City Council's decision in 2018 about what to do with our year-end surplus, we were forced to allocate $1 million to expenses related to the massively policed one-year anniversary of 8/12. This was at a time when the council's main interest was supporting affordable housing.

Schauer's writing is gnomic, which is how prominent law professors sometimes write, as if they're sending smoke signals to the Supreme Court to interpret the law in one direction rather than another. What I take Schauer to mean is that, in the future, *because of events like Charlottesville*, courts may very well start to allow cities to take things like cost and danger into account, whereas before, they were prevented from doing so because they would always been seen by courts as a backdoor for a heckler's veto. In other words, the law may be adapting, right before our eyes, toward Jackson's original position, even if we don't realize it.

As 2018 PROCEEDED, THE ACCOUNTABILITY BRUSHFIRE BURNED ON. In May, the councilors appeared at a press conference and, led by the new mayor, Nikuyah Walker, announced that City Manager Maurice Jones's three-year contract, which expired at the end of the year, would not be renewed. Walker said, "It has become clear to us that what our City needs at this critical juncture is a fresh perspective and a new direction."[27]

In August, the crucible produced ingots of wisdom. Earlier in the summer, I sat down for a long interview with A. C. Thompson of ProPublica, a leading investigative reporter on the alt-right. He had spent years carefully researching and trying to understand both the movement and its interface with government. I was struck by the depth and nuance of the questions. He seemed to really understand the nature of our government, what we had tried to do, and what we could and could not do. The hour-long *Frontline* documentary appeared a week before the one-year anniversary of Unite the Right and delivered a clear verdict on why the state and city had both appeared to be so clueless.[28] At long last, there was an accurate picture of events. The documentary's tone reflected informed, educated frustration. It did not scapegoat. It asked questions and pursued answers.

In the documentary, Thompson clarified the "credible threat" standard that Police Chief Thomas had referred to in the crucial meeting with the Virginia state troopers. An article published alongside the documentary began:

> On Aug. 2, 2017, Charlottesville Mayor Michael Signer convened a closed meeting of the City Council. The Unite the Right rally was days off, and Signer was concerned about how to manage the potential for trouble. The Virginia State Police were there. So, too, was the chief of the Charlottesville Police Department.
>
> Signer and the Council members asked the law enforcement officers present directly: Was there a "specific, credible threat" of violence?
>
> There was none, the elected officials said they were told.[29]

In the documentary, Thompson explained why the council had feared losing in court, and why we hadn't been able to stop the permits from being issued. In a tone of frustration, he asked why the entire federal apparatus that had been set up to address terrorism after 9/11 had failed in Charlottesville. The documentary quoted me saying, "I wish that we had known more. I wish that we had been given more information by the state intelligence apparatus." When Thompson asked whether the police had indicated that militias would be invading us, I said, simply, "No."

Thompson found that an anonymous researcher in the federal government said he had filed reports every two weeks from January to August 2017 chronicling clear evidence that extremists on the right and left were destined to meet violently. He said those reports were shared with the federal agency that hired him and, he believed, had made their way to the authorities in charge. "Because of the length of time that the groups had to organize, the extent of their networking, and the logistics in question, there were concerns expressed to law enforcement agencies about the potential for violence," he told Thompson. In other words, the Department of Homeland Security and the Federal Bureau of Investigation *had* tried to warn the state and Charlottesville police of the potential for planned violence. So perhaps the fusion center's August 9 report had been read. But it had failed to impact both the security plans and the federal court decision.

Worse, Thompson reported, federal and state authorities had made no use of an intelligence tool "typically vital for such events": confidential informants inside extremist groups on both sides. The documentary interviewed a retired FBI agent who said there were clearly breakdowns in intelligence gathering and sharing in Charlottesville. "People in this movement, many times they are ripe for development as informants," he said. "If you can catch them at the right time, when you get them realizing that this is stupid, you can knock it out of the park." Yet this did not happen.[30]

Clues as to why could be found in a blockbuster front-page *New York Times Magazine* article that came a few weeks later, providing evidence that the FBI had removed white nationalists from the scope of potential domestic terrorists. The reporter, Janet Reitman, found that white supremacists and other far-right extremists had been responsible for 70 percent of fatalities in domestic terror incidents between 2008 and 2017, as compared with 26 percent by Islamic extremists. Nevertheless, federal agencies were focused instead on "strident rhetoric around 'foreign-born' terrorists"—particularly under the Trump administration. In the article, Peter Singer, a national security expert, recalled meeting with a group of senior Trump administration officials about counterterrorism. "They only wanted to talk about Muslim extremism," he said. Even before the Trump administration, he recalled, "we willingly turned the other way on white supremacy because there were real political costs to talking about white supremacy."[31]

All this brought to mind a chilling conversation I had at the United States Conference of Mayors meeting in Miami in June 2017 with an official from the Office of Countering Violent Extremism at the US State Department. He told me, in a tone of lament, that the State Department, under the Trump administration, had basically taken white nationalist groups out of the scope of potential terrorists. He implied, in no uncertain terms, that this decision had been made for domestic political reasons. This was just after the Richard Spencer–led torch rally, and just before the KKK came to Charlottesville. At the time, I'd had no idea that decisions made in faraway Washington could affect my city so profoundly.

BUT THE MOST IMPORTANT MECHANISM FOR DELIVERING AC-countability was the criminal justice system—the largest gear in our machine of local governance, but the one that moved the most slowly. It finally delivered judgment on the most heinous acts committed at Unite the Right.

A year after the beating of DeAndre Harris at the Market Street Parking Garage, most of his assailants were convicted and sentenced for their crimes. Alex Ramos was sentenced to six years in prison, and Jacob Goodwin to ten years in prison with two years suspended. Later, in January 2019, Daniel Borden was sentenced to twenty years in prison, although, after time suspended, he would spend a little less than four years in prison. It had taken over a year, and it came through a different arm of government from the City Council, but justice was at long last being served.[32]

The trial of James Alex Fields Jr. was held in November 2018, more than a year after Unite the Right. The whole town was on pins and needles awaiting the outcome. His defense attorney employed elements of the conspiracy theory that had been circulated to argue that he was acting in self-defense—that one of the left-wing militia groups had brandished weapons in a threatening way, and that Fields had reacted by driving toward and into, and then away from, the crowd.

Fields was charged with first-degree murder, five counts of aggravated malicious wounding, three counts of malicious wounding, and one count of failing to stop at an accident involving a death. The prosecution assembled exhaustive evidence, including video evidence of the car's actions and eyewitness testimony from dozens of victims. Over the course of the twelve-day trial, the jury also saw a text message that Fields had sent his mother before the Unite the Right rally. It included a picture of Adolf Hitler and the words, "We're not the one [sic] who need to be careful." Fields described the crowd at Fourth and Water Streets to his mother as a violent group of terrorists and claimed the crowd was waving ISIS flags. He called Susan Bro, Heather Heyer's mother, an "anti-white communist" and said, "She's the enemy."

The jury consisted of nine women and seven men, including four alternates. The twelve who deliberated the case recommended a sentence of life plus 419 years.

Afterward, Susan Bro said, "My God, the kid's messed up and needs help. . . . Put him away, I'm sorry. . . . My daughter is still not here and the other survivors still have their wounds to deal with." She added, "We've all been damaged permanently but we do survive and move forward."[33]

I couldn't have agreed more. In July 2019, his sentence was confirmed. He will spend the rest of his life in prison.

Meanwhile, the accountability brushfire lapped up against the structure of government itself. Midway through 2018, the community and the council started to debate whether the city should shift to a "strong mayor" form of government, as Richmond did in 2004, after former governor Doug Wilder led a campaign for the change (he then became the first strong mayor there under the new system). Some community members felt that the events of 2017 meant we needed such a change, but they were, at best, a loud and small minority. Other citizens expressed hesitation about whether a small city could be best served by a highly paid, full-time mayor, and the imbalances that would then be created with the part-time city councilors.

Reflecting on the lessons of 2017, I concluded that the best structural response to the events would be to instead elect the city manager, as is done in some cities in Maryland. The city manager would then have to earn a constituency, and the voters could hold him or her accountable for any mistakes made in office. I argued for this repeatedly from the dais, but there was no appetite among the other councilors for such a radical change. People did not even favor electing the mayor, let alone making the mayor the chief executive of the city.

After a short period of debate, we went on as before, with a "weak mayor" and an unelected city manager.

THE FOURTH BRUSHFIRE OF THE DISORDER PROBLEM, THE RUN OF the passions against governance, still bedeviled us. "Civility" continued to be a straw man for people committed to the belief that there was a culture of "tone policing" that was really just a nefarious means of enforcing the status quo of white supremacy. Andrea Douglas, the director of the Jefferson School African American Heritage Center, told the local paper, "So you've got to ask yourself the question: Are you asking me to be civil so that you can control this discourse?"[34]

But there was a problem with this logic. Civility, as Robert's Rules envisioned, was not the end of democracy. It was only a means to an end. It was a device to enable people with strong opinions to get things done together. If you were looking substantively to improve people's lives through government, it was, in fact, a device to address oppression.

Jim Hingeley, the public defender, continued speaking in almost every meeting about civility. Usually, the audience loudly mocked him. The jeers included, "You're defending a murderer," "No civility for white supremacists," "We'll intimidate every one of them," "You're at the wrong meeting," "Cry me a river," "Poor babies," and "We have some reading for you."

During one meeting, Bellamy spoke out for incivility on the grounds that civility was oppressive. "When people are hurting, they are going to express themselves in the way in which they feel will get your attention, because the way they've been going about it before has been ignored," Bellamy said. "That does not make them bad people. That does not make them unruly."[35]

When the new council held a work session on our new governing procedures, despite all the controversy, and the fact that we had a new mayor who had risen to her position in part through attacks on the new rules, a surprising consensus developed that we did, in fact, need the rules, and that they needed to be stronger around the disorder problem. Our City Attorney's Office drafted a new set of expanded rules stating that "remarks and actions" disrupting the meeting would now be prohibited. These rules specified that interrupting a speaker who was addressing the council would not be permitted. Nor would interrupting a councilor who was speaking, or "shouting, and talking (either individually or in concert with others) in a manner that prevents a speaker or a Councilor from being heard or that otherwise hinders the progress of the meeting." This meant that any outburst, any talkback from the floor, was not allowed. And the rules went on to say that the mayor "*shall* call an individual to order when that individual goes afoul of these rules" (emphasis added). In other words, the mayor was *required* to prevent this behavior.

The new council passed these new rules unanimously. Now, it was up to the new mayor, Nikuyah Walker, to enforce them.

MAYOR WALKER, HOWEVER, DID NOT ENFORCE THE NEW RULES. What followed was instead months of meetings where there were open outbursts from the floor, heckling, jeering, finger-snapping, and open harassment of speakers and councilors alike.

Although many would say that enforcing civility was tantamount to enforcing white supremacy, many of the hecklers were not in fact lower-income African Americans. They were often graduate and undergraduate students, often white. Sometimes they were even well-heeled white residents who simply opposed a zoning decision that would put denser developments in their backyards. Taking cues from the new unruly environment, they would shout and cuss from the crowd. A young white man with tousled hair would come to council meetings with a small whiteboard and write slogans on it, often snapping his fingers and making audible outbursts. Another finger-snapper was the white chair of the local Democratic Socialists of America chapter, who would live-tweet proceedings, frequently while gasping, interrupting, and laughing out loud at speakers. Mayor Walker lectured her once from the dais about her white privilege. She was later hired as a columnist by the *C-ville Weekly*.

There was a particularly unruly council meeting on April 2, 2018. The disruptions began on a seemingly innocuous matter, the "West 2nd Project," a public-private mixed-use housing development on a city-owned parking lot adjacent to the Downtown Mall that included luxury condominiums. During the public comment period, several speakers in favor of the project were jeered, with plastic bottles being crinkled noisily to interrupt and distract them.

Jason Kessler was seated in the audience next to a balding man with a firearm openly strapped to his waist. Danger emanated from the pair, yet they sat there for over half an hour, waiting for their turn to speak. When Kessler's slot came up, he strode to the podium. In a shaky voice, he read well-rehearsed words, clearly intended to set the council up for another First Amendment challenge in court. He demanded of the councilors, "You all are seen as leaders by the mobs who have taken over the city. Many call them Antifa. If a federal judge grants me an injunction to hold another rally in support of the monuments, will you ask them not to block access to the park and to remain nonviolent?"

During his remarks, he was interrupted by both white and black members of the audience. Walker had to interrupt him to quiet the crowd. "Excuse me, excuse me!"

Kessler was followed by Chris Wayne, a supporter of his who first addressed the council and then turned toward the crowd, gesticulating toward them and openly antagonizing them. When Mayor Walker reminded him that our rules required him to address the council, he responded, "Sorry, ma'am, I just felt the peanut gallery needed to be addressed." The crowd kept shouting nonetheless. He turned back around and said, "I'll be right outside if anybody wants a piece of me when this is over."

Walker then declared a recess. As protesters crowded around Kessler and his friends, she directed officers to clear the chambers. There were screams of "Shut the fuck up, Jason!" There were also just open screams. Wayne shouted back, "Shut the fuck up, peanut gallery." When it was time to resume the meeting, we took our seats. But there were still shouts of "Fuck you!" and open jostling in the crowd. Walker did not want to remove anyone. She did not want to clear the chamber. But that's what she ended up deciding to do. "OK, so, we're clearing the room," she said. She told the officers, "You all can clear the room." Audience members exited angrily. "What the fuck?" one woman screamed, over and over. "Why? I'm sick of this shit! I can't fucking sleep at night! Fuck the police!"

"It's insane," Walker said from behind the dais, her words picked up by the live microphone. I understood. Life was different in the mayor's chair. She had needed to clear the chamber to keep order, just as I had done. She had needed to establish order in a chaotic meeting—just as I had done.

When we returned to the dais after a long break, Mayor Walker then told the crowd, "It is my duty as Mayor to now read rules." Her remarks were revealing:

> This is very difficult for me. I was hoping that we would find a flow to where people were doing things different naturally, that they felt like if there were people up here representing their values, that they would respond differently. While it has been better, it has been very difficult to conduct the meetings and have business take place. I really don't know the answers because I know every reason why it's happening, but then I know how other people feel, even for me, making this time valuable and getting business actually done, right. With that said, do I want to sit up here and tell people how to respond? I don't want to be that person.

She paused and took a breath, then continued: "But anyway, that's where we are." She went on to read the exact same rules I had relied upon—stronger now—that prevented interruptions and heckling both of councilors and anyone addressing them. She did so with a loud sigh. But she read every word.

She then ruminated on the difficulties she was facing as mayor. "My intention was to allow people to find their way. . . . I don't even raise my kids like this. I want them to be vocal and I want them to have a voice. At the same time it is very difficult up here." On the heckling that had taken place during the debate about the West 2nd Project, she said, "They have a right to speak. They have a right to voice their concerns." She continued, "The screaming, yelling, bottles crinkling, are not going to change that. . . . So, these are the rules. I have to now, not let things flow." She said she would now have to "just be firm with everyone."

Soon after that meeting, at a city council retreat, Bellamy angrily took on what he described as "white liberals"—many of the activists snapping their fingers and crinkling bottles in council meetings. He said their advocacy for communities of color actually set back racial progress. "We have this issue with white people in our community saying black people need XYZ and they don't ever come to First Street. Don't listen to that bullshit."[36]

It was around this time that meetings started to become quieter. Mayor Walker continued to send signals that she would in fact enforce the rules. I learned in a meeting toward the end of 2018 with our new police chief, Rashall Brackney, that she believed these changes were due to her own decision to intervene. She told me she had held meetings with both Bellamy and Walker to instruct them on the material dangers of the environment in council chambers—not just in terms of attrition among the police forces, but in terms of the dangers felt by council members.

It was around this time that our dais was finally bulletproofed—a three-foot-high strip of metal sheathing was wrapped around the back of the long curved desk that separated us from the audience. If something happened, the idea was, we would duck under the desk.

In the background of all this was a new national discussion about civility in the Trump age, led by figures like the best-selling psychologist Jonathan Haidt (previously a UVA professor). Haidt supported an effort called Civil Politics, which focused on "evidence-based methods for improving inter-group civility." Civil Politics defined civility as "the ability to disagree productively with others, respecting their sincerity and decency." But "by civility," said the organization's website, "we do NOT mean agreement." The group's work drew on scientific research to understand how moral disagreements become uncivil, and how we can recommend changes that can get people out of unproductive, uncivil disagreement. Its focus was on "indirect methods," such as changing contexts, payoffs, and institutions, rather than "direct methods," such as pleading with people to be more civil, or asking people to sign civility pledges.[37]

But the battle continued to frame and claim civility in Charlottesville. In March 2019, National Public Radio produced a piece on the civility debate. The piece unfortunately pitched in with the politics of symbolism, rehearsing the old complaint that the civility versus incivility line also followed white versus black and establishment versus social justice polarities. The reporter quoted Jalane Schmidt, who said, "Civility is actually used to shut down discussion. . . . It is often a way to 'tone police' the folks that don't have power and that don't speak in four-syllable words."[38]

The irony was that civility was becoming yet another football in our politics of symbolism. The logic was seductive and inescapable, particularly to the same white liberals whom Bellamy had recently attacked for their often counterproductive activism: if you supported "civility" (whatever it might be), you were also supporting the same establishment the anarchists were attacking, and so you were also supporting white supremacy, and so you also might be a racist. So you'd better not support civility, whether as a symbol or a concept, let alone as an actual practice.

Small surprise that in April 2019, the publisher of *Charlottesville Tomorrow*, a small news nonprofit, would casually refer to a "new generation of African American leaders [that] has ripped open an old conversation repressed by civility."[39]

Or that in 2019, when the regional tourism board (on which I sat as a member of city council) hired a North Carolina PR firm to rebrand the city—and it proposed a theme of "Cville-ization," which would have included ads celebrating "Cville-ity"—the concept was roundly bemoaned, satirized, and ultimately dismissed in favor of a new slogan: "More to C," referring to the "C" in "C'ville," but highlighting the city's many attractions.

Meanwhile, following UVA's victory in the NCAA college basketball championship in 2019, the *Daily Progress* published an article titled "UVa Fans' Peaceful Celebration Bucks National Trend," celebrating the fact that the town had experienced little property destruction and violence in the victory party that night.[40] In response, Jamelle Bouie, a UVA graduate and Charlottesville resident who was named a *New York*

Times columnist in 2019, then tweeted about the "civility fetish of liberal Charlottesville."

This was the same year that a delegate to the state legislature from Richmond, Delores McQuinn, a prominent African American leader in the General Assembly, proposed a bill declaring 2019 the "Year of Reconciliation and Civility."[41]

By the time of our city council meeting on November 5, 2018, after months of chaos and ineffectiveness, even Wes Bellamy had gone back to where we had started, pushing for order in our chambers. His speech was significant:

> I know that there's been a great deal of conversation about things that have transpired over the past 15 months or so. There have been a lot of emotional meetings, a lot of people who feel very passionately about things that have transpired. And I think all of that is welcome. However, the way in which we do so needs to be in a sense in which we are leaders in our community. Whether you want to be or not when you step up to this podium people are looking up to you as a community leader. While others are talking let's try and be . . . respectful. I've heard of a variety of people from the spectrum who feel as if they are not comfortable coming to the meeting for a variety of reasons. And these are people who are very passionate about social justice issues. One of which was at the meeting last week, a mother I knew, and she left the meeting because the climate that was here, which has been rather disparaging. When they see our meetings they are looked at as a circus or show. We've had a lot of traumatic events that have taken place. Let's try to get back to a place where we move forward not only with equity but with respect for all. We can be the leaders in doing that. I hope we can do that. Words matter.

It seemed that if we just gave up the word "civility," which had successfully been redefined as a sign of oppression, and instead started using the word "respect," we could again try and bring rules, order, and deliberation back to the chambers.

The contradictions revealed what civility had become. In the politics of symbolism, it had become a valuable commodity. It was no longer what Robert's Rules of Order is for thousands of government bodies around the world—impersonal rules of the road to help people in government work together to achieve results. It was instead a proxy for underlying battles about culture and identity.

Which means there was diminishing common ground for governing itself.

BUT IT WAS ON THE FIFTH BRUSHFIRE, THE DEMAND FOR EQUITY, that there was the most progress, albeit again with churning, confusion, and cost. Walker's election had made blindingly clear what the scores of agonized African Americans testifying to the council in the meetings since August 12 had been telling us: the invasion of white nationalists had been a unique horror for them. In the middle of December 2017, I took a walk with a young black man who had appeared before the council during the traumatic "take-over" on August 21. We knew each other personally. His angry demand for my resignation that night, dreadlocks swinging around his face, had been more painful than anything else.

It was a frigid day. We walked from one end of the mall to another. He expressed frustration that I'd sided with the police over the counterprotesters after the KKK rally. He asked why I hadn't been able to stop Unite the Right from happening despite evidence of violence. I responded to each of these points as factually as I could. He shook his head at everything, dumbfounded at the law, our form of government, how tied our hands had been.

As the tension eased and we continued walking, he became more confessional. I was most struck when he told me, with a tremor in his voice, about his fear not only that "they were going to come back," but that "they" would take over the city and eject all African Americans from it. I responded, with puzzlement, that this could never be the case. We had a black city manager, a black police chief, a black vice-mayor, and a black superintendent of schools. We were a progressive city, one that had voted, after all, to remove a statue of Robert E. Lee from the city. Didn't he agree?

He did and he didn't. It was clear that the fear was gut-deep; it was part of the air he breathed, the lens through which he saw our "charming" city. I was grateful that he'd been so honest with me about the consequences and the trauma of 8/12, especially the emotional landscape he and hundreds of others now shared.

OVER THE COURSE OF THE NEXT YEAR, DESPITE THE DIFFERENCES and divisions on the new city council, equity would assume a central role in a new consensus that developed among us for the priorities of our post–Unite the Right community. Even though we often had harsh disagreements, the new mayor and I did agree on the need for a new "equity lens" for many policy decisions. In the new budget, we dramatically expanded the city's tax credit for low-income homeowners experiencing increased property taxes due to gentrification. We also brought all city employees, including part-time school and pool workers, up to a $15 an hour wage.

We set in motion an entirely new approach to affordable and public housing, with our spending ballooning in the 2020 fiscal year to over $10 million. At long last, we were able to assist the independent Charlottesville Redevelopment and Housing Authority with millions of dollars of new funds to redevelop the crumbling stock of public housing— including Crescent Halls, which had been the subject of that fractious council meeting back in 2016, when the air-conditioning broke down. This only happened in partnership with the musician Dave Matthews and his longtime manager, Coran Capshaw, one of Charlottesville's most prominent real estate developers, who plowed millions into the project. Ironically, the same business success that some of the new dissenters would use to attack the city on equity grounds would be deployed to resolve one of our most intractable equity problems.

However, there were other setbacks and conflicts. A one-time allocation of $75,000 to the Downtown Business Association to help market businesses suffering a downturn because of 8/12 was scorched by advocates for taking away from work on equity. The long-planned mixed-use

West 2nd Project was effectively killed when Bellamy hectored the developer, one of Charlottesville's most prominent affordable housing owners, from the dais for not including more affordable housing in the project than the city itself had originally agreed to. Even though he had already invested $2 million in underground utilities, he abandoned the project. The Landmark Hotel, deprived of the city's support, continued to hulk, crumbling and overtaken by weeds, in the heart of the Downtown Mall.

Equity, in other words, was not a salve. It was not a rainbow. It was a journey with its own agonies, just like all the others.

THE DIFFERENT BRUSHFIRES, ALL STILL SMOLDERING, THREATened the city again in the summer of 2018 as we approached the one-year anniversary of August 12. It remained unclear whether Kessler and other alt-right supporters would try to invade the city again, despite his loss in court and his subsequent withdrawal of his permit application. It seemed highly unlikely that the alt-right would come back, but both the city and the state proceeded with massive preemptive plans anyway. It was very strange to watch the post–Unite the Right machinery be put into place to create a stadium plan per the Heaphy Report's recommendations. The community watched as cranes lifted dozens of concrete Jersey barriers along Market Street, creating a stone lane that would presumably channel protesters and counterprotesters along defined lanes toward fixed exit and entry points.

On the eve of August 12, 2018, Emily and I were walking near the barriers when we ran into a local part-time journalist named Hawes Spencer. He was very critical of the virtual "lock-down" the city was under at the time. We got into the topic of the internecine fighting among the city councilors. He looked at me for a long moment before saying that he had "always wanted" to tell me something: "You could have been Joan of Arc," he continued.

He went on to explain that if I had stuck to my guns, demanded the resignation of Maurice Jones and Al Thomas, and gone on to be censured or even expelled by my colleagues on the council, then, after the Heaphy Report came out, I could have been seen as the hero—the lone member who was bravely telling the truth. I looked back at him for a long moment. We were standing almost in the middle of the closed-off street. Cranes were lifting more Jersey barriers onto the street, which was otherwise deserted. It felt like a war zone before a war.

It wasn't the time to tell him about my faith in the agonistic engine of democracy. I told him instead something simpler: that I just couldn't have put the city through yet more drama and trauma, not at a time when our public meetings already felt like people's hearts were being ripped apart.

We said goodbye. And waited for the one-year anniversary of 8/12.

THE DYNAMIC THAT SWEPT OVER THE CITY ON THE ACTUAL ANNI-versary would have been mysterious to anyone who hadn't followed the events of the past two years, but it had an unnerving familiarity to anyone who had. Hundreds of protesters took to the streets, marching through neighborhoods, and up and down the Downtown Mall, seeking confrontation with the police. There was open anger and anguish about the failures a year before. But there was no real evidence of any police misbehavior. Despite videos of furious faces shouting at the impassive police officers for the "militarization" of Charlottesville, in the end only a handful of people were arrested. And there were no white supremacists. No Kessler fans. No neo-Nazis. Instead, Kessler went to Washington, DC, joined only by about two dozen supporters, in what USA Today's editorial board called a "pathetic showing."[42]

The change in Charlottesville was a direct result of the consent decrees from the lawsuit we'd launched with Georgetown University against the militias, which prevented any militia members from return-ing to the city in groups of two or more.

It was just the protesters and the police, locked in a dance of rage and catharsis from the failures and trauma from a year before.

IN THE WEEKS AFTER THE SPUTTERED-OUT ANNIVERSARY, THE city seemed to calm down to some extent. But then, as James Alex Fields Jr.'s trial got underway, a robocall was sent to thousands of land lines with the Charlottesville area code of 434 with a frightening message. Against a musical backdrop of "Another One Bites the Dust," a male voice droned:

> Who Killed Heather Heyer in Charlottesville? The Jew Mayor. His pet negro Police Chief. Together they conspired to create mayhem in order to shut down speech they didn't like by a group that had a permit. They conspired to allow physical assaults by violent leftists against the permitted group as an excuse to declare a public emergency. . . . Due to the anarchy created by the negro Police Chief on direct order of his Jew Mayor boss, a young man drove his car into a crowd blocking the streets.

The call ended with "A Jew mayor. A Negro police chief. Find them. Convict them. Punish them." I received alarmed calls from UVA faculty members, some Jewish, who had received the call. My first call was to the Anti-Defamation League, which informed me the call had been placed by a small ragtag group out of Idaho. My second call was to our new chief of police, who said no white nationalists had been sighted in the city, but to keep her posted if I had cause for alarm.

A family member, worried, said we might want to stay away from our windows. I gave a moment's thought to having the police over to our house to perform a safety evaluation. And I then got my bearings. It was a fringe group in Idaho. Fields was going to be convicted. The city was safe. We were moving on.

After Fields's conviction in December 2018, he pled guilty to other charges and waived all appeals, thereby avoiding the death penalty. Justice, at last, would be served.

27

OVERCOMING EXTREMISM

FOR THE SURVIVORS, INCLUDING THOSE WHO HAD BEEN PHYSI-cally injured in the car attack and in the street fighting, pain would erupt frequently in public. One African American woman who had been onsite at Fourth Street when the car plowed into the crowd would some-times shout and curse during meetings, even a year after the events. Thousands of others who were psychologically injured also had a hard time escaping the trauma. Months after 8/12, practicing local therapists continued to see patients for free who could not escape the memories. Congregation Beth Israel continued to pay for a full-time security guard. The anxiety of Jewish parents whose children attended the day care and played outside in the courtyard had driven that decision.

In 2018, as the convulsions rumbled through town like aftershocks following an earthquake, I read one book of the Bible late at night, again and again, when I couldn't sleep: Proverbs.

The book likens wisdom to a mysterious woman beckoning to us. "Does not wisdom call, does not understanding raise her voice?" (8:1). She calls out to us, "Learn prudence" (8:5). "Take my instruction," she urges, "for wisdom is better than jewels" (8:10). She can be cruel. If we do not attend to knowledge, she threatens, "I will mock when panic strikes you, when panic strikes you like a storm" (1:26–27). But if we follow wisdom's counsel, she will give justice. "By me kings reign, and rulers decree what is just" (8:15).[1]

What *would* be the result of witnessing, and surviving, the predations of the basest elements of humanity? It gave me comfort to think we might be gaining wisdom through our agony—and that the arc we were working to bend could ultimately lead to justice. The American experiment has always been a wrestling match between optimism and pessimism about our fate under our fragility, vulnerability, and prejudices. As America entered its third century, and as Trumpism swept the land, I felt democratic norms and institutions could still provide a way out. True, we could become that which we abhor, the horseshoe's polar extremes connecting. But we could also see fresh new growth rising from ashes.

Humanity featured this history. Jim Crow, after all, gave birth to a new era of civil rights. The Holocaust gave birth to Israel. World War II gave birth to international human rights. Watergate gave birth to transparency and accountability in government. And so Unite the Right could—and should—give birth to a new generation committed to pluralism, tolerance, and equity, and to confronting white nationalism and domestic terrorism.

Extremism had come from within democracy. It was a wily, slippery adversary, emerging like a virus among different hosts. But democracy could also provide the antidote. Democratic norms and institutions— and leaders—could be inoculated against the threat. Like the body politic's immune system, we citizens could innovate against hate. Under threat, democracy's principles could rebound, stronger than ever.

Through the fire and smoke of the afterburn, one such beacon blinked particularly brightly for me. Perhaps the hard-won wisdom gained through a crisis like Charlottesville could make a difference for others. In the summer of 2018, I was in Colorado to officiate at a friend's wedding when I received a call from Greg Fischer, the mayor of Louisville, Kentucky. A white nationalist group called the Three Percenters was coming to town for a confrontation with a far-left group occupying an Immigration and Customs Enforcement station. The mayor had fifteen minutes before a meeting with his police chief, he said. What could I tell him about Charlottesville?

A few lessons immediately came to mind. I told him to look into the "dark web" as much as he could to understand the intentions of those coming. I said to think about de-escalation rather than escalation—the long-term rather than the short. He should bring together as many stakeholders as he could into the broadest strategy possible. He could also establish strong connections to the far left—from within the police department, if at all possible. And he should pay as much attention to rogue actors as to organized groups. If there were silos between the city, state, and federal agencies, anyone directly involved in the security plan should engage in table-top exercises and simulations to rehearse the plan and anticipate contingencies. They should think about communications as much as actual strategy and tactics. And above all, as mayor, he should work with the police to ensure that the security plan separated the groups, and that it went above and beyond to anticipate the unexpected.

He thanked me. Later, when the event was successfully defused, he told me the advice had been very helpful. This was what experts call "capacity building": exchanges leaders have with each other in order to share information and create more capacity to solve problems.

What had begun as the "Civility Alliance" and had then become the "After Charlottesville Project" now became "Communities Overcoming Extremism: The After-Charlottesville Project," an endeavor that would seek to learn from experiences like Charlottesville's to build such capacity among leaders. It pursued that goal by creating alliances and sharing collective wisdom and best practices for both the public and private sectors. As founder and chair of the project from 2018–2019, I called on a lifetime of friends and colleagues to build a group of partners to support the initiative. The Anti-Defamation League came on board, serving as the project's home. The conservative organizations Charles Koch Institute and Defending Democracy Together also joined, showing the power of extremism to create new alliances. The Fetzer Institute from Michigan was a generous partner, and the Ford Foundation and John Pritzker Fund lent their support. Comcast NBC Universal and New America came on board as well, as did the Aspen Institute's Justice and Society Program and Georgetown University's Institute for Constitutional Advocacy and Protection.

I called many public luminaries on democracy to contribute, from Danielle Allen of Harvard to Khizr Khan, from Anne-Marie Slaughter at

New America to the *New York Times* columnist and former George W. Bush adviser Pete Wehner.

As we developed the project, the Georgetown anti-militia litigation became the model of how to innovate against hate, of how to confront extremism through democracy itself. But that was only one example. We started referring to the "hard" and the "soft" sides of strategy. Hard approaches involved litigation, intelligence, prosecution, counter-extremism, and policing. Soft approaches were societal, aspirational, and collective: healing, reconciliation, and compassion.

Law school teaches the distinction between inductive and deductive reasoning. Deductive reasoning applies a known rule to new facts. Inductive reasoning does the opposite, working from the facts to new rules. It grows organically, because you don't necessarily know going into a situation what you will know after it.

That's how we came to think of how the wisdom needed for confronting and overcoming extremism works. It's not deducing the answer from a five-point plan—because no confrontation will be exactly like any other one. Instead it's *inducing* insights from experience. Charlottesville, Berkeley, Portland, and Louisville differ from each other, just as statues in New Orleans differ from those in Charlottesville, Durham, and Richmond. In each case, the best leadership will emerge from principles in play and facts at hand, rather than through hard-and-fast rules. (This framework also aligns well with the new interest throughout public policy in "evidence-based" decision-making, where the proven effects of a policy provide its validation.)

Central to this enterprise is whether we believe democracy can overcome the challenge of extremism from within. *Can* struggle produce progress? In an interview for a podcast, I asked this question of Jesse Arreguín, the youngest-ever mayor of Berkeley, California, who had seen such strife and turmoil in 2017 that he had proposed prosecuting Antifa as a gang. "I'm hopeful," he told me. He explained: "I think that while it's enormously challenging, frightening for many of us, and we are in a period of immense instability, what I have seen is people who have stood up and spoken out, and who have done so peacefully and nonviolently. I really believe in the ability of our country to adapt and to defend our democratic rights." He took the charge personally as the leader of a dynamic, diverse city perhaps most famous for its tradition of untrammeled freedom of speech. He concluded, "The resolve and commitment of people to our democratic principles is inspiring and inspires me every day."[2]

In March 2019, I sat down with Susan Bro in the headquarters of the Heather Heyer Foundation in a small rented office off of Jefferson Street in downtown Charlottesville. Awards and recognitions stood on a shelf filled with books behind me. A large oil painting of Heather in purple hues looked down upon us. When I asked Heather's mom about the agonistic idea of progress, she took a long look at me and then told me about being diagnosed with cancer in 2009. She'd had surgery, which resulted in a massive infection. A week after the surgery, she said, it didn't feel right, but she was told it was normal. Then the wound ruptured. She told me how the surgeon had to reopen the wound to clean out the infection and dead tissue before it could successfully heal.

For her, it had become a metaphor for what was happening in our democracy today. "If we don't take the time to do that lengthy healing process we will have another rupture in a very short time," she told me. She began to cry, continuing over the tears: "I would never have made that sacrifice of Heather. . . . But Heather got caught up in this explosion of the infection coming out."

It was quiet in the office. It was a warm March day in a quiet rented office in a town that sometimes felt like the center of the universe, but at that very moment it felt like what it usually was—a small southern college town full of the contradictions and pains of America itself. Where the past, as the novelist William Faulkner said, was never past. Bro addressed my question about progress through struggle. "I get what you're saying about the agonistic part of history, because people are casualties of this infection. . . . So getting down to the nitty gritty, let's scrape out the infection, let's have healing from the bottom."

"We are just now really talking about it," she said.

In November 2018, we brought together 150 leaders from around the country for a Communities Overcoming Extremism summit at Washington University in St. Louis. The horrific massacre at the Tree of Life Synagogue in Pittsburgh had only just taken place on October 27, so we naturally began with insights into the nexus between extremism and terrorism. Tom Brzozowski, the engaging but grave counsel for counterterrorism at the US Department of Justice, spoke about the Dylann Roof massacre in Charleston in 2015, and the unfortunate reality that when such a crime is prosecuted as a hate crime, it distracts from its status as a terrorist event. We needed, he said, a federal domestic terrorism statute that Mary McCord of Georgetown proposed that would create a full federal apparatus against crimes that seek to terrorize.[3]

The next morning, Samar Ali, a bright and charismatic Muslim American Tennessean, spoke about Millions of Conversations, an organization she founded after becoming the target of vicious anti-Muslim trolling while serving as a senior aide to the Republican governor of Tennessee. Ali, the daughter of Syrian and Palestinian immigrant parents, had been a White House Fellow before taking the job working for international economic development for Tennessee. But this didn't stop bigots from suggesting she was a Muslim mole. In combating these attacks, she participated in focus groups, where she found she could break through by speaking individually and empathetically with people who had been taught to hate her. Millions of Conversations will replicate that lesson by recruiting Muslim American ambassadors in cities around the country to create similar breakthroughs.

Mayor Arreguín of Berkeley spoke on a panel chaired by Steve Benjamin, the mayor of Columbia, South Carolina, and the president of the United States Conference of Mayors. Arreguín spoke about lessons from the city's seven white nationalist events of 2017. It turned out that we had a lot in common. He, too, had decided on a strategy recommending that counterprotesters not take the bait—urging them to stay away from events populated by violent white nationalists. And he, too, was pilloried for his attempt to keep people safe and separate. The city had also found itself tossed and turned by the US Supreme Court's First Amendment requirements, playing host to expensive "free-speech" events—and, again, being angrily attacked for it. He also had concluded that the First Amendment needed to evolve to give cities the tools they needed to prevent disaster—the tools that Justice Robert Jackson, in his *Terminiello* dissent, had said we should have.

In a "wisdom circle" on pluralism and tolerance, Bernadette On-yenaka of the National League of Cities addressed the issue of white privilege. When a white attendee became agitated after feeling like she was being compared to Trump supporters, Onyenaka leaned forward from the other side of the circle. "It isn't that we want you to feel bad for having privilege," Onyenaka told the white folks there. "It's that we want you to recognize that you have privilege to spend. And that we want you to spend it." It was a generous vision of how to address the inheritance of loss and inequity we all share. I could see the room relax and come together. And it had happened in a way that's rare in conversations about race and privilege today.

Lisa Consiglio spoke passionately about Narrative 4, a nonprofit group she and the novelist Colum McCann launched to promote the power of individual stories to create bridges. She gave simple and profound examples. While tutoring in neglected public schools, she could connect with marginalized youth in a whole different way. In one-to-one interactions, she could break through to a student's humanity by simply asking him or her to "tell me your story." Everyone has a story. It's our ossified politics that has forgotten that.

Khizr Khan gave a powerful keynote speech about the power of legal innovation and about the rule of law in this age of domestic terror. Since his famous speech at the Democratic National Convention in 2016, he said, he had given two hundred speeches, and it had been exhausting. He told the story of sitting next to two Holocaust survivors while receiving an award in Boston. Both observed similarities in today's political and public discourse and the extremism they lived through during World War II. They made him promise that he would do his "humble part," he said, "to remind us to continue to stand against extremism and never forget."

Jane Campbell, the former mayor of Cleveland, Ohio, told us about helping to create Charter for Compassion—a movement that now includes over four hundred cities around the world that have embedded compassion as a governing value in their ordinances, resolutions, and operating plans.

Jorge Elorza, the driven, intellectual mayor of the diverse city of Providence, Rhode Island, shared his experience, in the wake of Donald

Trump's victory, of creating programs to express solidarity with embattled groups in the city. Providence had formally declared itself a "city of kindness" to embed the goal of kindness into its programming.

Ali Noorani of the National Immigration Forum described cutting-edge work creating a network of over three thousand evangelical Christians in red and purple states who believe immigration strengthens rather than weakens the country. These relationships help dissolve the "otherization" that pits us against one another, oftentimes with violent results. They instead nurture an attitude of warmth and compassion toward these human beings who have too often been the subjects of violence.

COMMUNITIES OVERCOMING EXTREMISM'S SECOND SUMMIT CONcentrated on how leaders in the private sector could act against extremism. In the weeks before Unite the Right, there had been a ton of publicity about an unusual action by Airbnb when the company had voluntarily decided to cancel the reservations of dozens of people coming to Charlottesville for Unite the Right.

As an executive and general counsel at a tech company myself at the time, I was deeply struck by the action. It's difficult for a company to design a system internally that allows it to strike out in such a way in public on such a quickly developing matter. That's one reason so many companies have chosen the opposite path when it comes to extremism: a laissez-faire attitude that views their platforms as passive, accessible public highways. Up until its announcement in June 2019 of a new approach where hate speech would be actively removed from its platform, YouTube had been the greatest exemplar of this approach, allowing unfettered access to hate groups and even terrorists to play and replay videos. Their algorithms even seemed to advantage inflammatory content. The change showed a different way was possible for all tech companies.[4]

Like the Georgetown litigation, the Airbnb decision was an example of how to "innovate against hate." We saw that we could build capacity among other companies looking to develop their own programs against extremism, so we began to get to work, moving from one tech company to another. The stories we came upon were rich, varied, and inspiring. In

July 2019, Airbnb would host a summit featuring over a hundred leaders sharing best practices for increasing the "trust and safety" practices of tech companies.

In preparing for the summit, we talked to Patreon, which enables artists and performers to crowd-fund their work through donations from supporters. Its CEO had recently made waves with a YouTube video announcing the company's decision to ban the far-right activist Lauren Southern because of videos she had made that openly incited violence against refugees seeking safe haven in European countries. This action stemmed from the company's new content policy, which concentrated on violence, not speech (even though, as a private company, Patreon and others are free to ban any kind of speech they want).

We also talked with Eventbrite, which allows for easy planning of events. The company's leaders realized the danger of extremists exploiting their platform after a Richard Spencer–driven National Policy Institute rally in November 2016. The rally gained infamy when its attendees used the "Heil" symbol in devotion to Trump. The tricky thing is that they know a lot more about such events after they occur than beforehand. Their new approach combines a content policy with a team dedicated to finding and examining violent content while also protecting free speech. They're striving to be sensitive toward the need for robust free speech, yet at the same time trying not to foster racist, exclusive speech and anti-Semitic speech.

We reached out to PayPal, which also has a content policy and a team dedicated to preventing extremist groups from processing payments. The company has worked to become a leader in the field by coordinating with organizations like the Southern Poverty Law Center (SPLC) and the Anti-Defamation League (ADL). The team was trying to root out far-right extremist organizations that used the platform for funding. The strategy had drawn the ire of conservatives, especially after Marc Thiessen, former director of speechwriting for President George W. Bush, criticized the SPLC in 2019. Conservatives claimed that PayPal's approach had an ideological bent and launched a boycott against the company.[5] But they were continuing the work, undaunted.

Another company, Storyful, employs journalists and technologists to advise tech companies and news organizations on trends in media. Its representatives told us that their methods could, in some cases, identify extremism before it started. They were studying the potential for extremists to migrate from traditional platforms, such as YouTube and PayPal, to new ones, such as online gaming platforms. That's where the new danger was.

At Mozilla, the nonprofit that makes the Firefox browser, the staff works to influence the tech ecosystem spanning the globe against extremism. Mozilla funds fellows at partner companies who advocate for systemic change. One works on how spam and malware can be countered. Another helped the European Union create a new code of practice around misinformation, which in turn led to more transparency around manipulative Facebook ads related to parliamentary elections. Another works on regulatory issues around intermediary liability—the responsibilities of companies to their users for the content running on their platforms—and the fact that companies can shelter behind Section 230 of the US Communications Decency Act of 1996, which protects online companies from liability for any third-party content they publish. But the world is changing as bedrock "intermediary liability protections" are being questioned. Indeed, an amendment to Section 230 has been proposed in Congress that would add restrictions to the immunities it provides.[6]

And we talked with people from Airbnb, which had taken the bold step of canceling the reservations of the Unite the Right attendees. Chris Lehane, an old friend of mine and a senior executive there, told us they had created a new "policy protocol" based on "community standards." They now have a team of dedicated engineers who spend their time "developing technological approaches to identify conduct and behavior and folks who aren't consistent with the values" Airbnb upholds. This leads to hundreds of "flags" that can pop up in their algorithms.

What had happened in Charlottesville? Six months out, the Airbnb algorithm began to notice a bunch of people getting flagged trying to make reservations in Charlottesville. Working with the ADL, Airbnb determined that a gathering of ultranationalists was about to take place. Lehane recalled receiving a phone call on a ferry in Maine, where he had to make a decision on whether to go forward. He knew they would be publicly attacked for barring people. "My answer, on the ferry," he told us, was, "Are you pro-Nazi or anti-Nazi?" He had his communications people make sure they knew about the decision in case Airbnb was attacked (the alt-right swiftly announced a boycott). But they were prepared to explain their actions.

Lehane saw this sort of action by a private company as part of a much broader effort. His theory, he said, was that there would be an evolution of a "global community sector." It would be different from the public or private sector. Social democratic countries—he referenced Norway and the other Nordic countries—already have a community sector, he said. That's not where the Internet *is* going, but that's where he *wanted* it to go, and he thought it would go in that direction through actions like Charlottesville and new programs that Airbnb and these other companies were voluntarily pursuing.

All of this was coming out of an age of turmoil and vast damage that this very same sector—the Internet—had enabled. I had as much despair as anyone about what the Internet and social media had wrought with Trumpism and the alt-right militias, particularly, of course, so horrifically with their violent invasion of Charlottesville. But here the same world was, giving birth to a new idea, through the will of resilient people who were committed to achieving the very principles of constitutionalism itself. At the summit itself, there was broad agreement among the midlevel tech companies in attendance that they could work better together to develop best practices and alliances among their "trust and safety" departments—that there would be strength in numbers, as they sought to turn the Internet in a more humane direction.

It was the same story as in the public sector, where new leaders were taking a clear-eyed look at the devastation around them before setting forth to build a better world.

IN APRIL 2019, I FLEW TO CHATTANOOGA, TENNESSEE, AT THE invitation of Mayor Andy Berke, whom I'd last seen in St. Louis during the Communities Overcoming Extremism summit. Four years earlier, a Muslim man had killed five people at two military recruitment installations in Chattanooga. It could have been a disaster, leading to a cycle of escalating fear and panic and setting off violence toward the city's minority populations. Instead, through calm and steady leadership and comprehensive engagement with police and the city's minority populations, Berke calmed tensions.

Now, he had a different set of concerns. In 2018, the University of Tennessee at Chattanooga had seen two instances of white supremacist flyers being distributed around campus. One featured Adolf Hitler and was placed on top of Black History Month flyers. In the other, the group Identity Evropa (which had come to the Unite the Right rally) distributed flyers that read, "Our Generation. Our Future. Our Last Chance." In 2016, two vehicles belonging to a Jewish organization were set on fire in the city. According to the Chattanooga Police Department, there had been 133 such "bias incidents" within the city since 2012.[7] Meanwhile, Tennessee ranked ninth in the country for hate incidents.

Berke had resolved to address the pattern through proactive policy—just what Communities Overcoming Extremism was about. He had invited me to the city to help announce a new Council Against Hate. The council, chaired by prominent local leaders Berke had recruited, was multifaceted and thoughtfully designed. In fact, Berke had woven a three-part "theory of change" into the council. This approach was designed to achieve a legal framework to deter hate crimes through enforced penalties; to engage influencers in the business and faith communities, in the media, and in other groups to set cultural expectations around shared values; and to drive generational change from the bottom up by educating young people. It had different teams to work on different areas of hate, from researching the problem to engaging young people to liaising with the private sector to increasing media literacy.

The event was not the press conference I expected. It was a working community meeting. After we announced the plan, the organizers invited the hundred-plus attendees to join different tables for the different action areas. There, Chattanooga citizens of every stripe and color excitedly brainstormed ideas for how to fireproof their dynamic city. When the meeting reconvened, there were specific ideas, from asking the CEOs of local companies to join in a coalition to remove hate from workplaces to creating community informational sessions about the dangers of fomenting extremism online among young people.

In recent generations, Chattanooga has reinvented itself from an industrial and railroad hub to a city with the fastest Internet in the country, a booming technology center, and a diverse, multiethnic population. On my visit, I walked along the riverfront. It has been transformed through powerful new infrastructure projects, including an aquarium, an art gallery, and a baby-blue pedestrian bridge—as well as installations meant to better embrace the city's complicated history of oppression. The Trail of Tears is repeatedly memorialized; a flowing water feature meant to memorialize the Native American population travels over a staircase under large medallions designed by Native American residents. And the city plans to add a memorial to a local lynching victim. Several dozen community meetings have been held, and the bulk of the project's $900,000 has already been raised, with no controversy—only a commitment to a more accurate telling of history in the present.

As I walked through this dynamic city, I reflected on how Berke's new Council Against Hate was a paradigm of leadership, of resilience against prejudice—and of our capacity to overcome extremism through the very mechanisms that make us a democracy.

CONCLUSION

WHEN THE HISTORIES ARE WRITTEN, THEY WILL SHOW THAT this era featured an extraordinary flaring-up of political furies. The gray area dwindled. Black and white took over. Passions reigned in the highest and lowest halls of government. I have tried to give the facts here as best as I could, but nobody will ever finally define what Charlottesville means because the stakes of another interpretation are simply too high. So the question becomes, instead, what can we make of it?

As I finished writing this book, Charlottesville remained a raw mass of contradictions, a microcosm for a nation wrestling to shake free from an angry and violent era. Spike Lee's Oscar-nominated *BlacKkKlansman* featured searing footage from Charlottesville in the last few minutes of the film, virtually soldering a connection between the story of a black man infiltrating the KKK in the 1970s and the violence of white nationalists in Charlottesville.

During the fateful year of 2017, I was often told that Charlottesville had become a "hashtag." Charlottesville was now #charlottesville. But what did that actually mean? Just as in the battle to frame Charlottesville, there is not one definitive answer. There are instead facets to the massive, morphing cultural phenomenon, the signifier, that is #charlottesville.

On the one hand, it was the most vivid exposé of the far right in our times, punctuated by violence and terrorism and a broader story of the rise of white nationalism in America and the world. As instances of right-wing violence became more common—a horrific massacre took place at a mosque in New Zealand in March 2019, for example—Charlottesville seemed to become more and more of a meme.

As domestic terrorism and white nationalism go, Charlottesville's meaning is alarming. The Southern Poverty Law Center has reported that the number of white nationalist groups in the United States increased from 100 chapters in 2017 to 148 in 2018. From 2017 to 2018, the Anti-Defamation League found a 182 percent increase in the distribution of white supremacist propaganda, along with an increase from 76 to 91 in the number of rallies and demonstrations by white supremacy groups. And the Center for Strategic and International Studies found that the number of terrorist attacks by far-right perpetrators quadrupled in the United States between 2016 and 2017, and that far-right attacks in Europe rose 43 percent over the same period.[1]

But #charlottesville also represented one of the bloodiest self-inflicted wounds of the Trump administration, the point when Steve Bannon was forced out of the White House, and a scandal that had every appearance of being Trump's Hurricane Katrina. It also represented, in Virginia, a quickening to the long slow death of the nexus of states' rights, Massive Resistance, and Dixiecrats that had poisoned Virginia politics in the modern era. The punishing defeat of Republicans in the fall of 2017, and the devastating punishment of Republican US Senate candidate Corey Stewart in his neo-Confederate campaign in 2018, are also each contained within #charlottesville.

So too does #charlottesville encompass contagious efforts to repudiate the alt-right's celebration of Confederate icons by removing them. Indeed, in January 2019, my alma mater, Washington-Lee High School in Arlington, Virginia, renamed itself Washington-Liberty High School in order to remove Robert E. Lee's name.

And #charlottesville holds the failures of policing, as well as the shortcomings of First Amendment law, revealed in the horrifying Vice News documentary. But at the same time #charlottesville contains teachable moments for police forces, prosecutors, mayors, and judges around the country who will absorb the lessons and evolve better ideas from them.

The multifaceted meaning of #charlottesville reinforces the unique power, the alchemy, even, of American constitutionalism. Dayton, Ohio, employed the successful anti-militia litigation technique from our lawsuit with Georgetown to sue the KKK in an attempt to prevent it from holding a rally in the city.[2] Following the example of the companies we were highlighting and connecting with through Communities Overcoming Extremism, Facebook announced that it would ban white supremacist content.[3] A new landscape is emerging from the madness and mayhem of Charlottesville as surely as wisdom is produced by trauma in ancient Greek tragedy.

As I review this journey, I remain haunted by the great paradox of history my grandfather described for me so many years ago: "*Everything becomes its opposite,*" he had said. It took me twenty years, and the experiences described in this book, to understand that his paradox was actually a challenge: if we can, we must stop democracy, too, from becoming its opposite.

The central challenge of democracy has always been resisting the lowest common denominator, and instead, supporting our norms and our institutions to enable democracy to provide solutions to problems, rather than just magnifying them. Our politics, and our governments, should challenge us and educate us, precisely when we want to be most impassioned. *Especially* when things are complicated. But if this story proves anything, it's that this approach doesn't cater to today's public opinion. It doesn't offer people the instant reassurance they seek nowadays as we are sucked into the maelstrom of extreme positions churning against one another. In the face of so many hurtling into the fray, such leadership can be attacked as inert, unresponsive, even cowardly. But we must still dare to do it.

Creating space for thought, challenging black-and-white absolutist positions, forcing leaders to consider substance rather than symbols, educating rather than flattering the public, choosing to wrestle in the gray areas—these can not only be unpopular, they can be politically hazardous. They can feel like attacks not only on a system, but on people's very emotions—on their desire to fall deeply in love with one side or another, with one symbol or another.

But this is all the more reason to think things through. To design our politics around the richness of the actual problems, and the solutions they actually require. The fact is that many issues government must address today—whether extremism or domestic terrorism, the First Amendment or the Second Amendment, climate change or infrastructure, nuclear policy or military alliances, trade agreements or workforce education, and yes, memorials, race, and memory—are complex, not simple. They will require leadership. The answers (and the politics of getting the answers) must be at once forceful and thoughtful. That doesn't mean bureaucratic or sclerotic, risk-averse, pencil-necked, or four-eyed. It does mean we can be at once conscientious and principled, and nuanced and pragmatic. Going back to those big philosophical words from my seminars at UVA, it means the deontological can involve the utilitarian (and vice versa), and that the transactional and the transformational are not necessarily mutually exclusive.

James Madison's political victories over two centuries ago prove that our democracy can deliberate rather than dumb things down. They suggest that even after this valley of death, even after the blood and chaos of Charlottesville, there's sunlight ahead. In a time when Sinclair Lewis's *It Can't Happen Here* became a best-seller eighty years after it was first published in 1935,[4] in a time of rising populist authoritarians, not only in the United States but around the world, deliberative democracy can still prevail. The victories to achieve it will be violent. They will come at great cost. Leaders will be battered, and the arc will be jagged. But the trajectory will be upward.

I was once at a funeral pyre at the "burning ghats" in Varanasi, India. In the early morning, along the banks of the murky Ganges River, I watched as a blackened corpse burned, surrounded by loving family members who murmured and chanted. I was told how the tradition is to query the patterns in the smoke for signs of destiny.

In the wisps of smoke that still twist up above the ash and agony of Charlottesville, there's hope for a burned, torn, scarred, but still indomitable country.

ACKNOWLEDGMENTS

As I was writing this book, two people close to me passed away. This book is dedicated to both of them. The first was my childhood friend Matt Seidman, who died after a tragic accident in 2018. He was a beloved confidant, the best man at my wedding, and someone who loved debating everyone and everything. He first suggested I write a book about Charlottesville. I am grateful he did, but dearly wish he could have actually read this book.

The second, Paul Nace, was a mentor of mine for twenty years before he passed away in 2017. In many early drafts, he was a sort of sage and conscience to me, even in death. As the book moved forward, I edited out some of the passages where his presence came through the most, but I did so only reluctantly. I keenly felt the old adage that in writing, you must kill your darlings. But I do know that Paul at least belongs in these acknowledgments.

Paul was a short, vigorous, occasionally impish guy with bright blue eyes and a gravelly manner of speaking. I met him while working on a congressional campaign in Massachusetts. He had been a sailor with the US Navy in Vietnam, along with John Kerry, before becoming a political consultant, real estate developer, and green technology entrepreneur.

Paul was a touchstone for many political leaders because, along with political savvy and personal charm, he had a powerful conscience. For example, Paul had it out with Kerry after Kerry voted in 2002 to authorize war in Iraq. A student of the errors of Vietnam and militaristic hubris, he hated everything about that bill and the war that followed. By Paul's report, the two men had a harsh phone call and did not speak for a year after the exchange. Yet Kerry gave the eulogy at Paul's funeral. When I was twenty-three, Paul took me under his wing. For the next twenty years, we would talk every six months, sometimes for a couple of hours, and I made most of my professional and personal decisions with his advice in mind. Paul would constantly return to conscience, the deepest source of one's ideas and purpose. At the same time, he would always remind me of the importance of practical considerations—data, insights into human beings, the impact our policies have on the world, the need to be useful. You could not have a conscience without wisdom, in other words, or wisdom without a conscience. You needed both.

When I learned he had died, I was besieged by memories of Paul's generosity during many inflection points in my life, whether Berkeley or law school or campaigns or the law, or getting married, facing challenging personal decisions, moving to Charlottesville—and anything and everything else. He had been my closest and most consistent mentor since college. He had listened closely, and he had been honest and tough, yet gentle. I realized how completely altered I had been by his character. I didn't realize it at the time, but Paul's death deprived me of a reliable compass that had always charted me through squalls just when I could have used such guidance most. So my thanks to Paul for the gifts of his guidance and conscience, which I can only hope are reflected throughout this book.

I would also like to thank the phalanx of friends, family members, and colleagues who offered incredibly helpful advice for and about this book: Andy Berke, Emily Blout, Ryan Chiachiere, Jim Coan, Bill Crutchfield, Frank DiStefano, Alvin Edwards, Mike Gubser, Dan Hunt, Sally Jackson, Stan Katz, Andy Kaufman, Susan Liautaud, Russ Linden, Frank Lovett, Jim Morin, L. F. and Susan Payne, Paige Rice, Marj Signer, Maggie Thornton, Mark Vlasic, and Henry Wiencek. I had helpful conversations about local and state government law with Rich Schragger.

Fred Schauer helpfully sent me an early draft of his article on the First Amendment.

My colleagues at Communities Overcoming Extremism: The After Charlottesville Project were wonderful at every stage of the work. Thanks to Jonathan Greenblatt, Ethan Ashley, Erika Moritsugu, Beth Nathanson, Sarah Ruger, Emilia Huneke-Bergquist, Sharif Azami, Bobby McKenzie, Joshua Dubois, Brandon Andrews, Mary McCord, Meryl Chertoff, and Elliot Majerczyk.

I've been fortunate to be part of three different groups whose structures and membership have helped develop the ideas in this book: the Aspen Institute's Rodel Fellows Program, led by Mickey Edwards; the Civic Collaboratory, led by Eric Liu; and Patriots and Pragmatists, led by Mike Berkowitz and Rachel Pritzker—all visionaries and friends.

I am indebted to my agent, Gail Ross, for her staunch support, friendship, and enthusiasm, and to my editor at PublicAffairs, John Mahaney, for his faith, loyalty, and constantly trenchant advice. Marj Signer, Bob Signer, Mira Signer, Rebecca Signer Roche, and Rachel Signer were unwavering in their love and support. Above all, I am grateful to Emily Blout and our sons William and Jacoby for just being themselves.

NOTES

Source notes are not included for quotations from Charlottesville City Council meetings; however, video archives of meetings can be accessed by linking from the City of Charlottesville's website to http://charlottesville .granicus.com/ViewPublisher.php?view_id=2. Meeting dates are provided in the text. The same web page includes videos of other meetings of Charlottesville city entities, including the planning commission.

INTRODUCTION: WINTER IN SUMMER

1. Ridge Schuyler, "Realizing the Dream: Family Self-Sufficiency in Albemarle County & Charlottesville. Virginia Orange Dot Report 2.0," September 23, 2015, 6, https://cvillechamber.com/wp-content/uploads/2015/09/2015-Orange-Dot-Report-2.0-Online-Edition.pdf.

2. Merriam-Webster Dictionary, online edition, 2019, https://www.merriam-webster.com/dictionary/firestorm.

3. Merriam-Webster Dictionary, online edition, 2019, https://www.merriam-webster.com/dictionary/crucible.

4. Hannah Arendt, *Men in Dark Times* (New York: Harvest Books, 1968), 4.

5. Ibid., 7–8.

6. See Michael Lloyd, *The Agon in Euripides* (Oxford: Clarendon Press, 1992), 1.

7. A. Thomson, "Polemos and Agon," in A. Schaap, ed., *Law and Agonistic Politics*, Edinburgh/Glasgow Law and Society Series (Farnham, UK: Ashgate,

2009), 105–118, 107. It is important to note that there is a rich and lively debate among political theorists about many critical nuances within the agonistic thesis, and it is at the nuances (such as whether the self or interest groups are principally engaged in agonistic struggle, or how agonism relates to pluralism) where much of the idea's importance lies. I am admittedly deploying the idea, and the term, at its most simple and surface level here. But for those interested in the richer applications, a world of insight awaits. Suggested sources include Dana Villa, *Politics, Philosophy, Terror: Essays on the Thought of Hannah Arendt* (Princeton, NJ: Princeton University Press, 1999); Chantal Mouffe, "Agonistic Democracy and Radical Politics," *Pavilion Journal*, December 29, 2014; Patricia Roberts-Miller, "Fighting Without Hating: Hannah Arendt's Agonistic Rhetoric," *Journal of Advanced Composition* 22, no. 3 (2002): 585–601; "The Optimistic Agonist: An Interview with Bonnie Honig," Open Democracy, n.d., https://www .opendemocracy.net/en/opendemocracyuk/optimistic-agonist-interview-with -bonnie-honig; Andrew Schaap, "Political Theory and the Agony of Politics," *Political Studies Review* 5, no. 1 (2007): 56–74.

CHAPTER 1: THE HOOK

1. The quotation is from Police Dept. of City of Chicago v. Mosley, 408 U.S. 92, 95–96 (1972).

2. John Milton, *Areopagitica* (pamphlet, 1644). The full text of the pamphlet is available at Project Gutenberg, https://www.gutenberg.org/files/608/608-h/608 -h.htm.

CHAPTER 2: "SIMPLY BECAUSE THERE'S PASSION" (JANUARY 2016)

1. We would in fact encode that requirement in the new rules we would pass, in part to stop councilors from doing end-runs around the city manager and causing staff to go on wild goose chases to handle their requests.

2. Regarding Albemarle County: in Virginia, cities and counties are entirely separate entities.

3. City of Staunton, "The Origin of the City Manager Plan in Staunton," 1954, www.icmaml.org/wp-content/uploads/2014/07/Origin-City-Manager-Plan-in-Staunton-VA.pdf.

4. Ibid.

5. "Council-Manager Form of Government," brochure, International City/County Management Association, 2017, https://icma.org/sites/default/files/18-027 %20Council%20Manager%20FOG%20Brochure_final%2010-16-17.pdf.

6. As tempting as it is to suggest the model should be thrown in the trash because it's unresponsive or ineffective, the research doesn't show that to be the case. On the contrary, in a comprehensive 2014 study examining over 1,600

American cities and towns, two political scientists found that "in contrast to the expectations of reformers, we find that no institution seems to consistently improve responsiveness." Chris Tausanovitch and Christopher Warshaw, "Representation in Municipal Government," *American Political Science Review* 108, no. 3 (2014): 2.

7. The attention paid to the ceremonial dimension of my role as mayor often reminded me of a book called *The King's Two Bodies*, somewhat fetishized by political theory graduate students, which describes the two different sides of kings in both their historical and ceremonial roles: their actual person, and the made-up, mythical "body" that transcends time, representing the mystical durability of the state itself. Ernst Kantorowicz, *The King's Two Bodies: A Study in Mediaeval Political Theology* (Princeton, NJ: Princeton University Press, 1957).

8. It serves the same broad historical purpose that John Adams alluded to in Congress when he argued that the new president, George Washington, should have the official title of "His Highness, the President of the United States, and Protector of the Rights of the Same." He was rebuffed when it was pointed out to him that the Constitution prohibited titleships. See Harlow Giles Unger, "How 'His Highness' George Washington Became 'Mr. President,'" *Huffington Post*, February 14, 2014, www.huffingtonpost.com/harlow-giles-unger/how-his-highness-presidents-day_b_4784011.html.

CHAPTER 3: "IS MIKE YOUR DADDY?" (FEBRUARY 2016)

1. Michael Signer, *Demagogue: The Fight to Save Democracy from Its Worst Enemies* (New York: Palgrave Macmillan, 2009).

2. As a Virginia Municipal League expert has written, "the agenda for a regular meeting should include only those items ready for decision. Until the facts and significance of a case are known, a Council meeting is not a good place to have a general discussion about how to dispose of a particular problem." Jack Edwards, "Effective Public Meetings Essential for Successful Governance," *Virginia Town and City* (Virginia Municipal League), May 2014, 16. See also Henry M. Robert III, Daniel H. Honemann, and Thomas J. Balch, *Robert's Rules of Order Newly Revised in Brief* (New York: De Capo Press, 2011), 20–23.

3. C. Alan Jennings, *Robert's Rules for Dummies* (Hoboken: John Wiley and Sons, 2016), 78.

4. Samantha Baars, "Winning the Lottery: City Council's New Commenting Policy Draws Controversy," *C-ville Weekly*, February 16, 2016.

CHAPTER 4: RACE, POLICY, AND THE PAST (MARCH 2016)

1. Naomi Zack, "Deontology, Utilitarianism, and Rights," in *The Ethics and Mores of Race: Equality after the History of Philosophy* (Lanham, MD: Rowman and Littlefield, 2011), 137–160.

2. "Virginia's Redemptive Moment," Brown v. Board of Education Scholarship Committee (Richmond: Virginia General Assembly, 2013), 8, http://brown scholarship.virginia.gov/pdf/reports/scholarship-program-report.pdf.

3. The legislature's 2016 report about the scholarship program showed the specific and human results of this tailored policy. In the ten years the program had been in operation, eighty-nine individuals had received the scholarship. Almost half had attended community colleges. Thirty had attended the historically black St. Paul's College. A handful had attended universities, including the University of Virginia. At an expenditure of $1,186,757.59, the program was within budget. Victims had been redressed. See "Brown v. Board of Education Scholarship Program: Fiscal Status Report, August 1, 2016," Brown v. Board of Education Scholarship Committee, http://brownscholarship.virginia.gov/pdf/reports/2016-08-07-Fiscal-Status.pdf. For more information on the scholarship itself, see http://brownscholarship.virginia.gov.

4. Southern Poverty Law Center, "Whose Heritage? Public Symbols of the Confederacy," June 4, 2018, https://www.splcenter.org/20180604/whose-heritage-public-symbols-confederacy.

5. "Mitch Landrieu's Speech on the Removal of Confederate Monuments in New Orleans," *New York Times*, May 23, 2017, https://www.nytimes.com/2017/05/23/opinion/mitch-landrieus-speech-transcript.html.

6. In 1932, an inscription was added to the monument explaining that the battle was for "white supremacy." The city then added a new plaque in 1974 explaining that the monument did not reflect modern attitudes. In 1993, the city relocated the monument from Canal Street to Iberville Street next to a parking garage. Andrew Vanacore, "Among Contested New Orleans Landmarks, Liberty Place Marker Has Always Been a Battleground," *New Orleans Advocate*, April 14, 2017, https://www.theadvocate.com/new_orleans/news/article_bf24c1d6-1fe4-11e7-a6c1-8b5611a8c879.html.

CHAPTER 5: "BROADEN THE APERTURE" (APRIL 2016)

1. Melissa Eddy, "Germany's Latest Bestseller? A Critical Version of Mein Kampf," *New York Times*, January 3, 2017, https://www.nytimes.com/2017/01/03/world/europe/germanys-latest-best-seller-a-critical-version-of-mein-kampf.html.

CHAPTER 7: "HEIL SIGNER" (JUNE 2016)

1. Rob Schilling, "Heil Signer: Charlottesville Mayor's New Totalitarian Police State," *Bearing Drift*, June 26, 2016, https://bearingdrift.com/2016/06/28/heil-signer-charlottesville-mayors-new-totalitarian-police-state.

2. Memorandum Opinion, Draego v. City of Charlottesville (W.D. Va. 2016), 26.

3. Ibid., 30.

4. Ibid.

5. Ibid., 32.

CHAPTER 8: "HAVE YOU EVEN READ THE US CONSTITUTION?" (JULY 2016)

1. Mark Tenia, "Descendant of Slaves Reflects on the Meaning of Robert E. Lee Statue," ABC 8 News, August 15, 2017, https://www.wric.com/news/descendant-of-slaves-reflects-on-the-meaning-of-robert-e-lee-statue_20180320012402648/1059562107.

CHAPTER 9: "TO UN-ERASE THIS HISTORY" (AUGUST 2016)

1. Dean Seal, "In Wake of Criticism, Petition in Favor of West Main ABC Store Drawn Up," *Daily Progress*, January 19, 2015, https://www.dailyprogress.com/news/local/in-wake-of-criticism-petition-in-favor-of-west-main/article_b70ba432-a05d-11e4-a0fa-672909af057b.html.

2. Tom LoBianco and Ashley Killough, "Trump Pitches Black Voters: 'What the Hell Do You Have to Lose,'" CNN, August 19, 2016, https://www.cnn.com/2016/08/19/politics/donald-trump-african-american-voters.

3. Public hearing, Blue Ribbon Commission on Race, Memorials, and Public Spaces, City of Charlottesville, August 24, 2017, audio recording available at https://soundcloud.com/cvillecitygov/blue-ribbon-commission-august-24-2016.

CHAPTER 11: "WE WILL BUILD THIS WORLD FROM LOVE" (OCTOBER 2016)

1. John Edwin Mason, "History: Mine and Ours. Charlottesville's Blue Ribbon Commission and the Terror Attacks of August 2017," in *Charlottesville 2017: The Legacy of Race and Inequity*, eds. Claudrena N. Harold and Louis P. Nelson (Charlottesville: University of Virginia Press, 2018).

CHAPTER 12: DIZZYING AND DESPONDENT (NOVEMBER 2016)

1. For a short time, it seemed that the math might work out. Folks were claiming there was a breakaway group of libertarian Republican electors who might join with groups of defecting electors in Texas (the home of Jeb Bush) and Ohio (the state of the other remaining Republican candidate, John Kasich) to get to the magic number of 37. If all 37 voted for the same alternative Republican candidate (it was inconceivable they'd vote for Clinton), and Clinton asked all of her 232 electors to vote for the same Republican alternative, then a majority of 269 electors could defeat Trump at the college.

2. Anna Higgins and Tim Dodson, "Homophobic, Sexist, Anti-White Language Abundant in Charlottesville Vice Mayor's Tweets," *Cavalier Daily*, November 28, 2016, https://www.cavalierdaily.com/article/2016/11/wes-bellamy-charlottesville-twitter.

3. Samantha Baars, "'Lightning in a Bottle': Statue Commission Chair Disappointed by Decision," *C-ville Weekly*, November 9, 2016, https://www.c-ville.com/lightning-bottle-statue-commission-chair-disappointed-decision.

CHAPTER 13: "IT'S AN ISSUE OF RIGHT AND WRONG, SIR" (DECEMBER 2016)

1. "Blue Ribbon Commission on Race, Memorials, and Public Spaces Report to City Council," December 19, 2016, 9, www.charlottesville.org/Home/ShowDocument?id=48999.

CHAPTER 14: "YOU GOTTA GET ME OUT OF THIS" (JANUARY 2017)

1. Importantly, these monies would be funded directly with cash, rather than financed through bonds, which would have required additional votes. In other words, we could get started on projects right away.

2. He went on to reel off a list of specific race-related budgetary and programmatic proposals in housing, education, workforce development, and community dialogue that he and I would describe later as an "equity package."

3. Because it was an event I'd organized personally, rather than on behalf of the council, I had to do it all on my own. The city manager had informed me that I couldn't even use the city's podium, lest the event be interpreted as one occurring with the city's official sanction and resources.

4. Lisa Provence, "Unprecedented Activism Galvanizes Charlottesville," *C-ville Weekly*, March 3, 2017, https://www.c-ville.com/unprecedented-activism-galvanizes-charlottesville.

CHAPTER 15: GRENADE GAME (FEBRUARY 2017)

1. Fenwick's actions, however, would not endear him to the Charlottesville voting public. In the Democratic primary election that was held in June 2017, he would lose decisively, and he would also lose decisively when he ran again in the Democratic City Council primary in June 2019.

2. Martijn Icks, Jennifer Keohane, Sergei Samoilenko, and Eric Shiraev, "Character Assassination in Theory and Practice: 2017 Conference Report," Character Assassination and Reputation Politics Lab, Georgetown University, 2017, https://s3.amazonaws.com/chssweb/documents/25632/original/Final_CARP_Report.pdf?1500493596.

3. Staff report, "Charlottesville Mayor and Gubernatorial Candidate Riggleman in Twitter Spat over Statue," *Daily Progress*, February 8, 2017, https://www.dailyprogress.com/news/virginia_politics/charlottesville-Mayor-and-gubernatorial-candidate-riggleman-in-twitter-spat-over/article_b37ae6f0-ee41-11e6-adcd-9bb08ae70cc6.html.

4. Walt Heinecke, "Opinion/Letter: 'Resist Council's Assault on Democracy,'" *Daily Progress*, February 8, 2017, https://www.dailyprogress.com/opinion/opinion-letter-resist-council-s-assault-on-democracy/article_ecfd73ac-ee00-11e6-b961-0f7fcd38af37.html.

CHAPTER 17: "OUR MAYOR IS A NEO-FASCIST" (APRIL 2017)

1. Chris Suarez, "Council Hopeful Leads Protest over Landmark Tax Breaks," *Daily Progress*, April 24, 2017, https://www.dailyprogress.com/news/local/Council-hopeful-leads-protest-over-landmark-tax-breaks/article_28455abe-294e-11e7-9d5b-37538d343ce6.html.

CHAPTER 18: "THAT DAY WE FINISH THEM ALL OFF" (MAY 2017)

1. See "'Hail Trump!' Richard Spencer Speech Excerpts," YouTube, posted by *The Atlantic*, November 21, 2016, https://www.youtube.com/watch?v=1o6-bi3jlxk; and Liam Stack, "Attack on Alt-Right Leader Has Internet Asking: Is It O.K. to Punch a Nazi?," *New York Times*, January 21, 2017, https://www.nytimes.com/2017/01/21/us/politics/richard-spencer-punched-attack.html.

2. Lisa Provence, "Lee Park Scene of White Nationalist Demonstration, Counterprotest," *C-ville Weekly*, May 15, 2017, https://www.c-ville.com/lee-park-scene-white-nationalist-demonstration-counter-protest.

3. Michael Edison Hayden, "Charlottesville Mayor Calls Pro-Confederate Rallies Horrific," ABC News, May 14, 2017, https://abcnews.go.com/US/Mayor-charlottesville-calls-pro-confederate-rallies-horrific/story?id=47404820.

4. Terminiello v. Chicago, 337 U.S. 1 (1949), 16.

5. Ibid., 21.

6. Ibid., 22.

7. Ibid., 4.

8. Ibid., 37.

9. "Justice Jackson Delivers Opening Statement at Nuremberg, November 21, 1945," Robert H. Jackson Center, n.d., https://www.roberthjackson.org/article/justice-jackson-delivers-opening-statement-at-nuremberg-november-21-1945.

10. *Terminiello*, 13.

11. Ibid., 23.

12. Ibid., 23–24.

13. Ibid., 28.

14. Ibid., 36.

15. Interview of Nicole Hemmer by Michael Signer conducted March 27, 2019, for "Overcoming Extremist" podcast, Anti-Defamation League, forthcoming in 2019.

16. Peter Beinart, "The Rise of the Violent Left," *The Atlantic*, September 2017, https://www.theatlantic.com/magazine/archive/2017/09/the-rise-of-the-violent-left/534192.

17. Tom Porter, "Berkeley Mayor Calls for Antifa to Be Classified as Crime Gang After Clashes at Weekend Protest," *Newsweek*, August 29, 2017, https://www.newsweek.com/berkeley-Mayor-calls-antifa-be-classified-crime-gang-after-clashes-sunday-656286.

18. Weeks later, in an event unrelated to the conflict with Antifa, the ex-con was on a light-rail train when he shouted at two teenage girls, "Get off the bus, and get out of the country because you don't pay taxes here." One of them was wearing a hijab; the other, her friend, was African American. Christian stabbed two men who defended the women. One bled to death on the train. The other died at a hospital. See Lee Moran and Andy Campbell, "2 Men Stabbed to Death Standing Up to Muslim Hate in Portland," *Huffington Post*, May 27, 2017, https://www.huffpost.com/entry/portland-attack-commuter-train_n_5929362ce4b053f2d2acaf56.

19. Beinart, "Rise of the Violent Left."

20. Jean-Pierre Faye, *Le Siècle des idéologies* (Paris: Armand Colin, 1996).

21. Showing Up for Racial Justice, https://www.showingupforracialjustice.org/why-surj.html.

22. City of Charlottesville et al. v. Pennsylvania Lightfoot Milita et al., Complaint for Injunctive and Declaratory Relief, Circuit Court of Charlottesville, Virginia, 2017, 56, available at https://www.law.georgetown.edu/icap/wp-content/uploads/sites/32/2018/02/lawsuit-charlottesville.pdf.

CHAPTER 19: "DON'T TAKE THE BAIT" (JUNE 2017)

1. Stephen Carter, *Civility: Manners, Morals, and the Etiquette of Democracy* (New York: Basic Books, 1998), 133; Peggy Noonan, "Rage Is All the Rage, and It's Dangerous," *Wall Street Journal*, June 15, 2017, https://www.wsj.com/articles/rage-is-all-the-rage-and-its-dangerous-1497571401.

2. One notable proponent of the "absolutist" view was Supreme Court Justice Hugo Black, who wrote, "The First Amendment's unequivocal command that there shall be no abridgement of the rights of free speech and assembly shows that the men who drafted our Bill of Rights did all the 'balancing' that was to be done in this field." Konigsberg v. State Bar of California (1961), 266 U.S. 36, 61; and legal scholar Alexander Meiklejohn, who authored "The First Amendment Is an Absolute" in *The Supreme Court Review* 1961 (1961): 245–266.

3. The Village of Skokie v. National Socialist Party of the United States (1978), 69 Ill. 2d 605, 616.

4. Ibid., 617.

5. "ACLU History: Taking a Stand for Free Speech in Skokie," American Civil Liberties Union, n.d., https://www.aclu.org/other/aclu-history-taking-stand -free-speech-skokie.

6. Dean Seal, "KKK Leader Seeking Charlottesville Rally Has History as FBI Informant," *Daily Progress*, June 6, 2017, https://www.dailyprogress.com/news /local/kkk-leader-seeking-charlottesville-rally-has-history-as-fbi-informant /article_d4f743b0-4b0b-11e7-9b0d-bf585dde11ff.html.

7. Buzz Bissinger, *A Prayer for the City* (New York: Random House, 1997).

8. Letter from John W. Whitehead, Rutherford Institute, to Charlottes-ville City Council, March 9, 2016, available at *C-ville Weekly*, www.c-ville.com /wp-content/uploads/2016/03/rutherford-to-city-council-3-09-2016.pdf.

9. Letter from John W. Whitehead, Rutherford Institute, to Chief Al Thomas, Charlottesville Police Department, and Charlottesville City Council, June 27, 2017, available at Rutherford Institute, https://www.rutherford.org/files_images /general/06-27-2017_Letter_Police-Chief-Thomas.pdf.

10. Lisa Provence, "Police Show Up at Activists' Doors," *C-ville Weekly*, June 27, 2017, https://www.c-ville.com/police-show-activists-doors.

CHAPTER 20: "SAILING INTO THE WINDSTORM" (JULY 2017)

1. This is in contrast to the "concealed carry" of firearms—where they're hidden in a coat or in a handbag or pocket. Concealed carry is more heavily regu-lated, requiring a Virginia state permit and local permission.

2. "Area NAACP Chapter Holds Counter Rally to the KKK," NBC 29, July 8, 2017, www.nbc29.com/story/35840245/area-naacp-chapter-holds-counter-rally -to-the-kkk.

3. My specific language was: "Our Police faced the great challenge of provid-ing for both the safety of our residents and visitors and the protections of the 1st Amendment. They did so through a sophisticated public safety strategy, involving over 200 officers and support from entities including the Virginia State Police and the University of Virginia."

4. Here is the full statement I put up:

Transparency and respect are at the core of good government. The Char-lottesville Police Department began their formal debriefings about the rally today. The Department, the Virginia State Police, and the City of Charlottesville owe our citizens an accurate account both of what happened on July 8 and why. The statement I issued on July 8 referring to pepper spray and tear gas was written in consultation with the Chief of Police and the City Manager and was based on information they had at the time. Police Chief Al Thomas has said he will thoroughly review Saturday's event not only to understand what went right, but also where we can improve. He will begin to answer questions from the press to-morrow and present a report on the event to the City Council in the near future, where he will also answer our questions. I know that July 8 was deeply distressing for many. For anyone who experienced trauma that day, I am sorry. I recognize that many in our community had different opinions about July 8, including whether to directly protest the rally, participate in other events or stay home. But I am deeply proud that we spoke with one voice in rejecting bigotry here. *This is a revised version of a post that appeared earlier*

5. "Independent Review of the 2017 Protest Events in Charlottesville, Virginia" ("Heaphy Report" hereafter), Hunton & Williams, December 2017, 59–61, http://ftpcontent.worldnow.com/wvir/documents/heaphy-review-dec-1.pdf.

6. Both letters are available online, posted by the Legal Aid Justice Center. See https://www.justice4all.org/wp-content/uploads/2017/07/Letter-to-Local -Officials-RE-July-8-Klan-Rally.pdf and https://www.justice4all.org/wp-content /uploads/2017/07/Letter-to-State-Officials-RE-July-8-Klan-Rally.pdf.

7. John Nagl, *Learning to Eat Soup with a Knife: Counterinsurgency Lessons from Malaya and Vietnam* (Chicago: University of Chicago Press, 2005).

8. Unless a "conflict of interest waiver" is signed, or some other permissible arrangement is made.

9. United for Peace and Justice v. Bloomberg (NY 2004).

CHAPTER 21: DOMESTIC TERRORISM (AUGUST 2017)

1. US Department of Homeland Security, Office of Intelligence and Analysis, "Domestic Terrorist Violence at Lawfully Permitted White Supremacist Rallies Likely to Continue," August 9, 2017, 1, https://www.documentcloud.org /documents/4404359-DHS-Bulletin-Aug-9.html.

2. Ibid., 2. The memo included an important footnote on the same page: "The Virginia Fusion Center (VFC) recognizes that all Americans are afforded the constitutionally-protected right to peacefully assemble as outlined by the First Amendment of the United States Constitution, and will take action accordingly."

3. "Transcript: Bin Laden Determined to Strike in U.S." CNN, April 10, 2004, www.cnn.com/2004/ALLPOLITICS/04/10/august6.memo.

4. Will Parrish, "Police Targeted Anti-Racists in Charlottesville Ahead of 'Unite the Right' Rally, Documents Show," Shadow Proof, March 7, 2018, https:/ /shadowproof.com/2018/03/07/documents-reveal-police-targeting-anti-racists -charlottesville.

5. Alan Zimmerman, "In Charlottesville, the Local Jewish Community Presses On," ReformJudaism.org, August 14, 2017, https://reformjudaism.org/blog/2017 /08/14/charlottesville-local-jewish-community-presses.

6. "Charlottesville Says It Provided Protection to Synagogue, Refuting Initial Account," Jewish Telegraphic Agency, August 18, 2017, https://www.jta.org/2017 /08/18/united-states/charlottesville-says-it-provided-protection-to-synagogue -refuting-initial-account.

7. Interview of Vegas Tenold by Michael Signer for "Overcoming Extremism" podcast, Anti-Defamation League, forthcoming in 2019.

8. Nathan Gutmann, "What a Jewish Journalist Saw in Charlottesville," *Forward*, August 12, 2017, https://forward.com/news/379780/what-a

-jewish-journalist-saw-in-charlottesville/?utm_source=rss&utm_medium=feed&utm_campaign=Main.

9. Sarah Rankin, "Chaos and Violence Rock Charlottesville as White Nationalists Rally; 3 Dead," Associated Press, posted at *Virginian-Pilot*, August 12, 2017, https://pilotonline.com/news/nation-world/virginia/article_260bf4f5-36d9-5cf1-98f7-adf1f002251a.html.

10. Sheryl Gay Stolberg and Brian M. Rosenthal, "Man Charged After White Nationalist Rally in Charlottesville Ends in Deadly Violence," *New York Times*, August 12, 2017, https://www.nytimes.com/2017/08/12/us/charlottesville-protest-white-nationalist.html.

11. My wife Emily would take on the hacking as an academic research project. By examining the city's IT data, she concluded we had been subject to a sophisticated distributed denial of service (DDOS) attack, whose origins could have included not only far left and far right actors but a foreign government. Emily L. Blout, "Nazis in Charlottesville: Notes from the Crucible." Conference paper, Society for Cinema and Media Studies, March 2018.

12. Interview with Chuck Todd, *Meet the Press*, August 13, 2017, NBC News, https://www.nbcnews.com/meet-the-press/video/full-charlottesville-mayor-it-s-on-the-president-to-say-enough-1023587395719.

13. Interview with Jake Tapper, *State of the Union*, CNN, August 13, 2017, posted on YouTube, https://www.youtube.com/watch?v=Qnrznkh43nM.

14. David A. Graham, Adrienne Green, Cullen Murphy, and Parker Richards, "An Oral History of Trump's Bigotry," *The Atlantic*, June 2019, https://www.theatlantic.com/magazine/archive/2019/06/trump-racism-comments/588067.

15. Melissa Chan, "Donald Trump Refuses to Condemn KKK, Disavow David Duke Endorsement," *Time*, February 28, 2016, http://time.com/4240268/donald-trump-kkk-david-duke.

16. Kristine Phillips, "'Look at the Campaign He Ran': Charlottesville Mayor Is Becoming One of Trump's Strongest Critics," *Washington Post*, August 13, 2017, https://www.washingtonpost.com/news/local/wp/2017/08/13/look-at-the-campaign-he-ran-charlottesville-mayor-is-becoming-one-of-trumps-strongest-critics/?utm_term=.8860cedeaa93.

17. "Full Text: Trump's Comments on White Supremacists, 'Alt-Left' in Charlottesville," *Politico*, August 15, 2017, https://www.politico.com/story/2017/08/15/full-text-trump-comments-white-supremacists-alt-left-transcript-241662.

18. Maegan Vasquez and Kevin Liptak, "Trump Defends His Charlottesville Comments After Biden Slams Them," CNN, April 26, 2019, https://www.cnn.com/2019/04/26/politics/charlottesville-donald-trump-joe-biden-robert-e-lee/index.html.

19. "Full Text: Trump's Comments."

20. Two scholars noted how we can come to one stance "pre-factum"—before a fact is known—and to another "post-factum"—after the fact is known, writing, "What we often forget is that those post-factum responses are premised on the existence of *pre-factum*, or before-the-fact, expectations and assumptions about the behavior of individuals, groups, and even nations." For instance, a car

accident "involves perceived errors of choice or judgment on the part of one party to a social relationship." Moreover, "relationships based on accountability, whether perceived as the ability to hold someone to account or the capacity to be held to account, require an awareness and appreciation of both pre-factum and post-factum dimensions." Melvin Dubnick and H. George Frederickson, *Public Accountability: Performance Measurement, the Extended State, and the Search for Trust* (Washington, DC: National Academy of Public Administration and The Kettering Foundation, 2011), 7–8, http://papers.ssrn.com/sol3/papers .cfm?abstract_id=1875024.

21. Ibid., 11.

22. Doug McKelway, "Your World," Fox News, August 14, 2017, https:// www.foxnews.com/transcript/ron-hosko-discusses-the-police-response-to -charlottesville.

23. Baxter Dmitry, "Police: Charlottesville Was 'Inside Job' to Ignite Race War," Your News Wire, August 15, 2017, https://web.archive.org/web/20170820131704 /http://yournewswire.com/charlottesville-inside-job.

24. Richard Godwin, "Sean Adl-Tabatabai on Being in the Eye of the 'Fake News' Storm," *Evening Standard*, February 16, 2017, https://www.standard .co.uk/lifestyle/london-life/sean-adltabatabai-on-being-in-the-eye-of-the-fake -news-storm-a3468361.html.

25. Daniel Funke, "Fact-Checkers Have Debunked This Fake News Site 80 Times. It's Still Publishing on Facebook," Poynter Institute, July 20, 2018, https://www.poynter.org/fact-checking/2018/fact-checkers-have-debunked-this -fake-news-site-80-times-its-still-publishing-on-facebook.

26. "Charlottesville Police Were Told to Stand Down During Protests-Reported as Fiction!" Truth or Fiction, August 21, 2017, https://www.truthorfiction .com/charlottesville-police-told-stand-down.

27. The requested language was, "I overstepped my role as Mayor. I had personal opinions that I misrepresented as the will of Council before meeting with my fellow Councilors. I posted those opinions and misrepresentations on Facebook on August 24 before a closed session. I apologize for overstepping my role and for putting the reputations of our City staff in jeopardy."

28. Aaron Davis, Joe Heim, and Laura Vozella, "How Charlottesville Lost Control Amid Deadly Protest," *Washington Post*, August 26, 2017, https://www .washingtonpost.com/investigations/how-charlottesville-lost-control-amid-deadly -protest/2017/08/26/288ffd4a-88f7-11e7-a94f-3139abce39f5_story.html.

29. Emma Eisenberg, "Charlottesville, 'Happiest City in America'—But for Whom?," *Salon*, August 20, 2017, https://www.salon.com/test/2017/08/20 /charlottesville-happiest-city-in-america-but-for-whom.

30. Merrill Perlman, "Passing the Blame: A Scapegoat by Any Other Name . . . ," *Columbia Journalism Review*, November 15, 2010, https://archives .cjr.org/language_corner/passing_the_blame.php.

31. John Early, ed., "Governor's Task Force Issues Final Report on Unite the Right Rally," NBC 29, December 6, 2017, https://www.nbc29.com/story /37009773/governors-task-forces-final-report-12-06-2017.

32. Governor Terry McAuliffe, *Beyond Charlottesville: Taking a Stand Against White Nationalism* (New York: Thomas Dunne, 2019), 141, 57, 135.

33. My statement also included as a "fresh start" four "protocols" we'd discussed in our closed session, where I had agreed to meet with senior staff only with another councilor present, to be "more mindful of" the time of our clerk's office, to divide up the Council meetings themselves to "reflect shared leadership" by giving other councilors announcements and public hearings (though I would still run the main meeting), and to consult with councilors and staff before making public announcements as mayor. It was at once embarrassing and bemusing. Looking over the items now, I'm struck by how directly they correlated with my attempts to shift the mayorship to a proactive role, and also by how inoperable and unenforceable they were. In the coming months, as events and demands for my leadership unfolded (more on this below), I ended up generally ignoring the "protocols," with the exception of dividing up some parts of our meetings.

CHAPTER 22: "DONALD TRUMP IS GOD!" (SEPTEMBER 2017)

1. Lisa Provence, "Do Robert's Rules of Order Mask White Supremacism?" *C-ville Weekly*, September 8, 2017.

2. "Disunity over Unity Is a Sign of Deep Fissures," *Daily Progress*, September 27, 2017, https://www.dailyprogress.com/opinion/opinion-editorial-disunity -over-unity-is-a-sign-of-deep/article_89f94790-a2ff-11e7-ae69-030b44073a1b .html.

3. Joseph Goldstein, "After Backing Alt-Right in Charlottesville, A.C.L.U. Wrestles with Its Role," *New York Times*, August 17, 2017, https://www.nytimes com/2017/08/17/nyregion/aclu-free-speech-rights-charlottesville-skokie-rally .html.

4. "Charlottesville Violence Prompts ACLU to Change Policy on Hate Groups Protesting with Guns," PBS NewsHour, August 18, 2017, https://www .pbs.org/newshour/nation/charlottesville-violence-prompts-aclu-change-policy -hate-groups-protesting-guns.

5. "ACLU Speaker Shouted Down," *Inside Higher Education*, October 5, 2017, https://www.insidehighered.com/quicktakes/2017/10/05/aclu-speaker -shouted-down-william-mary.

6. "ACLU Case Selection Guidelines: Conflicts Between Competing Values or Priorities," internal memorandum, American Civil Liberties Union, available from *Wall Street Journal* at http://online.wsj.com/public/resources/documents /20180621ACLU.pdf?mod=article_inline.

CHAPTER 23: FLASH MOB (OCTOBER 2017)

1. For video, see Richard B. Spencer, "Back in Charlottesville," Periscope, https://www.pscp.tv/w/1yoKMpodMMexQ.

2. Philip Zelikow, "The Domestic Terrorism Danger: Focus on Unauthorized Private Military Groups," Lawfare, August, 15, 2017, https://www.lawfareblog.com/domestic-terrorism-danger-focus-on-unauthorized-private-military-groups.

3. NAACP v. Claiborne Hardware Co., 458 U.S. 886 (1982), 927.

4. City of Charlottesville et al. v. Pennsylvania Lightfoot Milita et al., Complaint for Injunctive and Declaratory Relief, Circuit Court of Charlottesville, Virginia, 2017, available at https://www.law.georgetown.edu/icap/wp-content/uploads/sites/32/2018/02/lawsuit-charlottesville.pdf.

5. We allocated $900,000 to dramatically expand rental assistance vouchers for people living in affordable housing. We gave $1.4 million to build forty-eight affordable rental units at the Carlton Views II; $612,500 for the rehabilitation of thirty-five more affordable rental units; $480,000 to Habitat for Humanity of Greater Charlottesville to help finance sixteen homes to be purchased by households making between 25 and 60 percent of the area's annual median income; and $905,656 to the Albemarle Housing Improvement Program to rehabilitate between sixty and seventy existing owner-occupied homes. Those proposals went over our affordable housing annual fund by $645,000, but we authorized funding all of them anyway, directing staff to find the money elsewhere, which they promptly did (from our capital improvement budget's surplus fund).

6. Sean Tubbs, "Charlottesville Planning Commission Meeting Ended by Protesters," *Charlottesville Tomorrow*, October 10, 2017, https://www.cvilletomorrow.org/articles/commission-meeting-ended-by-disrupters.

CHAPTER 24: "UNMASK THE ILLUSION" (NOVEMBER 2017)

1. When the rules were ultimately passed by council a few months later, the limit was raised back to fifty after free-speech advocates raised concerns that the lower limit would inhibit protests; I was in the minority on the vote.

2. Governor's Task Force on Public Safety Preparedness and Response to Civil Unrest, "Final Report and Recommendations," December 1, 2017, https://www.policefoundation.org/wp-content/uploads/2018/08/Governors-Task-Force-on-Public-Safety-Preparedness-and-Response-to-Civil-Unrest.pdf.

CHAPTER 25: "LIKE TALKING TO A BRICK WALL" (DECEMBER 2017)

1. Heaphy Report, 153–166.

2. Ibid., 88.

3. Ibid., 98.

4. Ibid., 161.

5. Ibid., 163.

6. Ibid., 82.

7. Ibid., 24.

8. Ibid., 31.

9. Liz Robbins, "'Sanctuary City' Mayors Vow to Defy Trump's Immigration Order," *New York Times*, January 25, 2019, https://www.nytimes.com/2017/01/25 /nyregion/outraged-mayors-vow-to-defy-trumps-immigration-order.html.

10. Sines v. Kessler (W.D. Va., 2018), 53.

11. Heaphy Report, 155–156.

12. Ibid., 63.

13. Ibid., 156.

14. Ibid., 103.

15. Ibid., 174.

16. Aside from these questions of accountability, the report included several valuable recommendations for how to make similar events safer in a way that addressed the critical problems that had surfaced in Charlottesville. On the First Amendment, it recommended that attorneys in small cities needed "centralized expertise and guidance at the state level," which could be provided by state agencies such as the secretary of public safety and the Attorney General's Office (much as I had tried to arrange on my own in my contacts with the Governor's Office and the Attorney General's Office). On the security plan, the report recommended the creation of "stadium plans," where the entire perimeter of an area would be secured, with fixed points of entry and exit as well as barricades and buffer zones within the stadium for the separation of groups. On intelligence, it suggested that the US Department of Justice should facilitate information sharing between agencies, creating a clearinghouse of plans, after-actions, and other guidance; that such national-level coordination could also access intelligence through the fusion centers; and that local police departments should improve their intelligence-gathering capabilities through enhanced technology, including software to aggregate and sift open-source information as well as drones to monitor demonstrations as they occur. It recommended a unified command structure that would clearly identify decision-making authority across agencies, and said that state agencies should do a far better job of coordination. It recommended better training and information around responses to disorders, including training in de-escalation for officers interacting with protesters, smarter deployment of riot gear, and better preparation for arrests. Finally, it recommended better preparation for contingencies. The report recommended that operational plans be flexible enough to allow for rapid deployment of specialized units, and that commanders be enabled to receive and respond to real-time intelligence. Heaphy Report, 167–178.

17. Emmy Freedman, "Activist Group Protesting City Council's Plan to Offer Land Developer Tax Break," NBC 29, December 17, 2017, https://www.nbc29 .com/story/37087039/activist-group-protesting-city-Councils-plan-to-offer-land -developer-tax-break.

CHAPTER 26: THE CRUCIBLE (2018)

1. Jalane Schmidt, "No, I Won't Ignore the Alt-Right," *Medium*, November 1, 2017, https://medium.com/resist-here/no-i-wont-ignore-the-alt-right-3227 c4fc40c8.

2. "Antifa Is Winning: Richard Spencer Rethinks His College Tour After Violent Protests," *Washington Post*, March 12, 2018, https://www.washingtonpost .com/news/grade-point/wp/2018/03/12/antifa-is-winning-richard-spencer-rethinks -his-college-tour-after-violent-protests/?utm_term=.8080c76e36b8; Aiden Pink, "Does Richard Spencer's Disastrous College Tour Mean the 'Alt-Right' Is Fizzling Out?," *Forward*, March 8, 2018, https://forward.com/news/national/396027 /does-richard-spencers-disastrous-college-tour-mean-the-alt-right-is.

3. See Michael Klarman, *From Jim Crow to Civil Rights* (Oxford: Oxford University Press, 2006).

4. Martin Luther King Jr., *Stride Toward Freedom: The Montgomery Story* (Boston: Beacon Press, 2010).

5. Liam Stack, "Charlottesville Confederate Statues Are Protected by State Law, Judge Rules," *New York Times*, May 1, 2019, https://www.nytimes .com/2019/05/01/us/charlottesville-confederate-statues.html.

6. "The National Memorial for Peace and Justice," Equal Justice Initiative, https://museumandmemorial.eji.org/memorial.

7. Norah Mulinda, "Historical Marker Unveiled for Lynching Victim John Henry James," *Charlottesville Tomorrow*, July 15, 2019, https://www.cville tomorrow.org/articles/historical-marker-unveiled-for-lynching-victim-john-henry -james.

8. Erica Green and Annie Waldman, "'You Are Still Black': Charlottesville's Racial Divide Hinders Students," *New York Times*, October 16, 2018, https://www .nytimes.com/2018/10/16/us/charlottesville-riots-black-students-schools.html.

9. "Monument Avenue Commission Report" (Richmond: Office of the Mayor, 2018), 13, https://bloximages.newyork1.vip.townnews.com/richmond.com /content/tncms/assets/v3/editorial/9/8d/98dfbab1-3a10-52d4-ab47-f4a2d9550084 /5b3a9346537e5.pdf.pdf.

10. Ibid., 18.

11. Ibid., 33.

12. Ibid., 32.

13. Web staff, "Richmond Is Getting a New Statue; and It's in Direct Response to Confederate Monuments," WTKR, June 21, 2019, https://wtkr.com /2019/06/21/richmond-is-getting-a-new-statue-and-its-in-direct-response-to -confederate-monuments.

14. Memorial to Enslaved Workers at the University of Virginia, University of Virginia, https://www.virginia.edu/slaverymemorial; Carol Diggs, "Telling All the Stories: The People and Places Working to Restore Charlottesville's African American History," *C-ville Weekly*, February 6, 2019, https://www.c-ville.com/telling-all-the-stories -the-people-and-places-working-to-restore-charlottesvilles-african-american-history.

15. Ivana Krynkiw, "Judge Rules Alabama Confederate Monument Law Is Void; City of Birmingham Didn't Break the Law," *Alabama*, January 15, 2018, https://www.al.com/news/birmingham/2019/01/judge-rules-alabama-confederate-monument-law-is-void-city-of-birmingham-didnt-break-the-law.html.

16. Henry Wiencek, *Master of the Mountain: Thomas Jefferson and His Slaves* (New York: Farrar, Straus and Giroux, 2012).

17. Thomas Jefferson, *Notes on the State of Virginia* (Richmond: 1853), 149–152, 155.

18. Letter from Mark R. Herring to Julie Langan, Office of the Attorney General of Virginia, August 25, 2017, https://www.oag.state.va.us/files/Opinions/2017/17-032-Langan—Monuments—Issued.pdf.

19. Richard Schragger, "Stakes High in Statue Litigation," *Daily Progress*, May 19, 2019, https://www.dailyprogress.com/opinion/opinion-commentary-stakes-high-in-statue-litigation/article_6bf28f70-7820-11e9-a7d3-170db5da717d.html.

20. Sines v. Kessler (W.D. Va., 2018), 54.

21. Ibid., 55 (citations omitted).

22. Ibid., 53.

23. Fred Schauer, "When Speech Meets Hate," *Virginia*, Winter 2017.

24. Fred Schauer, "Costs and Challenges of the Hostile Audience," *Notre Dame Law Review* 94, no. 4 (2019): 1671–1698, https://scholarship.law.nd.edu/cgi/viewcontent.cgi?article=4848&context=ndlr.

25. Ibid., 1682–1683.

26. Ibid., 1687.

27. Hawes Spencer, "Charlottesville Won't Renew City Manager's Contract," WVCE, May 25, 2018, https://ideastations.org/radio/news/charlottesville-wont-renew-city-managers-contract.

28. ProPublica was founded in 2007 as a nonprofit to support true investigative journalism with the resources that traditionally had been provided by for-profit newspapers—outfits that have been demolished through the disruptions in journalism and the traditional advertising base that funded it. ProPublica strikes agreements with traditional newspapers and other media organizations—they do the investigations, and the products are copublished.

29. Ali Winston, "For Charlottesville Authorities, a Painful Post-Mortem on Preparedness," ProPublica, August 7, 2018, https://www.propublica.org/article/for-charlottesville-authorities-a-painful-post-mortem-on-preparedness.

30. "Documenting Hate: Charlottesville," ProPublica/Frontline, August 7, 2018, https://www.pbs.org/video/documenting-hate-charlottesville-1120-ie0mod.

31. Janet Reitman, "U.S. Law Enforcement Failed to See the Threat of White Nationalism. Now They Don't Know How to Stop It," *New York Times Magazine*, November 3, 2018, https://www.nytimes.com/2018/11/03/magazine/FBI-charlottesville-white-nationalism-far-right.html.

32. Though, as of this writing, two assailants remain at large. Ian Shapira, "Who Are the Last Two Attackers of DeAndre Harris in Charlottesville Parking

Garage?" *Richmond Times-Dispatch*, March 3, 2019, https://www.richmond .com/news/virginia/who-are-the-last-two-attackers-of-deandre-harris-in/article _212533a2-33c3-5445-94ee-004ce2f64cd3.html.

33. "Jury Recommends Life in Prison Plus 419 Years for Charlottesville Driver James Alex Fields," NBC News, December 11, 2018, https://www.nbcnews.com /news/us-news/jury-recommends-life-prison-plus-419-years-charlottesville-driver -james-n946536.

34. Kayli Wren, "Incivility at Council Meetings Defended," *Charlottesville Tomorrow*, January 14, 2018, https://www.cvilletomorrow.org/news/article /29570-incivility-at-Council-meetings-defended.

35. Ibid.

36. Nolan Stout, "Councilors Vent Frustrations at All Day Retreat," *Daily Progress*, December 18, 2018, https://www.dailyprogress.com/news/local/city /Councilors-vent-frustrations-at-all-day-retreat/article_cb4ccaee-0327-11e9 -b1fc-a30d9fb2d512.html.

37. "Civil Politics," CivilPolitics.org, www.civilpolitics.org.

38. Debbie Elliott, "Hear Me by Any Means Necessary: Charlottesville Is Forced to Redefine Civility," National Public Radio, March 20, 2019, https://www.npr.org/2019/03/20/704902802/hear-me-by-any-means-necessary -charlottesville-is-forced-to-redefine-civility.

39. Giles Morris, "Let's Talk: Positive Feedback," *Charlottesville Tomorrow*, April 4, 2019, https://www.cvilletomorrow.org/articles/lets-talk-positive -feedback.

40. Bryan McKenzie, "UVa Fans' Peaceful Celebration Bucks National Trend," *Daily Progress*, April 9, 2019, https://www.dailyprogress.com/news/local/ uva-fans-peaceful-celebration-bucks-national-trend/article_60d4d8f4-5b34 -11e9-aedb-179526f0ab4f.html.

41. "HJ 617 Year of Reconciliation and Civility," introduced by Delegate Delores McQuinn, January 3, 2019, https://lis.virginia.gov/cgi-bin/legp604.exe?191 +sum+HJ617.

42. "Unite the Right 2018 Divides into 4 Lessons," *USA Today*, August 13, 2018, https://www.usatoday.com/story/opinion/2018/08/13/unite-right-2018 -divides-into-4-lessons-editorials-debates/982692002.

CHAPTER 27: OVERCOMING EXTREMISM

1. Book of Proverbs, quoted from Revised Standard Version (New York: American Bible Society, 1980).

2. Interview of Jesse Arreguín by Michael Signer for "Overcoming Extremism" podcast, Anti-Defamation League, forthcoming in 2019.

3. Mary McCord and Jason Blezakis, "A Road Map for Congress to Address Domestic Terrorism," Lawfare, February 27, 2019, https://www.lawfareblog.com /road-map-congress-address-domestic-terrorism.

4. "YouTube Announces Update to Its Hate Speech Policy," Yahoo News, June 5, 2019, https://news.yahoo.com/youtube-announces-updates-hate-speech -001908256.html.

5. Caleb Parke, "Conservatives Call for PayPal Boycott After CEO Says Southern Poverty Law Center Helps Ban Users," Fox News, February 28, 2019, https://www .foxnews.com/tech/conservatives-call-for-paypal-boycott-after-ceo-admits-splc -helps-ban-users; Marc Thiessen, "Marc Thiessen: The Southern Policy Law Center Has Lost All Credibility," Fox News, June 22, 2018, https://www.foxnews. com/opinion/marc-thiessen-the-southern-poverty-law-center-has-lost-all-credibility.

6. Makena Kelly, "Internet Giants Must Stay Unbiased to Keep Their Biggest Legal Shield, Senator Proposes," *The Verge*, June 19, 2019, https:// www.theverge.com/2019/6/19/18684219/josh-hawley-section-230-facebook -youtube-twitter-content-moderation.

7. Rosana Hughes, "Andy Berke's Council Against Hate Unveils Proposed Strategies to Combat Hatred and Extremism in Chattanooga," *Times Free-Press*, April 11, 2019, https://www.timesfreepress.com/news/local/story/2019/apr/11 /Council-against-hate-strategies/492471.

CONCLUSION

1. Robert Farley, "The Facts on White Nationalism," FactCheck.org, March 20, 2019, https://www.factcheck.org/2019/03/the-facts-on-white-nationalism.

2. Jerry Kinney, "City of Dayton Sues to Stop Hate Group Rally," Cincinnati Public Radio, March 14, 2019, https://www.wvxu.org/post/city-dayton-sues-stop -hate-group-rally#stream/0.

3. Sasha Ingber, "Facebook Bans White Nationalism and Separatism Content from Its Platforms," NPR, March 27, 2019, https://www.npr.org/2019 /03/27/707258353/facebook-bans-white-nationalism-and-separatism-content -from-its-platforms.

4. Tracy Mumford, "Sinclair Lewis' 'It Can't Happen Here' Becomes Best-seller After Trump's Win," NPR News, *Fresh Air with Terry Gross*, November 23, 2016, https://www.mprnews.org/story/2016/11/23/books-sinclair-lewis-bestseller -after-electi.

INDEX

CAT THRASHER

THE HON. MICHAEL SIGNER, the award-winning former mayor of Charlottesville, Virginia, is a public scholar, practicing attorney, and executive.

Signer has served as an executive and general counsel at a major Virginia technology firm, as counsel to then governor Mark Warner of Virginia, as the national security director on the 2008 John Edwards presidential campaign, and as an associate at Wilmer Hale in Washington, DC. He was a 2009 candidate for lieutenant governor of Virginia. A longtime voting rights attorney, he traveled to wartime Afghanistan in 2010 to help monitor the parliamentary elections on behalf of the US government. He has served on the Virginia Board of Medicine and on the board of directors of the Center for National Policy, and was a founding principal of the Truman National Security Project.

Signer is the author of two previous books, *Demagogue: The Fight to Save Democracy from Its Worst Enemies* and *Becoming Madison: The Extraordinary Origins of the Least Likely Founding Father*, which have been assigned in classes at the University of Virginia, James Madison University, George Mason University, George Washington University, and Rutgers University. He has taught at the University of Virginia, Virginia Tech, and the University of California. He has written opinion pieces and essays for the *New York Times*, *The Atlantic*, the *Washington Post*, *Time*, *Vox*, *Democracy*, and *The New Republic*, and has been an invited speaker at SXSW, Renaissance Weekend, and the Aspen Ideas Festival.

From 2016 to 2018, Signer served as mayor of Charlottesville, an AAA-bond-rated city of nearly fifty thousand. During his tenure, the city had Virginia's lowest unemployment rate, was ranked #4 in the country for entrepreneurs by *Entrepreneur*, and was named the country's #1 place to visit by Expedia.

He received the Anti-Defamation League's Levenson Family Defender of Democracy Award in 2017, the Distinguished Alumnus Award from the University of California in 2018, the Courage

PublicAffairs is a publishing house founded in 1997. It is a tribute to the standards, values, and flair of three persons who have served as mentors to countless reporters, writers, editors, and book people of all kinds, including me.

I. F. STONE, proprietor of *I. F. Stone's Weekly*, combined a commitment to the First Amendment with entrepreneurial zeal and reporting skill and became one of the great independent journalists in American history. At the age of eighty, Izzy published *The Trial of Socrates*, which was a national bestseller. He wrote the book after he taught himself ancient Greek.

BENJAMIN C. BRADLEE was for nearly thirty years the charismatic editorial leader of *The Washington Post*. It was Ben who gave the *Post* the range and courage to pursue such historic issues as Watergate. He supported his reporters with a tenacity that made them fearless and it is no accident that so many became authors of influential, best-selling books.

ROBERT L. BERNSTEIN, the chief executive of Random House for more than a quarter century, guided one of the nation's premier publishing houses. Bob was personally responsible for many books of political dissent and argument that challenged tyranny around the globe. He is also the founder and longtime chair of Human Rights Watch, one of the most respected human rights organizations in the world.

·   ·   ·

For fifty years, the banner of Public Affairs Press was carried by its owner Morris B. Schnapper, who published Gandhi, Nasser, Toynbee, Truman, and about 1,500 other authors. In 1983, Schnapper was described by *The Washington Post* as "a redoubtable gadfly." His legacy will endure in the books to come.

Peter Osnos, *Founder*

in Political Leadership Award from the American Society for Yad Vashem in 2019, and the Rob DeBree & David O'Malley Award for Community Response to Hatred from the Matthew Shepard Foundation in 2019. He was recognized by *The Forward* magazine in its "Forward 50 2018" list of the fifty most influential Jewish leaders in America. He is also a member of the 2018 class of the Aspen Institute's Rodel Fellows.

He has been profiled by NPR, CNN, the *New York Times*, the *Washington Post*, and *The Guardian* and interviewed by *Meet the Press*, *Face the Nation*, *The Rachel Maddow Show*, and NPR's *Morning Edition*. He created the "Governing Extremism" podcast.

He founded and chaired Communities Overcoming Extremism: The After Charlottesville Project, a capacity-building project for leaders in the public and private sectors whose partners included the Anti-Defamation League, the Ford Foundation, the Charles Koch Institute, the Fetzer Institute, the John Pritzker Fund, the Kresge Foundation, the Soros Fund, Comcast NBC Universal, and New America.

Signer holds a PhD in political science from the University of California, Berkeley, where he was a National Science Foundation Graduate Research Fellow; a JD from the University of Virginia School of Law; and a BA in politics from Princeton University, where he was a work-study student and graduated *magna cum laude*. He lives with his wife and their twin five-year-old boys in Charlottesville, Virginia.